Canada
at the Polls,
1979 and 1980

AEI'S AT THE POLLS STUDIES

The American Enterprise Institute
has initiated this series in order to promote
an understanding of the electoral process as it functions in
democracies around the world. The series will include studies
of at least two national elections in more than twenty countries
on five continents, by scholars from the United States and
abroad who are recognized as experts in their field.
More information on the titles in this series can
be found at the back of this book.

Canada
at the Polls,
1979 and 1980

A Study of
the General Elections

Edited by Howard R. Penniman

WITHDRAWN

American Enterprise Institute for Public Policy Research
Washington and London

Library of Congress Cataloging in Publication Data

Main entry under title:

Canada at the polls, 1979 and 1980.

(At the polls series) (AEI studies ; 345)
Includes bibliographical references and index.
1. Elections—Canada—Addresses, essays, lectures.
2. Political parties—Canada—Addresses, essays, lectures.
3. Canada—Politics and government—1945—Addresses, essays,
lectures. I. Penniman, Howard Rae, 1916–   . II. American
Enterprise Institute for Public Policy Research. III. Series.
IV. Series: AEI studies ; 345.
JL193.C34   324.971′0645   81-19144
ISBN 0-8447-3474-8   AACR2
ISBN 0-8447-3472-1 (pbk.)

AEI Studies 345

Printed in the United States of America

216551

Contents

Preface

Canada at the Polls, 1979 and 1980: A Study of the General Elections is another in the continuing series of studies of national elections in selected democratic countries published by the American Enterprise Institute. Underlying the series is the belief that public policy makers and students of elections in each democracy can profit from a knowledge of electoral rules and practices in a wide variety of other democracies. The greater their understanding of the political consequences of the conduct of elections in other countries, the deeper their insight into the impact of electoral rules and practices at home.

This book is about two Canadian general elections nine months apart. In May 1979 the Progressive Conservative party (PC) finished 4.2 percentage points behind the Liberal party in the popular vote but won twenty-two more seats in the House of Commons. The PC formed a minority government—as it had in 1957, another election when it won more seats with fewer votes than its chief competitor. As in 1957, the government was short lived. In the election held in February 1980, the Liberal party again won a plurality of the popular vote but this time was rewarded with a majority of the seats in the House of Commons.[1] In the next few pages, I would like to use these results to highlight a few broad features of electoral politics in Canada.

The Two-Party System. Besides Canada, three large democracies—Britain, New Zealand, and the United States—have used the single-member-district/plurality system to elect their national legislators

[1] The nationwide popular vote, of course, legally has no impact on the outcome of an election conducted under a single-member-district/plurality system. The results in each district determine the winners. What sometimes draws attention to the national vote is a concern to give equal weight to every vote cast in the nation. Particularly when one of the major parties wins fewer votes nationally but more seats in the legislature than its nearest rival, the question whether the system itself should be changed tends to be raised.

since the Second World War.[2] Canada presents a significant contrast to the other three when it comes to the place occupied in the party system by the two largest parties. To clarify this contrast, let us adopt Douglas Rae's definition of a two-party system and see whether in our four countries (1) the two largest parties together have won at least 90 percent of the seats in the lower house of the national legislature and (2) the share won by the largest party has remained below 70 percent.[3]

Canada has had thirteen elections since the Second World War, and in twelve the Liberals and the PC together have gained less than 90 percent of the seats. In 1958—the only election that met the first of Rae's criteria—the PC took 78.5 percent of the seats and therefore overstepped the limits of the second. For all the elections since the war, the two major parties' average combined share of the seats has been 85.9 percent. In six elections, all between 1957 and 1980, no party won a majority in the House of Commons. The elections of 1979 and 1980 produced almost identical two-party results: 76 and 76.8 percent of the popular vote respectively and in both years 250 seats, or 88.7 percent of the total, in the House of Commons (though the distribution of those seats between Liberals and Conservatives was very different after the two elections).

Turning to Britain, we find that in none of the eleven general elections since the war has one party received an absolute majority of the national vote; yet in ten of the eleven, one party has taken a clear majority of the seats in the House of Commons. In February 1974 the Labour party, which lost the popular contest to the Conservatives, won only a plurality of the seats. Together, however, the two parties won 598 seats, or 94.2 percent of the membership. In 1974, a year with two general elections, the seats were divided so evenly between the major parties after the February poll that the small Liberal party and the regional parties held the balance of power, and they came close to doing so again after the October election.[4] The average combined two-party share of M.P.s since the war has been 97.1 percent, but neither party by itself has ever held more than 58 percent. Ob-

---

[2] David Butler, Howard R. Penniman, and Austin Ranney, eds., *Democracy at the Polls: A Comparative Study of Competitive National Elections* (Washington, D.C.: American Enterprise Institute, 1981), pp. 12-19. India adopted the same system but did not hold its first election until 1952.

[3] Douglas W. Rae, *The Political Consequences of Electoral Laws*, rev. ed. (New Haven: Yale University Press, 1971), p. 72.

[4] Howard R. Penniman, ed., *Britain at the Polls: The Parliamentary Elections of 1974* (Washington, D.C.: American Enterprise Institute, 1975), pp. 242-47; and Howard R. Penniman, ed., *Britain at the Polls, 1979: A Study of the General Election* (Washington, D.C.: American Enterprise Institute, 1981), pp. 334-35.

viously the two-party system as defined above has been securely entrenched in Britain since the war.

In three of New Zealand's twelve elections from 1946 to 1978, a major party won an absolute majority of the popular vote, and one party has always elected a majority to the parliament. In the 1978 election the National party lost the popular vote but won control of the House of Representatives. In general elections the voters have only twice elected a third-party member to the House: in 1966, when the two-party share of the seats dropped to 98.1 percent, and in 1978, when it was 98.9 percent. Both years a Social Credit Political League candidate was elected.[5]

In the United States the joint Democratic and Republican share of the popular vote for members of the House of Representatives has never fallen below 97 percent in any postwar election, and no third-party candidate has won a seat in the House since Vito Marcantonio's victories in a New York City district in 1946 and 1948.[6] Interestingly enough, the nearly total dominance of the House membership by two major parties has been a recent development. In the last seven decades of the nineteenth century, when the House averaged only 235 members, more than 400 candidates of lesser parties were elected to Congress. Although the number steadily declined in the first forty years of the twentieth century, lesser party representatives were regularly elected. Third-party representation decreased in large part because state after state adopted laws requiring that the major parties select their candidates by direct primary. Under this system a congressman owed his nomination not to a party organization but to local voters who had registered as Democrats or Republicans or, rarely, under the label of another party. A congressman elected under these circumstances was free to support whatever positions the voters of his district found acceptable, with almost no concern for the views of party leaders. As a result, there was little need to found a third party to promote a particular program: on the contrary, almost any platform could be sold more easily under a major party label. The use of the direct primary strengthened two-party supremacy in Congress, but it did so at the expense of party cohesion, which in any case had always been lower in the United States than in the other democracies.

[5] Howard R. Penniman, ed., *New Zealand at the Polls: The General Election of 1978* (Washington, D.C.: American Enterprise Institute, 1980), p. 154. Social Credit also has elected legislators in by-elections, once in 1978 and once in 1981.

[6] Marcantonio was a member of the American Labor party. Several congressmen have been elected as independents (usually because of a local division within a major party), but all have immediately arranged to join either the Republican or the Democratic caucus.

Canada, then, is the one country operating under the plurality formula where a two-party system has not flourished during the last three decades. The share of seats in the federal legislature captured by the Progressive Conservative and Liberal parties has regularly fallen below 90 percent, and the nation has suffered the weaknesses that accompany minority governments.

National Results, Regional Results, and the Urge for Electoral Reform. Canada's political problems have not been confined to the continued presence of relatively strong lesser parties. While the same two major parties have vied for control of the government for more than a century, it is hardly an exaggeration to say that the country today has no genuine national party. Since the war the Liberals have formed nine of the thirteen governments, six times with majority support in the House of Commons. As Stephen Clarkson has pointed out, however, the very electoral system that has often promoted the success of the Liberal party has also made the Prairie provinces its "zone of continuing weakness. . . . In these provinces the Liberal party suffers from the electoral system as if it were a 'third party' itself, receiving on average only 9 percent of the seats, despite retaining about one-quarter of the vote. Like the New Democratic party elsewhere in the country, it has a continuing base of electoral support with no prospect of winning corresponding representation in Parliament."[7]

In 1979 voters in Prince Edward Island in the east, Alberta and Saskatchewan in the west, and the Yukon and Northwest Territories elected no Liberal M.P.s. In 1980, even as the party won a comfortable legislative majority and gained two M.P.s from Prince Edward Island, it won no seats west of Manitoba, as British Columbia joined the western provinces where the Liberals were shut out. Of the 147 seats taken by the Liberals in 1980, 74 were in Quebec and 52 in Ontario. The remaining 21 came from Manitoba and the Maritime provinces.

The PC claims to be the only truly national party because it won at least one seat from every province. In fact, three of its four postwar victories produced only minority governments, and in those years it took only one of the seventy-five seats in Quebec (proportionately fewer than U.S. Republicans regularly obtained in the Solid South of the early twentieth century). In the four preceding elections Conservative candidates had won a maximum of four seats in Quebec districts. The PC has done relatively better elsewhere, but in twelve

[7] Howard R. Penniman, ed., *Canada at the Polls: The General Election of 1974* (Washington, D.C.: American Enterprise Institute, 1975), p. 66.

of the thirteen postwar elections, its average share of the national vote has been more than nine percentage points less than the Liberal party's.

Though interest in electoral reform increased considerably after the Conservatives' minority victory in 1979, the likelihood that the Canadians will enact significant changes in their system is slim. Inertia is always an obstacle to major electoral reform, and most democracies have clung tenaciously to the system to which they have become accustomed. France, in fact, is the only important exception to the rule that nations make minor modifications in their election rules but do not change the system itself. Most major party leaders have hesitated to throw out a system that has given them control of the government, well aware that a new system that was likely to strengthen their bid for seats in some regions would cost them seats in others. Moreover, where plurality arrangements prevail, a shift to a proportional system, which can be expected to prevent a single party from winning a majority, has little appeal for any but small parties.

Meanwhile, the voters at large feel little urge to reform the electoral system. Very few citizens are much concerned about the niceties of electoral arrangements. As two contributors to this volume have suggested, most Canadians think of election results in terms of seats and districts and pay little attention to the national vote. The reporting processes in Canada and elsewhere encourage this view. Information about seat distribution is readily available on election night, and by morning the public knows how many seats each party has won—while precise nationwide voting data are available only later when complete district returns are in, the mistakes corrected, and the totals compiled. By this time, only a handful of politicians and scholars care what the figures say about the relationship between the national vote and the party composition of the parliament.

At one time or another, Britain, New Zealand, the United States, and Canada have all witnessed elections in which the party that won the most votes nationally failed to get the most seats, but all these countries still use the system under which the discrepancies occurred. Most people have neither noticed nor cared. In each case there was no evidence of major corruption, the rules had been generally followed, the party that had won the most seats controlled the government. Most citizens ask no more of an electoral system.

The Contributors. Canadian political scientists have contributed all the essays in this volume. Alan C. Cairns, of the University of

British Columbia, discusses the constitutional and legal context of the 1979 election, and John Meisel, recently of Queen's University and now chairman of the Canadian Radio-television and Telecommunications Commission, provides the political context. William P. Irvine, of Queen's University, writes about the Canadian voter and his views before the 1979 election and in the epilogue summarizes the circumstances leading up to the 1980 election, the campaign, and the results. Robert J. Williams, of the University of Waterloo, describes the processes by which Canadian parties choose their candidates. John C. Courtney, of the University of Saskatchewan, Stephen Clarkson, of the University of Toronto, and Walter D. Young, of the University of Victoria, discuss the campaigns of the Progressive Conservative, Liberal, and New Democratic parties respectively. Vincent Lemieux and Jean Crête, of the Université Laval, explain the place and problems of Quebec within the Canadian federal system. F. Leslie Seidle, of the Office of the President of the Privy Council, and Khayyam Zev Paltiel, of Carleton University, analyze the operation and impact of the laws that governed Canadian campaign financing for the first time in 1979. Frederick J. Fletcher, of York University, discusses the coverage of the campaign in the mass media. M. Janine Brodie, of Queen's University, and Jill Vickers, of Carleton University, examine the role of women in the 1979 campaign. I am grateful to Jean-Marc Hamel, chief electoral officer of Canada, and to Christine Jackson, assistant director of operations in his office, for supplying the ballots reproduced in appendix A. Finally, the electoral data in appendix B were compiled by Richard M. Scammon.

HOWARD R. PENNIMAN

Canada
at the Polls,
1979 and 1980

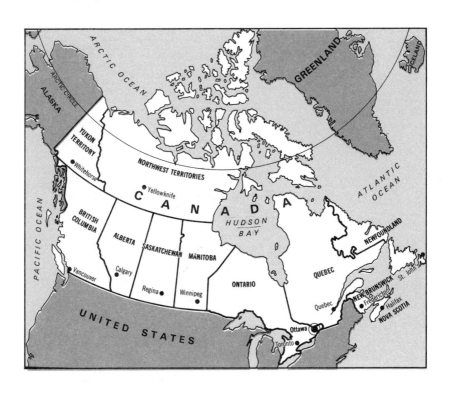

1

The Constitutional, Legal, and Historical Background

Alan C. Cairns

In the first general election in the Dominion of Canada, in 1867, 268,217 Canadians voted. In the thirty-first general election, in 1979, 11,455,702 Canadians cast valid ballots.[1] Eighteen of the thirty-one elections were won by the Liberals[2] and thirteen by the Conservatives.[3] Since 1921 the Liberals' electoral superiority has been especially pronounced, with thirteen victories in eighteen contests. The Liberal hegemony has been even more decisive in terms of years in office. The Conservatives have held office only twice since 1921, from 1930 to 1935 and from 1957 to 1963.[4] While there has been a third party in the field for the past sixty years, the two original parties that emerged at the time of Confederation have maintained their position as the leading contenders for national power. In recent federal elections third parties have consistently taken about one-quarter of the popular vote.

By virtue of this long experience of competitive politics and free elections, Canada has one of the oldest continuously functioning democratic political systems in the world. Canadians have always been able to change their rulers by electoral means. At the federal level, incumbent governments are defeated and replaced about one-third of the time. In the 1970s provincial governments were overturned

[1] Official figures.

[2] Counting 1896 and 1925 as Liberal victories. In 1896 the Liberals received thirty more seats, but 1.2 percentage points fewer votes, than the Conservatives and formed the government. In 1925 the Liberals remained in office with Progressive support, although they received fewer seats and fewer votes than the Conservatives.

[3] Counting 1957 and 1979 as Conservative victories, although in each case the new minority Conservative government was based on less voter support than the Liberal government it replaced.

[4] And for a short period in 1926.

1

in nine of the ten provinces. Only in Ontario, where the Conservative party has held office continuously since 1943, has the party of government escaped electoral repudiation.

In the 1979 election, 35.9 percent of the valid votes gave the Conservatives a minority government of 136 seats. The defeated Liberals, who had controlled the government since 1963 and were supported by 40.1 percent of the voters, received only 114 seats and became the official opposition. This capricious result, an illustration of the perverse capacity of the Canadian electoral system to bestow the gift of power on the voters' second choice, was accepted with no serious questioning as the verdict of the people, as had been the results in 1896 and 1957, when the party with the most seats, which formed the new government, had come in second in the popular vote. Indeed, so habituated are Canadians to assessing the victor almost exclusively in terms of seats that the fact that the Liberals received nearly half a million more votes than the Conservatives was scarcely noted, especially in English Canada, where the Liberals ran a clear second to the Conservatives. The change of government was procedurally smooth. Joe Clark and the Conservative party he had led since 1976 took power with 136 of the 282 seats in the House of Commons.

Its national government now controlled by the Conservatives for the first time since 1963, Canada was in the middle—or perhaps only at the beginning, or perhaps nearing the end—of a period of profound internal tension and malaise. Part of the frustration of leaders and disillusion of followers reflected the same perplexities, confusions, and contradictions that bedevil the governors and the governed elsewhere in Western democracies. The diverse conventional wisdoms that had provided adequate answers to yesterday's questions now seemed dated and irrelevant in a country beset simultaneously by inflation and unemployment, an energy crisis, and a weakening of political confidence. In addition, a constitution that had weathered a century of profound change, including war and depression, was now on the defensive. To many, not only in Quebec, it seemed little more than a museum piece. The constitution was criticized by some for its age, by others for its lack of appropriate democratic rhetoric; reformers said it stood in the way of a more effective management of public affairs, and the government of Quebec denounced it for shackling the Quebec people in an unrewarding relationship with an English-speaking majority. As the new Conservative government took office, it was clear that reality had finally caught up with the hitherto unfounded, somewhat indulgent assertion that Canada was a difficult country to govern.

In Canada as elsewhere, belief in the possibility and desirability of managing nature by the application of intelligence and confidence in the beneficence and competence of governments as the instruments of that intelligence were in disarray. The resultant widespread attack on big government was the most visible aspect of a profound pause in the political and intellectual evolution of the Western world. In Canada "a binge of state-worship,"[5] based on an exaggerated belief in the efficacy and potency of governments, was coming to an end.

More threatening, however, than this pervasive uncertainty about political activity in the 1970s was the Canadian version of yet another ubiquitous phenomenon—the explosion of ethnic feeling or nationalism, which, to the surprise of social scientists no less than politicians, challenged the existing constitutional order of virtually every developed political system in the world. The Canadian experiment in French-English accommodation could no longer be taken for granted as a modest success story. The breakup of the country through its inability to contain the aggressive nationalism of Francophone Quebecers was a serious possibility that had to be entertained even by the most cautious scholar and politician. The politics of the second-largest country in the world, which only two decades earlier had seemed stable to the point of boredom, had become confused, tense, and exciting.

Federalism

Maintaining agreement on a common political system for French- and English-speaking Canadians has been a constant challenge to Canadian political leaders for more than a century, and federalism has been largely responsible for their success in meeting that challenge until recently. The choice of federalism in 1867, rather than a unitary government on the British model, was an unavoidable response to the political necessity of accommodating Nova Scotia, New Brunswick, and Ontario, as well as Quebec. The opposition of the French Canadian population of Quebec to a unitary state, however, was much more deeply based than superficially similar sentiments elsewhere in British North America in the mid-nineteenth century.

French Canadian opposition was based on language difference, cultural distinctiveness, Catholicism, and collective memories of the victory of the English over the French a century earlier. The preserva-

---

[5] Donald Smiley, "Intergovernmental Relations in Canada: Where Does the Taxpayer Come In?" (Paper presented to the Annual Conference of the Institute of Public Administration of Canada, Winnipeg, August 1979), mimeographed, p. 4.

tion of some significant government authority under their own control was self-evidently necessary to the geographically concentrated French-speaking minority surrounded by an expansive, commercial Anglo-Saxon civilization.

The federalism developed out of the pre-Confederation discussions was an attempt to deal with the breakdown of the political system established by the 1840 Act of Union, which had brought English and French from Upper and Lower Canada (the future Ontario and Quebec) together in what was designed as an essentially Anglo-Saxon unitary state. That polity, which combined the English-speaking majority from Upper Canada and the French-speaking majority from Lower Canada under a common government in the United Province of Canada, was a response to Lord Durham's analysis of what he saw as the backward, unprogressive character of French Canada. In his *Report on the Affairs of British North America* (1839), Governor General Durham had advocated institutional engineering to submerge and obliterate the distinctive nationality of French Canada within the framework of a united colony, where the progressive, superior, commercial civilization of English Canada would overwhelm the less competitive culture of the French-speaking inhabitants, to the benefit of both.

By the mid-1860s the inadequacies of Durham's diagnosis were evident in the continuing French Canadian sense of nationality, the emergence of aggressive French Canadian leadership, and the developing recognition of French Canadian rights. The faltering political system of the colony was becoming unworkable. The inability of governments to survive hindered economic expansion. A new constitutional arrangement was necessary.

The power of ethnic feeling had triumphed over the institutions of a formally unitary political system, and constitutional engineering had failed to hasten the disappearance of French Canada. The next phase of constitutional craftsmanship showed greater sensitivity to the enduring national consciousness of the minority.

From an ethnic perspective, Confederation was designed to minimize competition between French and English by splitting the United Province of Canada into two provinces, Quebec and Ontario, to be dominated by French and English majorities respectively. Indeed, for many French Canadians, the significance of Confederation—an event never as symbolically important to them as to English Canadians—was the opportunity it allowed for an escape into provincialism.

The colonial societies of British North America and their local political elites did not insist on federalism out of any abstract conception of the desirability of diffusing and checking power. Their

4

separate histories led them to oppose any constitutional arrangement that would have required them to submerge their individuality in a majoritarian political system governed by a single central government. Federalism, with its tolerance for diversity, was for them a precondition of acceptance of the other part of the Confederation package, the creation of an overriding central government endowed with predominant authority over the great affairs of state. For the leading English Canadian Fathers, particularly John A. Macdonald and Alexander Galt, the latter was the essential objective, for the attainment of which they reluctantly conceded certain minimum powers and taxing capacities to the provinces. They sought and created a powerful central government to undertake the task of nation building, which was their central purpose.[6]

Thus, like all complex arrangements, the federal system of 1867 was valued for different reasons by different people. In particular, there was an implicit division of labor along ethnic lines between the governments of the federal system. The central government, viewed as the key instrument of nation building, economic growth, and territorial expansion, derived its impetus from the commercial culture of English Canada, while the provincial government of Quebec became one behind which the population could shelter under the protective guidance of the Catholic church. It was not a government expected to lead its people.

The Monarchy

The choice of federalism in 1867 was the only significant institutional borrowing from the United States. Apart from federalism, the basic components of the political system were derived from the British tradition. Canada, as the preamble to the British North America Act stated, was to have a "Constitution similar in Principle to that of the United Kingdom." The features of the British constitution the colonists borrowed were those with which they had already had experience.

The monarchy, represented by a governor general at the federal level and by lieutenant governors in the provinces, was not a matter

---

[6] In choosing a centralist variant of federalism, they were also responding to their own interpretation of the contribution of American constitutional arrangements to the American Civil War, which was the backdrop to their discussions. They concluded that too loose a federation, with residuary powers given to the states, strengthened centrifugal forces, led to doctrines of states' rights, and in extreme cases could lead to the carnage of civil war. To avoid the repetition of such a disaster, concessions to regional diversity were kept to a minimum.

of contention in the Confederation debates of the 1860s. There was no support for republicanism. On the contrary, the monarchy was valued as a bulwark for elitist tendencies against the possibly contagious heresy of democracy that had infected Canada's tumultuous neighbor to the south. The monarchy reflected the conservatism of the Fathers, "the social doctrine that public order and tradition, in contrast to freedom and experiment, were central to the good life."[7] In the North American context, it also symbolized Canada's distinctiveness and its continuing links with Europe.

In the 1970s the crown occupied a less central place. From the very beginning the monarchy in Canada was unavoidably weaker than in the United Kingdom: the representatives of the crown in Canada are appointed, not born to office, their tenure is limited, and they lack the aura of royalty. Recent developments have further reduced the significance of monarchical institutions. The decline of the British empire and its transformation into the Commonwealth, the diminished political role of the United Kingdom in world affairs, the greatly reduced importance of Britain as an export market for Canadian products and as a supplier of capital, and Britain's entry into the European Common Market have eroded both the utilitarian and the sentimental bases for the British connection.

Canada's evolution from colony to independent nation and the increasing ethnic diversity of English Canada have also contributed to the weakening of the monarchical tradition. Indeed, given the indifference or hostility of many Francophone Quebecers and the republican sentiment spilling across the border, it is arguable that the monarch, governor general, and lieutenant governor are no longer unifying factors in the country. What is beyond question, however, is that attempts to eliminate or officially downgrade the constitutional monarchy, no matter how subtle, are highly divisive and counterproductive.

In any case, in addition to their useful ceremonial, ritual, and social role, governors general and lieutenant governors have an overall responsibility for the constitutional health and the constitutional morality of the political process that might in certain circumstances require their personal intervention. The constitutional monarch is more than a link with the past, to be cherished or deplored as temperament dictates. The governor general possesses reserve powers essential to the smooth functioning of the Canadian parliamentary system, which might have to be wielded against the advice of his

---

[7] George Grant, *Lament for a Nation: The Defeat of Canadian Nationalism* (Toronto/Montreal: McClelland and Stewart, 1965), p. 71.

constitutional advisers in order to safeguard the constitution.[8] The election of minority governments in six of the last nine federal elections increases the possibility of the governor general's involvement in delicate and sensitive political situations.

Responsible Government

Responsible government, cabinet government, or parliamentary government—different names for the same phenomenon viewed from varying perspectives—was, like the monarchy, not selected in 1864–1867, but simply continued. Responsible government had been achieved in 1848 in Nova Scotia and in the province of Canada and shortly afterward in New Brunswick, Prince Edward Island, and Newfoundland. Canadians, according to Professor Brady's evocative summary, "could henceforth feel confident that the essential fabric of the British constitution was their own acquisition, secured through their persistent advocacy, fitted to their peculiar circumstances, and fostered as the substance and symbol of their political identity in North America."[9]

By the time of the Charlottetown, Quebec, and London conferences, which fashioned the Confederation agreement, responsible government, with its requirement that the political executive remain in office only as long as it received the support of a majority in the legislative assembly, was part of the habitual institutional environment of politicians in British North America. It was valued not only because it was British but for the practical contribution it could make to the decisive executive leadership required by a new country that faced daunting problems.

Although Canada was conceived when laissez-faire ideas were at their height in the United Kingdom, the Canadian Fathers were unimpressed by the idea of the state as night watchman or umpire, holding the ring for the contending social forces of a developing society. On the contrary, the state, especially the central government, was to play a leading role in territorial expansion across half a continent and in the political incorporation and economic development of the frontier. Given this orientation, there was negligible interest in establishing checks and balances on the American pattern of a separation of

[8] See Eugene Forsey, *Freedom and Order* (Toronto: McClelland and Stewart, 1974), pt. 1, esp. pp. 21-49.

[9] Alexander Brady, "Canada and the Model of Westminster," in William B. Hamilton, ed., *The Transfer of Institutions* (Durham, N.C.: Duke University Press, 1964), pp. 67-68.

powers, which might hinder the decisive exercise of executive authority by the prime minister and his cabinet.

The Canadian polity was not shaped either by fear of the state as an enemy of liberty or by awe of it as the enduring, mystical expression of the transient generations over whose destiny it presided. In fact, the very concept of the state (until recently in Quebec) has been somewhat alien to the Canadian political vocabulary. The idea of an active government playing a leading role has been widely accepted, however, and has justified the concentration of executive authority in a party-dominated cabinet.

The Fathers revealed their political elitism in their preference for a cohesive cabinet, based on an assured legislative majority, wielding the authority of a strong central government. This authority was to be employed in the creation of a Canadian society, a Canadian economy, and ultimately a new Canadian political identity. The cabinet-dominated central government was to be not a mirror to the social and economic facts of 1867, but the chief instrument for the transformation of the northern half of the continent into a great new transcontinental country.

The Senate

The blend of federalism, responsible government, and the monarchy that constituted the primary institutional fabric of the polity was supplemented by a diluted bicameralism. The establishment of the Canadian Senate was an essential part of the Confederation agreement, especially for the smaller provinces. Nevertheless, various features of its composition assured it a distinctly secondary role, reducing it almost to the status of spectator of the political battles fought out by the cabinet and the Commons.

The creation of an upper house satisfied both the desire to duplicate the British constitution where possible and a wish to placate the territorial interests that had necessitated federalism.[10] With its entire membership appointed by the central government, originally for life, the Senate clearly could not be an influential advocate of regional perspectives in the central government arena. It lacked the prestige that election brings in a democratic polity (a consideration much more

[10] "With Canadian experience of nearly a century, sectional representation and nomination by the central government seem irreconcilable in principle. . . . Macdonald and other leaders . . . granted the forms demanded by sectional sentiments and fears, but they made sure that these forms should not endanger the political structure." Robert A. MacKay, *The Unreformed Senate of Canada*, rev. ed. (Toronto: McClelland and Stewart, 1963), p. 43.

important now than in 1867); yet it was devoid of the aura aristocracy can bestow in a society with residual prebourgeois elements like the United Kingdom. Its sideline status was ensured by the conventions of responsible government that gave the lower house the power to make and unmake governments. Its most astonishing feat has been to survive and perform various useful functions in a society embarrassed at its continuing existence. It has combined weakness and longevity in a most impressive manner.

Institutions and Society: Part One

The institutional framework—federalism, responsible government, monarchical institutions, and bicameralism—has undergone little formal change since 1867. The functioning of Canada's institutions, however, is significantly different from that originally intended. The interaction between an evolving society and a network of institutions established in simpler times has inevitably transformed their meaning and modified their working. Since 1867 the population has grown from 3.5 million to nearly 24 million, and a predominantly rural nation has become predominantly urban, all within a formally unchanged constitutional order.

The political evolution of more than a century is a product of interactions too complex for detailed description. Only a general indication of the most important changes will be attempted.

The four provinces of 1867 had soon become seven, with the addition of Manitoba in 1870, British Columbia in 1871, and Prince Edward Island in 1873. Two more provinces, Alberta and Saskatchewan, were carved out of the Northwest Territories in 1905. Finally, Newfoundland, after a long history of rejecting association with Canada, became the tenth province in 1949 after two referendums, the second of which produced a narrow victory for the pro-Confederation forces led by Joseph Smallwood.

The federalism that was a necessary guarantee for the original participants in 1867 was no less necessary for the later arrivals. A unitary Canada would have encountered much more local resistance to its expansionist ambitions. Furthermore, as the nation expanded, distance became a consideration: Canada's new territories and new peoples needed governments closer at hand than Ottawa. They also needed governments attuned to their diverse interests. The great agrarian community specializing in the production of wheat for international markets that comprised Alberta, Saskatchewan, and Manitoba had economic interests often in conflict with those of central Canada. Prince Edward Island, British Columbia, and finally

Newfoundland were each more distinctive in economic interest, way of life, and political tradition than would have been compatible with a unitary state.

The development and expansion of the federal system altered the conditions of competition in the party system. The original two-party system, which had firmly established itself at the national level by 1900 in central and eastern Canada, was unable to take root with equal success in the agrarian communities of Alberta, Saskatchewan, and Manitoba that grew so rapidly in the early years of the twentieth century. Their special economic interests, heterogeneous population base, and developing political tradition were not well served by a party system that had developed in response to the very different requirements of Canada east of the Great Lakes. In 1921 the Progressive party returned sixty-five members to the House of Commons, including thirty-eight of the forty-three M.P.s from the three Prairie provinces. Support for farm movements in provincial politics and the successes of third parties in both federal and provincial politics in this area have been further indications of the contribution of regional diversity to the weakening hold of the two-party system.

Federalism has provided outlets for regional discontent at the provincial level and in doing so has increased the staying power of third parties, especially those able to gain control of provincial governments. Alberta had third-party government for fifty consecutive years, from 1921 to 1971, and British Columbia has been governed by third parties continuously since 1952. Since 1944 the New Democratic party (NDP) (originally the Cooperative Commonwealth Federation [CCF]) has held office for twenty-nine years in Saskatchewan, and since 1922 Manitoba has had thirty-six years of a shifting coalition government and eight years of NDP rule. In the periods 1936–1939, 1944–1960, and 1966–1970, Quebec was governed by the Union Nationale, and since 1976 it has been governed by the Parti Québécois, neither of which participates in federal politics. Only in the Atlantic provinces and Ontario (except from 1919 to 1923) have the old parties remained in control of government.

Some of the third parties operate only at the provincial level; the Parti Québécois in Quebec and Social Credit in British Columbia are the prime current examples. The different receptivity of national and provincial arenas to third-party activity has been one of the key factors in driving the federal and provincial party systems apart. Many voters express very different partisan preferences in successive federal and provincial elections. On the other hand, there is a spillover in both directions: more third-party activity in national politics, and more traditional party activity at the provincial level, than would occur if weak parties at one jurisdictional level were not sustained by their stronger namesakes at the other level.

There is a peaceful but never-ending struggle between institutions in Canada for power and influence. Those most capable of responding to the shifting imperatives of democracy, representativeness, efficiency, expertise, and leadership have gained power, while the less capable, such as the Senate and the crown, have lost it. It is powerfully argued, in Canada as in the United Kingdom, that recent prime ministers, partly because of the media's stress on personality politics, have acquired an exalted leadership role based on a direct relation with the electorate, which gives them a preeminence in cabinet and party not enjoyed by their predecessors.

The power of the House of Commons has been transformed by party discipline from a capacity to defeat and replace governments to a more diffuse ability to influence the climate of opinion on which success or failure at the next election depends. Ordinary M.P.s, lacking expertise, burdened by constituency duties, and treated as voting machines by their party leaders, are not significant actors in devising, criticizing, or controlling the passage of legislation or in influencing its subsequent administration. "In 'normal' circumstances of majority government," writes Mallory, "once a parliament is elected it is no longer independent, but a groaning beast of burden for the government's legislative program."[11]

Responsible government no longer means the location in the House of Commons of an effective capacity to defeat and replace the incumbent executive. Its contemporary meaning has been suggestively described by a close student as follows:

> The constitutional essence of responsible government in Canada today probably includes the following: the government must command a regular majority in the House of Commons; the government must attempt to answer questions and criticisms in Parliament; the government must allow the Opposition to scrutinize government action and to debate urgent and important matters at periods both timely and lengthy enough to expose the major arguments; and elections must be held at least once every five years.[12]

[11] James R. Mallory, "Responsive and Responsible Government," *Proceedings and Transactions of the Royal Society of Canada*, vol. 12, 4th series (1974), p. 209.

[12] Thomas A. Hockin, "Flexible and Structured Parliamentarism: From 1848 to Contemporary Party Government," *Journal of Canadian Studies*, vol. 14, no. 2 (Summer 1979), p. 14.

Far more important than any of the preceding changes has been the general drift of power and decision making from the market to government. The displacement of the market and the politicization of everyday life reflect the collectivist view that societies and economies, like factories, can and should be managed and manipulated. The evidence is ubiquitous. It is manifest in the scale of government employment, with federal, provincial, and local governments directly responsible for the employment of more than one of every nine Canadians in the work force (a ratio that has changed little in the last two decades) and indirectly responsible for many more.[13] Total government expenditures as a percentage of gross national product increased from 28.6 percent in 1958 to 41.1 percent in 1978, and detailed government regulations affect ever more spheres of activity.[14]

The expansion of government activity rearranges the relations of power and influence between the key actors in policy making and administration. A direct consequence of the transformation in the role of government has been the steady accretion of power in the nonelected administrative branch. Every advance in the role of government tends to increase the indispensability, power, and autonomy of the civil service. The day-to-day administration of the minutiae of policies instituted by the legislators of yesterday inevitably escapes political scrutiny in all but the rarest of times. At the highest levels of the civil service, senior officials have a crucial say in policy making as a result of their expertise, administrative skills, and political adroitness. That their nominal political superiors can often exercise only nominal control is not surprising.

The cumulative result of an expansion of government intended to serve the needs and hopes of society is a system that threatens to escape the control of the political strata possessed of formal power and therefore significantly to erode the capacity of the electorate to give direction to government. The report of the recent Royal Commission on Financial Management and Accountability concluded:

> After two years of careful study and consideration, we have reached the deeply held conviction that the serious malaise

---

13 David K. Foot, "Political Cycles, Economic Cycles, and the Trend in Public Employment in Canada," in Meyer W. Bucovetsky, ed., *Studies in Public Employment and Compensation in Canada*, Institute for Research on Public Policy Series on Public Sector Employment in Canada, vol. 2 (Montreal: Butterworths, 1979), pp. 68-71, 79.

14 Gérard Veilleux, "Intergovernmental Canada—Government by Conference?— A Fiscal and Economic Perspective" (Paper presented to the Annual Conference of the Institute of Public Administration of Canada, Winnipeg, August 1979), mimeographed, p. 5.

pervading the management of government stems fundamentally from a grave weakening, and in some cases an almost total breakdown, in the chain of accountability, first within government, and second in the accountability of government to Parliament and ultimately to the Canadian people.[15]

There is widespread agreement that the expenditure side of government is out of control and that many government operations have become almost immune to elementary considerations of economy. Cabinet ministers have more obligations than they can meet, including the normal constituency duties of M.P.s, performance in the House of Commons, the supervision and leadership of their departments, and participation in the cabinet.[16] Further, as Stewart points out, the reality is not that of spendthrift governments evading the control of tight-fisted legislators. The latter, no less than the former, see greater political gains in expenditure than in cutbacks.[17] As a result of these deep-seated pressures for expansion, government has become a major instrument for the misallocation of resources.

The impact of big government on the performance of cabinet and Commons is devastating. According to Robert Stanfield, the former leader of the official opposition, both the cabinet and the House of Commons are overloaded to the point where they are incapable of doing their job. The cabinet cannot control the bureaucracy, and the Commons cannot control the cabinet. "What is involved is recognition that democratic responsible government and all-pervasive government in Ottawa are not compatible. They cannot exist together."[18] The expansion of government, as we shall see, has also compounded the difficulty of making the federal system efficient.

Institutions and Society: Part Two

Federalism has made an indispensable contribution to the peaceful functioning of the Canadian polity. Nevertheless, it has proved

[15] Government of Canada, *Royal Commission on Financial Management and Accountability: Final Report* (Hull: Ministry of Supply and Services, 1979), p. 21.
[16] Ralph Heintzman, "The Educational Contract," *Journal of Canadian Studies,* vol. 14, no. 2 (Summer 1979), p. 2.
[17] John Stewart, "Strengthening the Commons," *Journal of Canadian Studies,* vol. 14, no. 2 (Summer 1979), p. 39.
[18] Robert L. Stanfield, "The Present State of the Legislative Process in Canada: Myths and Realities," in William A. W. Neilson and James C. MacPherson, eds., *The Legislative Process in Canada: The Need for Reform* (Toronto: Butterworths, 1978), p. 47.

impossible to keep all matters on which French and English differ safely within provincial jurisdiction. On key occasions the contending ethnic groups have disagreed over vital federal policies. In both world wars, the different meaning of the European connection for English- and French-speaking Canadians occasioned significant variations in their willingness to fight and die on foreign soil. Federal involvement in the construction of the welfare state in the past half-century has been less warmly received in Quebec than elsewhere. Divergent attitudes toward the role of the state, toward the federal system, and toward democracy itself have exacerbated French-English relations since Confederation. Canadian history has been punctuated by ethnic crises pertaining to language, education, civil liberties, military service, foreign policy, and other areas of government activity.

Nevertheless, until comparatively recently these divergences of belief and practice did not threaten the survival of the political system. Federalism, with disputes at the margin over the desirable degree of centralization and decentralization, seemed capable of responding flexibly to changing pressures for action by the provincial governments and the federal government in Ottawa. The fluctuation between periods of centralization and decentralization in response to the shifting strength of centripetal and centrifugal forces has, in fact, been a dominant theme for students of Canadian federalism.

The periods of unquestioned central government ascendancy have been limited essentially to the first decades after Confederation, both world wars, and the period of reconstruction from 1945 to the mid-1950s. This last period was shaped by the war experience and postwar conditions but also by the "lessons" of the Great Depression. The latter had a profound effect on the intellectuals of English Canada and the governing elites in Ottawa, who have had to grapple in recent years with the erosion of a federal hegemony they once thought destined to last.

The contrast between the depression of the 1930s, when government was paralyzed, allegedly because of the divided power structure of the federal system, and the war and postwar periods, with their notable successes in management and economic rehabilitation under the lead of a clearly dominant central government, made it easy for English Canadians to conclude that centralization was the wave of the future. In those halcyon days, which were really only yesterday, it was widely believed that a range of social forces and tendencies vaguely clustered under the label of modernization or secularization were driving the federal system toward centralization and reducing or eliminating the underlying diversity on which, it was thought, provincial power rested.

The numerous descriptions, predictions, and exhortations from the 1930s to the mid-1960s pointing to a more centralized future have, at least in the short run, been repudiated by the new reality of growing provincial power and a relatively weak central government. The attenuation of federal dominance in the last two decades has attracted varying explanations, the intricacies of which cannot be pursued here.[19] What must be noted is that the perception of a central government gravely weakened and in retreat is widespread. The recent report of the Task Force on Canadian Unity claimed that fifteen years ago the central government was regarded with respect, sustained by loyalty, and recognized as efficient and competent.

> Today, that is much less true; "Ottawa," as we found on our tour, is for many Canadians synonymous with all that is to be deplored about modern government—a remote, shambling bureaucracy that extracts tribute from its subjects and gives little in return . . . an unfair stereotype . . . but this view has . . . a widespread appeal today.[20]

Conversely, the escalating importance of the provincial governments of the large or wealthy provinces is universally attested. In recent decades there has been an indisputable increase in the power and status of the provinces, to which, accordingly, citizens are increasingly linked by a network of laws, services, benefits, and duties. The realities of the situation are inextricably intermingled with the fads and fashions of the intelligentsia responsible for explanation and evaluation. To compensate for the errors of their elders, who viewed the provinces as anachronisms, many contemporary scholars are almost blinded by provincialism and overlook the continuing power and responsibilities of Ottawa.

The attack on the central government is most vigorously mounted by the Parti Québécois government. Other provincial governments, however, are far from pleased with the functioning of a federal system they feel pays too little attention to their singularities, gives inadequate recognition to their competence, and provides insufficient opportunities for regional perspectives to be brought to bear on central government policy making.

The frustrations of both levels of government are directly related to that expansion of government activities of which they are simul-

---

[19] For a good analysis, see Donald V. Smiley, *Constitutional Adaptation and Canadian Federalism since 1945*, Documents of the Royal Commission on Bilingualism and Biculturalism, no. 4 (Ottawa: Queen's Printer, 1970).

[20] Task Force on Canadian Unity, *A Future Together: Observations and Recommendations* (Ottawa: Ministry of Supply and Services, 1979), p. 16.

taneously the major beneficiaries and the prime victims. Both levels of government are active and entrepreneurial in attempting to implement their competing visions of a desirable future. Both intervene vigorously in the overlapping societies and economies under their jurisdiction in the pursuit of divergent grand designs.

In a unitary state the decline of the market results in a straightforward displacement of private by public decision making. In a federal system with strong governments at both levels, the result is much more complex. What was hitherto handled by the processes of markets and by nonpolitical decision makers, for whom the federal division of powers was irrelevant, is not only politicized but federalized as well. Federal and provincial jurisdictional differences penetrate ever deeper. The sphere of activity outside the political, and therefore outside the federal, system constantly shrinks. Much of this federalization from above, which claims an ever-expanding ratio of citizen activity as federal or provincial, is a result of the internal dynamics of Leviathan at both levels of government. Much of the emphasis on regionalism, for example, reflects not any underlying territorial diversities but the power of provincial governments to structure the political world in terms of their self-interest.

In a federal state the displacement of the market generates intergovernmental conflict. The success of governments in enhancing their own authority multiplies the potential for intergovernmental conflict over anything from regulatory details to the most profound issues of public policy. To minimize the actual incidence of conflict, there has been a vast proliferation of federal-provincial committees with subject matters ranging from the most specific issues, which are handled by civil servants, to the most general questions of the economy and the constitution, which are on the agenda when the prime minister and the premiers of the eleven governments meet. The complexities of the system produce policy rigidities, bottlenecks that cannot be eliminated by the exercise of hierarchical authority, a decline in effective control by legislatures and electorates, and, frequently, serious costs to the citizenry the system is supposed to serve.[21]

In spite of the undeniable importance of these structural tensions, it is clear that the core of the threat to Canada's survival is elsewhere, in the area of Quebec/Ottawa or French/English relations. Since 1960 a succession of Quebec governments has constructed and employed the Quebec state as a powerful instrument of social and economic transformation. The institutional predominance of the

[21] Smiley, "Intergovernmental Relations."

16

Catholic church was quickly eliminated, and its link with the English business classes in Quebec, with whom it shared an interest in a weak provincial state, was broken. The bureaucracy was transformed into an efficient agency for the pursuit of public purposes; welfare was transferred from the church to government professionals; and the educational system was expanded, secularized, and taken over by the provincial state. In sum, a process was stimulated by which French Canadian Quebecers were transformed into a political people, whose nationalism no longer cast government as an enemy. On the contrary, state and society in Quebec were drawn into an intimate embrace.

From the mid-1960s on and particularly in the Trudeau years from 1968 to 1979, the federal government fought to preserve its authority and legitimacy with Francophones both within and outside Quebec. The basic strategy has been to increase the presence and visibility of French Canadians in the federal bureaucracy by extending the use of French as a language of work and by making services available, where numbers warranted, in either official language. The federal government has also attempted, with less success, to increase the availability of education in the French language in provincial education systems. The central government's objective has been to preserve the viability of Francophone communities outside Quebec, in order to redress the tendency of Quebec Francophones to see Quebec, not Canada, as their homeland.

Concurrently with the central government's attempts to strengthen the attachment of French Canadians, wherever located, to Ottawa, the internal politics of the province of Quebec were convulsed by the rapid growth of the Parti Québécois, which was formed in 1968 and attained power in 1976. After its severe defeat in the 1973 elections, the Parti Québécois deliberately severed its position on independence from the issue of good government. The party realized that its independence program hindered its bid for power in the province by frightening off many voters who were seeking a low-risk defeat of the unpopular incumbent government, the Liberal regime of Robert Bourassa. In the 1976 provincial election campaign the party stated that it would conduct itself in office as a provincial government and would give the electorate a separate opportunity in a postelection referendum to vote for or against independence.

The success of that strategy in its first phase—the attainment of office—precipitated a situation of profound constitutional uncertainty. The party used its assumption of provincial government power for an unrelenting assault on federalism, employing all the weapons that office makes available.

The Parti Québécois won its first provincial election on November 15, 1976, one of the great turning points in Canadian history. Since 1960 a succession of Quebec prime ministers had chipped away at the federal regime and made it clear that Quebec's allegiance to the idea of Canada was less than wholehearted. Nevertheless, all of them, from Jean Lesage to Bourassa, had been prepared to go along with federalism. With the victory of the Parti Québécois the old game of incrementalism, of ad hoc advances, was discarded. After 1976 political strategy in Quebec City responded to a set of guiding objectives that postulated an independent Quebec.

The Parti Québécois sought to make itself the only legitimate spokesman for the powerful nationalism that had long existed in Francophone Quebec. To do so it had to convince the electorate that federalism and nationalism were incompatible and that the latter must be clothed in the garments of an independent state.

The Electoral System and National Unity

The Canada that went to the polls on May 22, 1979, was not a nation in a state of equilibrium. It was widely assumed that major constitutional changes would be necessary to induce the people and government of Quebec to remain within Canada and that the constitution would have to be adapted to the new realities of provincial power. Canadians had just been told by a major government task force that time was running out[22] and that unless quick action were taken the fragmentation of the country was probable, some said inevitable.

Thus from November 15, 1976, when the Parti Québécois was elected to govern Quebec, up to the federal election in May 1979, there was an unusual amount of introspection: conferences on "whither Canada?" proliferated, academic assessments of the country's condition and prospects multiplied, federal-provincial conferences on the constitution were held, and parliamentary committees conducted hearings on constitutional changes proposed by the Trudeau government. The public was extensively consulted in a series of open meetings between September 1977 and April 1978 held all across the country by the Task Force on Canadian Unity. The commissioners' efforts to stimulate grass-roots feedback and to let the people speak produced "some 900 briefs and close to 3,000 letters."[23]

Meanwhile in Quebec the provincial government was approaching the referendum to be held in the spring of 1980, in which the

---

[22] Task Force on Canadian Unity, *Future Together*, chap. 2.
[23] Task Force on Canadian Unity, *A Time to Speak: The Views of the Public* (Ottawa: Ministry of Supply and Services, 1979), p. viii.

people of Quebec would be asked to contribute to the decision on their collective future. The wording of the referendum question had not been determined by the time of the national election, but it was bound to reflect the blend of integrity, partisan self-interest, and strategic advice from pollsters characteristic of political decisions in a democracy.

In these circumstances,[24] it might have been expected that the general election would be infused with high drama, as the parties confronted the electorate with clear, alternative constitutional futures. But no detailed proposals appeared. The Liberals identified Trudeau with strong leadership and national unity. The Conservatives portrayed Clark as a consensual leader with good relations with the Conservative premiers of six provinces. The NDP did not treat national unity as a priority issue, and it reduced the constitutional question to a superstructural reflection of economic problems caused by inept political leadership. The election made almost no contribution to Canadians' education in the causes and possible cures of the country's constitutional ailments.

Only loosely, therefore, could it be said that the election was about the constitution. On the other hand, concerned observers invested the outcome with great significance for the constitutional future of the country, not because of variations in the constitutional policy of the two major parties and only partly because of differences of personality and character in the party leaders, Clark and Trudeau. Concern was focused on the constitutional consequences expected to flow from the regional and ethnic biases of whichever governing party emerged when the votes were counted. In the graphic language of the Quebec correspondent of the leading English-Canadian newspaper:

> With foreboding I see the arrival of this election day, 1979. . . . French Canada will vote one way, English-speaking Canada another. The political process will reflect in the federal Government the drawing apart of the country's two language communities, who recognize themselves in different parties. The Progressive Conservatives and the NDP will by tonight be the only really significant political expressions of English Canada. . . . The rift in the country along the language fault line, where the tension has been building for years, opens tonight. . . . If Pierre Trudeau manages to form a minority government, with the massive support of

[24] See Edward McWhinney, *Quebec and the Constitution, 1960-1978* (Toronto: University of Toronto Press, 1979), for a useful corrective to the pessimism of many English Canadian writers on the "crisis."

French Canada, it will be seen as an outrage, a kind of alien occupation, by much of English-speaking Canada. The bitterness will go deep.

[Or] Joe Clark [will] . . . form a government without significant representation in French Canada. The composition of the House of Commons [will] divide largely according to language. René Lévesque [will] anoint himself the political spokesman for all francophones. He will say . . . that the two nations of Canada are now politically visible, the reality of the country no longer obscured by the masking presence of a French Canadian Prime Minister.[25]

Johnson's view that the election outcome would be disastrous for national unity was widely shared. It reflected a developing body of opinion, not yet a consensus, that some of the most destructive tendencies in the Canadian polity could be attributed to the bias in the transformation of votes into seats by the electoral system.

The electoral system, like much else in Canadian political life, had been taken over from Great Britain before Confederation and retained afterward with little thought for possible alternatives. Although proportional representation has always had a sprinkling of support in Canada and there has been occasional experimentation with other electoral systems in the provinces, the first-past-the-post system in single-member constituencies—known as ridings in Canada—has been little challenged at the federal level. It was British and good enough for the Mother of Parliaments. It was simple and easy for voters and candidates to understand. Finally, until 1957 it contributed to one-party legislative majorities and hence to executive stability.

From 1921 to 1957 the electoral system discriminated savagely against the Conservative party in Quebec and thus deprived one of the two main parties in the country of effective contact with French Canada, but this consideration was secondary. The Conservatives for all but five years had been confined to the opposition, where the regional and ethnic bias of their caucus apparently had minimal negative consequences for the political system. By contrast, the Liberal government in power for most of the period from 1921 to 1957 effectively straddled the two great language communities and also, with occasional exceptions, had politically adequate representation from western Canada.

From this and earlier historical experience going back to Confederation, a particular role in maintaining national unity was attrib-

[25] William Johnson, "Canada's Fate Looks Bleak," *Globe and Mail*, May 22, 1979.

uted to the party system. The governing party, in particular, and the federal cabinet were held responsible for the aggregation and conciliation of regional interests at the center. Conventional wisdom had it that it was in these two bodies, which were, of course, intimately linked, that political compromises and regional brokerage took place. Here, if anywhere, was the genius of Canadian politics—the power to reconcile French and English, center and periphery, provincial perspectives and national perspectives.

The period from 1957 to 1974, covering eight general elections, cast doubts on the contribution of the party system to political stability and national integration and by implication contributed to the erosion of support for the electoral system. Five of these eight elections produced minority governments. This undermined one of the prime virtues attributed to the electoral system, its capacity to manufacture a one-party legislative majority for a party receiving less than a majority of votes. More serious was the effect of the electoral system on the regional distribution of party members in the House of Commons. During this period the Liberals received on average only 32 percent of the seats "merited" by their electoral support from the Prairie provinces. The Conservatives in the same period received only 64 percent of their "entitlement" from Quebec, or 40 percent if their breakthrough in 1958 is excluded. Particularly significant was the fact that basic shortfalls in provincial representation now affected governing parties, the Conservatives in Quebec in 1957–1958 and 1962–1963 and the Liberals in one or more Prairie provinces, especially Alberta, from 1963 to 1979. Under the first-past-the-post electoral system, therefore, not only did parties move in and out of government, but regions and provinces, including the Francophone community concentrated in Quebec, also underwent the abrupt transition from the government to the opposition side of the House.

According to several analysts, a major aspect of the political weakness of the central government was the lack of significant representation for whole provinces and regions on the government side of the House. This in turn contributed to a developing provincialism, led by the governments of those provinces deprived of effective input into the governing party at Ottawa. Thus, as time ran out on the Liberal government, politicians and analysts became increasingly apprehensive about the possibility that a Conservative government with negligible representation from Quebec would be elected. This result, which evidence indicated was the outcome coveted by the Parti Québécois government, became known as the doomsday scenario. It was feared that this outcome, with English Canada apparently in control of the central government, would further mobilize Francophone Quebecers behind the banner of a provincial government possessed of new proof of the insensitivity, ineffectiveness, and illegitimacy of the Ottawa government.

More generally, as Watts noted,

> where the parties have become primarily regional in their bases, the parliamentary federations have been prone to instability. . . . In this respect one of the most ominous signs in the present Canadian scene is the apparent inability of each of the major political parties to attract support from some major regions of the country and thus to be truly representative of an interregional consensus.[26]

Even outside Quebec, the representational imbalances in the national party system were given extra salience by the centrifugal pressures at work in the federal system. Various provincial governments, possessed of a heady confidence, chipped away at a central government with weak representative credentials. Since it was becoming increasingly difficult to deny that the electoral system made a major contribution to the regionalization of the national party system, which in turn eroded the legitimacy of the central government, the electoral system itself was on trial in the recent election. The results gave little solace to the defenders of the existing system and further diminished the taken-for-granted quality it had previously enjoyed. Electoral reform is bound to remain a live issue as long as the existing system proves incapable of producing majority governments representative of the nation.[27]

The objective of electoral reformers is a more reasonable relationship between the percentage of votes and the seats received by each party in each province and region of the country. This goal is pursued not in the interests of justice, but in the cause of national unity. A more regionally representative central government would be a more legitimate and effective central government.

The thirty-first general election, on May 22, 1979, was fought under the old rules—what a recent Quebec government study sympathetic to proportional representation pointedly called the "English

---

[26] Ronald L. Watts, "Survival or Disintegration," in Richard Simeon, ed., *Must Canada Fail?* (Montreal and London: McGill and Queen's University Press, 1977), p. 52.

[27] For the most recent and best analysis available, see William P. Irvine, *Does Canada Need a New Electoral System?* Queen's Studies on the Future of the Canadian Communities (Kingston: Queen's University, Institute of Intergovernmental Relations, 1979).

system."[28] The election results provide a textbook illustration of the inequities and negative consequences the existing system is capable of producing. The defeated Liberals received nearly half a million more votes, and twenty-two fewer seats, than the party that replaced them in office. Although the new Conservative government was generally favored by the electoral system, the Conservatives were harmed in Quebec. They received 432,000 votes in Quebec, more than they received in six other provinces, but only two seats. In Prince Edward Island, by contrast, 34,147 votes gave the party four seats. Thus, although the Conservatives received 10.5 percent of their total vote from Quebec, only 1.5 percent of their seats were from that province. The Liberals, with 15 percent of their vote west of the Great Lakes, received only three seats, 2.6 percent of their total seats, in the four provinces of Manitoba, Saskatchewan, Alberta, and British Columbia.

The new Conservative government emerged from the May election to confront the nationalist demands of the Parti Québécois with fewer members from Quebec than any government party since 1867. The Conservatives also had fewer popular votes than the Liberals they replaced and the lowest percentage of the popular vote of any governing party since Confederation. The minority status of the Conservative party and the bias in the regional and ethnic composition of its caucus and cabinet not only would impinge on the legislative-executive relationship in Ottawa. They would also weaken the central government in that larger federal-provincial system of intergovernmental bargaining so crucial to the evolution of Canadian federalism. As it turned out, the country was saved from the consequences of an unrepresentative Conservative government by the return to power a year later of an unrepresentative Liberal government.

It was indeed a curious outcome. As noted earlier, the effective capacity of the House of Commons to control the government is minimal. In principle an elementary capacity to reward and punish belongs to the electorate. In reality the exercise of that capacity can be rendered nugatory by an inefficient electoral system that turns losers into winners and winners into losers, as it did on May 22, 1979. Few seem to have noticed this fact. Even fewer seem concerned. That the results of an election are easier to justify by the principles of a lottery than by any principle of equity is not, however, a trivial matter.

[28] Robert Burns, *One Citizen, One Vote: Green Paper on the Reform of the Electoral System* (Quebec: Ministère d'Etat à la Réforme Electorale et Parlementaire, 1979), pp. 16, 25, 28, 33.

2
The Larger Context: The Period Preceding the 1979 Election

John Meisel

It is easy to exaggerate the importance of events that command one's full attention and in the study of which one has made a heavy invest-ment of time.[1] One is nevertheless tempted to conclude that the 1979 general election was one of the most momentous electoral contests in Canada since World War II. The country and many of its chief political figures were approaching a number of critical crossroads, where the paths chosen would quite literally determine whether Canada would survive as a nation and, if it did, whether its political regime would any longer resemble the parliamentary system adopted at the time of Confederation or correspond in any way to the ideals on which it was based. The developments leading up to it, the elec-tion itself, and its aftermath would all affect how Canada would meet the unprecedented challenges of its immediate future.

Party politics are not conducted in a vacuum, and external factors such as economic conditions frequently exacerbate Canada's domestic travails. By way of illustration, trends in three important economic indicators—unemployment, the consumer price index, and the exchange rate—are plotted in figure 2-1, where they are related to monthly shifts in the polls conducted by the Canadian Institute of Public Opinion. Although the data suggest that short-run fluctuations in party popularity are not linked to variations in eco-

---

This chapter was completed while the author was professor of political science at Queen's University.

[1] The principal sources for this chapter are John Saywell, ed., *Canadian Annual Review of Politics and Public Affairs* (Toronto: University of Toronto Press, 1975, 1976, 1977); *Canadian Newsfacts* (Toronto: Marpep Publishing); and the author's recollections and file of clippings from various Canadian newspapers.

FIGURE 2-1

Party Support and Economic Indicators, July 1974–May 1979

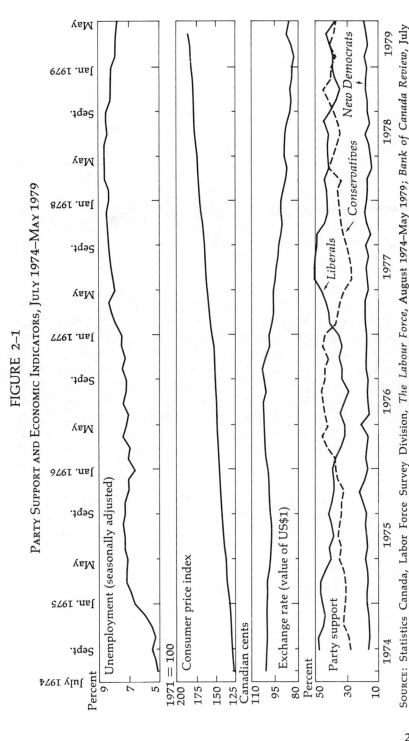

Source: Statistics Canada, Labor Force Survey Division, *The Labour Force*, August 1974–May 1979; *Bank of Canada Review*, July 1974–May 1979; and Canadian Institute of Public Opinion, *Gallup Report*, September 1974–May 1979.

25

nomic conditions, they do not conflict with the assumption that the ultimate drawing together of the Liberals and Progressive Conservatives in 1978 and 1979 may have been caused by growing anxiety about the economy as well as uncertainty about who was responsible for, and most able to cope with, the deteriorating situation.[2] Canada's acute economic difficulties are of course partly self-inflicted, but they also reflect North American and worldwide problems. The oil crisis hit Canada hard, as it has every highly industrialized country, despite the fact that Canada produces considerable amounts of black gold. Differences between the oil-producing provinces, particularly Alberta, and the Ottawa government, on the one hand, and the consumer provinces, notably Ontario, on the other, contributed to intense political tensions.

Inflation, which ran at annual rates of 10.9, 10.8, 7.5, 8.0, and 9.0 percent in the years from 1974 to 1978, also resulted in part from foreign developments, although Canadians and their government must bear some responsibility for the secular rise. Nor can they escape blame for the alarming unemployment rate. During the period between the 1974 and 1979 elections, the number of those seeking jobs exceeded, for the first time in Canadian history, the 1 million mark. In this period the unemployment rate rose from about 5 to over 8 percent. Although these figures are depressing, it should be noted that they cover a period in which the rate of job creation was also high. During the same period the value of the Canadian dollar dropped by about 16 percent in relation to the ailing U.S. dollar. Although this gave an impetus to the country's export trade, it also added to the already threatening inflationary pressures.

The interelection period, then, was marked by a combination of externally and domestically generated economic problems to which, as we shall see, the government was unable to respond adequately. It was, in fact, considered by many to be one of their causes.

The Political Community

Regional Tensions. One reason for the widespread enthusiasm that accompanied Pierre Elliott Trudeau's accession to the prime ministership and his electoral victory in 1968 was the sense that he would be able to heal the serious rifts between Canada's regions, particularly that between Quebec and the rest of the country. The high expectations met with disappointment: national cleavages deepened during Trudeau's years in office, and the federal government was unable to arrest the centrifugal forces, whose intensity only grew.

[2] See also figure 3-1, in chapter 3.

The election of the independentist Parti Québécois (PQ), under the charismatic René Lévesque, in the Quebec provincial election of November 1976 constituted a major escalation in the province's drive for independence. At the same time, Ottawa's preoccupation with French Canada and the predominantly eastern support base of the Trudeau government contributed to western alienation, which became extreme and found expression in the unaccommodating postures adopted by most western governments when they negotiated with Ottawa.

Canadian politics came to reflect more and more the rising strength of the provinces: the national political arena was made to include constant and increasingly demanding negotiations between the two senior levels of government. This process of redefinition of Canadian politics made it all the more difficult for Ottawa to evolve satisfactory solutions to the country's mushrooming problems.

No doubt for this reason, as well as for others, Prime Minister Trudeau announced in the autumn of 1974 that he would press for the resolution of outstanding constitutional issues within the life of the Thirtieth Parliament. The following year he proposed that the two most troublesome sets of problems be negotiated separately: those dealing with "patriation" (that is, making the written part of the constitution a Canadian rather than a British document) and amendment of the constitution and those redefining the respective jurisdictions of the two senior tiers of government. Trudeau indicated that in the absence of agreement Ottawa would act unilaterally in the matter of patriation. Strong opposition by the provincial premiers compelled the Liberal government to abandon its plan early in 1977. A new initiative followed in June 1978, when the government published its white paper *A Time for Action* and introduced Bill C-60, the Constitutional Amendment Bill. The latter included a lofty preamble, a charter guaranteeing a number of political and civil rights, proposals for the transformation of the upper chamber (which would have included some members appointed by provincial governments on the basis of proportional party representation), changes in the Supreme Court, and a commitment by the federation to reduce regional disparities. Opposition among the provinces and in the relevant parliamentary committee resulted in the abandonment of this major effort at constitutional revision.[3]

---

[3] For excellent, authoritative surveys of these and related developments, see Les Kom, *The Federal Year in Review: 1976-77*, vol. 1; and Douglas Brown, *The Federal Year in Review: 1977-78*, both published by the Institute of Intergovernmental Relations, Queen's University, Kingston. See also chapter 1 in this volume.

The government took another initiative designed to contribute to the resolution of the constitutional dilemma and to examine the question of national cohesion. In 1977 it appointed the Task Force on Canadian Unity, headed by a one-time Liberal cabinet minister, Jean-Luc Pepin, and John Robarts, the former premier of Ontario. But the manner in which the task force was announced, and subsequent reactions to changes in its composition as well as to its recommendations, suggest that in the cabinet's view this was never a serious attempt to find solutions to vexing problems. It was probably a gesture intended to meet the criticism that Ottawa was not responding effectively to the unity issue.[4]

Ethnic Cleavages. Although constitutional issues had a bearing on every facet of Canadian life, including the rights of and relations between members of the major language groups, they were generally seen as rather abstract and not likely to arouse passions. But some actions by federal and provincial authorities triggered public responses that demonstrated the magnitude of the problem. There were deep cleavages between Francophones and Anglophones that inevitably spilled over into the partisan political sphere. They centered on language use and language rights, an extremely sensitive matter likely to be associated with collective survival and to touch the wellspring of many an individual. The federal government's bilingualism program in the public service (civil service) had never been popular in some parts of the country, particularly the West and some sections of Ontario. It was also detested by a great many English-speaking bureaucrats. It became apparent, in the period between the two elections, that the federal government's extremely costly schemes to teach many Anglophone civil servants French had been largely ineffective and that parts of the program had been wrongly conceived.[5] The longstanding hostility of many English-speaking civil servants and other Canadians to the federal programs initiated as a result of the reports of the Royal Commission on

---

[4] The main report is nevertheless a document providing useful background to the constitutional and socioeconomic problems of Canada, as well as an interesting guide to possible solutions. See the Task Force on Canadian Unity, *A Future Together: Observations and Recommendations* (Ottawa: Ministry of Supply and Services, 1979). For a critique of the report and of other constitutional initiatives, see Alan C. Cairns, "Recent Federalist Constitutional Proposals: A Review Essay," *Canadian Public Policy*, vol. 5, no. 3 (Summer 1979), pp. 348-65.

[5] An informed assessment from a sympathetic source is in Commissioner of Official Languages, *Fifth Annual Report, 1975* (Ottawa: Information Canada, 1976).

Bilingualism and Biculturalism thus appeared justified because of their poor administration and so fanned resentment against French Canadians.

If ineffective language teaching in the public service angered primarily Anglophones, both of Canada's major language groups were profoundly disturbed by the dispute about whether only English or both languages could be used in the cockpits of aircraft flying over Quebec. The initial incident, precipitated and then mishandled by the Department of Transport under Jean Marchand and later Otto Lang, developed into a major confrontation involving a national air strike a few days before the opening of the Olympic games in the summer of 1976. It is no exaggeration to say that rarely in recent memory had English and French Canada been so dangerously pitted against one another. It has been argued by serious observers that the electoral victory of the Parti Québécois would have been very much less likely had many in Quebec not become exasperated by the treatment accorded the champions of French—the *gens de l'air*.

English Canadians, on the other hand, and not only in Quebec, were outraged by the language legislation introduced by Robert Bourassa in 1974, which limited the use of English in Quebec. Even more offensive, Bill 1 (later renumbered 101)—the major language law of the PQ government—compelled virtually all immigrants to Quebec to send their children to French schools, removed all English signs from public view, and ensured that French would be spoken in all major economic enterprises in Quebec. Beyond the many complex constitutional aspects of the legislation was the question whether English was going to be tolerated in the public life of Quebec and whether Ottawa would go to bat on behalf of Anglophone Canadians living in that province, whose constitutional rights, many believed, had been violated by the Quebec government. Anglophones in provinces attempting to improve the status of French in their jurisdiction, particularly in Ontario and New Brunswick, were dismayed because they recognized that it would prove increasingly difficult to provide better services to Francophones outside Quebec if Anglophones within the province were going to be coerced into the use of French. Whatever the merits of the case and its ramifications,[6] the central fact from our perspective is that serious antagonism was generated by the efforts of Quebec governments to protect the French language, by the weaknesses of the federal government's

[6] See John R. Mallea, ed., *Quebec's Language Policies: Background and Response* (Quebec: Les Presses de l'Université Laval, 1977); and Camille Laurin, minister of state for cultural development, Quebec, *Quebec Policy on the French Language* (March 1977).

language training program, and by the major confrontation between the *gens de l'air* and the English-speaking pilots and controllers, provoked largely by the ineptitude of the Department of Transport.

Class Antagonism. Politics in Canada, as in the United States, is not based primarily on class cleavages, although there is, of course, some relation between the economic status of individuals and their political affiliation.[7] Among voters choosing the New Democratic party, blue-collar workers have always been most numerous, but the other parties always receive a significant proportion of the labor vote.

A number of events following the 1974 election indicated that class conflict was becoming more sharply defined and that organized labor was taking a more aggressive role vis-à-vis the federal government and the older political parties. The event precipitating this sharpening of class tensions was the Liberal government's introduction of wage and price controls. During the 1974 election campaign, the Progressive Conservatives had called' for a price and wage freeze, during which anti-inflation measures would be designed and adopted. Prime Minister Trudeau made the matter an important element in his campaign and mercilessly ridiculed the opposition's proposal on the grounds that it was impracticable: Canadians would never accept controls. Some fifteen months after the election, the government introduced its own anti-inflation program, which imposed limits on the amount by which individual incomes could rise annually and attempted directly to restrict the rise in prices.

The Canadian Labour Congress (CLC) vigorously opposed the measures, arguing (correctly, as it turned out) that they would hit wage and low-salaried employees much harder than anyone else and that industry would still be able to get away with huge profits at the expense of the consumer.[8] To underline its displeasure with the government and its adamant rejection of the anti-inflation program, the CLC instructed its representatives to resign from all government boards and commissions of which they were members. It also called for an unprecedented one-day national work stoppage: on October 14, 1976, over 1 million workers, according to reliable estimates, stayed off the job.

[7] Mildred Schwartz, "Canadian Voting Behavior," in Richard Rose, ed., *Electoral Behavior: A Comparative Handbook* (New York: Free Press, 1974), pp. 383-92; and Harold D. Clarke, Jane Jensen, Lawrence LeDuc, and Jon H. Pammett, *Political Choice in Canada* (Toronto: McGraw-Hill Ryerson, 1979), pp. 107-19.

[8] Reginald S. Letourneau, "Inflation and Incomes Policy in Canada," Executive Bulletin, no. 9 (Ottawa: Conference Board of Canada, May 1979), and "Did We Expect Too Much from Controls?" *Canadian Business Review*, vol. 6 (Spring 1979), pp. 11-16.

This was in effect a one-day national strike, and it indicated that the alienation of labor from the older parties (both of which supported the anti-inflation program) had reached a new high point. But this should not be exaggerated. The basic absence of militancy in the CLC is evident in its proposal, made in 1976, for a powerful tripartite council of labor, business, and government to play a key role in the planning and execution of national economic policy. Opposition soon developed, however, even among some of the CLC affiliates. One of the arguments against it urged that the most effective way of achieving a planned and more equitable society would be for unions to do more to support the New Democratic party (NDP), which was considered by many to be labor's political arm. Three years later the CLC did in fact decide to give much greater aid to the NDP election campaign than it ever had before.

But the CLC was not the only body toying with quasi-corporatist ideas. John Munro, the minister of labor, had been pressing for a tripartite consultative body, and there were also suggestions for a more representative council composed of other interests—farmers and consumers, for instance. The various ideas entertained by the government were never brought even close to implementation, in part because they met with strong opposition from most politicians, no doubt including Liberals, who feared that the new structures would undermine the power of Parliament. In any event, it was never envisaged that the new body's role would be anything but consultative. The federal government did, of course, seek the views of various economic interests from time to time and went so far as to arrange regular meetings with selected business leaders, who were expected to react to its ideas about future economic policies.

The prime minister created a major brouhaha when, in a 1975 television interview, he stated that Canadians had not been able to make the free market system work and that greater government intervention was to be expected. These comments, and a later similar speech to the Canadian Club, unleashed a storm of protest from all sides and united business and labor against him. The intensity of the reaction led Trudeau and the government to abandon any further *dirigiste* initiatives or musings.[9]

Class rifts, as we have seen, intensified in the period between the 1974 and the 1979 elections. The strengthened ties between the unions and the NDP pointed to the importance of the party's per-

[9] Transcript of the prime minister's interview with Bruce Phillips and Carol Taylor on the CTV program "A Conversation with the Prime Minister," taped December 23 for broadcast December 28, 1975, mimeographed (Office of the Prime Minister, press release, January 19, 1976).

formance in the forthcoming election. Its strength in the new Parliament in relation to the other parties could be expected to affect the role of labor in Canadian politics as well as the role of the new government in mediating the relations between social classes in the country. But the conflicts here were much less virulent than the two discussed above. On regional tensions and ethnic cleavages, the Liberal and Conservative positions differed dramatically, as did the manner in which they approached the outstanding problems. It was clear that the election would decide which of fundamentally divergent approaches would be adopted by the new government. The election would determine how the federal government would henceforth handle the effort to redefine the Canadian state.

The Political Process

Canada's centennial celebrations in 1967 and the concurrent success of Expo had created an atmosphere of optimism throughout the country on the eve of Pierre Trudeau's accession as leader of the Liberal party and prime minister. In many eyes, the advent to power of an exceptionally intelligent, forceful, and stylish leader was the crowning event of this heady era, guaranteeing that Canada would indeed become the "just society" to which Lester Pearson's successor had dedicated himself in the 1968 campaign. The high hopes of the euphoric late 1960s were, as we have seen, soon dissipated and resulted in the near defeat of the Liberals in the 1972 election.[10] Despite the government's return to power with a majority in 1974,[11] however, the former optimism never returned. This was not, of course, surprising in view of the troubles the industrialized countries were encountering as the result of the energy crisis and other economic problems.

In Canada, however, the growing anxiety and unease had their roots not only in the threatening economic climate but also in two other developments: the decline, which appeared to many to be of major proportions, in the fundamental democratic safeguards and the decline in the capacity of the government to function effectively.

Democratic Safeguards. Conditions necessary for the adequate operation of parliamentary democracy were seen to be threatened in several

[10] John Meisel, "Howe, *Hubris,* and '72: An Essay in Political Elitism," in John Meisel, ed., *Working Papers on Canadian Politics* (Montreal: McGill and Queen's University Press, 1975), chap. 6.

[11] Howard R. Penniman, ed., *Canada at the Polls: The General Election of 1974* (Washington, D.C.: American Enterprise Institute, 1975).

areas. Three, in particular, attracted a good deal of attention: ministerial responsibility, access to government information, and individual freedom.

It is doubtful whether the general public was greatly concerned about these matters. There is some evidence, derived from the reaction to the Royal Canadian Mounted Police (RCMP) scandals, that the niceties of civil liberties and proper democratic procedure are of little interest to the majority of people.[12] But they arouse passionate reactions from politicians (particularly but not only those in opposition), the media, and the legal profession. Among these groups they assume quite extraordinary importance and, because of the strategic position occupied by the concerned individuals, they influence the perception the general public has of the political process and the government. In this instance, the decline in support for Trudeau among the media, many academics, and other elite groups was almost certainly associated with what was to them his much too casual approach to many procedural aspects of the democratic process. This seemingly cavalier attitude was all the more disappointing since the prime minister had long and widely been known as a strong civil libertarian and since in other respects he had expressed great concern for human rights, many of which, as noted above, he had hoped to enshrine in the constitution.

It has long been a cardinal principle of parliamentary government that individual ministers take full responsibility for everything that is done by their departments. Under Trudeau, and particularly during the Thirtieth Parliament, this principle was increasingly violated by members of the cabinet. The most striking example concerned revelations that the Royal Canadian Mounted Police had committed a number of illegal acts, many of which ministers, including the prime minister, had denied in the House, only to have to claim later that they had been misinformed or kept in the dark. The government used a number of stratagems for the sake of gaining time and immunity.

One consisted of exploiting the existence of the McDonald Royal Commission Concerning Certain Activities of the Royal Canadian Mounted Police, which was exceedingly slow in getting started and in doing its work and to which the government itself provided information only most grudgingly. But it furnished an excellent excuse to the prime minister and his colleagues: many questions in the House about the RCMP scandals were not answered by the

---

[12] About two out of three Canadians thought that the RCMP should be allowed to open mail and that the power they had was not excessive (*Gallup Report*, August 29, 1978, and January 14, 1979).

responsible ministers on the grounds that a response would have been improper while the matters at issue were before the commission. Certain documents requested by provincial attorneys general were denied them on the same grounds. Another device was to exploit the rules of the House that make it possible for ministers to refuse to respond to oral questions put to them and for former ministers not to have to discuss matters that occurred in their departments while they were in charge of them. Since Trudeau shuffled his ministers from portfolio to portfolio frequently (there were, for example, five solicitors general from 1968 to 1979), many questions asked by the opposition about the RCMP remained unanswered.

The RCMP case was only the most notorious instance in which the government, after a variety of dubious decisions, refused to take responsibility for the actions of its agents. There were other cases—the awarding of aircraft contracts, for instance—in which ministers and the cabinet as a whole refused to accept responsibility for actions taken by the government. Furthermore, the growing importance of quasi-independent crown agencies enhanced the opportunities for public business to be conducted in a manner that escaped the scrutiny of Parliament and for which the cabinet could not be held responsible. Thus Atomic Energy of Canada paid millions of dollars in commissions under highly suspicious circumstances suggesting that a large part of these funds had been used for bribes, and Polysar—a publicly owned chemical company—paid kickbacks to some of its customers to enable them to avoid taxes in their own country. The government could not be held directly responsible, nor could the parliamentary committees that examined these cases extract the needed information from agency officials.

Ministerial responsibility was undermined in yet another manner, one that was not, as such, unusual but that reached dangerous proportions in the Thirtieth Parliament. The question period in the House of Commons is among the most effective means available to Parliament for bringing attention to weaknesses in the government's activities. It depends on skillful questioning by the opposition and on ministers providing information to members on whatever governmental activities interest the House. The Trudeau cabinet, probably more than any of its predecessors, resorted to evasion, obfuscation, and a host of other means to protect its members from revealing potentially harmful information.

It is likely that one of the reasons for this was the serious decline in trust among the major parties. It is, of course, normal and common for them to have a low opinion of one another, but the degree to which the political atmosphere degenerated in this context was extraordinary. There is ample evidence to suggest that the prime minister and his chief lieutenants thought that a Conservative government under Joe Clark would literally destroy Canada. Similarly, the Conservatives appeared quite convinced that the Liberals, if returned to power, would fatally mishandle the national unity crisis and at the same time destroy the democratic safeguards and procedures required for the survival of Canadian parliamentary institutions. The NDP seemed to a certain extent immune to both these sets of fears and, while clearly unimpressed by the older parties, managed to avoid doomsday scenarios. But even so, both government and opposition members of Parliament, under these conditions, tended to abuse the question period in a manner that often undermined the credibility of Parliament and made it look plain silly.

The government's growing tendency to seek refuge under a cloak of secrecy was also displayed in its refusal to introduce a much needed and promised Freedom of Information Act. The matter had been raised by John Turner, then minister of justice, as early as 1969. At that time the idea was to provide public access to government documents in all but a few cases and to allow for judicial review in disputed cases. Although such legislation was paid lip service by many, it was not introduced until the year of the election and then in an insipid form. It was accorded such low priority that it never became law. The only achievement the government could boast in this area was the Human Rights Act, which proscribes discrimination in areas under federal jurisdiction on grounds of race, religion, age, sex, marital status, and physical handicap and which also set up the Canadian Human Rights Commission. This act enables individuals to obtain some access to information the government may hold about them. In a somewhat different but related field, the auditor general (an official responsible to Parliament) was given increased powers to investigate government spending.

These concessions notwithstanding, the administration's nervousness about people's finding out too much about what it was doing was alarming to many. The government went so far as to invoke the Official Secrets Act on two occasions against a newspaper and a former official, only to find that in each case the courts upheld appeals against it.

The greatest apprehension about what was happening to individual freedom was aroused by the conduct of the RCMP. A series of revelations showed that during the preceding decade the Mounties—heretofore regarded as unassailable models of propriety and rectitude—had committed a whole series of illegal acts. They had planted wiretaps, broken into the offices of the Parti Québécois to steal lists of members and also into a left-wing news agency, used confidential medical information to disrupt organizations they deemed subversive, stolen dynamite and burned a barn, published a phony provocative advertisement in the name of a Quebec radical organization, opened mail in the post office, and obviously lied to their political masters about what they had been doing. In the eyes of most people concerned with civil liberties, the government took a remarkably relaxed position after these facts came to light. Its most decisive action was to procure legislation that legalized a heretofore forbidden act—the opening of mail. Thus civil libertarians were shocked on two counts: by what the RCMP had done and by the government's seeming unconcern over the consequences these developments could hold for the rights of Canadians. No member of the Liberal administration, under which the law was repeatedly broken by the RCMP, acknowledged any negligence or wrongdoing, no one resigned, nor has a single officer involved in any of the RCMP's illegal acts and acting on the instructions of his superiors been brought to trial.

The Capacity of the Government to Govern. It is one of the paradoxes of the 1979 election that, despite the view, shared by virtually all the mass media and the pundits, that the Liberal government had become incompetent and dangerous and despite its electoral defeat, the popular vote (as William P. Irvine shows in chapter 3) was anything but a public repudiation. This was no doubt caused primarily by the steadfast loyalty of Francophones and the unappealing image projected by Joe Clark. But the actual performance of the government during the Thirtieth Parliament was also a factor. The government managed to increase pensions, to improve some other social measures, and to outlaw, as we have seen, certain forms of discrimination. It had made possible an open and fair-minded inquiry, under Mr. Justice Thomas Berger, into the likely consequences of the projected MacKenzie Valley pipeline.[13] It also succeeded, in the face of persistent and vigorous lobbying, in ending the tax advantage heretofore enjoyed by *Time* and *Reader's Digest*, thus helping to increase the advertising revenue of Canadian publications. A variety of measures were introduced helpful to farmers generally and to Prairie wheat growers in particular. Petrocanada, the publicly owned oil company, was established and given major regulatory powers under the Petroleum

---

[13] Thomas R. Berger, *Northern Frontier, Northern Homeland: The Report of the Mackenzie Valley Inquiry*, 2 vols. (Ottawa: Ministry of Supply and Services, 1977).

Administration Act. The government also extended its activities in the field of lotteries. In addition to augmenting the powers of the auditor general, measures to increase the effectiveness of government included the Financial Administration Act, which created the new post of comptroller general. A popular decision of the prime minister's was to recommend the appointment of Ed Schreyer, the young former NDP premier of Manitoba, as governor general.

A number of measures of the Trudeau government during the Thirtieth Parliament were received well by some sections of the Canadian public but were much resented by others. The abolition of the death penalty seems to have been opposed by the majority of the people, while the reaction to other measures was more mixed.[14] Limiting the federal contribution to medical and hospital insurance—which are provincial responsibilities—and tightening the eligibility rules guiding unemployment insurance probably pleased the majority of people who knew about them but naturally displeased the potential beneficiaries of these programs.

Much of the good will created by these programs and decisions was offset, however, by the obvious failures and indications that the government had become accident prone. In the eyes of the business community and probably also in those of most taxpayers, one of the most damaging indicators of the Liberals' inefficiency was their incapacity to reduce public expenditures. And when, at last, the prime minister announced that $2½ billion would be cut from the next budget in an effort to bring about a major reduction in the rate of growth of government spending, the reaction was largely hostile. There were two main reasons: some of the ostensible cuts were in fact merely reductions in *projected increases* in estimated expenditure, and such cuts as were made revealed that the government had no effective criteria by which to discriminate between essential and expendable programs.

One of the most dramatic indicators of Ottawa's loss of control was chronicled in the rise in the federal deficit. In 1974 it was $676 million; by 1978 it had reached $11.8 billion—a sum greater than the total annual budget when Trudeau came to power. The value of the Canadian dollar, in relation to its American cousin, dropped from above parity to around eighty-five cents. Efforts to reduce energy consumption met with anything but spectacular success, and some

[14] A Gallup poll in August 1977 reported that 75 percent of those questioned favored the imposition of capital punishment for killing a prison guard or an on-duty policeman and 68 percent supported executions for people convicted of killing an "innocent person."

were badly botched. Thus a scheme to assist homeowners in insulating their houses was so badly timed and prepared that its chief result seemed to be to drive up the price of insulation material. Promises made in 1974 to help cities and intercity travelers· by providing massive assistance to the development and improvement of energy-saving public transport remained largely unfulfilled. Another sign of the growing inefficiency of the government was the difficulty it was experiencing in getting legislation through Parliament. The number of bills successfully piloted through the legislature declined, and the number of important pieces of legislation that died on the Order Paper before the end of the Parliament rose. There was a forty-two-day postal strike, and mail service deteriorated until it became a national joke.

Some of the problems reflected the general deterioration of the political atmosphere, some were caused by the inefficient functioning of the cabinet and its members, and some resulted from the unwillingness of the government to antagonize powerful economic interests. Thus the first phase of a proposed new competitions policy was launched by amending the Combines Investigation Act so that it would apply to services, but the centerpiece of the program—controls on mergers and monopolies—was withdrawn after it met with stiff opposition from the business community. Although a new version was introduced in the session of Parliament preceding the election, it was never called for debate.

The most damaging failure of the government was its handling of inflation. The controls, already mentioned, had been instituted despite violent opposition from labor and to some extent also from industry. The latter came to accept the program more readily as the nature of its operation became clear. But in any event, the government had from the beginning insisted that it too found controls unpalatable and that they were imposed only to provide the breathing space within which structural solutions to the problem would be found and launched. The time available was completely wasted, and the controls were abandoned in response to massive popular pressure without any long-term solution's having been devised.

The government also lost face as a result of scandals over the improper conduct of ministers or their departments. Several of these concerned the relations between members of the cabinet and the judiciary. André Ouellet, minister of consumer and corporate affairs, was found to have been in contempt of court in 1976 for criticizing the decision of a Quebec judge in a price-fixing case. He resigned but later reentered the cabinet. Another minister got himself into difficulties over this incident. C. M. Drury (public works) called the judge who was to hear the case and subsequently offered to resign from the cabinet. The prime minister refused the offer, but Drury withdrew from the cabinet later and resigned his seat in 1978. He was then appointed chairman of the National Capital Commission. John Munro, the minister of labor, had, in 1978, also called a judge in a manner deemed improper and so had to resign. The solicitor general, Francis Fox, confessed to the House in the same year that he had signed someone else's name on a hospital document, and he too withdrew from the government. A different breach occurred when Alastair Gillespie, the minister of energy, Marshall Crowe, the chairman of the National Energy Board, and some of their staffs spent several days fishing in the Arctic as the guests and with officials of an oil company that was preparing an application for permission to construct a northern pipeline. Another minister who was widely censured by the press was Otto Lang: he was accused of using government jets for his own private purposes and those of his relatives and employees. In the period from 1974 to 1976, the cost was estimated at nearly three quarters of a million dollars.

Numerous other revelations diminished the credibility of the Trudeau administration. Among them were the news that the Ministry of Supply and Services had circulated a blacklist intended to keep individuals considered by the RCMP to belong to an "extraparliamentary opposition" from being employed by the government; evidence that a former Hamilton harbor commissioner had received large kickbacks from dredging contracts; suggestions that a Liberal senator had engaged in influence peddling with respect to the awarding of concessions for duty-free shops; and indications that the government had let large contracts without calling for tenders. These and similar disclosures were interpreted by many as indicating that the government had gone into a decline that affected not only its sense of propriety but also its ability to govern.

The impression of growing impotence was enhanced by the serious hemorrhaging experienced by Trudeau's cabinets. We have just seen that a number of ministers were compelled to resign because they had committed certain indiscretions. Others found the federal government uncongenial and withdrew either for "personal reasons" or because of disagreements with government policy. Two of the prime minister's chief Quebec friends and allies—Jean Marchand and Gerard Pelletier—left the cabinet. The most serious losses, however, were among English-speaking ministers: departing members included not only such old hands as Mitchell Sharp and C. M. Drury but also James Richardson, one of the party's very few western members, who resigned over his disagreement with the cabinet's language policy; Ron Basford and Bryce Mackasey, who were generally seen as being particularly sympathetic to the less favored members of society; and John Turner and Donald Macdonald, two former ministers of finance and among the ablest and most respected members of the Trudeau administration: These and other resignations and retirements strengthened the impression that the government was faltering, an impression particularly strong in Ontario and the Toronto area, where a great many people thought that their representatives in Ottawa lacked luster. It was in precisely this part of the country that the 1979 electoral contest was most competitive and the Liberals suffered their greatest losses.

For all these reasons, as the election approached, a large number of concerned Canadians were wondering whether the Liberal government had not been in office too long for its own and for the country's good. Inadequate concern for individual rights, the gradual attrition of ministerial responsibility, growing inefficiency and inability to cope, and constitutional rigidity all tended to be ascribed to two factors: the prime minister's personal characteristics and power and the long tenure in office of the Liberal party. There were many who believed that another term in office for the government would threaten the conditions required for the proper functioning of democratic institutions in Canada. For them a change was seen as imperative.

This being the case, how can one explain the closeness of the outcome and the substantial Liberal vote? Later chapters address themselves to this question in some detail. The only factor we need to note here is the paucity of available alternatives. If the Liberals seemed inefficient and possibly dangerous, how did the NDP and the Conservatives strike the electorate? Polls and results alike indicate that for quite different reasons the two opposition parties had trouble exploiting the disillusionment with the government. A very large proportion of the Canadian electorate found the mildly social democratic alternative of the NDP, or possibly its labor-oriented image, unacceptable. The party was, at any rate, woefully weak in Quebec and was given no chance at all of forming the next government. It was, in consequence, not seen favorably by a large enough proportion of the electorate to become a viable alternative to the Liberals. The Conservatives had two major problems. Like the NDP, the party had only slim support in Quebec, and throughout the country Joe Clark was perceived by many voters as unsuitable for the prime ministership.

While the NDP had developed a program that could be seen as an alternative to that of the Liberals, the Conservatives, during most of the period preceding the opening of the election campaign proper, appeared excessively negative and seemingly unable or unwilling to state with any precision how they would cope with the country's problems. The party was reluctant to become very specific before the campaign was fully under way for fear that the government would simply take over its proposals. Its policies, with the exception of the popular mortgage-rebate scheme, were not revealed until well after the issuing of the writs. The unrelieved, indiscriminate, and unceasing criticism of every act of the government by Conservatives also turned away many who were seeking a serious alternative to Trudeau. Their leader met with wholesale skepticism and was constantly bucking unfavorable comparisons between him and the prime minister.

The issue confronted by many voters was, therefore, the question of what constituted the greater risk: returning the Liberals for another term or entrusting the country to the Conservatives under Clark. Either course struck many as exceedingly dangerous.

Parties and the Party System

Many of the failings of the Liberal party were, as noted, blamed on its long period in office. Although the problem was probably not seen by the majority of the population as the result of one-party dominance, there was an awareness of the dangers to all parties of being too long either in or out of power. The election was therefore important, and was seen as being important, in terms of the future character of the country's party system.

Indicators of Realignment. Opinion polls, as we saw in figure 2–1, fluctuated in the period between elections and made it clear that the final outcome would be close. A minority government was almost a certainty as the polling day approached, and the weakness of the Liberal party, in terms of the number of seats it could win, was becoming apparent. Because so much of the appeal of the party was concentrated in Quebec and the French constituencies generally, the lead the government enjoyed over its chief rivals in the overall national figures could not be translated into a parliamentary advantage. It was becoming increasingly likely that, party support being essentially stable elsewhere, the outcome would be determined in southern Ontario, particularly in the Toronto metropolitan area, and British Columbia. And it was in these two regions, as we saw, that the government appeared to be encountering its most acute difficulties.

The scandals and numerous resignations from the ministry suggested that the prime minister was having trouble applying as much talent to the national problems as was needed and that longevity was having its effects on the government. If these indicators were somewhat impressionistic, there were others that could be taken as hard evidence of the mounting difficulties of the government party.

Provincial elections. Although the link between national and provincial parties in Canada is often tenuous, there is some connection between them. At election time most activists at one level usually participate at the other, and the tangible and intangible assets of one organization are likely to benefit the other. Among the most telling advantages for a federal party campaigning in a given province is, of course, the access to patronage available to its provincial sister organization, if it happens to be in power. Who forms the provincial governments therefore has some consequences for federal elections.

In this perspective the Liberal party had experienced a secular decline. Even at the time of the 1974 election, there were only three Liberal governments left: in Prince Edward Island, Nova Scotia, and Quebec. By the time of the 1979 contest, as can be seen in tables 2–1 and 2–2, they had all been defeated, and Trudeau's was the only Liberal administration left in the country. Although the Conservatives were the chief beneficiaries of Liberal provincial misfortunes, they were to some extent also wounded by the Quebec result. The latter not only spelled the defeat of the Bourassa Liberal government but also increased the bifurcation of the provincial party system between the former government party and the Parti Québécois. The Union Nationale, a conservative party that had on occasion helped the federal Conservatives, was nearly wiped out.

The NDP also suffered provincial losses. The party's governments were defeated in Manitoba (by Conservatives) and in British Columbia, where the Social Credit party returned to power.

By-elections. Table 2–3 shows that between the 1974 and the 1979 federal elections there were twenty-five by-elections. The net gains and losses were as follows: Liberals, −6; Conservatives, +5; NDP, +1; and Social Credit, no change. A number of these by-elections produced particularly painful results for the government. Thus in Hochelaga, Gerard Pelletier's former seat, the Liberal candidate was Pierre Juneau, who had replaced Pelletier as communications minister but without having previously secured the necessary parliamentary seat. His defeat was, therefore, a serious repudiation of the government. The Conservative who defeated Juneau later, however, crossed the floor of the House to join the government benches. Another blow was registered in Ottawa-Carleton, where John Turner's former seat was taken by a Conservative.

No fewer than fifteen by-elections were held on October 16, 1978, and this feast was not unnaturally considered a minielection. Interest in these contests, which were being held in all regions of Canada, was particularly great, since a federal election could not be delayed much longer; the results were eagerly awaited as an indication of who would be likely to form the next government. There were a number of surprises. In Newfoundland the NDP candidate replaced a Conservative incumbent by winning his party's first seat in the province. The Conservatives also did badly in Quebec but retained the ridings they had held in the Maritimes, British Columbia, and Hamilton. Of the greatest interest were the seven contests in the greater Toronto area, in St. Boniface in Manitoba, and in Ottawa Centre. The NDP held on to its Toronto seat (Broadview), but the Conservatives took all the others from the Liberals. With the exception of the Quebec results, therefore, the outcome constituted a serious blow to the government.

Activities and Events

The Liberals. Since the two old Canadian parties are chiefly electoral and not programmatic, their national extraparliamentary organizations tend to be inactive when the party holds office. The National Liberal Federation therefore was not much in the news in the interelection period. Among its routine events were a convention in the autumn of 1975, a policy workshop in March 1977, a policy convention about a year later, and a candidates' workshop in January 1979. For all practical purposes, these activities were of little electoral consequence. The program, strategy, and personnel of the party were largely determined by the cabinet and particularly the prime minister, with the obvious exception of the selection of local candidates. But even here the influence of the effective nerve center of the party—the entourage of Trudeau—was felt.

After the Conservative leadership convention early in 1976 the polls showed the Liberals badly eclipsed by the Tories, but this changed after the PQ victory in the November Quebec election (see figure 2–1). Both Lévesque and Trudeau made highly publicized speeches in the United States at the beginning of 1977, which appeared to have had a strong impact on English Canada. They were, at any rate, followed by the popular resurgence of the Liberals. Trudeau had been urged to go to the country as early as 1977, but he refused. In the spring and again in the autumn of 1978, all signs pointed to an early dissolution. A number of patronage appointments indicated an imminent election. Candidates were nominated in large

TABLE 2–1
PROVINCIAL ELECTION RESULTS, 1974–1979

Province and Date of Election	Seats in Legis- lature	Lib. % of Seats	Vote	PC % of Seats	Vote	NDP % of Seats	Vote	Other % of Seats	Vote
Newfoundland									
September 16, 1975	51	20	49	30	46	0	4	1	1
June 18, 1979	52	19	41	33	50	0	8	0	1
Prince Edward Island									
April 29, 1974	32	26	54	6	40	0	6		
April 24, 1978	32	17	52	15	47	0	1		
April 23, 1979	32	11	46	21	53	0	1		
Nova Scotia									
April 2, 1974	46	31	49	12	38	3	12	0	1
September 19, 1978	52	17	39	31	46	4	15		
New Brunswick									
November 18, 1974	58	25	47	33	47	0	3	0	3
October 23, 1978	58	28	44.5	30	44.5	0	6	0	5
Quebec									
November 15, 1976	106	27	34					79	66 [a]
Ontario									
September 18, 1975	125	36	27	51	44	38	29		
June 9, 1977	125	34	31	58	40	33	28	0	1
Manitoba									
October 11, 1977	57	1	12	33	49	23	39		
Saskatchewan									
June 11, 1975	61	15	31	7	28	39	40		
October 18, 1978	61	0	15	17	37.5	44	47.5		
Alberta									
March 26, 1975	75	0	5	69	63	1	13	5	19
March 14, 1979	79	0	6	74	57	1	16	4	21
British Columbia									
December 11, 1975	55	1	7	1	4	18	39	35	50
May 10, 1979	57			0	6	26	46	31	48

[a] Includes the Parti Québécois: 66 seats, 41 percent of the popular vote.

SOURCE: Pierre G. Normandin, ed., *The Canadian Parliamentary Guide* (Ottawa, 1974-1978); and *Canadian News Facts*.

TABLE 2-2
PROVINCIAL ELECTION RESULTS, CHANGE SINCE LAST ELECTION, 1974–1979
(in seats and percentage points)

Province and Date of Election	Lib.		PC		NDP		Other	
	Seats	Vote	Seats	Vote	Seats	Vote	Seats	Vote
Newfoundland								
September 16, 1975	+11	+12	−3	−15	0	+4	0	−1
June 18, 1979	−1	−8	+3	+4	0	+4	−1	0
Prince Edward Island								
April 29, 1974	−1	−4	+1	−2	0	+6		
April 24, 1978	−9	−2	+9	+7	0	−5		
April 23, 1979	−6	−6	+6	+6				
Nova Scotia								
April 2, 1974	+8	+3	−9	−9	+1	+5	0	+1
September 19, 1978	−14	−10	+19	+8	+1	+3	0	−1
New Brunswick								
November 18, 1974	−2	+1	+2	−4			0	+3
October 23, 1978	+3	−2.5	−3	−2.5	0	+3	0	+2
Quebec								
November 15, 1976	−75	−21					+72	+21[a]
Ontario								
September 18, 1975	+16	+1	−27	−8	+19	+6	0	+1
June 9, 1977	−2	+4	+7	−4	−5	−1	0	+1
Manitoba								
October 11, 1977	−4	−7	+12	+12	−8	−4	0	−1
Saskatchewan								
June 11, 1975	0	−12	+7	+26	−7	−15		
October 18, 1978	−15	−16	+10	+9.5	+5	+7.5		
Alberta								
March 26, 1975	0	+4	+20	+17	0	+2	−20	−22
March 14, 1979	0	+1	+5	−6	0	+3	−1	+2
British Columbia								
December 11, 1975	−4	−9	−1	−9	−20	0	+25	+18
May 10, 1979	−1	−7	−1	+2	+8	+7	−4	−2

a Includes the Parti Québécois: +60 seats, +11 percentage points.
SOURCE: As for table 2-1.

TABLE 2–3
Federal By-Election Results, 1975–1978

Date	Constituency	Results					Comparison of Results
		Liberal	PC	NDP	SC	Other	
Oct. 14, 1975	Hochelega (Que.)	5,649[a]	8,236	675	1,729	666	L → PC
	Restigouche (NB)	9,158[a]	6,049	1,392	1,140	—	L → L
Oct. 18, 1976	Ottawa-Carleton (Ont.)	18,796[a]	34,477	12,777	—	1,318	L → PC
	St. John's West (Nfld.)	3,971	11,119[a]	8,597	—	—	PC → PC
May 24, 1977	Malpèque (PEI)	4,657	4,532[a]	393	—	46	PC → L
	Temiscaminque (Que.)	7,422	3,136	377	9,603[a]	495	SC → SC
	Verdun (Que.)	15,208[a]	2,003	8,151	173	175	L → L
	Terrebonne (Que.)	25,006[a]	15,539	1,299	1,949	1,608	L → L
	Louis-Hébert (Que.)	30,763[a]	9,142		1,652	1,021	L → L
	Langelier (Que.)	12,171[a]	3,952	1,104	618	446	L → L

Oct. 16, 1978

Humber-St. George's-St. Barbe (Nfld.)	10,322	5,851[a]	12,386	—	—	PC → NDP
Halifax-East Hants (NS)	10,161	18,767[a]	1,697	—	355	PC → PC
Fundy-Royal (NB)	12,241	17,327[a]	3,434	—	—	PC → PC
Lotbinière (Que.)	11,955	6,916	962	16,358[a]	—	SC → SC
St. Hyacinthe (Que.)	21,515	16,559[a]	1,259	889	—	PC → L
Montreal Westmount (Que.)	17,214[a]	9,391	1,817	—	305	L → L
Hamilton Wentworth (Ont.)	18,282	20,263[a]	14,105	—	301	PC → PC
Toronto Broadview (Ont.)	3,466	7,968	8,388[a]	—	204	NDP → NDP
Toronto Eglinton (Ont.)	7,996[a]	19,485	2,246	—	—	L → PC
Toronto Parkdale (Ont.)	5,721[a]	6,759	4,806	—	190	L → PC
Ottawa Centre (Ont.)	7,361[a]	12,078	7,470	—	254	L → PC
York-Scarborough (Ont.)	21,431[a]	55,455	7,681	—	912	L → PC
St. Boniface (Man.)	13,804[a]	18,552	9,570	1,204	442	L → PC
Toronto Rosedale (Ont.)	10,114[a]	18,732	3,008	—	471	L → PC
Burnaby-Richmond-Delta (BC)	4,713	30,395[a]	11,308	—	1,467	PC → PC

[a] Party of incumbent.

SOURCE: Normandin, *Canadian Parliamentary Guide*; and *The Report of the Chief Electoral Officer on Federal By-Elections Held in 1978*.

numbers, and some very strong new contenders were brought into the Liberal camp. But the prime minister still had doubts about the appropriate date. This led ultimately to the withdrawal of a number of new candidates who could no longer postpone making decisions that precluded a political career. The delay in the voting day also strengthened the impression held by some of its enemies that the government was too power-hungry and unable to bring itself to relinquish its grasp on office.

This impression was reinforced by the large number and kind of patronage appointments made by the Trudeau administration. When Trudeau came to power, it had been widely expected that the exceptionally well qualified and independent-minded leader would inject a new element of rationality and imagination into the political life of the country and that he would cleanse it of some of the less palatable features of party life. While, on the one hand, the traditional structures and personalities in the Liberal party were downgraded in favor of the prime minister's personal advisers in the Privy Council office and the prime minister's office, patronage for retiring or defeated Liberal candidates and various other party hangers-on was dispensed on a scale unprecedented within recent memory. A careful analysis by two investigative journalists revealed that by the middle of summer in 1977, at least 200 of the order-in-council appointments (the appointments a government can make outside the civil service framework) made by the Trudeau government had gone to former Liberal candidates in federal and provincial elections or to their spouses. No fewer than fifty-nine judges appointed by the government were previous Liberal candidates.[15]

As the successive possible election dates approached, the number of these appointments increased, and their electoral purposes became more blatant. Claude Wagner, the occupant of the Conservatives' only safe seat in Quebec, was appointed to the Senate, and several other Conservatives holding marginal seats in other provinces were equally neutralized. The weakening of the newly elected Social Credit leader in Quebec, Fabien Roy, was achieved through the appointment of one of his lieutenants to the Canadian Grain Commission. Electoral opportunities were enhanced through wholesale appointments to the International Joint Commission, the National Parole Board, the National Energy Board, the Immigration Appeal Board, the Canadian Pension Commission, and similar bodies.

[15] Hugh Winsor and Dorothy Lipovenko, "Patronage: The Trudeau Government Says Thanks," *Globe and Mail* (Toronto), June 13, 1977; Ottawa Bureau of the *Globe and Mail*, "Losers and Winners Occupy List of Liberal Appointments," *Globe and Mail*, June 13, 1977.

One aspect of the patronage appointments just noted provides eloquent testimony to the acrimonious atmosphere between the parties. The Liberals, as everyone knew, were genuinely and passionately devoted to the cause of national unity and to the satisfaction of French Canadian demands within confederation. From the Liberals' point of view, it was clearly in the national interest for the Conservatives to gain some support in Quebec, particularly if they were going to form the government, which was a distinct possibility. Yet the Liberals tried every means available to shut the Tories out of Quebec. Clark had made it clear that if he were elected with only a small number of Quebec seats and potential ministers, he would appoint suitable Quebecers to the cabinet and, for the time being, bring them into Parliament by appointment to the unfilled seats in the Red Chamber (the Senate). Trudeau virtually demolished this possibility after he had called the election, by filling most (but not all) of the available Quebec Senate seats with Liberals, including Dalia Wood, his own campaign manager.

The Progressive Conservatives. Robert Stanfield, the greatly respected but electorally unsuccessful Progressive Conservative leader, decided to resign after his third defeat at the hands of Trudeau in 1974. By far the most momentous event in the party's history, during the period under discussion, was therefore the leadership convention held in October 1975. An exceptionally large number of candidates came forward, among whom about half a dozen were seen as serious contenders. They included Claude Wagner, a former ranking Quebec Liberal, who had been persuaded, under conditions that subsequently caused much embarrassment, to run for the Conservatives during Stanfield's tenure as leader; Paul Hellyer, a former Liberal cabinet minister and contender for the party leadership against Pierre Trudeau; Brian Mulroney, a young, bilingual Montreal lawyer, greatly favored by some powerful business interests; Jack Horner, a prominent and outspoken western Conservative, well known for his implacable opposition to the government's language policy; Sinclair Stevens, the conservative financial critic of the party; Flora Mac-Donald, a widely popular former party secretary who had run afoul of John Diefenbaker and had been an influential member of the group backing Stanfield for the leadership at the previous convention; and Joe Clark, a young Alberta progressive Conservative.

The convention was the most democratic ever run by the Conservatives; it was structured so as to guarantee the substantial (but by no means equitably representative) inclusion, among its 2,575 delegates, of young people, Francophones, and women. Among its most important features three stand out: (1) In choosing Joe Clark, the party settled on a compromise candidate whose major appeal was that he alienated fewer people than his opponents. He was therefore selected not because of what he stood for but, in a way, for what he did not stand for. A relatively unknown M.P., he was frequently referred to in the press as Joe Who? (2) Flora MacDonald was a strong candidate who did surprisingly badly on the first ballot. She had enjoyed an excellent press and had made a very good impression during the convention. Her weak showing can therefore most plausibly be ascribed to the Conservative party's not having been ready, at that time, to consider a woman as a serious candidate for the leadership. (3) Despite the ultimate defeat of Claude Wagner, it is of extraordinary importance that the party that had had such weak links with Quebec and French Canada came within sixty-five votes of picking a French Canadian leader who, furthermore, only a few years before had been a Quebec Liberal cabinet minister and a candidate for the leadership of the Quebec Liberal party.

At any rate, Joe Clark emerged from the convention as a person who had been interested more in party organization than in policy and who embarked immediately on the task of building an effective electoral machine. The polls, as we have seen, showed that the Canadian public was at first very favorably disposed toward the party under its new leader. It was only after he had been in office for some time, and when the issue of national unity loomed very large in the minds of many Canadians after the PQ victory, that the Liberals under Trudeau regained public favor.

Among the reasons for this reversal were the problems that beset the new leader and the manner in which he dealt with them. One of these concerned the constituency in which he was going to contest the next election. Because of redistribution, a number of M.P.s found that their ridings were about to disappear and that they had to seek a new electoral base. Clark clashed over his own nomination in Bow River with Stan Schumacher and backed away from an open confrontation with his rather truculent colleague. The incident was interpreted by many as indicating that the leader could not even command the respect and consideration due to him from a fellow Albertan and that he did not have the strength to assert his position in the matter. There were other problems. Jack Horner, miffed at having lost the leadership to Clark and at not being guaranteed an uncontested nomination in the Crowfoot riding, crossed the floor of the House to sit on the Liberal front benches—a reflection as much on the Liberals' lack of principle as on Clark's incapacity to dominate his party.

Claude Wagner, also disaffected because he failed to carry the convention, was a critical, divisive colleague and eventually, as we have seen, accepted a Senate seat from Trudeau. Clark's one decisive act at this time, asserting his leadership, was directed at the extremely popular Prince Edward Island member, David MacDonald, whom he removed from the party's strategy planning committee after he had voted independently of the party on a matter of principle. This was seen as an unnecessary slap at a liberal, able colleague, one that probably cost the party the Malpèque seat in the 1977 by-election. Another by-election embarrassment arose as a result of the nomination in a Quebec constituency of a candidate who, it turned out, had made some strongly anti-Semitic statements in a book he had written. Clark was criticized for tolerating this candidacy and was compared unfavorably with Stanfield who, in somewhat similar circumstances, had deprived an anti-French candidate in New Brunswick of the right to contest an election under the Conservative banner.

Although the new Conservative leader managed eventually to acquire a reasonable measure of credibility, he never completely shed a certain aura of incompetence and awkwardness and of being jinxed. A world trip, undertaken to give him the image of an experienced statesman, was plagued with mishaps and turned into something of a disaster. That it did not wipe out the party's electoral chances attests to the degree to which Clark had previously been able to win acceptance among Canadians as well, of course, as to the appeal of many Conservative candidates. In addition to effectively restructuring and revitalizing the organization of his party, Clark had been unceasing and painstaking in his attacks on the government's record and position. He offered a more decentralized view of federalism than that of Trudeau and, in 1977, launched a five-point economic program that seemed to have found some support in the country. It expressed his commitment to the elimination of overlapping and duplicating federal-provincial programs, greater parliamentary control over federal spending, a "sunset law," a systematic review of the necessity to continue crown corporations, and a review of the virtues of universality in welfare programs.

The Conservative leader's stature was enhanced by a well-publicized conference he had held with the four Conservative premiers from Ontario, Alberta, New Brunswick, and Newfoundland. The joint statement issued by the five Tory politicians rejected much of the Liberal approach to current constitutional problems by stressing that the central attack must be economic. By the time the party held its general meeting in November 1977, Clark's position had been sufficiently consolidated to bring him a 93 percent vote of confidence, couched in terms of whether or not there should be a leadership review. Finally, the young westerner clearly benefited from the practice, started in October 1977, of televising House of Commons debates. He showed up well, particularly during the question period, and so won his spurs as a plausible, if somewhat wobbly, challenger for the prime ministership.

The New Democratic party. Like the Conservatives, the NDP had to find a new leader after the 1974 election. David Lewis, the dynamic party chief, decided to retire after suffering a personal defeat in his York South constituency. He was replaced as House leader by Ed Broadbent. The latter had performed impressively in this role but hesitated before deciding to seek the arduous and time-consuming task of heading Canada's social democratic party. He finally reversed an earlier decision and declared that he was a candidate for the leadership, a move strongly supported by the majority of the party caucus and the leadership of the national party organization and of the unions close to the NDP.

Unlike the other parties, the NDP imposed a limit of $15,000 on what a leadership candidate was allowed to spend, and it also subsidized each aspirant to the tune of $1,000. A national tour of all the hopefuls was organized, with the result that all-candidate meetings were held in seventeen cities. Attendance at these gatherings was, however, disappointingly low. When the convention opened in Winnipeg in early July 1975, almost 2,500 delegates were eligible to attend, but only about 1,600 showed up, more than 700 of the missing people representing organized labor.

The establishment candidate had to ward off three principal challengers: Rosemary Brown, the most ideological and left wing of the three, who sat in the British Columbia legislature for Vancouver-Burard; John Harney, a bilingual professor who had been an M.P. and had come in third in the 1971 leadership race; and Lorne Nystrom, a young Saskatchewan M.P. Broadbent was ahead from the beginning but did not secure his election until the fourth ballot, when he received 59 percent of the vote and Rosemary Brown took 41 percent. The center-right of the party had triumphed over the more radical elements.

Broadbent continued to provide effective leadership in Parliament and was generally credited with proposing more concrete and precise alternatives to the government than the Conservative leader.

In various speeches, particularly at the party's 1977 convention, he staked out the NDP's position on major national issues in a manner that differed clearly from those of his opponents. The NDP was as centralizing as the Liberals, although it did speak of decentralized administration, without indicating quite what this meant. Like the Conservatives, the party saw the solution to the national crisis in better economic arrangements, but the policies here diverged completely from Clark's, favoring labor and low-income groups rather than business.

As a result of this position, organized labor decided to go all out in supporting the NDP's election campaign. The Canadian Labour Congress, claiming 2.3 million members or affiliates, promised, in 1978 and again in 1979, to furnish not only funds but also election manpower and organizational effort on behalf of the NDP.

The Social Credit party. Réal Caouette, the once fiery Quebec leader of the Social Credit party, resigned in 1975 because of ill health and was replaced in November by the popular member from Lotbinière, André Fortin. The latter was killed in a car accident, however, and was in turn replaced temporarily by Caouette's son Gilles. Another convention, this time held in Winnipeg in May 1978, selected Lorne Reznowski as leader. Numerous internal divisions, some of which had developed under Fortin, scandals, and other mishaps plagued the party and culminated in the resignation of the new leader in February 1979. Fabien Roy, a member of the Quebec National Assembly representing a splinter party (the Popular National party), assumed the leadership shortly before the election and had very little time to organize the party forces before their strength was tested on May 22.

In 1979 each party confronted a test much more critical than the challenges of a routine election. The Liberals were perceived increasingly as a French party and as one that had been in office too long. Although there was widespread and often intense hostility to the government, at least in English Canada, the opposition appeared to offer an uncertain alternative. It was, in the first place, divided among three parties, each enjoying certain advantages and suffering severe handicaps in different regions of the country. Their attractiveness also varied for other reasons. The Conservatives suffered most as the result of the low appeal of their leader, who, many feared, was simply not up to the task of leading the country through the impending troubled times. Ed Broadbent was seen as more forceful and impressive, but his ideas and party were rejected by many on ideological and strategic grounds: the party had no chance of replacing the

Liberal administration. Social Credit had to all intents and purposes retained a foothold only in Quebec and had been weakened there and elsewhere by a series of misfortunes.

The outcome of the election was therefore seen by many as determining the future of Canada and of the Canadian party system. It would decide whether the one-party-dominant pattern would continue, with consequences many feared disastrous for the well-being of the country's traditional parliamentary form of government, or whether there would be a realignment leading toward the evolution of a new party system. The character of the latter could not be foreseen but was likely to grow out of the profound changes that would affect both the Liberals and the Conservatives should their respective power positions be reversed. Important consequences were also likely to flow from expected changes in the status of the NDP and Social Credit. The former, it was thought, would test once and for all the extent to which it could benefit from the muscle of organized labor, and the election would also show whether the party could increase its electoral base enough to become a major party. As for Social Credit, its demise was expected by many and with it some sort of realignment in Quebec.

May 22 and its aftermath were therefore seen as events of quite extraordinary importance, surpassing even the conventional psephologists' concern over whether the contest was a realigning, deviating, or maintaining one,[16] or even whether it was "critical" in the classic sense developed by V. O. Key.[17] There was a strong possibility that the 1979 contest would in the long run be seen as a systems-altering election in the sense that the Canadian polity would develop quite differently after a Liberal than after a Conservative victory.

---

[16] Angus Campell, "A Classification of the Presidential Elections," in Angus Campbell, Phillip E. Converse, Warren Miller, and Donald E. Stokes, eds., *Elections and the Political Order* (New York: John Wiley and Sons, 1966), pp. 63-77.

[17] V. O. Key, Jr., "A Theory of Critical Elections," *Journal of Politics*, vol. 17 (February 1955), pp. 3-18.

3

The Canadian Voter

William P. Irvine

The typical Canadian voter of 1979 had been either a young parent or a child during the baby boom of the 1940s. Though older voters had memories of the 1929 depression, most had been raised in a period of prosperity when jobs were easy to find, inflation was relatively low, and a university degree provided an almost certain entree to the job market. These comfortable expectations have changed in the past five or ten years as society itself has seen significant changes. More and more people live in large urban centers. The population in metropolitan areas grew from 46 percent in 1951 to 51 percent in 1961 to 55 percent in 1971 to 59 percent in 1976. The electorate is becoming younger as the baby boom children reach voting age, which was reduced in 1970 from twenty-one years to eighteen years. In 1962 less than 30 percent of the electorate was under thirty-five; by 1976 this had grown to 37 percent. Finally, more and more of the electorate is having some experience, increasingly a disappointing one, of being in the labor force. In 1961 Canada had a labor force of 6.5 million, of whom 1.7 million were women. In 1971 the corresponding figures were 8.6 million and 2.8 million, while the April 1979 labor force estimates reported 10.8 million having or seeking work. Of these, 4.2 million were women, as the labor force participation rate for women continued its dramatic increase.

Impressive as these figures are, they are by no means unique to Canada. Similar changes have taken place in most industrialized countries, with significant consequences for politics, electoral and nonelectoral, in the late 1960s and early 1970s. They have been accompanied by increasingly bitter strikes, protest marches and demonstrations, and organized violence. Canada has shared in all these manifestations of alienation, more than might have been expected in view of its history as the "Peaceable Kingdom." From 1951 to 1964, the labor time lost in strikes had exceeded 0.2 percent of total time worked in only two years. Between 1965 and 1975, time lost was

TABLE 3–1

POLITICAL PROTEST IN CANADA, 1948–1967

Indicator	1948–57	1958–67	Total
Number of peaceful protest events	3	25	28
Number of armed attacks	18	95	113
Number of riots	6	23	29
Deaths from political violence	0	8	8

SOURCE: Taylor and Hudson, *World Handbook*, tables 3.1-3.4.

equally low in only one year. In four others years it exceeded 0.4 percent of total working time, and in four of the remaining years it was between 0.3 percent and 0.4 percent.[1]

Canada has never scored very high in protest or political violence. In the 1948–1967 period as a whole, Canada ranked 47th among 110 countries in peaceful protest, with 28 events; 47th of 122 countries in the existence of armed attacks, with 113 events; 73d of 128 in riots, with 29 events; and 105th of 120 in deaths from political violence, with 8 for the period.[2] As we see in table 3–1, however, almost all of this activity took place in the second half of the period.

In electoral politics similar disruption has occurred in most Western democracies—manifested as declines in voter turnout, the incursion of new actors into the party system, or both. In the United States, voter turnout in presidential elections fell continuously from 63 percent in 1960 to 54 percent in 1976.[3] In Denmark, Norway, Belgium, and Holland, voter turnout has held up, but the attraction of established parties has not.[4] Denmark and Norway saw a significant

[1] Statistics Canada, *Perspective Canada II*, 2d ed. (Ottawa: Statistics Canada, 1977), chart 6.25.

[2] Charles L. Taylor and Michael C. Hudson, *World Handbook of Political and Social Indicators* (New Haven, Conn.: Yale University Press, 1972), tables 3.1-3.4.

[3] Thomas E. Cavanagh, "Changes in American Electoral Turnout, 1964-1976" (Paper presented to the Annual Meeting of the Midwest Political Science Association, April 19-21, 1979), pp. 1-2.

[4] On Denmark, see Ole Borre, "Recent Trends in Danish Voting Behavior," in Karl H. Cerny, ed., *Scandinavia at the Polls* (Washington, D.C.: American Enterprise Institute, 1977), pp. 3-37; for Norway, Henry Valen and Willy Martinussen, "Electoral Trends and Foreign Politics in Norway," in Cerny, *Scandinavia at the Polls*, pp. 39-71; for Belgium (where voting is compulsory and the absence of decline in turnout is, therefore, not in itself highly significant), the data are summarized in Wilfrid Dewachter, "Recent Changes in the Belgian Party System," mimeographed (European University Institute, 1978); on Holland, see Hans Daalder, "The Netherlands," in S. Henig, ed., *European Political Parties*, 2d ed. (London: Allen and Unwin, 1979), pp. 175-208.

drop in support for the main socialist or labor parties in the decade from the early 1960s to the early 1970s. This was coupled with the rise of new antitax parties and splits in the parties on the right. The Dutch Catholic party also lost its preeminent position. New parties were the main beneficiaries. In Belgium the demands of new linguistic groups weakened established party organizations and spawned new parties. Both types of change took place simultaneously in Great Britain, where voter turnout declined from 87 percent in 1950 to 73 percent in October 1974, while the combined vote shares of the Conservative and Labour parties fell from 90 to 77 percent. As a result, the two-party share of the eligible electorate dropped twenty percentage points, from 76 percent in 1950 to 56 percent in October 1974. While these declines were partially arrested in 1979 (turnout increased to 76 percent and the two-party share increased to 81 percent of the vote and 61 percent of the electorate), the British party system has been significantly weakened.[5] In all these countries, these behavioral changes seem to be symptomatic of increasing alienation and cynicism.[6]

Canada: Support for the System, Skepticism about the Parties

This brief tour of comparative election results illustrates a general political malaise of the early 1970s that passed the Canadian voter by. Despite the economic and social changes of the period, electoral results from the last Progressive Conservative government in 1962 to the new one in 1979 showed only minor perturbations. The first two lines of table 3–2 confirm that turnout in Canada has generally fluctuated within quite narrow bounds—from 75 to 79 percent of the eligible voters.[7] Though 1974 saw a drop below this range, this may have been the result of a summertime election in a country where it is difficult to cast ballots other than personally on election day.

[5] Ivor Crewe, "Do Butler and Stokes Really Explain Political Change in Britain?" *European Journal of Political Research*, vol. 2 (March 1974), pp. 47-92; Ivor Crewe et al., "Partisan Dealignment in Britain, 1964-74," *British Journal of Political Science*, vol 7 (April 1977), pp. 129-36; and Austin Ranney, "British General Elections: An Introduction," in Howard R. Penniman, ed., *Britain at the Polls, 1979: A Study of the General Election* (Washington, D.C.: American Enterprise Institute, 1981), pp. 1-29, especially tables 1-3 and 1-4.

[6] Borre, "Recent Trends," pp. 33-37; on the United States, see Arthur H. Miller, "Political Issues and Trust in Government, 1964-70," *American Political Science Review*, vol. 68 (September 1974), pp. 951-72.

[7] The range across provinces is typically very much greater. In 1979 turnout varied from 61 percent in Newfoundland to 82 percent in Prince Edward Island. In most provinces, variation across time is also larger than the national figure.

Canada's major parties, the Liberals and the Progressive Conservatives, are now almost a century old and arose out of even earlier formations. It is not surprising that their vote, too, should be well established. Like the turnout, their combined share typically fluctuates within a four-point range, from 72 to 76 percent. Their one excursion beyond this range in the last two decades also took place in 1974, when the combined vote attained 78 percent through a combination of factors peculiar to that year. The provincial wing of the largest of the federal "third" parties, the New Democratic party (NDP), had won the 1972 election in British Columbia. It embarked on a series of policies and incurred a series of mishaps that polarized the province.

British Columbians could not vent their anger on the provincial government until 1976, but they were able to take it out on the party's federal counterpart in 1974. The slump in the federal NDP vote hit all provinces in a small way but was devastatingly large in British Columbia. It largely accounts for the 1974 increase in the major-party share of the vote. Since turnout fluctuates relatively independently of the fortunes of the major parties, their share of support in the total potential electorate shows no dramatic movement, remaining in the range of 54 to 59 percent. The governing parties in Canada typically have a support base only as high as that of the British parties at their worst and substantially below the peaks of popularity for the Labour and Conservative parties in Great Britain.

TABLE 3–2

THE CANADIAN VOTER'S ATTACHMENT TO THE POLITICAL SYSTEM,
1962–1979
(percent)

Indicator	1962	1963	1965	1968	1972	1974	1979
Turnout	79	79	75	76	77	71	76
Major party share of total vote	74	75	72	76	73	78	76
Major party share of total electorate	58	59	54	58	55	55	58
Mean political efficacy score[a]	—	—	2.9	2.9	—	2.6	—
Mean political cynicism score[b]	—	—	2.2	2.3	—	—	—

TABLE 3–2 (continued)

Indicator	1962	1963	1965	1968	1972	1974	1979
Survey findings							
Those agreeing that it makes a "great deal" or "some" difference which party forms the federal government	—	—	82	62	—	79	—
Those agreeing that the federal government handles the most important problems[c]	—	—	73	70	—	60	64
Those agreeing that the federal government handles personal problems[d]	—	—	42	44	—	52	40

Dash (—): Not available.

[a] On a scale of 0 to 4, the number of times respondents agree: that government doesn't care what they think; that politics and government are too complicated for them to understand; that people like them have no say in what government does; and that those elected to government generally lose touch with the people.

[b] On a scale of 0 to 5, the number of times respondents say: that quite a few people in government are a little crooked; that government wastes a lot of money; that one can trust the government to do what is right only some of the time; that government pays more attention to big shots; and that quite a few people running the government don't know what they are doing.

[c] In 1965 and 1968, the respondent was asked which level of government handled the most important problems facing Canada; in 1974, to which level of government he paid most attention; and in 1979, which level of government the respondent considered "his" government.

[d] The respondent was asked to which level of government he looked to handle the most important problems affecting him and his family.

SOURCES: First three lines calculated from reports of the chief electoral officer for relevant elections; 1965 and 1968 survey data from a national survey organized by John Meisel; 1974 survey data from a national survey organized by Harold Clarke, Jane Jenson, Lawrence LeDuc, and Jon H. Pammett; 1979 data from a national survey done for the English and French CBC television networks.

We have many fewer data points for our measures of dissatisfaction, but there again "little change" seems to be the most plausible generalization. Few think that the party battle is a sham: around 80 percent in both 1965 and 1974 felt that it made at least some difference which party formed the government. For both political efficacy and political cynicism, Canadians' mean scores (defined in table 3–2) are somewhat beyond the midpoint: on average, Canadians agreed with more than two of the questions designed to measure these feelings. The 1974 decline may be a harbinger of things to come, but in general one finds little movement in the summated scores and contradictory movement on the individual items.[8]

Since the election of the Parti Québécois in Quebec in 1976, political leaders have felt very strongly that national unity in Canada is under grave threat. To explore this in any detail would take us too far afield, but the last two lines of table 3–2 give some insight into the problem. Canadians clearly feel that the federal government deals with weightier issues than the provincial governments; around two-thirds of those willing to make a choice between the two levels of government say that the federal government handles the most important problems. Many fewer feel they have a personal stake in the federal government; generally the proportion of "federalists" on this question has been only slightly above 40 percent among those willing to make a choice. The 1974 finding of 52 percent is difficult to explain. Evidence for the apparent downward trend in the proportion of people selecting the federal government as most important is not conclusive, since the format of the question and the proportion of respondents making a clear choice changed considerably over the period.[9]

Canada has apparently been unaffected by the forces that shook other Western party systems. Before celebrating this, however, it is important to consider the absolute levels of these indicators of attachment. The direction of party identification, shown in the first part of table 3–3, is broadly consistent with what we have already seen.

[8] From 1965 to 1974 there was a small but steady decline in the proportion agreeing that politics and government were too complicated for them to understand. The three other items of political efficacy (that M.P.s lost touch with constituents, that government didn't care what people felt, and that the respondent felt he had no say in what government did) declined slightly from 1965 to 1968, but then took large jumps to hit their 1965 to 1974 high points in the latter year. Of the five political cynicism items, tapped only in 1965 and 1968, two (trust in government and the belief that some people in government are crooked) were essentially stable, two more (the waste of tax money and breaks given to big shots) increased, and the last (the belief that quite a few government officials don't know what they are doing) declined. These findings are offered as rough indicators and do not take account of the methodological literature now dealing with these items.

[9] The choice between federal and provincial governments on the handling of "important problems" was made by 71 percent of the sample in 1965, 78 percent in 1968, 50 percent in 1974, and 87 percent in 1979. On the level of government that best handled personal concerns, the base for the percentages in the last line of table 3-2 was 74, 71, 67, and 71 percent of the 1965, 1968, 1974, and 1979 samples respectively. As to response format, respondents to the 1968 and 1974 surveys were invited to consider "local government" as a further potential response category; those interviewed in the other surveys were not.

TABLE 3–3

THE CANADIAN VOTER'S ATTACHMENT TO THE FEDERAL PARTIES,

1965–1979

(percent)

Indicator	1965	1968	1974	1977	1979
Party identification					
Liberal party	37	45	46	35	36
Progressive Conservative party	25	23	22	19	21
New Democratic party	11	10	10	10	11
Social Credit	6	4	3	3	3
Other parties	1	2	—	—	1
No identification, don't know,					
no answer	20	16	20	32	27
Strength of party identification					
Very strong	23	24	27	—	—
Fairly strong	41	43	40	—	—
Not very strong	15	15	13	—	—
No identification, don't know,					
no answer	21	18	20	—	—
Always identified with same party	49	52	66	—	—
Always voted for same party	46	52	49	—	—
Stable and "very strong" or "fairly					
strong" identification with:					
Major party	34	38	37	—	—
Minor party	7	6	6	—	—

Dash (—): Not available.

SOURCES: For 1965-1968 see table 3-2; 1977 data are taken from a national Quality of Life Survey done by the Institute of Behavioural Research at York University; 1979 data appeared in the *Toronto Star*, May 14, 1979, p. A6.

The surveys up to 1974 were all postelection soundings and may have led to an overstatement of support for the Liberal party after its majority victories of 1968 and 1974. The 1977 poll was taken without any electoral context, while the 1979 figures are taken from a Canadian Institute of Public Opinion (CIPO) survey commissioned by the *Toronto Star* during the election campaign.

A party system is the most important stabilizing and legitimating institution in a large bureaucratic state, though its effect depends less on the direction of partisan attachment than on its quality. How many feel linked to the party system, and how strongly? In immediate postelection surveys only about 20 percent feel no links, but without an electoral stimulus or before a clear winner has emerged the figure is closer to 30 percent. We must wait for the results of the 1979 postelection survey to discover whether the proportion of unaffiliated voters has really increased. Canadians are in general more partisan than Americans, one-quarter of whom were calling themselves "independents" in postelection surveys as long ago as the 1950s; by 1972 that figure had reached 35 percent, where it leveled off, increasing by only one percentage point in the next four years.[10] Survey questions probing the strength of party identification follow different formats in Canada and the United States and are hard to compare. Two-thirds of Canadians claim to be "very strong" or "fairly strong" supporters of some party, a figure significantly below the 72 percent of British respondents in 1974.[11] Strength of party attachment in the United Kingdom had dropped sharply in a decade, whereas the Canadian figure remained constant at the low level.

These professions of party attachment are belied, however, by the behavior of the voters. Only two-thirds, and *not* the same two-thirds who are strong supporters, have been constant in their party affiliation. Even this figure is a dramatic increase over 1968. Putting the professions of strength and stability together, we find that only slightly more than 40 percent of Canadian voters can be described as having deep roots in the party system. In figures largely constant over time, around 37 percent of Canadian voters are strong, stable supporters of the major parties. A further 6 percent have a similar attachment to the minor parties.[12] That these provide good estimates of the quality of partisan attachment in Canada is further indicated by the fact that only about half the Canadian voters claim always to have voted for the same party since becoming eligible.

The Volatility of Public Opinion. The impression of a highly stable electorate given by tables 3–2 and 3–3 might seem to be confirmed by a quick comparison of countrywide aggregate vote distributions in

[10] Norman Nie, Sidney Verba, and John R. Petrocik, *The Changing American Voter* (Cambridge: Harvard University Press, 1976), pp. 48-49; and Arthur H. Miller, "Partisanship Reinstated? A Comparison of the 1972 and 1976 U.S. Presidential Elections," *British Journal of Political Science*, vol. 8 (April 1978), p. 131, fig. 1. For 1972 and thereafter, the figure for "independents" is the sum of pure independents, Democratic leaners, and Republican leaners.

[11] Crewe et al., "Partisan Dealignment," table 14, p. 162.

[12] Harold Clarke, Jane Jenson, Lawrence LeDuc, and Jon Pammett have suggested measuring partisanship in Canada along dimensions of strength, stability over time, and consistency as between federal and provincial party sytsems. On theoretical and comparative grounds, I am not persuaded of the value of the consistency dimension. See their *Political Choice in Canada* (Toronto: McGraw-Hill Ryerson, 1979), pp. 155-61.

1974 and 1979 (shown in figure 3–2 below). The Progressive Conservative and Social Credit parties seem to have moved hardly at all, the Liberals to have dropped three points, and the NDP to have gained a similar amount. In fact, the Canadian voter is not nearly so rooted in the party system as these figures suggest. This is illustrated for the interelection period in figure 3–1, which charts the monthly change in responses to the Canadian Institute of Public Opinion (Gallup poll) question: "If a federal election were held today, which party's candidate do you think you would favor?"

After the 1974 election, the party preferences of the Canadian electorate covered a lot of territory before returning to approximately their original pattern (on a nationwide basis). Only NDP support remained relatively stable, with month-to-month movements rarely exceeding sampling error and not usually being in the same direction for two successive months. The movement of the voters is mainly back and forth between the established parties. Although we do not have data enabling us to relate shifts to events, certain inferences can be drawn from figure 3–1.

Professed support for the Liberal party increased after the July 1974 election—a quite normal "halo effect" for a party that had won a parliamentary majority—and this support remained above its election total until March 1975. The disjunction between government popularity and the inflation rate, which was such an issue in the 1974 election, is perhaps surprising. Liberal popularity coincided with the period October 1974 to February 1975, when double-digit inflation reached its highest levels. By March and April inflation had dropped almost a whole percentage point, and support for the Liberal party suffered a sharp two-month drop of six points, four of them apparently going to the Progressive Conservatives. This movement seems best interpreted as a correction in "surplus" or "deficit" popularity, rather than a response to economic or other issues. The parties were returning within range of their general election levels, where they remained until February 1976. The Liberals' conversion to wage and price controls in October 1975 did not have a major impact on the party's popularity.

Liberal popularity seems to coincide more closely with large movements in unemployment figures. The seasonally adjusted rate was below 6 percent from March to November 1974. It reached 6.0 percent in December and soared to 6.6 percent in January 1975 and 6.8 percent in March. These increases may have helped precipitate the decrease in Liberal popularity that began in that month. Unemployment crossed the 8 percent barrier on a long-term basis in July

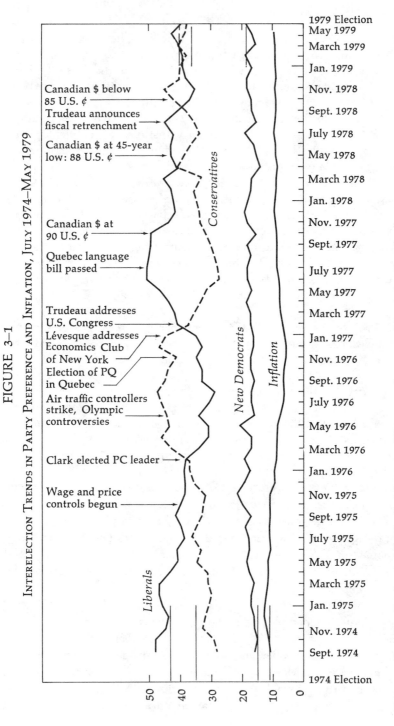

FIGURE 3–1

INTERELECTION TRENDS IN PARTY PREFERENCE AND INFLATION, JULY 1974–MAY 1979

Canadian $ below
85 U.S. ¢

Trudeau announces
fiscal retrenchment

Canadian $ at 45-year
low: 88 U.S. ¢

Canadian $ at
90 U.S. ¢

Quebec language
bill passed

Trudeau addresses
U.S. Congress

Lévesque addresses
Economics Club
of New York

Election of PQ
in Quebec

Air traffic controllers
strike, Olympic
controversies

Clark elected PC leader

Wage and price
controls begun

Conservatives

New Democrats

Inflation

Liberals

1979 Election
May 1979
March 1979
Jan. 1979
Nov. 1978
Sept. 1978
July 1978
May 1978
March 1978
Jan. 1978
Nov. 1977
Sept. 1977
July 1977
May 1977
March 1977
Jan. 1977
Nov. 1976
Sept. 1976
July 1976
May 1976
March 1976
Jan. 1976
Nov. 1975
Sept. 1975
July 1975
May 1975
March 1975
Jan. 1975
Nov. 1974
Sept. 1974
1974 Election

50   40   30   20   10   0

SOURCES: Canadian Institute of Public Opinion, monthly news releases; and Statistics Canada.

1977, and this too coincides with a persisting reversal of Liberal party fortunes.

But neither inflation nor unemployment seems decisive in the major opinion movements of 1976–1977. More decisive in the Liberal drop in popularity was the Progressive Conservative leadership convention that elected Joe Clark party leader in February. If an election campaign generates initial popularity for the winner, the ballyhoo surrounding a leadership convention attracts support for the party generating all the publicity. This was strikingly evident in early 1976. Progressive Conservative support went from 37 percent of declared voting intentions in February 1976 (interviews taken before the convention) to 46 percent in April, giving the party a fifteen-point lead over the Liberals.

Support then fluctuated around those levels until the end of the year. To be sure, the Liberal government was also facing serious challenges that helped keep its popularity low. Unemployment rose above 7 percent permanently in April 1976. On June 20, less than a month before the start of the Olympic games in Montreal, Canada's air-traffic controllers went on strike to protest bilingual air-traffic control in the province of Quebec. This strike was supported by many Canadian and foreign airline pilots who refused to come into Canadian airspace. The strike lasted nine days before the government capitulated and suspended bilingual air-traffic control pending an inquiry. The political atmosphere was highly charged, particularly at the elite level, and ethnic conflict was more bitter than at any time since World War II. Nor were the government's Olympic troubles over. Canada refused to allow Taiwan's athletes to compete under the name "Republic of China." The United States threatened to pull out its team, and the International Olympic Committee considered withdrawing its official sanction. These potential blows to the success of the games were averted by a hasty compromise, but no solution could be found to the demand of many African nations that New Zealand be barred from the games for having sent a rugby team to South Africa. Thirty African, Middle Eastern, and South American states—a quarter of the total number of teams—withdrew from the games. This combination of events may have helped to push Liberal support below 30 percent in August 1976, but no long-term damage to Liberal fortunes was evident.

On November 15, 1976, the province of Quebec elected a government whose avowed aim, though slightly unclear, was to end federal government in Canada, at least as far as Quebec was concerned. The Parti Québécois wanted a sovereign state bound to the rest of the country by no more than ties of friendship and economic advantage, with details to be worked out in bilateral institutions. Initial voter reaction in the country as a whole was eerily quiet. Liberal support was essentially unchanged from September 1976 to January 1977. Support for the Progressive Conservative party did show a five-point jump from November to December 1976 but fell back slightly the next month. In mid-January 1977, Prime Minister Lévesque of Quebec spoke to the Economic Club of New York. He attempted to convince his audience that his party's goals were in the line of normal evolution for a society and that the corresponding date in American history was 1776. Many in his audience saw greater resemblance to 1860. About a month later, Prime Minister Trudeau addressed the U.S. Congress on Quebec independence, calling that type of nationalism a potential crime against humanity. While it may seem incongruous that Canada's destiny was being fought out on the playing fields of the American establishment, both events were widely televised in Canada and no doubt starkly underlined the seriousness of the threat coming from the Parti Québécois. Certainly the purposefulness of the Lévesque government in language matters could not be in doubt after its introduction of language legislation, symbolically Bill 1 of the new Parliament, at the end of April 1977.

In any case, the Liberal party pulled ahead of the Progressive Conservative party in February 1977 in the first step of a trend reversal that saw them reach 51 percent in June and July, while the Progressive Conservatives fell to 27 percent in each of those two months. In August the Parti Québécois language bill passed the Quebec National Assembly, and the provincial government began to adopt a lower profile in the hope of dissipating the social tensions it had generated. With the cooling of the Parti Québécois issue, support for the Liberal and Progressive Conservative parties began to move back to normal countrywide levels.

Increasing inflation may now have become a factor, moving up from 6.1 percent in January to 7.6 percent in April to 8.8 percent in October and to 9.5 percent in December. Though the October to December increase coincided with a large exchange of votes between the Liberal and Progressive Conservative parties, the change in support may have been simply a correction of previously abnormal levels. Support for the Liberals remained within sampling error range of its 1974 vote from November 1977 to August 1978. So did Progressive Conservative support, with one noteworthy exception. It rose dramatically the month after the Canadian dollar fell to U.S.$0.8814, the lowest level since 1933. That occurred in March 1978. In April the two parties were tied at 41 percent of expressed voting intentions. Progressive Conservative support remained high the next month as well but then fell back to normal levels.

Liberal support only really began to fall after Prime Minister Trudeau's announcement of retrenchment in August 1978, an announcement that began a period of improvisation, reflecting more hope than well thought out policy. By September the Liberals were barely ahead of the Progressive Conservatives. At the end of that month the Canadian dollar fell below U.S.$0.85 on three occasions, and in October the Progressive Conservatives took the lead for two months. From December 1978 right through polling day, however, support for the two parties was statistically indistinguishable.

There were major and sustained opinion changes after the Progressive Conservative leadership convention of February 1976 and after the election of the Parti Québécois at the end of that year. One can also discern antigovernment reaction in the month or two after important economic or social challenges: the introduction of wage and price controls, the air-traffic control and Olympic controversies, and the breaking of supposed psychological barriers in the value of the Canadian dollar or the level of unemployment. The only large and sustained movement plausibly attributable to economic or political mismanagement was the August to November 1978 reversal in the positions of the Liberal and Progressive Conservative parties. In eight by-elections in October, the Progressive Conservatives had obtained 49 percent of the popular vote, the Liberals 30 percent. While party fortunes did converge after the by-elections and the November CIPO poll, the Liberals were unable to come back far enough to win a parliamentary victory.

Weak Social Bases of Parties. In many countries of Europe, party loyalties are buttressed by other personal and social linkages: Roman Catholics vote for Christian democratic parties; trade unionists vote for socialist parties. Though less so since the advent of television, support for "community-based" parties is little affected by short-term events. Interpretation of such events is typically provided by a party, church, or union press, which rarely forces readers to reassess their loyalties. Though Canadian and American parties do generate identifications in their own right and there do arise psychological pressures for political consistency, these are much less powerful than the traditional partisan subcultures of many European states.

The fact is that the major Canadian parties do not stand for much of anything, at least in economic matters.[13] Hence it is not

[13] There are differences in approach to constitutional issues and perhaps also on some economic matters. The differences may be important to political scholars and commentators but do not play major roles in political campaigns. Subtleties are then sacrificed to competitive claims of competence, loyalty to an undivided country, and ability to make changes. Longstanding and well-understood ideological differences do not emerge during campaigns.

surprising that few feel a long-run commitment to any party. In social terms, both the Liberals and the Progressive Conservatives are aggregates representing most segments of the country. In the Low Countries, Scandinavia, or Austria, a person's partisanship in the late 1960s was highly predictable from his occupation, religious beliefs, or region of residence.[14] Though predictability has declined in Europe, it is still much higher than in Canada, where only about 10 percent of the variance in the 1974 vote could be predicted from social characteristics.[15]

In a country where the government is called upon to assist old people and the unemployed and unemployable and to underwrite business investment and scientific research, it is remarkable that social class has so little effect on party loyalties. Party support does not vary even as much as 8 percent across the categories of education, income, and class identification. Although the 1974 survey found many more Liberals than did that of 1965, this increase went right across the board, with social class characteristics no more strongly related to partisanship in the former than in the latter year.

Regional, cultural, and religious differences are evident and may be growing, though the evidence is clouded by the large Liberal shift. In both 1965 and 1974, support for the New Democratic party increased as one moved from east to west. In 1965 Progressive Conservative support showed two conspicuous gaps: Quebec and British Columbia. By 1974, the party had gained strength in British Columbia. Though it had suffered setbacks east of the Prairies, it was particularly weak in Quebec. In 1965 Liberal support did not reach far beyond the Ontario-Manitoba boundary. By 1974 it had become triple tiered: very strong from Quebec eastward, more competitive in Ontario, and weak in the West—no doubt somewhat weaker than the figures reported in table 3–4 suggest.

Differences between English speakers and French speakers sharpened in the nine-year period, at least in support for the Liberal party. Neither the Progressive Conservatives nor the NDP saw much change in their group support, and Liberal gains were largely at the expense of the unaffiliated. Rather more interesting differences emerged with respect to the various religious groups. In 1965 the difference was between the various Protestant denominations and all others. There was a smaller difference in the latter group. Roman Catholics were almost exclusively Liberal if they were anything. Jewish voters,

---

[14] Richard Rose, "Comparability in Electoral Studies," in Richard Rose, ed., *Electoral Behavior: A Comparative Handbook* (New York: Free Press, 1974), pp. 16–20.

[15] Clarke et al., *Political Choice*, pp. 124–27.

TABLE 3–4
PARTY IDENTIFICATION IN SELECTED REGIONS AND
SOCIOECONOMIC GROUPS, 1965 AND 1974
(percent)

	1965				1974			
Category	Lib.	PC	NDP	(N)	Lib.	PC	NDP	(N)
Atlantic	42	38	4	(229)	50	30	6	(220)
Quebec	42	11	7	(797)	58	7	5	(702)
Ontario	40	32	12	(1,052)	44	26	11	(878)
Prairies	25	33	13	(395)	30	34	13	(393)
British Columbia	24	17	22	(256)	37	22	16	(252)
English-speaking	34	31	12	(1,867)	44	28	12	(1,700)
French-speaking	43	10	7	(745)	60	7	5	(565)
Roman Catholic	49	12	7	(1,144)	62	10	7	(1,003)
Anglican	25	42	9	(350)	43	33	7	(280)
United, Presbyterian	27	40	13	(745)	36	38	11	(539)
Other Protestant	30	24	16	(308)	32	36	13	(259)
Other	47	20	18	(98)	43	13	21	(223)
Primary education	38	22	9	(941)	50	23	6	(471)
Secondary education	36	26	12	(1,255)	48	24	11	(1,102)
Postsecondary education	39	28	11	(534)	47	20	12	(613)
Low income	36	29	7	(489)	53	24	7	(340)
Medium income	36	23	12	(7,660)	46	23	11	(1,401)
High income	42	27	11	(487)	52	21	10	(532)
Middle-class identification	40	26	10	(1,290)	55	19	8	(693)
Working-class identification	35	23	12	(1,325)	48	17	13	(334)

NOTE: Other, don't know, and no answer, though not given in the table, are included in the percentage base and in the number of cases (N).
SOURCE: Figures are taken from the 1965 and 1974 surveys cited in table 3-2.

Eastern Catholic or Orthodox, Oriental and nonreligious, lumped together as "other" in table 3–4, were as strongly Liberal as Roman Catholics, but more strongly politicized. They also gave very strong support to the NDP and respectable strength to the Progressive Conservatives. The largest and most socially prestigious Protestant denominations were strongly Conservative, the others more evenly divided, with somewhat stronger support for the NDP.

By 1974 Roman Catholics were still single-mindedly Liberal, but that party was also doing well among the leading Protestant denominations. Liberals had a quite commanding lead in the high-status Anglican group and equaled Conservative strength among members of the United and Presbyterian churches. Members of other Protestant faiths were now predominantly Conservative, while the residual grouping was becoming polarized between the Liberal and New Democratic parties at the expense of the Progressive Conservatives.

Regional and cultural differences have strong public impact in Canadian politics but are not issues of policy. No important parties were anti-Quebec or anti-French, though the Liberal claim to be for these groups was more convincing when the party was headed by a French Quebecer. Although energy problems, particularly since the 1974 election, have set western interests more clearly against those of the East, the differences in the percentages in table 3–4 have a much wider base. There are longstanding regional grievances and prejudices in Canada, to which parties appeal covertly or by nominating particular leaders. A party can obtain an image as "pro-Prairies" or "anti-French" without explicitly clarifying the issues involved or seeking to mobilize any particular group. Because of the mathematics of winning federal office, however, no party can excessively indulge its best regions.

The result of this is the electoral volatility already noted. Quite clearly no group in Canada could get all it wants. Policy compromises are necessary. Unfortunately, since the parties do not make public campaign promises to regions or to ethnic groups, it is impossible to predict just what compromises they will be prepared to make. What is needed in Canada, and will increasingly be so, is election campaigns in which parties articulate economic and social strategies and explain to various groups precisely where they fit and how much they can hope to attain in any area. In the absence of such campaigns, voters can only react to the fit between the image they had on election day and the current behavior of the party in view of the challenges facing it and the country. Or they can react to other symbolic stimuli, such as the election of a new leader after months of focused media attention. Either way, the result is an electorate with few roots in the party system.

The Canadian Voters and the 1979 Campaign

It is always difficult to disentangle the motives behind a vote. Was there an issue on which one party had the popular position? How important was the party leader? The local candidate? Voters themselves might be hard pressed to reconstruct their own decision making.

Certainly the observer and recorder of bits and snatches of campaign lore is at a disadvantage. Writing before the results of an extensive academic survey, we have to rely on two sources: newspaper reporters, reporting locally on constituencies and nationally on crowd reactions, and polls commissioned during the campaign and publicly released.

Both sources tend to agree on the nature of the "big issues." They were inflation and unemployment. As we have seen, the former went from 9.2 percent in February and March to 9.8 percent in April —a figure announced just three days before polling day. The unemployment figures were slightly more encouraging. The seasonally adjusted rate dropped from 8.1 to 7.9 percent and remained at that level through the campaign. A survey in the metropolitan Toronto region found those issues far overshadowing all others. When asked to name the most important problem about which the federal government should do something, 65 percent mentioned inflation or high prices, 54 percent unemployment, 17 percent national unity, 7 percent cutting government spending, and 4 percent energy problems.[16] A national poll done for the Canadian Broadcasting Corporation (CBC) by the Carleton School of Journalism found 18 percent each mentioning unemployment and inflation and 13 percent seeing national unity as most pressing.[17]

The important issues were certainly Progressive Conservative issues, at least among English speakers. A poll on party competence on issues was taken by the CIPO twice during the campaign—shortly after it began and shortly before it ended. The findings are reported in table 3–5. Responses in the first report are broken down by first language of the respondent, showing that the Liberals were seen as the best party by both French and other language speakers on all four issues; but among English speakers almost twice as many chose the Progressive Conservatives as chose the Liberals on inflation and unemployment. Those two issues were repeated in the May poll, and the aggregate figures remained stable over the month's interval. We may presume that the cultural breakdowns did likewise. The selection of an issue as of paramount importance was itself a product of cultural differences. Certainly the May CIPO survey confirms that, had the Liberals been successful in making national unity the central election issue, the outcome might have been quite different. Its importance seems to have been limited to voters in Quebec, however.

The parties did try to raise other issues. As gasoline lines were lengthening in California during the campaign, the Liberals made

16 *Toronto Star*, May 7, 1979, p. A14.
17 Ibid., April 24, 1979, pp. A1, A6.

TABLE 3–5

PARTY PERCEIVED AS BEST ON ISSUES, APRIL AND MAY 1979

(percent)

Issue	Lib.	PC	NDP
April 1979			
Inflation	22	24	11
English speakers	17	30	13
French speakers	31	13	5
Other	25	20	11
Unemployment	21	24	16
English speakers	16	30	19
French speakers	28	13	8
Other	25	20	19
Strikes and industrial disputes	24	20	19
English speakers	18	24	22
French speakers	35	12	8
Other	27	15	28
Trade relations with United States	36	18	8
English speakers	33	24	8
French speakers	43	8	5
Other	39	11	11
May 1979			
Inflation	24	26	14
Unemployment	24	24	17
National unity	45	21	7
Energy	29	20	11

NOTE: Other, none, don't know, and no answer, though not given in the table, are included in the percentage base.

SOURCES: April figures from the April Gallup poll, results published in the *Toronto Star*, May 9, 1979, p. A9; May figures from questions commissioned by the *Toronto Star* for the May Gallup poll, results published in the *Toronto Star*, May 14, 1979, p. 6.

much of having created a state-owned oil company that was both developing Canadian sources and negotiating long-term arrangements with countries such as Mexico and Venezuela. The NDP tried to claim credit for forcing this on the Liberals in the 1972–1974 minority Parliament and also tried to outbid the Liberals in affirming a commitment to the Canadian Medicare scheme. The Progressive Conservatives had an attractive proposal of their own: allowing home mortgage interest and property tax to be deducted from taxable income. Much was made of the importance of this issue by newspaper reporters, who claimed that candidates saw it as very important. Though undoubtedly popular, it was not prominent among the unprompted responses of at least one of the groups at which it was targeted: the metropolitan Toronto voters.[18] Nor were energy and Medicare. Toronto is not a random sample of Canada, but it seems unlikely that the issues were more salient elsewhere.

Another element discerned more clearly by reporters than by pollsters was more a mood than an issue—a Proposition 13 desire to restrict government spending. The Liberal party had certainly felt this before the election and attempted to exploit it by reducing unemployment insurance and by other government cutbacks. Progressive Conservative leader Joe Clark, in his turn, spoke of balancing the budget and cutting the civil service. It is hard to know how widespread this mood was, and one suspects that the Progressive Conservatives may have lost more seats (two in the Ottawa area) than they gained by it. Another issue, local in its immediate electoral impact, became the number one issue a week after the swearing in of the new government. This was the Clark promise to move the Canadian embassy in Israel from Tel Aviv to Jerusalem.

Apart from the issues, there were the leaders. Here the "views from the bus" and the views from the punched cards diverge considerably. The reporters described the electorate as anti-Trudeau. Voters in previous elections had seen Trudeau as arrogant and aloof. He confirmed this impression during the campaign, suggesting that he might hold office without the plurality of parliamentary seats, calling farmers "whiners," and inviting the unemployed to "get off their butts" and find work. But reporters also found among voters a feeling that he had been in office too long, that he was obsessed with national unity at the expense of other concerns, and that he had unduly postponed the election.

In the polls, however, Trudeau's continued attractiveness remained evident. When the Carleton University School of Journalism

---

18 Ibid., May 7, 1979, p. A14. Note, however, that in December 1978, in a question specifically focused on mortgage deductibility, the Gallup poll found 74 percent in favor, 15 percent against, and 11 percent with no opinion (Canadian Institute of Public Opinion, release of December 27, 1978). A postelection academic survey found 8 percent of Ontarians calling this the most important issue in the election (Jon Pammett et al., "Change in the Garden: The 1979 Federal Election" [Paper presented to the Annual Meeting of the Canadian Political Science Association, Montreal, June 2, 1980], mimeographed, p. 27). Subsequent analysis suggests some small net benefit (0.4 percent) to the Progressive Conservatives from this issue (Pammett et al., "Change in the Garden," pp. 57-58).

TABLE 3–6

LEADER PERCEIVED AS BEST PRIME MINISTER, MAY 1979

(percent)

	Trudeau	Clark	Broadbent	Roy
All Canada	43	21	11	2
Atlantic provinces	48	17	13	—
Quebec	59	8	6	6
Ontario	36	27	11	1
Prairies	31	30	11	1
British Columbia	36	26	19	1

SURVEY QUESTION: "Forgetting for a moment which political party you happen to prefer or like right now, which of the following do you feel would make the best prime minister for Canada today?"

Dash (—): Less than 1 percent.

SOURCE: Questions commissioned by the *Toronto Star* for the May Gallup poll, results published in the *Toronto Star*, May 13, 1979, p. A26.

poll conducted for the CBC in April asked respondents to name the most competent leader, 38 percent chose Trudeau, 15 percent Clark, and 9 percent Broadbent. In the same survey, 47 percent felt that Trudeau had the most attractive personality; he was far ahead of Clark's 11 percent or Broadbent's 8 percent.[19] A May Gallup poll came up with similar results. Asked who would make the best prime minister, 43 percent chose Trudeau, more than twice as many as chose Clark. The breakdown in table 3–6 shows that this sentiment extended across all regions and, by inference, across all cultural groups. Only on the Prairies were the two perceived as equally able. Trudeau was certainly the overwhelming favorite among those who remained Liberal voters but was also seen as best by one Conservative voter in every six and by one minor-party voter in every four.

We are now better informed about what was in the voters' minds as they approached May 22 but still uncertain about how they made up their minds. Many did not vote for the leader the polls indicated they had thought best. Why? Canada's economic misfortunes, unemployment, inflation, and a falling dollar, told against Trudeau and his party—or did they? Voters' views of ability to deal with these issues may have been determined by commitments that had some other basis, such as cultural background. Perhaps it was simply "time for a change." A Gallup poll taken before the election was

[19] *Toronto Star*, April 24, 1979, pp. A1, A6.

called found 63 percent dissatisfied with the way Canada was going and 27 percent satisfied. Members of all language groups shared this unease, the non–French speakers by more than two to one, French speakers by 48 to 32 percent.[20]

Writing in 1962, Murray Beck said that Canadian elections effectively kept a balance between conflict and consensus. His study of elections up to that year found that every change in government was preceded by a period during which

> the floating voters in all regions have found the image of the incumbent party repellent and that of its major opponent more attractive. Under these circumstances no region can complain that it is having its governmental leaders dictated by another region, and the results of any election are generally acceptable.[21]

The notion that all regions in Canada move in the same direction at the same time is no longer tenable. Canadian voters did not speak in chorus on May 22, 1979. One can discern four, perhaps five, types of response to the issues, parties, and personalities in the election. More encouraging from the point of view of consensus building, the types do not coincide with the regional divisions of the country, with one significant exception. (See figure 3–2.)

What did happen? There were three provinces that the Progressive Conservative party clearly won: Prince Edward Island, Ontario, and Alberta. In each of these, the Liberal party vote percentage dropped from that achieved in 1974, and only the Conservatives made substantial gains. Though the aggregate figures may conceal quite complex exchanges of votes, on the whole the shift was from one of the traditional parties to the other.

In two other provinces, one can say only that the Liberals lost. In Saskatchewan the Liberal party lost nine percentage points, but this was divided almost evenly between the New Democratic party and the Progressive Conservatives. British Columbia was more clearly a province of NDP victory: the Progressive Conservatives increased their vote by only two points, while the NDP returned to its traditional third of the electorate in federal elections. The anger against the NDP provoked by its provincial government had finally been

---

[20] Ibid., April 7, 1979, p. C3.

[21] J. Murray Beck, "The Democratic Process at Work in Canadian Federal Elections," in James H. Aitchison, ed., *The Political Process in Canada* (Toronto: University of Toronto Press, 1963), p. 63. For a contrary argument, that Quebec has often frustrated the electoral desires of the rest of Canada, see Pierre Drouilly, *Le paradoxe canadien* [The Canadian paradox] (Montreal: Les Editions Parti Pris, 1978), pp. 112-16.

FIGURE 3–2

Popular Vote in Canada and the Provinces, 1974 and 1979

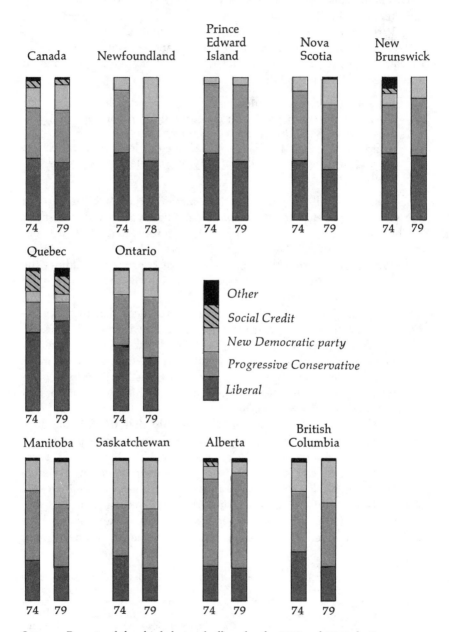

Source: Reports of the chief electoral officer for the 1974 and 1979 elections.

appeased by the defeat of that government in 1976. (British Columbians voted twice in May 1979, since a provincial election had been
called for May 10, 1979. Though the Social Credit government was
reelected, its majority was reduced, and the NDP provincial vote
increased.)

Another province ought perhaps to be included in this set of
results. In New Brunswick the Liberals lost relatively little support,
winning 45 percent of the vote, down from 47 percent in 1974.
The Progressive Conservatives picked up seven percentage points
and the New Democratic party six, largely from the Social Credit
party and an independent candidate who had been victorious in 1974
but did not run in 1979.

In three other provinces, Newfoundland, Nova Scotia, and Manitoba, both the Liberals and the Progressive Conservatives lost to the
NDP. In Nova Scotia the Liberals lost the most, but in the other two
provinces the vote was heaviest against the Progressive Conservatives.
Some of this may have been anger at Progressive Conservative provincial governments—or at least current provincial leaders. Under
a new leader, the Conservatives won a new provincial mandate in
Newfoundland a month after the federal election. In Manitoba, however, the government had been most strongly committed to reducing
the role of government in the provincial economy and had taken
stringent measures in a time of economic slowdown. The private
sector did not move to invest as a result of the new political climate.
While one would want much more evidence than simply the federal
vote returns, this may be a signal that the Proposition 13 mood is
unlikely to be sustained over the long run.

In Quebec the Liberal party won, and the three main opposition
parties lost. The Progressive Conservative party was the major loser.
Not only did its share of the vote decline by eight percentage points,
but its vote fell in absolute terms as well. The party had 520,000
votes in Quebec in 1974; it could keep only 430,000 five years later.

Clearly then, the various parts of Canada were marching to quite
different drummers. Looking only at the fate of the Liberal party,
one could quickly conclude that there really is an English Canada and
a French Canada. Only in Quebec did the Liberal party vote increase.
In the other nine provinces, it fell. The appearance of English-French
cleavage in Canada is somewhat moderated if we examine the results
in those constituencies, largely in New Brunswick and Ontario, where
there are large French Canadian minorities. Of the 207 constituencies
outside Quebec, fourteen are more than 25 percent French speaking.
A further thirteen have between 10 and 25 percent of their populations claiming French as their mother tongue. Table 3–7 indicates

TABLE 3–7

CHANGE IN PARTY SUPPORT, BY LINGUISTIC COMPOSITION OF
CONSTITUENCY, 1974–1979
(percentage points)

French Speakers in Constituency	Lib.	PC	NDP	SC	Number of Constituencies
Quebec					
Less than 67 percent	+10	−11	−3	+1	(14)
More than 67 percent	+6	−7	−1	−1	(61)
Rest of Canada					
Less than 10 percent	−7	+3	+5	−1	(180)
10–25 percent	−5	+2	+4	−1	(13)
More than 25 percent	−2	+5	+4	−3	(14)

NOTE: Changes may not add to zero because other candidates are omitted.
SOURCES: Calculated from unpublished data on the 1974 and 1979 elections supplied by the chief electoral officer of Canada. Constituency language data taken from the 1976 census.

that Liberal support fell in all types of constituencies outside Quebec, but it fell least—only two percentage points—in the most French constituencies. By contrast, the drop was seven points where French speakers constitute less than 10 percent of the population. Within Quebec the situation was reversed. The least French constituencies were even more strongly attracted by the Liberal party than the most French ones.

English-French polarization outside Quebec was reduced by withdrawals of minor party and independent candidates in New Brunswick. The Progressive Conservatives made strong gains there, though we cannot be sure that the gains came from French speakers. It is clear that the impression of linguistic polarization outside Quebec rests largely on effects of the electoral system. Liberals won all but two of the most French constituencies, nine of the thirteen in the 10 to 25 percent range.

The election was not just about polarization of linguistic groups, however. Economic issues were the most prominent, but their impact is harder to gauge, since it is virtually impossible to get good current economic data at the constituency level. Based on figures from the 1976 census, giving a nationwide rate of 6.1 percent unemployment among males, table 3–8 roughly classifies constituencies as having "low," "medium," or "high" unemployment, depending on whether

TABLE 3–8

CHANGE IN PARTY SUPPORT, IN CONSTITUENCIES WITH LOW, MEDIUM, AND
HIGH UNEMPLOYMENT, BY REGION, 1974–1979
(percentage points)

Unemployment Level	Lib.	PC	NDP	SC	Number of Constituencies
All Canada					
Low	−5	+3	+3	−1	(102)
Medium	−3	a	+3	a	(150)
High	−1	−4	+7	−3	(30)
Atlantic					
Low	—	—	—	—	(0)
Medium	−5	+3	+6	a	(18)
High	−4	−7	+13	−2	(14)
Quebec					
Low	+10	−10	−2	−1	(13)
Medium	+7	−8	−2	a	(50)
High	+4	−1	a	−4	(12)
Ontario					
Low	−10	+6	+4	a	(43)
Medium	−8	+5	+3	a	(52)
High	—	—	—	—	(0)
Prairies					
Low	−5	+3	+3	−2	(43)
Medium	−4	−5	+10	−1	(6)
High	—	—	—	—	(0)
British Columbia					
Low	−7	−2	+9	0	(1)
Medium	−10	+3	+9	−1	(23)
High	−8	−1	+10	−1	(4)

NOTE: "Low," up to 4.9 percent male unemployment, according to the 1976 census; "medium," 5.0 to 9.9 percent; "high," 10 percent or more. Neither Ontario nor the Prairies had constituencies of high male unemployment as defined here, and the Atlantic region had no low unemployment.
a Less than 0.5.
SOURCES: As for table 3-7.

the constituency was below, around, or significantly higher than the national figure. Since much unemployment in Canada is structural, what we are picking up is the chronically depressed or chronically favored areas. It is doubtful that many constituencies would have to be reclassified if 1979 data were available.

Looking at the figures for Canada as a whole, we find that the NDP does better in least-favored constituencies, the Liberals also do better (or at least less badly), and the Progressive Conservatives do increasingly poorly as unemployment gets worse. These generalizations must, however, be qualified.

When we control for region, Liberal fortunes seem generally unrelated to the economic status of constituencies everywhere outside Quebec, but the Progressive Conservative/NDP difference remains sharp, particularly in the Atlantic provinces and the Prairies. Unemployment is chronic in the Atlantic provinces. Where it is worst, the Conservatives lost seven percentage points, and the NDP gained thirteen. Where unemployment is not much worse than the Canadian average, both the Progressive Conservatives and the NDP gain marginally. On the Prairies there are no longer any constituencies with very high unemployment, but everything is relative. In the six least favored constituencies, the Progressive Conservatives again lost five points while the NDP gained ten. In Ontario and British Columbia, Progressive Conservative and NDP support is largely unrelated to unemployment categories.

If we combine all constituencies outside Quebec, we can confirm the impression that Liberal support was largely unrelated to these categories: losses of seven points in each of the first two and a loss of five points where unemployment is worst. Such a combination again implies that there is an "English Canada." On the constituency evidence this English Canada is becoming increasingly split according to economic fortune. The Progressive Conservatives gained five percentage points over 1974 in the most favored areas and three points in average areas but lost five points in areas of chronically high unemployment. The NDP gained across the board, but moderately (2 percent) in economically favored constituencies and spectacularly—by twelve percentage points—in depressed ones.

Interestingly enough, Quebec is also split economically. Here the Liberals, as the locally dominant party, suffer as unemployment increases, and, significantly, it is the Progressive Conservatives who benefit. In the context of overall 1974–1979 trends, this gets translated into a lesser gain for the Liberals and a lesser loss for the Conservatives as economic conditions worsen. The Parti Crédit

Social has lost its capacity to capture and channel economic grievances in Quebec.

With the Atlantic area, Quebec is the region that suffers most from chronic unemployment. The NDP is clearly moving to capture the grievances generated by unemployment in the four most easterly provinces of Canada; yet it is unable to do so in Quebec. Who can? One cannot rule out yet another third party, most likely one with a much more nationalistic bent than the Créditistes had when they tapped economic grievances in the early 1960s. There was a separatist party contesting the 1979 federal election in Quebec, but it did not have the support of the provincial Parti Québécois and gained only 20,000 votes in the whole province. This failure could be reversed if the economy continues to be in trouble.

The Progressive Conservative party is the only established party that could profit from this Quebec discontent with the Liberals. The figures in table 3–8 suggest that they have done so to some extent; yet their policy instincts appear to be all the other way, leading them along avenues that, though not "anti-Quebec," are irrelevant to the needs of dissatisfied Quebecers. In the area of unemployment policy, it is no doubt too soon to expect innovation. What the government has done, however, is to maintain the restrictions enacted by the previous Liberal government and to announce new ones.

One instance of a policy commitment unlikely to appeal to Quebec was the promise of tax relief for homeowners,[22] since home-ownership is much less common in Quebec than in the other provinces. In 1976 barely 50 percent of Quebec dwelling units were owned by the occupier, while the figure for the rest of Canada was 66 percent. Table 3–9 indicates the effect of this promise in the different regions. From the distribution of cases, it is clear that the significance of homeownership in the Atlantic provinces is different from its meaning in the rest of the country. It is not a rich region, and although two-thirds of the constituencies have high homeownership, this does not imply a large investment, hence no great benefit to be derived from tax relief. Thus it is not surprising that the pattern of vote switching in the Atlantic provinces is largely unrelated to

[22] After this was written, the Progressive Conservative government announced a program of income-tax credits to be phased in over four years. The program was more equitable as among homeowners than the party's campaign promise, particularly in that it gave a flat-rate credit of $250 (in the fourth and subsequent years) for local property taxes. The program had no subsidies for renters; so the point made in the text is still valid. The government fell before this measure could be enacted.

TABLE 3–9

CHANGE IN PROGRESSIVE CONSERVATIVE VOTE,
BY HOMEOWNERSHIP AND REGION, 1974–1979
(percentage points)

Proportion of Homeowners in Constituency in 1976	Change in PC Vote	Number of Constituencies
Atlantic provinces		
Less than 60 percent	−2	(4)
60–75 percent	+1	(6)
75 percent or more	−2	(22)
Ontario		
Less than 60 percent	+4	(28)
60–75 percent	+6	(44)
75 percent or more	+7	(23)
Prairies		
Less than 60 percent	−1	(8)
60–75 percent	+1	(20)
75 percent or more	+4	(21)
British Columbia		
Less than 60 percent	−2	(5)
60–75 percent	+4	(16)
75 percent or more	+2	(7)
Quebec[a]		
Less than 33.3 percent	−12	(18)
33.3 to 66.7 percent	−6	(29)
More than 66.7 percent	−6	(28)

[a] Different cutting points are used for Quebec because barely 50 percent of dwellings in the province were owned by occupants in 1976.
SOURCES: As for table 3-7.

this issue. Elsewhere, the higher the proportion of homeowners, the larger the Progressive Conservative gain (the less the loss, in Quebec). In every region except Ontario where homeowners are a relatively small proportion of the population, the Progressive Conservative party lost votes. While it is a long step from table 3–9 to confident conclusions about voter motivation, it does appear that the Conservatives' tax relief plan worked as they intended it to. With more certainty, one can conclude from tables 3–8 and 3–9 that the Progressive Conservatives were strongly favored by the wealthier areas of the country in 1979.

The Canadian Voter: Not Alienated but Not Enthusiastic. From the run-up to the election, it seemed to reporters that the political malaise that we have earlier seen affecting other democracies had now reached Canada. Against a background of inflation, energy shortage, and separatism, the election offered one candidate who had angered or disappointed most Canadians and another who had failed to impress many Canadians. The time was ripe for large-scale voter alienation.

In fact, there were two elections being fought on May 22. Neither was as negative as commentators expected. Neither produced an outcome describable as a national mobilization in support of a particular line of policy.

The election in Quebec was about national unity. It was a vote of confidence in Pierre Trudeau's, and the Liberal party's, ability to defend the interests Quebecers feel they have in a countrywide union. At 76 percent, turnout in the province was almost five points above the average turnout for the three previous Trudeau elections. It was identical, however, with the turnout in 1972—another election in which it appeared that French speakers' national interests were threatened. The 62 percent Liberal vote was the highest since 1940, when conscription loomed. The Liberals had invited Quebecers to "Speak Up"—and so they had, loud enough to give the Liberal party a plurality of the national vote though not to guarantee a lead in Parliament.

It was an election some Quebecers must have felt they lost. "Their" party was out. The one that was in appeared to be adopting a policy of benign neglect, with little offered to Quebec but toughness during the campaign followed by an insistence that Quebec's basic constitutional option must be decided by the Quebecers themselves. This proposition, reasonable in itself, illustrates the disadvantage of having a federal government containing few Quebecers: the effect is to say that Quebec's basic future can be discussed only by provincial politicians, a much more debatable proposition.

In fact, it is a mistake to say that Quebec lost the election, for the rest of Canada was holding quite a different one. That election was about rising prices and falling dollars. It was won by the Progressive Conservative party, not against Quebec but without Quebec and without a number of other provinces where the Conservative message fell on deaf ears. Where the Liberals had succeeded in angering almost everyone, their opponents' positive messages divided English Canadians. Those living in poorer regions, areas of more than 10 percent unemployment in the now seemingly good year of 1976, and areas with much rental accommodation switched to the New Democratic party. The better off preferred the Conservatives.

It would be an exaggeration to say that 1979 mobilized English Canadians along class lines. True, turnout went up, but from an unusually low base. Comparing 1979 turnout with the 1968–1974 average, five English-speaking provinces were below that average, three others were within two percentage points of it, and only one—Manitoba—was much more than two points above average turnout. In the poorer provinces, excluding Quebec but including Manitoba, NDP support reached new highs. Only in Manitoba did this involve above-average turnout.

Moreover, the election was not about class politics—even in the NDP. Though their campaign gave some prominence to the issue of preserving Medicare, they too were talking about industrial strategy and energy supplies. Though the Progressive Conservative party had planks whose benefits would accrue mainly to the middle class, their campaign was far from mobilizing the middle class.

Though all issues have implications for social classes, the overt conflicts for this government, as for the previous ones, would be inter-regional. The election campaign did little to clarify the issues. The federal stance had not been articulated, and no groups of voters were mobilized behind any settlement. The campaign did not reinforce the federal hand. No party sought any particular mandate, and there was none to be claimed when the election was over. Yet, in seeking settlements for regional conflicts, the Progressive Conservative government had one important resource—popular support. Though we were able to identify only three provinces where that party fully captured the anti-Liberal vote, two of these, Ontario and Alberta, were key ones. Any new government would have been faced with defining an industrial and energy strategy. As demonstrated in 1980, no Liberal government in 1979 would have had effective spokesmen from the contending sides in its own cabinet and caucus. The Progressive Conservative government did. Ontario is the leader of the energy-consuming provinces, Alberta of the producers. Both were well represented in the new government.

Reconciling the interests of the two while maintaining Canada's international position is not easy. Indeed, it proved to be a contributory factor in the defeat of the Clark government. But, in May 1979, it seemed that Canada had a government with a political base in economically crucial regions and with a less confrontationist style and commitment than its predecessor. It seemed, therefore, that Canadians had elected a government well equipped to formulate national economic strategies, albeit strategies of which poorer Canadians were skeptical.

The government was weak, however, in its ability to extend its economic coalition into Quebec. Both its constitutional and its economic policies could expect to find support in that province, but the party, with just two elected members, was unable to mobilize it. This was particularly serious as the provincial government was expected to call a referendum on what sort of political/economic relationship the province should have with the rest of Canada.

While the Clark government appeared to be in a strong position to deal with economic challenges, it seemed far too weak to end the "two elections on the same day" phenomenon we have observed. Immediate postelection prognostications focused on these two large questions of strength and weakness. Unnoticed by many, including those in the new government, was an even more elementary deficiency: it did not have a majority in the new Parliament.

[23] For case studies of the process during the 1960s, see Richard E. B. Simeon, *Federal-Provincial Diplomacy* (Toronto: University of Toronto Press, 1972).

4

Candidate Selection

Robert J. Williams

From the popular perspective, the 1979 general election campaign was a struggle between three titans who criss-crossed the country by chartered jet in an effort to gain top billing on the late-night television news. In reality, however, the choice was not just among the three or four major parties and the mushrooming fringe parties or even among the high-profile party leaders: it involved winnowing 282 men and women out of the 1,424 whose names appeared on the ballots across the country that day. One writer has said of this process that

> trench warfare fought constituency by constituency by the individual candidates . . . is a frustrating and frequently boring exercise which often gains a candidate little, reveals hardly anything about his or her suitability to be a member of Parliament, but can kill his or her chances if not entered into with gusto.[1]

In this other election, as in the national campaign, the objective is to meet voters, to be seen, and, above all, to be remembered. Sometimes the candidate has the advantage of a household name or the reputation attached to a job well done in a visible role in the community; others succeed by virtue of having a fresh face or a convincing campaign. Being a successful candidate usually means being familiar yet out of the ordinary, being typical yet distinctive. Even in the conduct of the election campaign, the tried and proven methods of door knocking, attendance at community events, and factory gating (or its equivalent) may be topped off with the extra gimmick, the unanticipated appearance. One Liberal candidate in metropolitan Toronto, for example, disrobed to campaign in a steambath,[2] while a Progressive Conservative candidate in southwestern Ontario was found waving to

[1] Hugh Winsor, "Little Gain for a Lot of Effort," *Globe and Mail* (Toronto), May 14, 1979, p. 7.
[2] Ibid.

motorists (and press cameras) in the morning rush hour from a cherry picker overhanging an expressway. Such ingenious episodes are highlights in local campaigns where the standard efforts are rounds of coffee parties, radio phone-in programs, and all-candidates meetings. As in any advertising effort, though, the product and the promotion become intertwined to such an extent that victory is often a reflection of both. At the same time, the campaign is not the only place in which there are winners and losers, perseverers and dropouts. It is only the final and most overt stage of selecting members of Parliament.

Even before the official election campaign gets under way, a screening process has already taken place, since of course the actual number of contestants does not equal the number of people eligible to serve in the House of Commons. In Canada the process established by law and by custom to elect members of Parliament is fairly well understood and is open to analysis. The filtering process that placed those 1,424 names on the ballots—and more particularly the 949 Progressive Conservatives, Liberals, New Democrats, and Social Creditors—is less well understood and much more shadowy in its operation. This reduction in the number of people who could be elected to the House of Commons usually takes place within the major political parties, which operate in a supply-and-demand world where the prize commodity is an individual believed to be attractive to the electorate.[3] In contrast to the election-day routine, the early screening process is not closely regulated by law, nor are the choices that are made as predictable as those made in the polling booth.[4] Furthermore, it appears to be a part of the electoral process that is highly variable yet capable of producing consistent and identifiable patterns among those selected.

On the face of it, the barriers to becoming a parliamentary candidate are quite low: with the exception of people convicted of certain crimes and people holding certain public offices or appointments, "any person who, on the date he files his nomination paper at an election, is an elector . . . may be a candidate at the election."

---

[3] The term "attractive" is used here in its traditional electoral sense, not in the oversimplified and restrictive analytical sense employed by William Mishler in his "Nominating Attractive Candidates for Parliament: Recruitment to the Canadian House of Commons," *Legislative Studies Quarterly*, vol. 3 (November 1978), pp. 581-99.

[4] An observation made by Peter G. Richards in describing British selection practice is relevant here. He noted that candidate choice "is a highly personal business and the grounds for the decision will vary for each case. . . . The final decision rests with the electors, but their actions are far more predictable." Richards, *Honourable Members: A Study of the British Backbencher* (London: Faber and Faber, 1959), p. 33.

This means—broadly speaking—men or women who are eighteen years of age or older and who are Canadian citizens.[5] To be nominated, the candidate must submit a nomination paper containing the signature of "twenty-five or more persons qualified as electors in the electoral district in which an election is to be held" and a deposit of $200, plus a witnessed statement of consent to the nomination and other documentation.[6]

Many practitioners and observers feel that these qualifications are, in fact, too easy to meet. Some candidates whose intentions or crusades are rather frivolous can gain a legitimate place in a most serious business. Others, who espouse political ideologies of marginal appeal, have found that they cannot even win the votes of all the people who placed them in nomination: thus, candidates of the Marxist-Leninist party in North Vancouver–Burnaby in British Columbia and in Halton, Ontario, received only twenty and twenty-three votes respectively[7] on May 22, even though they had been allowed entry into the campaign by twenty-five nominees. It is not clear, however, whether a more restrictive requirement for nominations would discourage such candidates or only cause them to renew their efforts to gain a place in what many regard as the essence of a democratic political system. Unfortunately, in elections more is not always better, particularly from the point of view of administering the event or of giving voters a fairly straightforward choice.

In reality, then, most of the barriers to entry into an election contest are psychological rather than legal. Blue-collar workers are not precluded from running, but few do. Professionals are not given preferred places, but many who run are professional people. While the age limit sets a starting point for participation, most candidates are years—if not decades—past the age of eighteen. Women are fully eligible to be candidates, but in 1979 only 195 candidates (13.7 percent of the total) were women.[8] Local residency is not required by the election laws, but most candidates are resident in their constituency. While party service is not set out as a qualification for serving in the House of Commons, the bulk of candidates nominated

[5] Canada Elections Act; s. 14 defines electors, s. 20 indicates the qualifications for candidates, and s. 21 describes persons ineligible to be candidates. All references drawn from the indexed copy of the act (Ottawa: Information Canada, 1974).
[6] Ibid., s. 23. It is interesting to note that the requirement of a deposit of $200 accompanying nomination papers has not changed since 1882, when it was increased from $50. See Norman Ward, The Canadian House of Commons: Representation, 2d ed. (Toronto: University of Toronto Press, 1963), pp. 155-56.
[7] Chief Electoral Officer, 1979 General Election: Preliminary Statistics, June 15, 1979, table 10.
[8] Chief Electoral Officer, Preliminary Statistics, 1979, table 5.

are drawn from a very small stratum of society: those who belong to and work for a political party.[9] In its essence, candidate selection in Canada is characterized by systematic biases, a local focus, and a party presence; it is idiosyncratic, highly decentralized, and partisan in its operations. It is difficult to generalize about the process of candidate selection, however, because no two cases are precisely the same and there may be considerable variation between the written rules and the actual practices followed. This is one of the main differences between candidate selection by the political parties and the electoral choice of the voter: the latter is strictly supervised by public officials, and the former is left to the discretion of party members and officials, both professional and amateur.

The two processes are also different in that the selection stage is characterized more by supply-and-demand considerations than is the election itself, although a couple of specific factors have contributed to a sharp rise in the number of people who have sought places in the House of Commons over the last four elections. In 1968 there were 967 candidates (a slight drop from the three federal elections of the 1960s); in 1972 there were 1,116; by 1974 the figure rose to 1,209; and, with an enlarged House in 1979, the official figure was 1,424.[10] It is now rather unusual for a federal constituency to have a contest that involves only candidates from the three or four largest parties. In 1979 only 70 constituencies, out of a total of 282, were three-way (that is, Progressive Conservative–Liberal–NDP) fights, and "major party" four-way struggles (that is, the three parties named above plus Social Credit) happened a mere 11 times. In 38 contests there were four candidates where the fourth was not a Social Creditor. In well over half of all Canadian federal constituencies (163, to be precise) there were more than four candidates nominated.

The main point is that the large increase in candidacies has not come about solely because of the enlarged House: it appears to have

[9] Many of the general characteristics of candidates and members of Parliament can be drawn from previous research. See, for example, Ward, *House of Commons;* Allan Kornberg, *Canadian Legislative Behavior* (New York: Holt, Rinehart and Winston, 1967); Roman R. March, *The Myth of Parliament* (Scarborough, Ont.: Prentice-Hall, 1974); and David Hoffman and Norman Ward, *Bilingualism and Biculturalism in the Canadian House of Commons* (Ottawa: Queen's Printer, 1970), all of which discussed M.P.s. On both successful and unsuccessful candidates, see Joachim E.-C. Surich and Robert J. Williams, "Some Characteristics of Candidates in the 1972 Canadian Federal Election" (Paper presented to the Canadian Political Science Association, Toronto, 1974).

[10] The figures are drawn from J. Murray Beck, *Pendulum of Power: Canada's Federal Elections* (Scarborough, Ont.: Prentice-Hall, 1968); *Report of the Chief Electoral Officer,* 1972 and 1974; and Chief Electoral Officer, *Preliminary Statistics,* 1979.

come from the large number of candidates representing less traditional parties who have ventured into the field. In 1979, under the provisions of the Canada Elections Act (1974), nine parties claimed official status in the parliamentary elections, since they had nominated more than the prescribed fifty candidates and had filed appropriate supporting documents. There appear to be two basic reasons for the rise of these new parties. First, the revisions to the Canada Elections Act in 1970 made it possible to list party names on the ballot for the first time. The 1974 election saw the participation, for example, of both the Communist party of Canada and the Marxist-Leninist party of Canada under the provisions of these rules, with subsequent publicity and perhaps even some form of legitimacy resulting from their designation on the ballot. In that context, a minor party could benefit from nominating sufficient candidates to allow each of them to "show the flag" in a location previously impervious to partisanship, the polling booth. Second, the 1970 amendments and the 1974 financial provisions provided more incentives to minor political parties, since they might qualify for free television time (in 1974) or a share in the time allocated by all broadcasters (in 1979), as well as direct financial support for any candidate receiving 15 percent of the total valid votes cast in the constituency.[11] Many smaller groups responded to these incentives and fielded sufficient candidates to qualify for these benefits, even though their best strategy for actually electing someone to the House of Commons might have been to concentrate their effort in a handful of constituencies.[12] Many candidates apparently enter the election contests merely to assist in the completion of a party slate—and this applies to some candidates in the traditional parties as well—but make no real impact in the election contest itself.

Proof of this is not hard to find: together, the 475 assorted candidates who were not Progressive Conservatives, Liberals, New Democrats, or Social Creditors amassed a total of 173,441 votes, or 1.51 percent of the total valid votes cast on May 22. Although the largest of these parties (the Marxist-Leninists) fielded more candidates than the smallest of the four traditional parties (Social Credit), and although in several instances fringe candidates outpolled candidates nominated by the traditional parties (for example, in Quebec, where Rhinoceros candidates often placed well ahead of NDP candidates), not one fringe candidate was elected to the House of Commons. Candidate selection in these parties was conducted in a fashion con-

[11] See John C. Courtney, "Recognition of Canadian Political Parties in Parliament and Law," *Canadian Journal of Political Science*, vol. 11 (March 1978), pp. 40-46.
[12] This is an application of Courtney's argument about broadcasting strategy in the area of candidates; the logic appears valid in both contexts.

siderably more obscure than in the remaining four parties, and no generalizations appear to be possible, even if it could be demonstrated that the candidacies had some bearing on the outcome of the election.

The Selection Process

The procedures used by Canadian political parties to select parliamentary candidates are obscure in their origins and variable in their operations. In the four parties under consideration the choice is normally made at a special meeting of the constituency party association, often called a nominating convention, which is usually devoted exclusively to selecting a candidate. In these meetings, members of the local party organization (however membership is defined) conduct an elimination or runoff election by secret ballot to determine the party's nominee. This individual is then entitled to formal party endorsement for the election (with concomitant campaign support from party headquarters), to have the party name included on the ballot next to his or her name, and to qualify for financial assistance under the Canada Elections Act. In cases where the constituency association is inactive, disorganized, or nonexistent, the parties may use regional or provincial bodies to designate a candidate. The whole business is, however, much more complex than this capsule description, and the screening process and individual party practices will be discussed in greater detail below.

Origins and Variations. The present selection process is the result of more than a century of evolution, combined with unchanging external factors in the Canadian political tradition. No comprehensive survey of candidate recruitment practices has yet appeared, though there has been some preliminary research, which forms the basis of this chapter.

Early Canadian federal elections were boisterous and often rowdy affairs. Norman Ward describes how a candidate for Parliament in the 1860s and 1870s could be nominated orally at an appointed time, although some partisan returning officers did their best to inhibit opposition nominations.[13] Later on, candidates were nominated by petition (along with a deposit), and balloting in the election became secret. Part of the tradition of local control over nominations probably developed in this period as a carry-over from the older, more open nominating and voting procedures. The custom of local nomination was later reinforced by the need of certain communities or classes (the farmers come to mind immediately) to emphasize that candidates were

---

[13] Ward, *House of Commons*, pp. 154-56.

chosen to serve as local spokesmen in Ottawa. Sometimes they even went to the extent of forming their own party groupings to avoid the dominance of the old parties. At the same time, however, the "parliamentary parties"[14] went out into the electorate seeking support; it was often desirable for them to have candidates whose loyalty was unquestionable or to be in a position to place certain candidates in favorable constituencies. To those ends, a certain amount of centralized influence over the selection of the party's candidates was retained. Intertwined with these organizational and political factors were the regional variations in customs and values that appear in most parts of Canadian political life.

It is thus possible to identify two broad traditions in candidate selection in Canadian political history. Even though the second approach described below has become the norm, the influence of the first has not been eliminated.

The centralized approach. At one extreme of the scale was the practice of having candidates selected by the party leader or a central party apparatus of some sort. In the 1935 provincial election in Alberta, for example, the fledgling Social Credit held that it was essential for the leader, William Aberhart, and his associates to choose all candidates. Local involvement was allowed by having constituency conventions nominate three or four candidates, from whom the leader would select an appropriate person. This technique allowed the party to conduct a thorough investigation of the various nominees and, in the end, "to ensure that real, not fraudulent, Social Creditors would be presented."[15] It may be noted that the same kind of control was exercised over the selection of candidates in the early days of the

---

[14] The distinction made here is between political parties whose origins were as "parliamentary coteries seeking the rewards of office" and those that began as "extra-parliamentary groups created in times of upheaval." The Liberals and (Progressive) Conservatives trace their origins to nineteenth-century parliamentary roots, while all other national parties began outside the parliamentary arena. The phrases quoted are from Conrad Winn and John McMenemy, *Political Parties in Canada* (Toronto: McGraw-Hill Ryerson, 1976), p. 1. The distinction is also discussed in Frederick C. Engelmann and Mildred A. Schwartz, *Canadian Political Parties: Origin, Character, Impact* (Scarborough, Ont.: Prentice-Hall, 1975), and, in terms of electoral organization, in Allan Kornberg and William Mishler, *Influence in Parliament: Canada* (Durham, N.C.: Duke University Press, 1976), pp. 39-40.

[15] Michael B. Stein, *The Dynamics of Right-Wing Protest: A Political Analysis of Social Credit in Quebec* (Toronto: University of Toronto Press, 1973), p. 38. The Alberta party's arrangements are discussed in more detail in C. B. Macpherson, *Democracy in Alberta: Social Credit and the Party System*, 2d ed. (Toronto: University of Toronto Press, 1962), p. 158, and in John A. Irving, *The Social Credit Movement in Alberta* (Toronto: University of Toronto Press, 1959), pp. 181-82.

Union des Electeurs, the forerunner of the contemporary Social Credit party in Quebec. Michael Stein argues that this was done to allow the founders of the party to dominate the organization as it expanded and to ensure its ideological purity.[16] The technique of leadership control did not become a permanent part of the Social Credit modus operandi in Alberta; it apparently did not survive Aberhart's death in 1943.[17]

In Newfoundland, between 1949, when it joined the Canadian federation, and 1968, there were "no public selection procedures" for Liberal party candidates in either federal or provincial elections. The premier, Joseph R. Smallwood, "made no secret of his ability to nominate candidates as part of his personal prerogative."[18] In his autobiography, Smallwood described his role this way:

> For a hundred years in Newfoundland, the leader of a political party exercised an authority that disappeared in mainland Canada long ago. It was the leader who selected and appointed every individual candidate of the party in each election. . . . I followed the normal Newfoundland practice and selected every candidate in every constituency in every provincial General Election while I was leader. With two exceptions, I selected and appointed every federal candidate of our Party in the first seven federal General Elections in Newfoundland.[19]

This is not to suggest that Newfoundlanders were somehow tricked out of their rightful role in candidate selection; as has already been indicated, there is no state monitoring of the process at all, and public participation is a customary or conventional feature. Furthermore, in provincial contests in Newfoundland at least, the majority of outport (that is, fishing village) voters were content to have as their candidate someone with "only the most tenuous connections with the constituencies," since these Liberals were sent to them as "Joey's men."[20]

---

16 Stein, *Dynamics*, p. 38.

17 Macpherson, *Democracy in Alberta*, p. 196.

18 S. J. R. Noel, *Politics in Newfoundland* (Toronto: University of Toronto Press, 1971), p. 282.

19 Joseph R. Smallwood, *I Chose Canada: The Memoirs of the Honourable J. R. "Joey" Smallwood*, vol. 2, *The Premiership* (Toronto: Signet, 1975), p. 186.

20 Noel, *Politics in Newfoundland*, p. 284. It should be pointed out that, according to one authority, Smallwood's nomination was announced "usually after some informal consultation with either trusted party agents or individuals from the district." See Steven B. Wolinetz, "Party Organization in Newfoundland: The Liberal Party under Smallwood" (Paper presented to the Canadian Political Science Association, Edmonton, 1975), p. 4.

These two examples will suffice to demonstrate that centralized control has been practiced in candidate selection in Canadian parties. Today this role is still possible, but only in exceptional circumstances. Ironically, under present electoral law, the party leaders or designated substitutes play a part in the endorsement of locally selected candidates that enhances their position beyond what tradition has allowed in the more recent past.

The decentralized approach. It is much easier to discover examples of the decentralized tradition in candidate selection in Canadian political parties; they are seen across the ideological spectrum and in various regions of the country. For the sake of brevity, only two examples will be noted.

Throughout their brief history, Canadian Farmers' parties operated with very strong local autonomy, and this logically meant that responsibility for the selection of an appropriate farmer candidate rested with members of the local organizations. In some cases, such groups would endorse a candidate already selected by one of the existing parties (Liberal or Conservative) who was known to be sympathetic to farmers; in others, individuals "untainted" by previous partisanship were nominated. It is clear that the Progressive party that fought in the federal election of 1921 and the various provincial Farmers' parties of that era were founded to follow a different course from the two old parties. Their selection of candidates by constituency associations is thus consistent with other features of their organizational life, such as a belief in direct democracy, recall, and—for a time—primaries.[21] As the first successful extraparliamentary party in the House of Commons, the Progressives were borne on the shoulders of local party activists. The party's very creation "had been forced from below by the spontaneous action of the rank and file of the members of the organized farmers in Ontario, Alberta, Manitoba, and indeed throughout the movement."[22] Despite the political failure of the Progressive movement, its legacy of opposition to the ideals and interests of the old parties and its adherence to strong principles of populist localism survived in the Cooperative Commonwealth Federation (CCF), founded in 1933.[23] Thus, since the CCF was "a movement with agrarian anti-party and non-partisan antecedents," its constitution

[21] A brief reference to this last-mentioned experiment is found in David Smith, *Prairie Liberalism: The Liberal Party of Saskatchewan, 1905-71* (Toronto: University of Toronto Press, 1975), p. 91.
[22] William L. Morton, *The Progressive Party in Canada* (Toronto: University of Toronto Press, 1967), p. 106.
[23] Morton, *Progressive Party*, pp. 283-84.

was designed to ensure that the new party would be free from the disabilities of the old ones. Part of the constitution's purpose was the demonstration of effective internal democracy in the face of the autocratic and elitist Liberal and Conservative parties.[24]

In a way, this internal democracy prevented the maintenance of consensus and ironically led to the need for some kind of control by the leadership over policy, tactics, and structures. Still, despite the potential powers of the central party institutions that developed over the party's life, great constituency autonomy existed over such matters as the selection of parliamentary candidates.[25] Once again, as in the case of the early Social Credit movement, there is a playing off of central and local influences against each other, except that in the case of the CCF the weight fell on the local side.[26]

While it is difficult to generalize with certainty, some of the old-line parties' approaches to candidate recruitment were clearly less autocratic and elitist than critics like the Progressives and others would have us believe. In the Saskatchewan Liberal party, for example, David Smith has demonstrated that "local associations were sensitive about their prerogative in the matter of selecting candidates and forthrightly rejected any candidate whose selection might be interpreted as the result of 'boss or clique rule.' "[27] As a result, overt intervention by the provincial party was apparently rare in the early days of the party's existence and into the 1920s, even though the party is widely viewed as a true machine organization.[28] Yet throughout this period there was also a rapid turnover of Liberal M.P.s at the provincial level, which, by inference, Smith attributes to behind-the-scenes maneuvering by "the central office and the party chiefs."[29] Still later, after the party had been out of office provincially for the twenty years from 1944 to 1964, the Liberal leader, Ross Thatcher, became a major stimulus to candidacy for many people: he actively sought out candidates and personally encouraged many to seek nomination in constituencies in which the Liberal party organization

[24] Walter D. Young, *The Anatomy of a Party: The National C.C.F., 1932-61* (Toronto: University of Toronto Press, 1961), p. 141.

[25] This argument is made in John Richards, "The Decline and Fall of Agrarian Socialism," in Seymour M. Lipset, ed., *Agrarian Socialism: The Cooperative Commonwealth Federation in Saskatchewan*, rev. ed. (Garden City: Doubleday, 1968), p. 374.

[26] Young, *Anatomy of a Party*, p. 299.

[27] Smith, *Prairie Liberalism*, p. 37.

[28] Ibid., p. 170.

[29] Ibid., p. 172.

had apparently gone into hibernation. It must be presumed that, by this time, even in the weakest of constituencies, selection nominally remained in the hands of local party activists; but the process was open to pressures and, to put it delicately, assistance from both the party's leadership and its central apparatus. In effect, most local organizations capable of functioning—and this does not apply only to Saskatchewan—jealously guard their nomination responsibilities, while the central party, responsible for the ongoing management of the organization and resolved (by definition) to bring the party electoral success, itches to get its hands on less-than-zealous constituency organizations to get "electable" candidates nominated.[30] Once again, a tension or a playing off of two traditions and two interests in the nomination process can be observed. Most evidence points to local autonomy as the norm in modern selection procedures.

Evolution and its effects. Evidence of a kind of developmental process can be seen in party selection practices. In present circumstances, the centralized approach is much less common than it used to be, though not unknown. Just as practices begun in one party— such as selecting the party leader in open conventions [31]—spread gradually to the others and into the ten provincial systems, so, too, decentralized approaches to candidate selection appear to have spread into all parties and provinces in normal circumstances. For example, the once-centralized Union des Electeurs was transformed into the Quebec wing of the Social Credit party and by 1962 boasted procedures allowing for the nomination of party candidates by bona fide party members.[32] Similarly, a formalized constituency role in candidate selection appears to have been established in the major Newfoundland political parties after 1968.[33] In other words, through a subtle process of evolution and imitation, the practice of selecting candidates through constituency conventions has come to be regarded as the acceptable method in all major parties and in all regions of the country, even though it is not always possible to put it into practice. In addition, it should be recognized that the variations noted reflect not only regional values and customs but the basic assumptions

---

[30] March, *Myth of Parliament*, p. 88.

[31] See John C. Courtney, *The Selection of National Party Leaders in Canada* (Toronto: Macmillan, 1973).

[32] Maurice Pinard, *The Rise of a Third Party: A Study in Crisis Politics* (Englewood Cliffs, N.J.: Prentice-Hall, 1971), p. 10.

[33] See Wolinetz, "Party Organization in Newfoundland"; and Susan McCorquodale, "Newfoundland," in Martin Robin, ed., *Canadian Provincial Politics: The Party Systems of the Ten Provinces*, 2d ed. (Scarborough, Ont.: Prentice-Hall, 1978), pp. 164-66.

and purposes behind the several political parties. As party organizations evolved and adapted themselves to changing fortunes and external considerations, so, too, did selection procedures change to reflect those conditions.

The major Canadian parties are organized today basically as cadres of local supporters who have only intermittent responsibilities. In addition, highly decentralized structures, usually focusing on the provincial units, coexist with an ongoing parliamentary party headed by the party leader. Traditionally, an extraparliamentary party bureaucracy has devoted its energies to maintaining the visibility of the party in the constituencies by aiding local associations through newsletters, research, visiting speakers, and the like. A more significant, but more obscure, function was the raising of funds for election campaigning; in the past, at least for the Liberals and Progressive Conservatives, this amounted to canvassing large corporations, individuals, and groups for contributions to the party treasury. The new conditions set by the 1974 legislation on election expenses may change such practices substantially, but the principle of top-down funding for expenditures in the area of national media campaigns and the strategic planning of the leader's tour (or that of prominent party figures) remains and ensures some degree of centralized direction for the party's election activities. In addition, the provisions relating to official designation of party candidates provide a continuation of an overseeing role for the central organization. Finally, the growth of public attention and of centralized sources of information gives the Canadian parties an apparent cohesiveness that belies their true mode of operation and the "natural" bias of the cadre party.

On the other hand, at the constituency level, Canadian political parties are election-oriented entities that lapse into inactivity between contests. Efforts are made to keep the local associations functioning—and this is easier if the sitting M.P. is their man—so that they can be more easily revived as an election approaches. Yet for the average party worker this is the real party, the place where he or she can have some influence over the party's direction and leadership. In the complex world of parliamentary and federal politics, ordinary party members recognize their limitations in imposing policy directions, ideological orientations, or bargaining strategies. They must be content with the trench warfare and the tactical implementation of electoral campaigns, with the knowledge, though, that they hold one key power in the whole electoral process: the right to nominate the party's candidate. As has been demonstrated, this prerogative has not always been made available to party members, but it seems clear that once it has been established, it is very difficult to remove. Rank-and-file selection of the candidate now serves as a symbol—if not the reality—of the democratic ethos of Canadian political parties and has become entrenched in party practices wherever the local organization is able to perform the task. Its lack of harmony with ongoing party direction, with fund-raising practices, and with the cult of leadership only illustrates how the party organizations are the result of piecemeal changes, evolutionary modifications, and the grafting of practices from one system onto those of another. The net result is nomination practices that are a kind of cross between an American local primary and a British party branch selection, with none of the close controls by state or party of either method.[34]

In effect, the tensions between local autonomy and centralized management have now been resolved in favor of the former largely because a successful modern party could not openly deny the local party membership a role while its major competitors operated with some form of open candidate selection. This is not to argue that the four major parties use precisely the same procedures, merely that each one pays homage to the principle of local control over candidate selection and tries to use it wherever possible. Centralized direction is carried out at some risk where a local association wishes to resist it but must be held in readiness should the local process falter.[35]

The net result is that there are four broad approaches to candidate selection—one corresponding to each party—but an infinite number of variations in specific constituency practices permitted under the party constitutions.

Operations and Practices. In the 1979 Canadian federal election, 949 men and women were officially endorsed candidates for the Liberal, Progressive Conservative, New Democratic, and Social Credit parties. This means that each one was permitted by the leader of the party to have the party's name on the ballot and also that the leader, or someone designated by him, was satisfied that the individual had the backing of the party association in the constituency. When political commentators try to explain how an individual obtains that backing, difficulties begin to emerge, for, as one former member of Parliament said, "Why one person is chosen and another rejected, why one steps forward and a better holds back, is without logic." [36]

---

[34] The same comparison was made more than a decade ago in Leon D. Epstein, *Political Parties in Western Democracies* (New York: Praeger, 1967), pp. 230-31. It is also made by Engelmann and Schwartz, *Canadian Political Parties*, p. 229.

[35] See Engelmann and Schwartz, *Canadian Political Parties*, p. 229, and March, *Myth of Parliament*, p. 88.

[36] Gordon Aiken, *The Backbencher: Trials and Tribulations of a Member of Parliament* (Toronto: McClelland and Stewart, 1974), p. 11.

While the various studies of federal nominees and members of Parliament reveal certain characteristics and styles associated with successful participants, "there is no comprehensive study of the circumstances of federal elections, and especially their competitive circumstances." [37] It is evident that views about a party's prospects have a profound impact on the number and caliber of candidates who come forward, on the turnout and enthusiasm of nomination meetings, and on the myriad influences converging in the process of selecting a parliamentary candidate. This process can be considered in terms of three phases of filtering: first, the searching and screening activities, then the selection proceedings themselves, and finally authorization by the national party.[38]

It is important to note that the last phase (here called authorization) is a recent addition to the selection process. For the most part, parliamentary nominees have been designated in the constituency parties, with only a general form of monitoring provided by the party's executive officers and central bureaucracy.

Searching and screening. From the point of view of a local party organization, two factors initially influence the task of candidate selection. The first of these, frequently found in 1979, is the readjustment of constituency boundaries since the last election. When they have been readjusted, new organizations need to be created from old, with the addition of new districts and the loss of old ones. For the Progressive Conservatives, this is a matter of some concern, since a nomination meeting cannot be held until a constituency association has been officially "chartered" with a constitution approved by the membership and an inaugural meeting held to elect officers. Furthermore, with redistribution, elected M.P.s may be required to play a game of musical chairs to determine who will seek nomination in the various new constituencies, which may also be fewer or more numerous than previously.

The second factor is the presence or absence of an incumbent M.P. in the constituency. For unsuccessful parties, the choice is usually open to renominate their former candidate or to seek a fresh face. There are, of course, varying opinions on the wisdom of the two choices. Some argue that "a loser is always a loser" and so the

37 Engelmann and Schwartz, *Canadian Political Parties*, p. 232.

38 Much of the information used in the rest of this discussion is drawn from interviews conducted with party officials in Ottawa in August 1979 and with other party activists and officials elsewhere who have wide experience in the local operations of various political parties. In the interests of open dialogue, some of those interviewed preferred not to be named. This courtesy will be extended here to all who assisted in providing information even though many had nothing controversial to add to the investigation. My thanks go to all of them; the errors of fact and interpretation are my own.

party should try to find someone who is not tainted by defeat. In other organizations (and many old-time New Democrats apparently held this view), previous candidates are presumed to represent an investment in time and money that should be built upon in subsequent campaigns. There is no particular pattern to be found here, but in situations where the prospects are good, parties would not normally have to accept a defeated candidate unless they chose to do so, while those facing hopeless odds might have to make do with conscripted ex-candidates.

For a party with a sitting M.P., the task is rather different. It is widely conceded that an incumbent M.P. who wishes to be renominated usually can be, although exceptions have been known—even among well-placed members.[39] Two studies of the Liberal party suggest that during the years of the party's hegemony in federal politics (from 1935 to 1957), nomination practices were often "empty formalities," since incumbent M.P.s "were virtually assured of renomination," defeated candidates "had the inside track," and where there were neither sitting members nor available experienced candidates, "the local cabinet minister and his organizers would normally anoint the man they wanted for the nomination. The association would then ratify the choice."[40] As a result, some constituencies would not have a real candidate search "for as long as fifteen or twenty years because they continued to elect the same candidate."[41] Furthermore, contemporary party officials have to keep a sharp eye on some constituencies where longtime M.P.s may attempt what one termed "the laying on of hands" regarding a successor. In this context, party officials think it important to encourage a genuine nomination contest, unless there is a risk attached to such a conflict in the constituency organization.

Most local party organizations, however, have a wide-open field in selecting a candidate since there are no incumbents, interested previous candidates, or others in an advantageous position. The process may then be viewed as a kind of marketplace, in which the prospective candidates need to be identified and persuaded to run and the local organization to be convinced of the merits of certain individual aspirants. Often—particularly when the party's electoral record is poor and its prospects the same—real inducements need to

[39] See Beck, *Pendulum of Power*, p. 402, for two exceptions in 1968.

[40] Reginald Whitaker, *The Government Party: Organizing and Financing the Liberal Party of Canada, 1930-1958* (Toronto: University of Toronto Press, 1977), p. 413.

[41] S. Peter Regenstreif, "The Liberal Party of Canada: A Political Analysis" (Ph.D. diss., Cornell University, 1963), p. 160.

be used in recruiting candidates. In 1979 Social Credit, for example, agreed in some instances to pay the $200 deposit required for candidacy as a way to minimize out-of-pocket expenses for candidates. Other parties, especially those with access to patronage at the federal or provincial level, may be able to return the favor to an unsuccessful candidate at a later point. Other people are persuaded to take on a candidacy by party officials, a cabinet minister, or even the party leader. These inducements are for reluctant candidates—in some cases conscripted candidates—who are found to take nominations in less-than-promising constituencies. Other individuals could be described as volunteers or self-starters. These are people who make their intentions known and go about persuading a local association to accept them. While such people relieve the local officials of some headaches, their presence is not without its problems. For example, the New Democratic party has always been suspicious of recent converts and values loyalty and involvement with the party over a reasonably long period of time in its candidates. Similarly, a Progressive Conservative official spoke of encouraging a local party executive to delay a nomination convention just because an ambitious and electorally attractive young candidate was pushing for an early meeting. The problem, he said, was that it would be very messy to try to "denominate" the candidate if they found a better person closer to the time of the election.

Many local parties, if they are sufficiently motivated and organized, establish a candidate search committee some time before an election is expected. The job of such a committee varies from party to party, but essentially the group serves to encourage candidates, to talk to potential nominees (such as municipal politicians or known supporters of the party), and to see to it that, in the end, there is at least one candidate willing to be placed in nomination. In the NDP, such committees invite people to run (avoiding any guarantees of success) and are usually charged with making sure that potential candidates know the party's rules about such matters as nomination meetings.[42] Progressive Conservative search committees may try to

---

[42] In an unusual arrangement, the Essex-Windsor (Ontario) NDP Association apparently invited an experienced candidate then living in Ottawa to seek its nomination. The candidate, who had finished ahead of former Liberal cabinet minister Bryce Mackasey in a by-election in Ottawa in October 1978, ran a close second to incumbent Liberal agriculture minister Eugene Whelan in 1979. The conventional method of "parachuting" outsiders into parliamentary seats (which will be discussed only briefly) is normally attempted at the instigation of the central party apparatus or is undertaken when prominent individuals require a seat in Parliament. It was through "local invitations" that, for example, both former Liberal prime ministers, Louis St. Laurent and Lester

interview prospective candidates but may not use that opportunity to screen out aspirants.

What these committees look for in potential candidates can be determined by inference through an examination of successful nominees. It is clear that the competitive position of the party influences the process, since successful parties are able to be more scrupulous and demanding than parties expecting to have to live with their candidate only for the duration of the campaign. At the same time, party expectations will also vary in systematic fashion. An NDP official, for example, spoke of contributions to the local party as significant in candidate selection.[43] Liberals, on the other hand, speak positively of having an open party, one in which long-term party activity is less important than "lots of desire and interest." As one official put it, "I don't think a person who has been involved in the party for a longer time has a greater claim to a nomination. Too often those kinds of people have blinkers on." Such questions have been discussed in other studies, some of which are listed in footnote 9 to this chapter.

Finally, observers have recognized that such things as search committees will work in certain kinds of ridings—in fact they may be essential in large urban areas—but would be frowned upon in other constituencies where, for example, the rank-and-file members believe themselves to be in a position to judge aspirants directly.

It should also be noted that central party offices, both federal and provincial, may serve to channel interested people into the local selection process. Most employ organizers (called field officers by the Progressive Conservatives) who are in regular contact with local parties to help in the persuasion of reluctant people, to encourage prominent party supporters to run, and to see to it that preliminary work is going on in plenty of time for an election call. People who inquire at, say, Liberal Federation headquarters are given the name of riding presidents in the area where they live or work and are asked to initiate discussions at that level. The role of Progressive Conservative officers has been described as that of broker between those who are in touch with the central office ("people who obviously

Pearson, found parliamentary seats and the former leader of the NDP T. C. Douglas found a seat in British Columbia after being defeated in Saskatchewan, where he had been premier for more than fifteen years. The Essex-Windsor case, which may not be unique in 1979, should not be considered a case of parachuting since the local association was apparently not being pushed to "take" the candidate.

[43] This point is supported in previous empirical research on parliamentary candidates and M.P.s, as seen in, for example, Mishler, "Nominating Attractive Candidates," pp. 589-91.

do not understand the process and likely have no constituency experience") and local people who will ultimately have to make the choice. All parties—with the possible exception of Social Credit—disclaim attempts to interfere with the local process of candidate selection. As an NDP source said, "We keep our hands off an established riding association." A Liberal spokesman suggested that interventions tended to go against the person who intervenes. While it would be naive to accept all such assertions at face value, the ethics of central-local relations are clearly understood by the participants.

In the end, the searching and screening that go on produce uneven results, in that some candidates are clearly more attractive than others and some constituencies will have an abundance of prospects while others must scramble to find someone—anyone—to carry the party banner. The two factors reinforce one another, since those who have the most to offer usually want to run for the most promising or safest seats, creating keen competition and often exciting nomination meetings. As Mishler has suggested, "parliamentary nominations are controlled by local party organizations whose choice of candidates is largely circumscribed (by choice as well as necessity) by the availability of local talent." [44]

Selection. Nomination meetings are the spectacles on the local campaign trail—at least for the victors. They are often the high point for those who later fail in the electoral struggle, while for many incumbents, for whom the outcome is a foregone conclusion, they are quite low-key affairs. These meetings may be enlivened by the presence of a visiting party notable who lends support—and may gain some media attention—but they are not without their own excitement and party enthusiasm, even if it is managed.

Once again, the competitive position of the party plays a large part in determining what kind of meeting will occur. The feeling of a party on the upswing is well described in Howard Scarrow's discussion of the Liberal nomination meeting in 1962 in "Urban Riding," [45] while the varying prospects and moods of competitors are captured in Brian Land's examination of the four meetings in Eglinton (an urban constituency in Toronto) in 1962. [46] In 1968 the Trudeau-

[44] Ibid., p. 585.

[45] Howard A. Scarrow, "Nomination and Local Party Organization in Canada: A Case Study," *Western Political Quarterly*, vol. 17 (1964), pp. 55-62, and "Three Dimensions of a Local Political Party," in John Meisel, ed., *Papers on the 1962 Election* (Toronto: University of Toronto Press, 1964), pp. 53-67.

[46] Brian Land, *Eglinton: The Election Study of a Federal Constituency* (Toronto: Peter Martin Associates, 1965), pp. 13-24. A summary version appears as "The Campaign in Eglinton" in Meisel, *Papers on the 1962 Election*, pp. 68-90.

inspired fervor for participatory democracy blossomed in several nomination meetings resembling full-scale leadership conventions.[47] But the essential starting point for a discussion of the nomination convention is the recognition that it is a reflection of the sovereignty of the local party.

As Peter Regenstreif has suggested:

> The variation in the organization and customs of the constituencies across the country is best demonstrated by the different practices connected with the selection of candidates for national elections. Ideally, nominating conventions are held. These may be public gatherings in which all may participate; they may be open only to party supporters; or, in very rare instances, the polling subdivisions of the riding may send accredited delegates and only these are permitted to attend and vote.[48]

The choice of format is dictated by the size and traditions of the constituency, and the arrangements may be described in the local party's constitution. Broadly speaking, there are three types of nominating meetings found in the four Canadian federal parties. Gordon Aiken, a former M.P., has described them this way: "Conventions . . . may be classed as dangerous, safe and half-safe. An open convention, where everyone present gets a vote, is dangerous." The second type—the safe convention—is a delegate convention in which access is strictly controlled by selection within the constituency subdivisions. It is a safe convention in that "it cannot be packed by outsiders or any one candidate" but may be viewed as undemocratic since participation is restricted. "So the half-safe convention was devised. Everyone who holds a membership card can vote." [49]

The open convention appears to have been the most common method for candidate selection before the concept of continuous party membership was established in Canada. Thus Scarrow's Liberal nomination meeting in "Urban Riding" was an open convention in which "anyone who lives in the constituency and who is a 'Liberal supporter' can attend the nomination convention and cast a ballot." [50]

---

[47] Beck, *Pendulum of Power*, p. 401.

[48] Regenstreif, "Liberal Party of Canada," pp. 158-59.

[49] Aiken, *The Backbencher*, pp. 11-12.

[50] Scarrow, "Nomination and Local Party Organization," p. 56. Other forms of nomination meetings were also known in even earlier times. For example, Peter Oliver writes about "charges of irregularities concerning the election of delegates" to a provincial Conservative nomination meeting in Grenville County in eastern Ontario in 1905. See his *G. Howard Ferguson: Ontario Tory* (Toronto: Ontario Historical Studies Series, 1977), p. 28.

Moreover, the method was prescribed by the party's constitution and had been used "as long as anyone could recall." Thus about 1,200 people turned up for the meeting and participated in the choice of the Liberal candidate with little or no screening by party officials. Such meetings are, of course, open to "neutral persons, and even opponents to select, or influence the selection of, the candidate," but they also "offer ample opportunity to ambitious candidates for packing the convention with their own supporters."[51] It is this feature that prompts Aiken to call these conventions dangerous, and he offers an example of how disasters might happen even though Meisel found no such cases in 1957.[52] On the positive side, Scarrow argued that such a convention was a good test of the organizational skills of the prospective candidate and would be an appropriate practice in situations where "the idea of dues-paying membership is rather artificial."[53] Indeed, officials in two federal parties pointed out that this fact had a bearing on the variability of selection practices. Said one Liberal, "There is no such thing as paid party memberships in Cape Breton." A Progressive Conservative organizer suggested that, in his experience, a membership is rather meaningless in areas such as eastern Ontario "where they will tell you 'I don't have to pay a dollar to prove I'm a Conservative.'" Thus, as Regenstreif noted, open conventions are usually held in those areas "where personal political dispositions are often public knowledge and there is little danger of opposition party members packing the meeting."[54] It is probable that the new provisions for election funding and accountability will gradually force the establishment of party memberships in such areas and that the open convention will be replaced by the membership convention.

The contrasting selection method, in terms of general accessibility and numbers of participants, is the delegated convention. It is curious that the actual number of constituency organizations employing this method is not known by party officials in Ottawa, although some provincially based people should know the practices in their own constituencies. Generally speaking, these conventions are held in the largest constituencies, where population centers are scattered and small (for example, in northern parts of Ontario or Quebec) or where the constituency has no natural focus or cohesion and the selection of

[51] John Meisel, *The Canadian General Election of 1957* (Toronto: University of Toronto Press, 1962), pp. 121-22.
[52] Aiken, *The Backbencher*, p. 11.
[53] Scarrow, "Nomination and Local Party Organization," pp. 55-56.
[54] Regenstreif, "Liberal Party of Canada," p. 159; but see note 50.

a particular site for the nomination meeting might prejudice the actual outcome of the contest.[55] Unfortunately, the distinction between a delegated convention and other kinds of nomination gatherings is not very clear to the press, and it is often impossible for an outsider to determine whether a convention actually took this form. Once again, the provisions for a delegated nomination convention would be contained in the local party's constitution and could vary considerably.

Basically, the principle of a delegated convention is that "only members of the party actually express their view as to who should represent it in the forthcoming election" [56] and that each polling subdivision, or perhaps some other set of geographic zones of the constituency, should be entitled to a specified number of votes. In this way, a fixed number of votes can be cast, although some associations include a provision for a minimum attendance or the presence of delegates from a certain number of the subdivisions before proceedings can commence. In effect, the polling area designates perhaps two or four people to go to the nomination meeting on its behalf. Whether these people are given directions on voting preferences is not clear—this may also be a local custom—but since balloting is secret, no sanctions can be applied. In theory, all party members living in a polling area will meet to select the delegates, but in practice delegates are appointed by the constituency party itself. It is for this reason, according to a Progressive Conservative source, that "you can be accused of rigging or packing the meeting." Without a viable and relatively permanent organization, the process becomes a sham. In both instances, a membership convention can reduce criticism and defuse potential feuds.

The third method retains features of both the other two. The membership convention is predicated on restricting participation in the selection proceedings to those who possess party membership but allows memberships to be sold to nonmembers until a specified deadline before the beginning of the nomination meeting. In certain circumstances, however, Liberal and Progressive Conservative associations have been known to make memberships available at the door, so that membership cards are really just tickets to the nomination meeting. These provisions have been tightened in many areas.

---

[55] Such practices are not exclusively used in remote areas (as suggested in note 50). For example, a conglomeration such as the old southern Ontario constituency of Wellington-Grey-Dufferin-Waterloo, which brought together sections of four counties, required the use of a delegated method—by the Progressive Conservatives at least. One way to get around this problem is to hold a "traveling ballot," as discussed below.

[56] Meisel, *General Election of 1957*, p. 121.

This characteristic of relatively open access to the selection process caused Epstein to refer to Canadian party meetings as having "an ill-defined eligible attendance." [57] It is conceded by sources in all major parties that the dues-paying membership of a party (as Scarrow called it) fluctuates, depending on how close the nation is to an election. Unfortunately, figures that would indicate the extent of this fluctuation are either not available or not shared with outsiders. An NDP official conceded that national party membership might rise by about 5 percent in an election year but argued that this was substantially less than in the Liberal or the Progressive Conservative party, since "people just don't join the party to help nominate someone—not like they do in the other parties. Besides, it would cost $10 to $15 to join an NDP association, not a dollar or two, so it doesn't happen very often." There is some feeling, though, that fluctuating membership may be a thing of the past, at least in the magnitude known in recent times. One reason for this is that the parties are eager to regularize their membership base for planning and financial purposes. Consequently viable local associations are busy renewing memberships during nonelection years, and national party offices try to encourage local associations to amend their rules to minimize the wholesale marketing of party memberships as a way of influencing nomination proceedings without, as one Liberal put it, "taking away from the democratic process in the local parties."

Not only is the format for the nominating convention open to modification by local parties, but the actual qualifications for party membership (for nomination purposes) may be open to local alterations in certain respects. The two key elements here are the membership fees and the cutoff date for purchasing a membership so as to be eligible to participate in a nomination contest.

The New Democratic party seems to have the most rigorous requirements for membership, and it is estimated that 75 to 80 percent of all ridings adhere to the same basic rules. These include requiring memberships to be purchased at least fourteen days before the announced date of the nomination meeting (although some associations use a thirty-day rule) to allow proper records of eligible participants to be drawn up and to minimize packing or manipulation of meetings. Party rules permit only residents of the constituency to vote in a nomination contest, and members of trade unions affiliated with the NDP can vote in nomination meetings only if they have taken out personal memberships within the time limits and live within the constituency. The New Democrats are very concerned about

---

[57] Epstein, *Political Parties in Western Democracies*, p. 230.

members' belonging to competing political groups or parties (this originated with fears of infiltration of the party by various communist groups), and thus the party's federal constitution (Article III, 1) indicates that an individual member may not be "a member or supporter of any other political party." Known violations of this principle would result in the voiding of an individual's membership in the NDP. Finally, individual membership fees are traditionally much higher than for the Liberals and Progressive Conservatives since they were a significant source of the party's funding before the new provisions for party finances. These high fees—often ten to fifteen dollars per year as opposed to two or three dollars in the other parties—may be reduced for senior citizens, families, students, and the unemployed, according to local custom or circumstances.

In the Progressive Conservative party, a model constitution is provided for local associations to use in developing their own. Thus certain elements may be common to most associations, but variations must be set out in the local party's constitution. In Article 12 of the model constitution, it is forbidden to issue memberships "during the 72 hours immediately prior" to a nomination meeting, although previous party members may renew their memberships "which were valid for the last meeting of the Association."[58] Thus some membership fees may be paid at the door of a Progressive Conservative nominating meeting, but only by those holding expired membership cards (or, as may happen, blank membership cards sent out to past members, which can be validated only by the payment of the annual fees before the meeting). The model constitution also sets out a requirement that the quorum for a nomination meeting is the presence of twenty-five resident members of the association. Efforts are made to be sure that people attending the convention are not activists in other parties, but in hotly contested nomination fights memberships may be sold to people with only marginal interest in the party. Finally, in a campaign to sign up supporters for a nomination contest, the accepted form is for the candidate's organization to *sell* such memberships to nonadherents and not to buy or distribute them. If there are any questions about such matters, a credentials committee may be established for the nomination meeting to screen dubious cases before election proceedings get under way.

In the Liberal party, practices also vary from association to association, but these are really variations on basic themes set out in

[58] Progressive Conservative Association of Canada, "Model Constituency Constitution," Ottawa (Document PCHQ 2662), p. 5. Some associations may cut the period down to forty-eight or even thirty-six hours in certain circumstances, while others have extended the period to as much as two weeks.

the provincial party constitutions. A model constitution is provided, which local associations may adapt to their own circumstances, but some provisions are regulated from the center. For example, in Ontario memberships may not be purchased within the seven days preceding a nomination meeting when no writs have been issued for an election; in fact, even when writs have been issued and no emergency is said to exist, the limitation of seven days stays in force. In contrast, in the awkward nomination period for the 1980 election, the Ontario party executive did declare an emergency and allowed memberships to be sold until seventy-two hours before nomination meetings. As in the case of the Progressive Conservatives, renewals can be sold at the door of the meeting hall, but in all cases nonresident members of local associations must have been properly enrolled fully six months before a nomination meeting to be allowed a vote. In that respect, rules for the resident components are also set out in the model constitution, with a 75 percent rule suggested. It may be noted that some associations do not allow any nonresident members, while others set levels to accommodate special situations; for example, in the Kitchener-Waterloo (Ontario) area, where many Liberal party members live in one federal constituency and work in another, the two local associations allow up to 10 percent of the members to be nonresident (which may mean that some people belong to both associations). Every local association executive contains a membership secretary whose duties include monitoring the level of nonresident membership. It is presumably within the prerogative of that person to refuse to allow certain people to join the party if the quota has been filled, although this may be done in some instances only with the approval of the entire executive. For the most part membership questions are not controversial, but a local party executive is always aware that irregularities may give the provincial party executive cause to void a nomination meeting. Finally, the Liberal party is moving toward making membership more exclusive than it has been in the past by suggesting to local associations that (in 1980 and subsequent years) members sign a pledge card based on one in the model constitution, confirming that they are not members of any other federal political party. To repeat, many of the provisions described may be different in provinces other than Ontario, and local autonomy is still the hallmark of party organization.

Finally, what information is available about the Social Credit party suggests that individual memberships are necessary for participation in the selection of the candidate. One source indicated that memberships must be obtained at least fourteen days before the nomination meeting, but specifications are not found in the 1978 constitution of the federal party. On the other hand, the constitution does indicate that no person "who is not a member of the party in good standing may hold any elected or appointed office in the party," and this is understood to apply to the party's candidates as well. None of the other parties makes this point as explicitly, although they assume, of course, that the candidates are supporters of the party they are seeking to represent in Parliament.[59]

It is important to recall that there are no provisions in Canadian electoral law requiring candidates to be resident in the constituency in which they choose to seek election. This applies to all parties. On the other hand, candidates may be nominated only by bona fide members of the local association, most of whom, as has been suggested, are local residents. Once again, arrangements vary from area to area, but the basic practice is for nominations to be called for at a properly convened meeting. In the Social Credit party, nomination papers for each candidate must include the signatures of twenty-five party members. The Progressive Conservative model constitution provides for the calling of nominations at the meeting, but it also stipulates that "each nomination must be moved and seconded by voting members in writing."[60] In terms of planning requirements, some associations suggest that aspirants notify the president or secretary in writing of their intention to stand some time before the nomination meeting, but it is not clear what provisions there are for unannounced nominations from the floor of the meeting.[61] In many associations twenty-five nominators are required; so a spontaneous nomination would be awkward to bring about. In the New Democratic party it appears that nominations from the floor are the norm although, as one New Democrat said, "there are not really many surprises—once you get to the meeting you usually know who is in the race." In most local parties, the call for nominations provides an opportunity for speeches in support of the candidates nominated, often with strict time limits to maximize the time for voting. This appears to be the

---

[59] Some surveys have found that a small fraction of candidates claim never to have been a member of the party before seeking nomination; but this is usually related to financial contributions to the party rather than to holding a membership card (since the practice is not universal in all associations), and it cannot be taken to be a general practice. See Surich and Williams, "Some Characteristics of Candidates."

[60] Progressive Conservative Association, "Model Constituency Constitution," article 12(4)(d)(i), p. 5. The subsequent part notes that "each nominee must consent to the nomination in writing and pledge support to the successful nominee."

[61] In one constituency association that has been observed, this period was ninety-six hours.

case even when a nomination is uncontested, giving party members an opportunity to stir up enthusiasm for the prospective candidate and the coming campaign. With the contestants duly identified, the selection takes place.

The standard practice is for secret ballots to be held until one candidate has won a majority of the ballots cast. When a contest is expected, arriving party members are provided with a number of authorized ballot papers, and their names are checked off on the membership lists prepared after the closing of the period for enrolling members. One member of the party is charged with the responsibilities of the returning officer, that is, to oversee the entire election apparatus for the nomination. This person will choose deputy returning officers (in the Liberal party these are usually volunteers from neighboring associations), who look after ballot boxes in which marked ballots are deposited. The number and location of these will depend on the size of the crowd and the logistics of the meeting room. They may be arranged in various corners of the room or in adjacent areas or, in some meetings, may be circulated to allow people to deposit ballots without creating crowding and unnecessary movement in a congested hall. Since presumably only legitimate party members have been issued ballots, no checking is necessary at this time, although a tally of the number of ballots issued is made against the marked membership lists in well-attended meetings. Balloting takes place for a specified length of time, after which the deputy returning officers, together with the returning officer and as many as two scrutineers (poll watchers) for each candidate adjourn to a sealed room to count the ballots. If no one emerges with a majority of the ballots cast, the person with the lowest number of votes is dropped, and another ballot is conducted in the same manner. This process is repeated until eventually a winner is declared and the results are announced to the waiting faithful.[62]

This is, of course, a signal for a show of party support from defeated candidates and a message from the victor—the first shot in the real campaign. If the balloting has proceeded smoothly or the nomination has been determined by acclamation, time will be spent seeking financial pledges from party supporters and urging assistance in the campaign from volunteers who will staff the election machine. It is important for the local party that any differences over the nomination proceedings and any disputes that may have occurred be

---

[62] It is apparently the custom in some Progressive Conservative associations for a "symbolic ballot" to be cast in the case of an acclamation. This was observed in practice in the research for this paper and is also noted by Land, *Eglinton*, p. 20.

resolved at the nomination meeting (probably behind the scenes), since any appeals against the verdict or confusion about the practices followed can only be taken up at the next highest level of the party, usually the provincial election committee, which has ultimate responsibility. As was suggested earlier, every effort must be made by the local association to conduct a fair and orderly convention and "to be seen to have done so." While the local associations normally designate the candidate in the kind of process described here, a higher level of authority can in certain circumstances overturn that process.

There are two sorts of constituency in which no nomination convention of the kind described here will actually take place. In one case, nomination proceedings are held, but they are spread out over several communities or over two or more days. This is known as a "traveling ballot" or "traveling convention," in which, presumably, the aspirants and certain party officials conduct a series of nomination meetings in widely dispersed centers within the constituency (thereby dispensing with the need for a delegated convention), taking the sealed ballot boxes along until party members in all corners of the constituency have had an opportunity to see and hear the candidates. It is my understanding that Joe Clark was first chosen as a Progressive Conservative candidate for the seat of Rocky Mountain (Alberta) in the 1972 election in this way. And in a remarkable departure from standard patterns, an incumbent member of Parliament was denied the Progressive Conservative nomination for the 1980 election in a northern Manitoba constituency in a traveling ballot.[63] It is interesting to note, also, that new technology may develop unique forms of nomination meetings, such as the one held in January 1980 in the remote centers of Frobisher Bay and Rankin Inlet in the eastern Arctic (some 700 miles apart), in which Peter Ittinuar of the NDP was renominated by means of a telephone hookup. The fact that he was the sitting member of Parliament for Nunatsiaq and unopposed for the nomination made the arrangement perhaps less startling.[64]

In the second case, to all intents and purposes, no candidate has come forward for a party nomination. Party officials do not like to talk about the sequence of actions that follows such a failure of the local organization (assuming that there is a viable one, which may not be the case at all). Intervention by the party hierarchy in local nomi-

---

[63] See "Manitoba Tory Incumbent Ousted in Nomination Vote," *Globe and Mail*, December 31, 1979, p. 9. The story reported that about 800 votes were cast over a two-day period and that this was the first nominating convention in the constituency in eleven years.

[64] See "Telephones Link Two Meetings 700 Miles Apart," *Globe and Mail*, January 10, 1980, p. 9.

nation activities in the face of opposition from the local association is rarely successful. As the Liberals found in 1979 in Scarborough Centre, efforts to bump a locally selected candidate in order to place a star candidate rebounded against them when this second candidate suddenly resigned the nomination.[65] Yet there are times when direct intervention by the party leadership is both necessary and normal, though not well publicized. Usually these are in areas of acute party weakness where, for instance, a special effort is needed to provide a full slate of candidates. In the case of the NDP, the provincial executive has a right to intervene in the local selection process where there is no organization. It may choose to act simply as a search committee to determine whether there can be a proper nomination procedure arranged; in more extreme cases it has the right to appoint a candidate on behalf of the party. In either event the provincial executive takes care to document its activities carefully to avoid running up against local people who may be surprised and annoyed at having the process taken out of their hands. Progressive Conservative sources also agree that party headquarters must be more deeply involved in the nomination process when the party is weak, although the onus is still on the local association to come up with someone.

The need for such activities in 1979 was apparently most frequent in the Social Credit party, to a great extent even in its area of strength, the province of Quebec. A party official suggested that conventions were used to select most Social Credit candidates (and a substantial fraction of these were contested nominations), but sometimes these were controlled situations in the sense that "if there is no candidate, the president of the riding association—or some other member of the executive—should take on the job." Thus many candidates are drawn from the local executive by default even though they may be nominated by the traditional convention method. It appears, though, that the regional party organization can step in if there is no local organization duly mandated to do the job and that some have been willing to select or even appoint persons interested in serving as candidates. Furthermore, where there are gaps, the provincial executive and, in extreme cases, the party leader can nominate a Social Credit candidate. There is some evidence that the party's new leader, Fabien Roy, took major responsibility for the nomination of Social Credit candidates in 1979. He did this in consultation with his own aides and some local people, but in many instances those chosen were not, in the view of some sources, real Social Creditors. There is a degree of leadership control over candi-

---

[65] A brief reference may be found in the *Toronto Star*, April 10, 1979, p. A3.

date selection in the contemporary Social Credit party that is not found in the other parties discussed here. It would not be correct to say that this is part of the normal structure of the party—a belief in a decentralized structure is affirmed by the constitution and other practices of the national party. Rather, it reaffirms the importance of the party's competitive position in the electoral arena.

Authorization. The final aspect of the selection process is the confirmation of support for the designated candidate by the national party and its leader. This acceptance has two related features: first, the rather informal oversight of local practices and selections and, second, the application of the new provisions of the Canada Elections Act.

As we have seen, the responsibility for generating candidates is highly decentralized in Canadian politics. Not only do the national parties refrain from screening and channeling candidates into local contests, they rarely pass critical judgment on those who have survived the local selection process. In this sense, the national party's role is rather passive and discretionary; only when there is evidence that local responsibilities were not handled properly or when there is obvious incompatibility between a local candidate and the party's or the leader's views on key matters will something be done about a locally generated candidate. Even then, careful action is necessary to avoid harming the party's electoral chances.

Canadian national parties appear to be totally trusting of their component parts and of the inherent testing of an individual's qualifications the nominating convention provides. A New Democrat, for example, said, "We tend to know the people we run; therefore we don't need to check them. Even when we do draw in candidates who are not longtime party people, they tend also to be fairly well known people. So there is no formal check on these people. As it happens, we have no experience of unknown people winning NDP nominations." Another suggested that there is no screening at all, "especially in smaller communities, since they are pretty reliable judges of people when they live and work together so much. Besides, the woods are full of ex-NDP candidates; so there is no need to explain to them what makes a good candidate!"

A Liberal official took the same approach, saying:

> There are no formal checks made on candidates. We accept the inherent wisdom of the local party on this. There is no formal program to screen people, and if anything goes on, it is most likely of the "grapevine" variety—we find that if there are any skeletons in the closet, or bad habits, et cetera,

the grapevine is very effective in bringing them out. We must accept that people who win an open nomination meeting are good enough for us.

Generally, then, the provincial and federal levels of the party do not carry out a formal review of candidates—except for the NDP's election planning committee, which is supposed to approve nominations, though this is normally quite routine, especially in the heat of a campaign. The national or provincial party is best seen as a recourse in the event of a dispute or of some question about the propriety of procedures followed in a nomination meeting. In such cases, the usual concern is merely to see that the association's constitutional rules have been followed and that the nominated candidate really has the confidence of the local association. It is quite possible, of course, that some provisions may not have been met—and that everyone concerned is quite prepared to accept that situation. To put the matter in the opposite way, "as the party's chances of winning the election increase in any constituency, so will its nomination procedures become more formalized and more carefully controlled." When a party nomination is tantamount to electoral victory, all the procedures must be closely followed. When the party nomination is viewed as a gesture on behalf of the party, a local association "can afford to be more relaxed, more casual, about the whole process." [66] Thus the higher levels of the party will only intervene upon the request of dissatisfied local members, and very often they will tacitly agree to overlook variations in normal practices when these are necessary. Finally, if it develops that a chosen candidate is unsuitable, there are few overt means of counteracting the difficulties this might bring. If the selection is made early, there may be an opportunity for local people or party officials to persuade the candidate to retire from the field. If this is done by party officials, however, the efforts may rebound against the party. In the end, a decision to step aside is voluntary; if it is not made, the candidate and the local organization may merely find that promised help from provincial headquarters, such as materials, organizational expertise, publicity events, and the like, is somehow overlooked or channeled into other constituencies. In this sense, the role of the national party is discretionary, and power is exercised cautiously so as not to interfere with local autonomy.

[66] Terence H. Qualter, *The Election Process in Canada* (Toronto: McGraw-Hill, 1970), p. 65. The point is also made in Meisel, *Canadian General Election of 1957*, p. 122.

Until very recently, the process of candidate selection stopped at this point. Since the revisions to the Canada Elections Act in 1970, however, candidates have been able to list their party affiliation on the ballot. It thus became necessary to determine how such affiliations could be upheld in law—not just in informal practice, as had been the case before that time.[67] Now it is necessary for the parties themselves to identify their own candidates for designation on the ballot and for other benefits under the revised legislation. Thus section 23(2)(h) provides for a statement to be filed with the other nomination papers, "signed by the leader of the party or by a representative designated by the leader of the party," to confirm that the nominee is "endorsed by the party." In 1979 the three major parties operated this provision through an official rather than the party leader, but it must be assumed that in no instance did these gentlemen act without the authorization of their respective leaders.[68] In the Social Credit party, responsibility for designating candidates outside Quebec was delegated to the provincial party presidents, while Fabien Roy retained the prerogative within Quebec.· Roy apparently selected and endorsed a number of Social Credit candidates who were viewed less than favorably in some party circles, but this may have been a result of the internal divisions that have racked the federal party since the death of former leader Réal Caouette in late 1976 and the provincial party since the episode of Yvon Dupuis in 1970.[69] In a general

[67] Before these changes a candidate could refer to himself or herself in campaign literature as, for example, an Independent-Liberal or an Independent-Conservative. These terms could be used without the permission of the official parties or candidates and were often adopted by individuals who had been denied the party nomination. The new provisions prevent anyone from using a party designation that could be confused in any way with that of an existing party. See Courtney, "Recognition of Canadian Political Parties," p. 48, for a discussion of the problems arising from having two communist parties.

[68] In 1979 the Liberal letters were signed by Gordon Ashworth, national campaign director, those for the Progressive Conservatives by national campaign chairman Lowell Murray, and those for the NDP by federal secretary Robin Sears. The only time that party approval was withheld was the famous case of Leonard Jones, who was refused party endorsement by Robert Stanfield to contest the seat of Moncton (New Brunswick) for the Progressive Conservatives in 1974. See Courtney, "Recognition of Canadian Political Parties," p. 53, and George Perlin, "The Progressive Conservative Party in the Election of 1974," in Howard R. Penniman, ed., *Canada at the Polls: The General Election of 1974* (Washington, D.C.: American Enterprise Institute, 1975), pp. 114-15.

[69] This incident involved "untimely and ill-considered intervention" by Caouette to have the newly formed provincial wing of the party accept his handpicked choice as leader, the former Liberal M.P. Yvon Dupuis, who had been forced to leave federal politics because of a scandal. The attempt to promote someone who had been vehemently anti-Créditiste in his active political life indicated an apparent lack of confidence in the existing provincial leadership group and probably

election this endorsement requires merely a letter of sponsorship from the leader or the designated representative, but in a by-election the letter must be signed by the party leader.

This new provision restores a greater measure of central oversight of the nomination process than had been evident in recent party practices (except possibly in the case of Social Credit). For the most part, local associations will continue to be charged with the responsibility of seeking and selecting the party's candidates, but the new arrangement "obviously enhances the position of the leaders of recognized parties in so far as they have been granted a power whereby they may accept or reject candidates nominated by the local constituency association." [70] There are two interests to be served in the selection of party candidates—the local and the national—and the new regulations have restored a measure of centralized supervision that had been eroded by local customs and the reality of a highly decentralized political system.

With the blessing of the national party bestowed through the letter of sponsorship and the endorsement of the local party association won in the nomination meeting, the candidate is officially launched into the trench warfare that will last until election day. The contest emerges from the shadows of the party's own conventions and codes into the glare of public scrutiny and the controlled atmosphere of the Canada Elections Act. The public struggle by the party for victory in the constituency begins when the more private struggle has been resolved. Party victory determines who will have a hand in governing the country, but it is the nomination contest that gives human faces to the political struggle. While, ironically, it is widely believed that "the characteristics and qualities of particular candidates have only a minor effect on the outcome of an election in any given constituency," the process still has great importance in that "the picture the public has of a party is probably influenced by the sort of candidates it nominates to represent it in successive

---

weakened the party's credibility in the provincial election of 1970. The party never really recovered from that faltering start. A full discussion of the Dupuis affair is found in Stein, *Dynamics*, pp. 110-18. It is also interesting to note how Caouette exercised his powers in the selection process when he was leader of the party. It was apparently his practice to give blank letters of sponsorship to party organizers, who would then fill in a name when a person was found to run. This scheme caused some embarrassment in 1974 when two candidates filed nomination papers in Labelle (Quebec) as Social Credit candidates and each one submitted a letter of sponsorship signed by Caouette. The cause of this mix-up is discussed in Michael Stein, "Social Credit Party in the Canadian General Election of 1974," in Penniman, *Canada at the Polls, 1974*, pp. 169-70.

[70] Courtney, "Recognition of Canadian Political Parties," p. 52.

elections." [71] It is the local activists working through their search committees and nominating conventions who give flesh to the "symbolism conveyed by the party label." [72]

Evaluations and Expectations. Despite the validity of some of his generalizations, Epstein's conclusion that Canadian political parties manage to select candidates "without primaries and without membership organizations" [73] appears no longer accurate. It has been demonstrated here that the concept of formal party membership has grown in importance and in stability in the last decade, even though one would still have to regard Canadian parties as essentially cadre-style organizations, in the sense that they lapse into relative inactivity between elections. Furthermore, while it is true that there are not direct primaries open to nominal or relatively inactive partisans, the membership convention is a kind of party primary in which rank-and-file members of the party can make the effective choice of the parliamentary candidate.

It was suggested earlier in this chapter that Canadian nomination practices seem to be a hybrid of the American primary and the British branch selection methods without the close controls of either. If the process is looked at from another perspective, however, the conclusion is quite different. It is possible to emphasize the contribution of *committed* party members to the performance of a key responsibility in the political system and to the fairly open operations of candidate selection in the major parties. Public control is not essential in Canada to ensure that a local party operates fairly and effectively, and rigorous internal supervision would be an unnecessary inhibition on political parties in a diverse federal political system. Thus Canadian candidate selection practices have been firmly established to accommodate the social and political realities of the parties themselves; they now have an aura and a mythology of their own that are shared by activists in all parties in the mainstream of Canadian political life. It is really only when the local selectors fail that the responsibility is taken up by others on behalf of the larger party interests. Most local party associations resist such takeovers as long as possible, and spirited nomination activities would be one of the first real signs of a reinvigorated local party.

The need to involve a core of organized and committed local partisans, willing to step forward to undertake the task of candidate selection on behalf of the larger party whenever required, may be

[71] Meisel, *Canadian General Election of 1957*, p. 120.
[72] Scarrow, "Nomination and Local Party Organization," p. 55.
[73] Epstein, *Political Parties in Western Democracies*, p. 231.

seen as a major weakness of Canadian selection procedures or as one of their greatest strengths. This most important responsibility provides a reason for local organizations to flourish and to remain relevant in a political age dominated by leadership, by centrally determined election strategies, and by the apparent decline in significance of the individual member of Parliament they are striving to elect.

It is apparent to most observers and practitioners that recent changes in electoral rules, in particular the provisions for party funding, have had some effect on the selection practices of the major parties. Memberships are now more clearly established in the minds of Canadians, and the parties are looking for more extensive and regular financial contributors (and hence, it is hoped, members). This has increased the spread of membership conventions in place of open conventions, even in areas where traditions die hard. The next logical step is to consolidate the membership recruitment activities so as to curtail the current practice of allowing people to join the party until a few days before a nominating convention. This might mean some other means of selecting candidates, such as a full-scale poll of all registered party members (in effect, a primary election). Given the present reluctance of Canadian election officials to get involved in internal party matters, however,[74] the development of such schemes would probably remain in the hands of the parties themselves. And since present practices are influenced by local tradition, regional variation, and party differences, it would be difficult to establish by law a uniform system suitable for the whole country.

On the other hand, changes in the formal rules of the game, such as the development of a permanent voters' list or more stringent qualifications for nomination, could pave the way for more official supervision of selection procedures. Canadians already face the possibility that the election laws themselves will tilt the normal balance of central-local relationships through the endorsement provisions; it is not a great step to requiring closer scrutiny of the previous selection stage. If that happens, of course, there could be important new situations to cope with. John Courtney has correctly pointed out that

> as the act of choosing the party candidate is undoubtedly the most important single task that riding associations perform, and as the reference in the Act to a candidate "endorsed by the party" could be interpreted in a variety of ways, the seeds have been sown for potential intraparty disputes over the use to which that power might be put.[75]

[74] See Courtney, "Recognition of Canadian Political Parties," p. 52, n. 41.
[75] Ibid., p. 52.

Not surprisingly, though, candidate selection will continue to take center stage in the constituency parties and will continue to serve as the prime means of involving party activists in the creation of the image the party will present to the community at large. It is, ultimately, one of our most important democratic resources.

A Note on the 1980 Election

The unexpected parliamentary defeat of the Clark government in December 1979 started the process of candidate selection all over again. It was, in most respects, similar to the process described in the preceding pages, the main exception being that it took place within constituency boundaries unchanged from those of 1979. In another respect, the task of the parties was rather compressed in comparison with that of 1979; more correctly, the 1979 selection period was inordinately long because of the numerous false starts and the many rumored dissolutions of the Thirtieth Parliament. Several local associations were consequently forced to make a second selection when their initial choice was unable to sustain the candidate's responsibilities for so long. In at least one case, a Liberal association had three different selection meetings in the lead-up to the 1979 campaign (see footnote 65). It is no wonder many candidates lost whatever momentum they had gained in the nomination contest as the election was deferred time and time again.

In 1980, of course, everything was completed in about six weeks, and the search for candidates was much more intense and challenging. At nomination day (three weeks before voting day), 1,496 Canadians had filed papers, another new record.[76] The selection process was highlighted by the defeat of one sitting M.P. (see footnote 63), by the predictable querying of local procedures by defeated aspirants, and, most important, by the reaffirmation by thousands of Canadians of their faith in the political system, demonstrated by their participation in nominating conventions in the depths of winter.

[76] "1496 Run in Federal Election," *Globe and Mail*, January 29, 1980, p. 1.

5

Campaign Strategy and Electoral Victory: The Progressive Conservatives and the 1979 Election

John C. Courtney

At the time the 1979 general election was called, Joe Clark had been leader of the Progressive Conservative party for little more than three years. Thirty-six years of age when he was chosen in 1976, Clark had become the youngest party leader in the country's history.[1] His youth, combined with his short stint as leader of a party notorious for its internal squabbles, prompted many heated discussions about his ability to lead the country. During the election campaign the Liberals, who knew they could ill afford to pass up any opportunity to score points, launched an all-out attack on the Conservatives on the grounds that Clark's statements on party policy were confused, indecisive, and contradictory. The Tory leader's problems stemmed, so the Liberals suggested, from his immaturity and inexperience. Joe Clark had clearly moved front and center by the time the election was called; he was precisely where the Conservative political stategists had wanted him. They were confident that for the first time in over twenty years a federal election was going to be fought on their terms, one of which was to make Joe Clark the object of public scrutiny and the center of political debate.

The Legacy

The labors of his two immediate predecessors as party leader had left Clark in 1976 a Conservative party substantially different in structure and support base from any that had existed previously. John Diefenbaker and Robert Stanfield had each transformed the party according

[1] Material on Clark is not plentiful. For the only book-length study, see David L. Humphreys, *Joe Clark: A Portrait* (Ottawa: Deneau and Greenberg, 1978).

TABLE 5–1

PROGRESSIVE CONSERVATIVE PARTY VOTE, BY REGION, 1945–1979

Share of National PC
Vote Cast by Region
(percent)

Year	Atlantic provinces	Quebec	Ontario	West, Yukon, and territories	Total PC Vote
1945	15.4	8.3	52.7	23.6	1,435,747
1949	15.9	22.6	43.6	17.8	1,736,226
1953	16.5	26.0	44.2	13.3	1,749,579
1957	14.8	21.7	42.9	20.6	2,572,926
1958	12.4	25.7	36.2	25.7	3,908,633
1962	14.2	21.6	36.9	27.4	2,865,582
1963	14.5	16.0	37.9	31.8	2,591,614
1965	15.7	17.3	37.4	29.6	2,499,913
1968	16.5	18.2	36.9	28.3	2,554,880
1972	13.3	13.5	41.6	31.8	3,383,530
1974	11.4	15.5	37.2	36.0	3,369,335
1979	10.7	10.1	42.1	37.1	4,089,953

SOURCES: J. Murray Beck, *Pendulum of Power: Canada's Federal Elections* (Toronto: Prentice-Hall, 1968); Howard A. Scarrow, *Canada Votes* (New Orleans: Hauser Press, 1962); Hugh G. Thorburn, *Party Politics in Canada*, 4th ed. (Toronto: Prentice-Hall, 1979), app.; and *Star-Phoenix*, May 25, 1979, pp. 34-35.

to his own interests and priorities, so much so that on Stanfield's retirement in 1976 the party bore little resemblance to what it had been when Diefenbaker became leader twenty years earlier. Their changes enabled Clark to start with a more solid base of electoral and parliamentary support and a more respectable party organization than any other Conservative party leader of this century had enjoyed on taking office. It was up to Clark to solidify that support, augment it with new supporters, and staff the streamlined party apparatus.

Under John Diefenbaker the Conservative party had enlarged its support considerably beyond its traditional twentieth-century base in Ontario. In the three elections immediately preceding Diefenbaker's victory in 1957, 47 percent of the total votes cast for the party were received in Ontario (see table 5–1). The "national" Conservative party was, to all intents and purposes, an Ontario Conservative party

TABLE 5–2

TOTAL PROGRESSIVE CONSERVATIVE SEATS BY REGION
FOR THE FIVE ELECTIONS 1957–1965

Region	Number of Parliamentary Seats	Number of Seats Won by PC	Seats Won by PC as a Percentage of Seats in Region
Atlantic	165	97	58.8
Quebec	375	89	23.7
Ontario	425	215	50.6
West	360	229	63.6

SOURCE: Reports of the chief electoral officer, Ottawa, 1957-1965.

in parliamentary representation as well as in votes. Only nineteen seats in 1945, sixteen in 1949, and eighteen in 1953 had been won by the party outside Ontario. One of Diefenbaker's contributions to the Conservative party, a contribution that would remain a more or less permanent feature of Canadian politics through the 1979 election, was to improve the party's fortunes in the hinterland, particularly the West.[2] In the five elections under Diefenbaker's leadership (1957–1965), the party took 63.6 percent of the 360 possible seats in the four western provinces, a greater proportion than its share of seats in any other region during that period (see table 5–2).

While the shift in a westerly direction was occurring in the late 1950s and 1960s, the kinds of voters and candidates attracted to the Conservatives changed accordingly. The "ethnic" voters, who had previously spurned the Conservative party, now embraced it as their own. Diefenbaker's appointment of Michael Starr to the cabinet in 1957 had gained widespread notice because it was a first for Canadians of Ukrainian ancestry. Yet the number of Conservative candidates and elected members of Ukrainian, German, and Polish ancestry grew so markedly after the 1957 election that they quickly became an integral part of the Conservative party in western Canada. By the 1970s their presence was taken for granted, as evidenced by the absence of comment on the ancestry of the Prairie ministers appointed by Clark to his cabinet after the 1979 election: Jake Epp, Ray

[2] Throughout this chapter the term "western Canada" includes, for the purposes of parliamentary representation, the Northwest and Yukon territories, and the term "Progressive Conservative party" is shortened to "Conservative party."

123

Hnatyshyn, Steve Paproski, and Don Mazankowski. With few exceptions, they and close to a dozen other Conservative M.P.s elected from the West in 1979 were born in the 1930s or early 1940s in Canada of first- or second-generation immigrants from Central and Eastern Europe. A major influence in their political socialization, as for thousands of others with similar ethnic backgrounds, had been the Diefenbaker victories of 1957–1958 and the rhetoric accompanying them. The Conservative party had claimed to champion the interests of "the little man" and to promote the cause of "unhyphenated Canadianism." It was rewarded accordingly in the West.

For the vast majority of immigrant settlers, virtually their only contact with Canada had been with the West. They and their descendants were reminded for the first time by Diefenbaker that their region was built on a foundation of cultural and linguistic diversity without parallel in the rest of the country. Their relative isolation from the developments in central Canada as well as their success in preserving their languages and much of their culture combined to make them chary of outsiders calling for support of a bilingual policy in which their languages had no place. Through Diefenbaker's eyes they had come to view Lester Pearson, and after him Pierre Trudeau, with a mistrust bordering on open hostility. The Canada these men claimed to lead was not the Canada of which they had come to feel a part.

That the changes under Diefenbaker were effected at the expense of the party's traditional support base in Ontario was most clearly seen in the first election following his replacement as leader by Stanfield. In the 1968 election only seventeen of eighty-eight Conservative candidates were elected in Ontario, the smallest number in the party's history; twenty-six of seventy were elected in the West. The party's principal support base had shifted from one region to another, but in net parliamentary terms it was barely ahead of its pre-Diefenbaker position. As Conservative fortunes in Quebec had once again dipped to their pre-Diefenbaker level, prospects of victory during Stanfield's leadership were not bright. Stanfield's attempts to gain support in Quebec failed, and when Clark, after his selection as leader in 1976, sought with equal diligence to win Quebec allies and supporters, he too was rebuffed. If the Conservatives were to win in 1979, it would have to be without Quebec.

Stanfield's contributions to the Conservative party were of a different sort from Diefenbaker's. Confident that the West, particularly the Prairie provinces, and Atlantic Canada would continue to support the Conservative party, Stanfield set about rebuilding the Ontario wing of the federal party. In part because of his deliberate policy and in part because of the appeal of his personality, Stanfield succeeded in recruiting to the Conservative party candidates who gave it much-needed credibility in Ontario. At no time was this truer than in the 1972 election, when the Conservatives won forty seats in Ontario. Many of the "class of '72" from Ontario quickly gained national attention as opposition spokesmen. They made it possible for journalists and commentators to envisage, for the first time in some years, a potential Conservative cabinet of some intellectual substance and political acumen.

Clark's debt to Stanfield's recruiting success became apparent with the 1979 election. Fully one-third of the fifty-seven Ontario Conservatives elected in 1979 first entered Parliament under Stanfield in 1972. All but a few of the Ontario stars of the much-heralded "Clark team" of the 1979 election were, in fact, first attracted as candidates by Stanfield and had been elected between 1968 and 1974, during his leadership. No fewer than nine of them ultimately entered Clark's cabinet: Lincoln Alexander, Ron Atkey, Walter Baker, Perrin Beatty, Bill Jarvis, Allan Lawrence, Flora MacDonald, Sinclair Stevens, and John Wise. Stanfield had managed to lay the groundwork for the Clark victory by revitalizing the federal Conservatives in the country's most important electoral area.

When Stanfield became leader, he also had to turn his attention to the state of the party's organization, both inside and outside Parliament. It was common knowledge at the time that the organization of the Conservative party was faltering and archaic. By the time he stepped down in 1976, it was clear that Stanfield's endeavors had met with mixed success. Caucus continued to operate much as it had under Diefenbaker. Although Stanfield had attempted to streamline its internal operations by introducing a committee system, it turned out to be an unwieldy and uncoordinated structure. Caucus still lacked direction, discipline, and an apparent will to bring about a change in government. In a widely publicized speech in 1975 Jim Gillies, then a leading member of the Conservative opposition front bench, drew attention to this fact: "The Tories are perceived by the public and the press in Ottawa as a body of individuals rather than a well-run, well-organized, well-structured team that knows what it is doing and where it is going." Gillies labeled his party "incompetent," "opportunistic," and bereft of "discipline and professional experience," claiming that "the only ingredient holding the party together in the House is a shared dislike of the Liberals."[3] Few individuals familiar enough with the Conservative caucus to assess its operation challenged Gillies's verdict.

[3] *Globe and Mail* (Toronto), September 3, 1975, pp. 1, 2.

In marked contrast to the parliamentary caucus was the vastly improved extraparliamentary apparatus with its small army of enthusiastic recruits familiar, in many cases, with the techniques of contemporary politics. After the impressive display of organizational skill by Premier William Davis's "big blue machine" in the 1971 Ontario provincial election, Stanfield and his staff had persuaded many of its members to work on the party's behalf in the coming federal election. That the Conservatives were so much better equipped organizationally to fight the 1972 election than they had been previously was a direct result of Stanfield's success with the Ontario group. For the first time the party was able to match the Liberals in many areas of political strategy and organization. They made use of public opinion research on issues, personalities, and policies, as well as informed advance people, knowledgeable speech writers, and professional media advertising on a scale never before attempted by the Conservatives. By the time Stanfield retired in 1976, not only had the party's electoral machinery been brought full force into the twentieth century, but the skilled personnel, professional as well as volunteer, needed to make it operate had been drawn into the party.[4] This was most conspicuous at the senior level in the case of Lowell Murray, the man without whom the Conservatives might well have failed in the 1979 election.

Described by the *Toronto Star*'s syndicated columnist Richard Gwyn as "perhaps the canniest political strategist in the country,"[5] Lowell Murray was no stranger to the Conservative party when Clark persuaded him to take on the crucial position of national campaign chairman in 1977. Clark and Murray had become active in the Conservative party at the same time, as young men in the late 1950s, and their paths had crossed frequently during the years that followed. Fellow members of Stanfield's staff in Ottawa for three years, Clark as a political adviser and speech writer and Murray as chief of staff, the two men had come to know and to respect each other's political talents. Clark was convinced, soon after he became leader in 1976,

---

[4] Among the party activists responsible for establishing the new political organization under Stanfield were many whose names continued to feature prominently in Conservative politics throughout the remainder of the 1970s. Some were attracted directly from the "big blue machine"; others had joined Stanfield's staff after he won the party leadership in 1967, many of them having worked previously for E. Davie Fulton; others were disgruntled Liberals who had left their party as an expression of their dissatisfaction with Trudeau's leadership.

[5] Richard Gwyn, *Star-Phoenix* (Saskatoon), June 15, 1979, p. 45. For more on Murray, see also Jeffrey Simpson, "Tory Jack-of-All-Trades Is Back in Harness," *Globe and Mail*, April 18, 1978, p. 9; Philip Teasdale, "How the Tories Got Back into the Running," *Financial Post*, November 11, 1978, p. 6; and Humphreys, *Joe Clark*, pp. 69-77, 241.

that Murray's political judgment, intuition, and skills (all of which have since assumed legendary proportions in the party) should be put to their fullest test. He appointed him national campaign chairman, free to establish an organization and to plan the strategy for the forthcoming election.

Joe Clark and the Political Momentum, 1976–1979

Writing on the eve of the 1979 election, the *Globe and Mail's* respected political columnist Geoffrey Stevens gave his assessment of the Conservative leader:

> Mr. Clark is one of the most determined men I have ever met. It was determination, more than anything else, which carried him, then a little-known and lightly regarded backbencher of only 36, to the national leadership of the Progressive Conservative Party in February 1976. It was determination which caused him to reject everyone else's doubts about his prospects and his competence during the low periods of his 39 months of leadership. It is determination—determination to confound the critics and skeptics who dismiss him as a disaster looking for a place to happen, determination to prove the Liberals *can* be beaten—which has brought him to the point where he is within reach of becoming prime minister of Canada.[6]

Stevens had noted the essential contradiction in Joe Clark's character: his resolute ambition was matched by an inability to generate widespread public confidence in his potential for victory.

The highlights of Clark's parliamentary career had followed a similar pattern. In 1972 he had won the party's nomination for Rocky Mountain only after having beaten two much better known contenders in an unusual series of ten nominating meetings. He had won the seat in the parliamentary election later that year, but to do so he had had to defeat one of the rarities of Alberta politics, a popular Liberal incumbent. In the 1976 leadership race, he was not considered a serious contender until the final weeks of the campaign, and although he was ultimately successful on the fourth ballot at the convention, he won only by overcoming an unprecedented third-place start on the first ballot. Again in 1979 Clark had to overcome the widely held view that he could not win.[7]

[6] *Globe and Mail*, May 16, 1979, p. 7 (italics in original).

[7] For details see Humphreys, *Joe Clark*, chaps. 9, 11. For two columnists' assessments of Clark, see Walter Stewart, "Joe Clark: The Tory on the Tip of Your Tongue," *Maclean's*, October 1974, p. 8, and Richard Gwyn, "A Guy Named Joe," *Canadian*, March 24, 1979, pp. 2ff.

Unexpectedly, Clark's honeymoon as Conservative leader lasted a full year, a comment perhaps more on the state of the governing Liberals than on the opposition Conservatives.[8] For the twelve months following their new leader's selection in February 1976, the Conservatives enjoyed what for them was a rare treat: a consistent lead in the Gallup poll, with some 42 to 47 percent of the voters to the Liberals' 29 to 35 percent. By October 1976, 36 percent of Canadians believed that Clark would make a better prime minister than Trudeau, who was preferred by only 28 percent. This was the first time Trudeau had trailed an opponent in such a poll since he had become prime minister in 1968.[9] Two autumn by-election victories for the Conservatives, one in the supposedly "safe" Liberal seat of Ottawa-Carleton, seemed only to confirm the new-found strength of Conservative support.

Yet all was not right. The Parti Québécois victory of November 1976 gave the Trudeau government a new lease on political life and effectively froze the Conservatives out of the debate over the province's future. In no area of public policy were the Tories more deficient than with respect to Quebec's place within a united Canada, a deficiency that was not corrected by the time the 1979 election campaign drew to a close. By early 1977 it was apparent that the Conservatives were all but irrelevant in Quebec itself, where the national unity debate was being waged in true gladiatorial style by the chief protagonists, Lévesque and Trudeau.

The party's drop in popularity was swift. By March 1977 Canadians no longer believed that Clark would make the best prime minister. Their preference, once again, was Trudeau by a margin of three to two.[10] By midsummer, Gallup poll support for the Liberals had reached a level nearly twice that for the Conservatives, 51 percent to 27 percent. Without a single Conservative victory in any of the six by-elections of 1977, some Tories talked openly of a "dump Clark" move as part of a salvage operation in preparation for the expected 1978 general election. The defection to the Liberal front benches of Jack Horner, prominent right-wing Albertan and a man the Liberals claimed had a considerable following in many parts of the country, seemed all but to seal the fate of the Tories.

By mid-1977 the weaknesses in the leader's office had become apparent. From the time Clark had become leader of the opposition,

[8] For a penetrating though brief analysis of the Liberal defeat in 1979, see Jeffrey Simpson, "Lengthy Slide into Defeat Started for Trudeau in '76," *Globe and Mail*, May 29, 1979, p. 9.

[9] Canadian Institute of Public Opinion, *Gallup Report*, October 16, 1979.

[10] Ibid., March 5, 1977.

his staff had spent a good deal of time on activities of questionable value. The much-heralded twenty-one-member "Policy Advisory Council," composed of academics, businessmen, and M.P.s, for example, made no significant contribution to the party; yet a considerable effort had gone into its operation.[11] For months on end Clark had undergone a particularly grueling travel and speaking schedule for no good reason, flying thousands of miles to deliver countless speeches of little substance. Clearly this was an exercise undertaken without much in the way of strategic planning. There was, in fact, no framework within which the leader and his party were expected to operate.

To Lowell Murray the task at hand was a formidable one, though not without hope. He engaged a young political scientist with experience in public opinion polling, Allan Gregg, as national campaign secretary and put him in charge of the party's polling surveys. With Clark's chief of staff, Bill Neville, and an experienced but publicly unknown politico of the Stanfield period, Rich Willis, Murray began in mid-1977 to put together an election campaign organization.[12] By the end of January 1978, planning had proceeded far enough to enable the top organizers from across the country to gather for a two-day closed meeting at Château Montebello in Quebec. Many of those in attendance had first been drawn to the Conservatives when Stanfield was party leader. At the meeting they were presented with the broad plans formulated by Murray and his small group for what, at that point, was generally expected to be the 1978 general election. That the election was delayed a full year did not alter in any substantial way the campaign planning presented at Montebello. If anything, the delay gave the organizers more than they had reason to hope for. They were given extra time to alter their plans to keep abreast of changing public attitudes, and they were given a chance to test their organizational capacity in a set of fifteen by-elections later that year.

The campaign organization was to be basically two-tiered. The Ottawa group under Murray was to establish the national priorities and goals and to have overall responsibility for realizing those goals; the provincial campaign organizations were to be responsible for carrying out the national campaign as it affected their particular areas

11 For more on the council, see "Clark Names 21 to Advise on PC Policy," *Globe and Mail*, January 20, 1977, p. 1.

12 Neville had been one of the key advisers to Clark over the three years since the 1976 leadership convention. For his background and role in the Conservative party, see Humphreys, *Joe Clark*, pp. 231ff. The Robert Teeter polling organization was once again engaged by the Conservatives to carry out surveys of public opinion as it had for the federal elections under Stanfield and for several provincial elections in the 1970s.

and to oversee the proper functioning of the local constituency campaigns. This meant that there would be only *one*[13] campaign at the national level, with decentralized operations at the provincial level to meet local requirements. Every provincial campaign organization was expected to parallel the national organization and to have, as a minimum, a tour director, advance personnel for tour arrangements, and a director of legal services, in addition to a provincial chairman and his committee.[14] For its part, Murray's organization assumed responsibility for (1) the leader's tour and its scheduling, (2) national media advertising, (3) national news and press relations, and (4) candidate services such as training and policy research. Power to determine the ultimate course of the national campaign was without question concentrated in the hands of Murray's small group in Ottawa, particularly as the all-important tour–news–speech–media advertising component was its private preserve. For their part, the provincial organizations had been assigned important operational tasks. This rational allocation of duties and responsibilities, which in itself was a testimonial to the premium Murray placed on planning, was thought by many Conservatives to be a first within their party. It was, in any event, a logical extension of the organizational reforms introduced during the three election campaigns under Stanfield's leadership.[15]

With Murray safely ensconced in the party's key organizational post and given free rein to manage the campaign, Clark had time to devote his own considerable organizational ability to the parliamentary party.[16] He began by establishing a full-fledged committee system under the chairmanship of Jim Gillies. Caucus committees were set up, one each for six broadly defined areas of public policy: social, economic, cultural, food and resources, government operations, and transport and communications. Each committee was headed by a lead-

[13] The word, underscored in the original party document, was no doubt emphasized to add weight to the point the organizers wanted to get across: too often in the past the Conservatives had been criticized for waging different and contradictory electoral campaigns in different parts of the country. Murray's preoccupation with tight centralized control under his direction was a clear signal that the same criticism would be leveled at Clark's campaign only if orders were disobeyed.

[14] Progressive Conservative party of Canada, "Campaign '78" (Meeting of January 25-27, 1978, Château Montebello, Quebec), chap. 1, p. 2 (hereafter cited as Montebello Report).

[15] Interview with Allan Gregg, national campaign secretary, Progressive Conservative headquarters, Ottawa, July 17, 1979.

[16] Richard Gwyn reported that Clark did not stop meddling in the party's organization until Murray, in effect, threatened resignation. See Gwyn, "A Guy Named Joe," p. 4.

ing member of the party's front bench and was composed of a varying number of M.P.s who were themselves given special areas of responsibility. Clark cleverly designed a system that had the great advantage of assigning some direct responsibility for the party's parliamentary performance to over one-half of his ninety-five-member caucus. Regular morning meetings of the committee chairmen to plan strategy for the daily question period were open to any Conservative M.P. who wished to attend. The result was a Conservative caucus more disciplined and less self-destructive than any observers could remember.[17] Questions asked of the government were markedly improved, sharper and more probing than had previously been the case. As the changes coincided with the introduction of television coverage of the House of Commons, Clark began to appear in the living rooms of the nation in a different context. The artificiality of the press "scrum" was replaced by the drama and excitement of the main political arena. On balance Clark performed well. He was a good deal more at ease leading the attack of a supportive and apparently harmonious group against the government on the floor of the House of Commons than he had been when pitted against a questioning mob of reporters in the parliamentary corridors. To the surprise of many and to the delight of his colleagues, who had argued the point for some time, Clark came across as a competent debater and an effective critic. His performances generally matched, and occasionally outshone, those of the prime minister. Televised parliamentary proceedings proved an unexpected bonus for the Tories.

By the time the April 1978 Gallup poll was released, it became clear why Trudeau had not called a spring election. The two major parties were tied with 41 percent of the decided voters, the first time in over a year that the Tories had moved out of the range of 27 to 36 percent and that the Liberals had fared so badly. Murray's top aides assessed the situation closely. One key indicator of renewed interest in the Conservative party was the increase in financial contributions. Fund-raising dinners were attracting larger crowds, and direct mailings requesting individual donations to the PC Canada Fund were proving a considerable success.[18] By the end of 1978 the

[17] By March 1978 a harsh critic of the Stanfield caucus, Jim Gillies, had become an avid supporter of Clark's new system: "We've really turned it around. . . . Caucus used to be hell, [but] it's a pleasure now." Quoted in Stephen Duncan, "Tories Getting Pumped Up for Next Election," *Financial Post*, March 4, 1978, p. 6.

[18] The PC Canada Fund was set up in 1974 during Stanfield's leadership as a nonshare capital corporation to take full advantage of provisions of the amended Canada Elections Act to allow income-tax-deductible donations to political

TABLE 5–3

NUMBER OF DONATIONS AND TOTAL FINANCIAL CONTRIBUTIONS TO
PROGRESSIVE CONSERVATIVE AND LIBERAL PARTIES, 1977 AND 1978

Party	Number of Individual Donations	Contributions from Individual Donors (dollars)	Party Receipts: Individuals, Corporations, and Other Organizations (dollars)
Progressive Conservative			
1977	20,339	1,742,964	3,774,448
1978	35,615	2,661,175	5,464,510
Liberal			
1977	21,063	1,983,687	4,423,566
1978	22,350	2,101,716	4,779,694

SOURCE: Registered parties' fiscal period returns for 1977 and 1978, filed with chief electoral officer, Ottawa.

number of individual donations to the party had increased by some 15,000 over the previous year, while the figures for the Liberal party had remained virtually the same. The total number of donors as well as the amount of money raised from individual contributions both surpassed the Liberal figures for the year, a direct contrast to the situation in 1977 (see table 5–3). The Conservatives would clearly have no difficulty financing their election campaign, whenever it was to be waged.

By early 1978 it had become apparent that there was a lessening of interest outside Quebec in the national unity question. Without question the Liberals stood to lose the most in that regard. As the government came under increasing criticism from all quarters for its handling of the economy in general and inflation and unemployment in particular, the Conservative strategists were cheered by the prospect of fighting an election on issues on which they were convinced the government was vulnerable. The results of the Conservatives' polling research of April and May 1978, perhaps some of the most sophisti-

---

parties. The Conservatives pioneered the direct mailing technique in Canadian politics under the supervision of David Macmillan. At Stanfield's urging, Macmillan had visited party offices in the United States to study the American direct mailing technique and had incorporated some of the best features of the American system into that used by the PC Canada Fund. It obviously paid off. According to Macmillan the party averaged $45 per new donor, compared with the average American response of $18 per new donor (Macmillan interview by L. Seidle, Oxford D.Phil. candidate, June 20, 1979, Ottawa).

cated polling in the history of Canadian parties, confirmed the strategists' impressions. Moreover, they produced evidence for the first time of a measurable level of public cynicism over the way the government was going about its business.

A substantial media-oriented program had been launched by the Liberal government during the fall of 1977, and it had lasted several months. It showed the prime minister in economic consultation with the provinces, in foreign speeches related to Canadian national unity and the economy, in fighting campaign style at a national Liberal conference, and in pleasant home surroundings with his children. According to the Conservatives' polling data, none of these moves helped the Liberal cause. If anything, they may have hurt it. An internal party summary circulated at the time described the Canadian population, on the basis of the polling results, as having grown increasingly dubious of such public relations operations as those undertaken by the Liberals. Among its conclusions were the following:

> Their PR campaign helped do them in because it was unmatched by real actions or results.
> Equally significant, Trudeau also failed in his relentless campaign to persuade the country that our economic problems originated outside Canada and that their solutions lay outside the federal government's hands. His strategy backfired, badly. There were too many contrary arguments being advanced—by the press, by the Opposition, by private sector spokesmen. And there was too much contrary evidence. The people not only do not believe Trudeau's story, they do not *want* to believe it. This contention is borne out by our research data. Fine communicator that he is, Trudeau has made himself not only the advocate of that nothing-can-be-done position: he personifies it.[19]

An important finding had come to light. Throughout the ten years of Trudeau's prime ministership, an increasingly familiar lexicon of adjectives had come to be applied to the Liberal leader: arrogant, cold, distant, haughty, and argumentative, to name a few of the more common ones. The Conservatives found in their early 1978 polls, as they expected, that the public readily associated those terms with Trudeau and recognized them as flaws in his character. But they also discovered that the negative comments being made about Trudeau by one segment of the population (dubbed by the Conservative planners "the reluctant Tories") were different for the first time. The prime minister was described as ineffectual in coping with the country's

---

[19] Progressive Conservative party of Canada, "Perspective," internal campaign summary of May 16, 1978, p. 2 (italics in original).

problems not because he was removed from them and uncaring about the people affected by them (as had previously been the case) but rather because he was perceived as lacking the ability to solve them. An internal document circulated among the senior Conservative strategists in the summer of 1978 deserves special attention, for it served as the basis for the party's "election writ plan," soon to be implemented on a trial basis in the October by-elections and made fully operational in the advertising, news, speaking, and tour segments of the 1979 campaign. Part of it read:

> The research showed the level of cynicism and despair concerning the state of the economy was never more widespread or acute among the Canadian electorate. Negative assessments of Trudeau were also qualitatively and quantitatively different. Dislike of Trudeau the man and disapproval of Trudeau the Prime Minister pervaded the responses of a majority of the sample but more importantly Canadians, for the first time, were beginning to perceive Trudeau strengths as weakness and were associating Trudeau's style with the problems that they were so readily acknowledging. In short, the electorate perceived that the economy and the nation were in worse shape than ever before and that they were holding the Liberal Government—and Trudeau, as the persona of that Government—directly responsible.
>
> The data also revealed that while this cynicism was being translated into blame, it had a spin-off effect not wholly anticipated. Canadians overwhelmingly agreed that while things were bad, they were "tired of always being told how bad things are." The Liberals [in their own research] took this finding to mean that Canadians wanted to hear how good things were, or were going to be. As a consequence they began a campaign of accusing us of being "Gloom and Doomers" and they attempted to shift the blame to international factors and influences outside of their realm of control. With hindsight, it is clear that this strategy badly backfired. Canadians were not saying "I'm tired of hearing how bad things are, I want to hear how good things are." They were saying "I know how bad things are, you don't have to tell me" . . . therefore they did not want to hear it because they did not need to. Also, because the voter associated the Liberals with the problems they perceived, Trudeau and Chrétien's abdication of responsibility simply added insult to injury and led to a further perception of uncaring, incompetence and wrong headedness.[20]

[20] Progressive Conservative party of Canada, "An Election Writ Plan" (no date), p. 1.

The direction that the Conservative campaign would take had now become a good deal clearer to its planners.

The final major political event of 1978 enabling the Tories to claim that fortune favored them was the set of fifteen by-elections in October. The press and the political parties alike viewed the occasion as a "mini–general election," in part because the fifteen vacant seats were spread across the country and the mood of a sizable cross section of the voting public could be tested accordingly and in part because it was known that the ultimate electoral test was only months away. Although they lost two seats they had formerly held (one to the Liberals, the other to the NDP), the Conservatives came out the big winners. They took ten seats in all, a net gain of four over their 1974 total in the fifteen contested seats. Five of the constituencies won by the Conservatives had previously been held by Liberal cabinet ministers, including four in the crucial swing vote area of metropolitan Toronto. None of the Liberal stars had been elected, but of the Conservative star candidates the two most prominent (David Crombie in Toronto Rosedale and Robert René de Cotret in Ottawa Centre) were elected easily in former Liberal seats. The total Conservative popular vote for the fifteen seats increased by nearly nine percentage points over its 1974 level to 48.7 percent, whereas the Liberal vote dropped by eleven points to 30.5 percent. In the five metropolitan Toronto ridings, the Conservatives captured nearly 60 percent of the vote, compared with 36 percent in 1974. Combined with the Gallup poll figures of the next several months, which showed the Conservatives once again in the lead nationally with between 40 and 45 percent of the decided voters, the by-election results gave the Tories the chance to assert that the political momentum going into the general election was with them. The kind of campaign they subsequently waged in 1979 was designed specifically with that in mind. Confident that they could take the key marginal seats of southern Ontario, the Conservative strategists saw their party as the one the others would have to beat.

Although 1978 closed on a markedly better note for the Conservatives than 1977, the by-elections brought to light serious concerns that they could not ignore. The Tory weakness in Quebec had been made painfully obvious with the loss to the Liberals of St. Hyacinthe, the only Quebec seat to have voted consistently Conservative since 1958. Had it occurred as a single event, that loss might well have renewed the debate that has raged on and off throughout this century about the Conservatives' ability to make any headway in Quebec and to form a government composed of both principal language groups. In the event, it tended to get lost in the political shuffle, for by far the greatest media attention was centered on the Liberals' dismal performance across the country as a whole. Where it was noted, it only confirmed the view of most observers that Quebec was on the verge of voting overwhelmingly Liberal in 1979, with the rest of Canada voting largely Conservative.[21]

Moreover, even though the parliamentary party was a visible improvement over its former self, doubts were still being expressed about Clark's ability to lead. With the devastating reports soon to be filed by journalists en route with Clark on his world tour of early 1979, the reservations surfaced again before the election. It was virtually certain that the Liberals would launch a major attack against Clark. The Conservatives had given some thought to this possibility as early as June 1978, when they analyzed the Liberals' own public opinion research, the "Goldfarb Poll." The Conservatives found that

> there are more questions about Joe Clark than there are about Trudeau. Not only are there more, but the substance of these leaves little doubt that the Liberals are quite prepared not only to wage a negative but potentially vicious campaign against Clark. In short, they may attempt to turn the uncertainties surrounding Clark's leadership into real negatives. If this is to be the case . . . we may have to employ the "positive" aspect of the campaign for "defensive" rather than "offensive" reasons.[22]

Finally, it was also acknowledged by the Conservative planners that the party had done well in the 1978 by-elections as a result not so much of its own strengths as of the undeniably weakened condition of the Liberal party outside Quebec. If that should change for any reason, the Conservatives could be in considerable danger. A memorandum circulated among the top strategists earlier that year had drawn attention to the fact that

> the apparently favourable trend in public opinion is obviously not accounted for by a groundswell of positive support for us. The continuing size of the "undecided" (Gallup) or "soft" (our research) vote is instructive. Nevertheless, our own credibility, including Joe Clark's, has improved. The Party has looked more cohesive. There has been a sense of momentum recently, particularly in Ontario.[23]

Virtually the same words could have been chosen to describe the party's position when Parliament was dissolved and the election called in March 1979.

[21] See, for example, Jeffrey Simpson, "Liberals Trace Their Defeat to Trudeau," and Geoffrey Stevens, "A Lot of Thinking to Do," *Globe and Mail*, October 18, 1978, pp. 1, 6.

[22] Memo from Gregg to Murray, "Re: Goldfarb Poll," June 12, 1978.

[23] Progressive Conservative Party, "Perspective," May 16, 1978, p. 1.

Target Groups and Campaign Strategy

The Conservative election plans came into effect as soon as the election date was announced. The plans had been on the books for some time. For the better part of a year, the party strategists had agreed that the Conservative campaign would be based on the theme that Canada's potential was wasting away under the Liberals. The four basic components of the Tory campaign—tour, speeches, news, and media advertising—were tied together to emphasize the "wasted potential" theme. The campaign was broken down into four distinct phases, each with its own rationale and objectives. The strategies and plans were based on the party's reading of the nation's mood by means of periodic sampling of public opinion that continued with increased frequency throughout the campaign. Nothing about this was novel when judged by contemporary standards. For the Tories, however, the sophistication of the surveys, the detail of the political plans, and the professionalism in designing the surveys and executing the plans combined to give their campaign the sharpest organizational focus in the party's modern history.

For three years leading up to the election, the Conservatives had carried out extensive research on the party support of Canadians. An in-house polling capacity had been developed within party headquarters for this very purpose. On the basis of past voting behavior and attitudinal predispositions of those sampled, it was determined that there were three demographic groups in which the party had an obvious interest. These three were identified as the party's target groups, from which it was hoped that a winning electoral coalition could be constructed.[24] The groups were found to exist only in "English-speaking Canada" and were described in the following general terms:

• *Traditional Conservatives* were the core party supporters, who numbered between 15 and 20 percent of the total electorate. They were characterized as a "generally Waspish, non-professional, suburban or rural" group strongly opposed to government in general and Trudeau in particular. Their principal interest in government stemmed largely from their desire to see it operated efficiently and managed properly. Although the group lacked "an overly positive assessment" of Clark, it could, barring some major political catastrophe to the Conservatives, be counted on to vote Tory in 1979.

• *The reluctant Tories* were numerically and demographically similar to the traditional Conservatives except that as a group they nor-

[24] The general description of each of the three groups is to be found in the Montebello Report, chap. 2, pp. 5-8.

mally tended to vote Liberal. They were people largely between the ages of thirty and forty-five with nonprofessional occupations. They tended to be upwardly mobile small businessmen and middle-class white- and blue-collar workers. Since they subscribed to the view that "the government that governs least, governs best," they had become increasingly distrustful of the Liberals' performance. They regarded many of the government's economic policies as excessively interventionist and regulative. This was especially true of the wage and price control program, which was enormously unpopular with organized labor. The reluctant Tories were no longer confident that the Trudeau cabinet had the ability to cope with the economic problems of the time. On another level, however, this group displayed an equally strong concern for stability and security—both personally and socially. On this ground they found Trudeau very appealing when the political focus was on the national unity question. This issue they saw as his. He was considered a tough politician and a competent crisis manager when dealing with Quebec. If national unity were held out as the yardstick by which this group could gauge leadership ability, Trudeau would win their support; if it were economic management and the government's performance, he would lose it.

• *The little men and women* were not usually Tory voters, although they had supported the party in large numbers at the height of Diefenbaker's leadership in 1958. Since then their votes had more often gone to the Liberals and to the NDP than to the Tories—that is, if they had voted at all, for this group was the least likely to vote of any. Both attitudinally and demographically the group stood in marked contrast to the others. It consisted largely of "the young, poor, workers, a significant share of the female population," and the new urban-ethnic Canadians. Collectively these people displayed little attachment to the political process and to political parties. It was discovered after the 1976 Tory leadership convention, however, that they had been won over to the Conservatives by qualities of Clark's character that they found appealing. Clark was seen as an energetic young individual "who was diligent and hardworking for the right reasons—he was concerned and wanted to 'do good.'" He was attractive to this group because his leadership qualities were seen in nonpolitical terms and because he was judged to be honest and trustworthy.

The Conservative surveys showed that the party had gained the support of all three groups during the months immediately after the 1976 leadership convention. Their combined strength had provided the party with the substantial lead in the Gallup polls that it had enjoyed for a year after Clark's selection. That lead had disappeared when conditions changed. Following the Parti Québécois victory in November 1976, the reluctant Tories returned to the Liberal fold because the qualities they most admired in Trudeau, toughness and experience, were then much in evidence. The little men and women, on the other hand, deserted the Conservatives when they began to see Clark more as a politician than as a "good man." Arbitration of internal party squabbles and increased attacks on the government showed a more political leader than they had believed Clark to be. Given their notion of politics, they perceived Clark as less honest and less trustworthy than when he had first come to their attention in 1976.

If victory was to be achieved in 1979, the best hope lay in reassembling the tripartite coalition of 1976. The strategists made the reasonable assumption that the traditional Conservatives had nowhere else to go electorally and that they could be counted on to vote Tory. For the Conservatives to come to power, a campaign that would win the support of both the reluctant Tories and the little men and women was required. Campaign strategy was everything. The situation was summarized in the following terms:

> The challenge that faces us is to employ a strategy that will overarch the attitudinal and demographic differences of these two groups, for each group, unto itself, does not contain the requisite number of voters needed for us to win. . . . We must, therefore, at one and the same time, appeal to the latent antipathy towards Trudeau demonstrated by the reluctant Tories, and project a leadership alternative in Joe Clark, the Man, for the so-called "little people.". . . A strictly negative approach for the reluctant Tories would undoubtedly be insufficient to pull them towards us in the required numbers. We therefore must project the leadership image that emphasizes toughness and decisiveness but, given the penchant of the latter group, a toughness and decisiveness that is displayed, once again, for *the right* reasons. For example, we must relate to the public that while our party and our Leader would perhaps prohibit strikes by firefighters we would do so not because we were anti-labour but because such strikes would cause people to lose their homes, etc. Overall, it would seem that we must use the Trudeau Record and the perceived mismanagement of this country as a base upon which to contrast the leadership styles of the two leaders and in doing so, project a leadership style that is sufficiently different enough from Trudeau's to attract the little people and at the same time sufficiently similar enough to Trudeau's to attract the reluctant Tories.[25]

25 Ibid., pp. 8, 9 (italics in original).

The political high wire on which homeowners and striking firemen were to be asked to balance together would not be easy to construct. If successful, however, the act itself would follow in a long Canadian tradition of political gymnastics.

To accomplish their goal of winning the support of the three groups, the Tory planners laid out specific objectives for each of the four phases of their campaign. It was in every sense of the term a detailed game plan. The tour, speech, news, and (in the final twenty-nine days) national media advertising components were tied together in each phase according to the particular objectives it was hoped to accomplish at that stage. One example chosen from the many features of each phase illustrates the sort of campaign the Conservatives waged. Phase one highlighted the Tories' attack on the Trudeau government—its record of broken promises and its eleven years of mismanagement. Phase two saw the "Man," Joe Clark, traveling on a chartered bus to meet the little men and women of southwestern Ontario. Phase three introduced a devastating set of television commercials designed to reinforce in the viewer's mind the criticisms Clark had leveled at the government in the first stage of the campaign.[26] Phase four brought with it a more leisurely, confident, and philosophical Clark who talked in positive terms about the kind of country he wanted Canada to be in the future.

The "wasted potential" theme was common to all four phases. It was a clever slogan in that the message it conveyed could vary according to the context within which it was being used. It allowed for both a negative ("wasted") and a positive ("potential") interpretation. Clark's speeches in the early part of the campaign read like a catalog of Liberal incompetence and mismanagement but, as the cam-

---

[26] The "symbolic" thirty-second and sixty-second television advertisements showed, among other things, a maple leaf (symbolizing Canada) drifting aimlessly down a stream and a hockey goalie (the typical Canadian, especially well timed as the advertisement ran throughout the Stanley Cup play-offs) being subjected to countless brutal shots from the stick of Trudeau. A negative "buzz word" commercial presented, in slow motion, an actual film clip from the televised proceedings of the House of Commons. It showed Trudeau being applauded by his backbenchers and gesturing at the opposition as key words chosen to recall numerous government and ministerial blunders ran overscreen: Sky Shops, Lang Air, Judges Affair, Nannygate, and so on. The creative genius behind most of the commercials was Nancy McLean, a Conservative with experience in two former federal campaigns under Bob Stanfield and in several provincial campaigns, including recent ones in New Brunswick, Manitoba, and Ontario. Media Buying Services of Toronto, headed by Lowell Murray's director of media operations, Peter Swain, was the agency responsible for the overall media campaign. For brief comments on all parties' advertising campaigns, see Peter Jeffrey, "Why the Election Campaigns All Bombed Out," *Marketing*, June 18, 1979, p. 10, and Donn Downey, "PC Ads Take Potshots at PM's Track Record," *Globe and Mail*, April 28, 1979, p. 12.

paign wore on, they became more visionary and hopeful. The transition had been from waste to potential. The television and newspaper photo sessions, usually arranged early in the day to guarantee nationwide coverage that evening, were of the same sort. Visuals were shot of Clark visiting an oil field, a shipyard, a mine, an abandoned rail line, and other sites carefully chosen to portray graphically the particular claim that was to be made at that stage of the campaign. The election theme song and logo carried with them the double-barreled message of the wasted past and the potential of the future: "Let's Get Canada Moving Again." The news-tour-speech-advertising operation was orchestrated with its very special audience in mind: the reluctant Tories and the little men and women. The appeal was so wide ranging and so calculated that it would be easy for large numbers of those groups to find something to which they could relate.

To the Conservative strategists it was apparent that the issue of political leadership could not be avoided. Indeed they were confident that, if that issue was defined in their own terms, the Conservative campaign would be strengthened. The Liberals could be counted on to play Trudeau as their trump card by arguing, as in fact they did, that the prime minister's experience, intellect, and forceful personality were precisely the qualities of leadership that the country needed to see it through the difficult years ahead. If they tried to match the Liberals on their own ground, the Conservatives knew that would be the undoing of their campaign, for Clark was not seen as Trudeau's match in experience, intellect, or strength of personality.[27] The Conservatives, however, were not without options. Some hope obviously lay in appealing to the reluctant Tories on the grounds that Trudeau no longer effectively employed the leadership qualities for which he had become famous.[28] Such an appeal was almost certain

---

[27] Little had changed since early 1978, when a Gallup poll had found that Trudeau vastly outranked Clark in "experience" (47 percent to 7) and "strength of personality" (43 percent to 8) (Canadian Institute of Public Opinion, *Gallup Report*, February 25, 1978). The Montebello Report reported on the Conservatives' own findings: "Our data also reveal that on some (perhaps many) indices of leadership, Joe Clark head-to-head against Trudeau is a clear loser" (chap. 2, p. 15).

[28] A memo from Gregg to Murray shortly before the election summarized the situation: "Traditional assessments of Trudeau usually follow that he is tough, decisive, charismatic, experienced, aloof, uncaring and arrogant. Our media campaign should put these traditional assessments into question. . . . There is a substantial body of evidence to indicate that voter preference shifts from Liberal to PC when the individual reassesses his perception of Trudeau. More specifically, when the individual realizes that Trudeau is weak rather than strong they shift their vote. The best example of this realignment has been the growing belief that Trudeau is ineffective or incapable of dealing with the separatist position" (memo from Gregg to Murray, "Creative Strategy," January 30, 1979).

141

to help, but of itself it would not be sufficient. To it was added a more important strategy that the news-tour-speech-advertising specialists incorporated into their respective parts of the campaign: "Change the notion of what constitutes the right kind of leadership" for Canada.[29]

If the political strength of Trudeau had brought the country in eleven years to the point where the economy was stagnant, unemployment and inflation were high, a separatist government had been elected in Quebec, and the rest of the provinces were dissatisfied with Ottawa for a variety of reasons, then qualities other than strength were needed in a prime minister. Accordingly, Clark was presented in the Conservative campaign as a conciliator. Canadians were told that Clark was a man who intended to cooperate with the provinces rather than confront them, who promised a government more open and responsive than Trudeau's, and who laid claim to a team of candidates and potential cabinet ministers unmatched by the Liberals.

The Tory campaign was deliberately designed to invite comparisons between the two major party leaders, a tactic that may well have had more far-reaching consequences than were recognized at the time. Certainly it placed the Liberals in a bind. Committed Liberal supporters were known to be highly motivated by the issue of leadership. Above all else they admired a strong political leader.[30] For the Liberals to ensure the highest possible voter turnout from their core supporters, they had to run a campaign featuring a noticeably strong and forceful Trudeau. But in doing so they risked losing a sizable body of their previous supporters, for as Trudeau's strengths became more obvious, the reluctant Tories could be counted on to defect to the Conservatives in increasing numbers.

The contrasting qualities of leadership were seen in the televised debate of the party leaders. The Tories at that point in the campaign knew from their recent samplings that at least 70 percent of the voters expected Trudeau to perform better in the debate than either of his two opponents. At the same time, the Conservative research indicated that the Tories were then leading in all major non-Quebec metropolitan areas, where in fact the outcome of the election was going to be determined. Since the surveys also established that few voters believed the debate would influence their vote one way or another, it became apparent to Lowell Murray and his group that Clark had to perform in a very special way. The Tory

---

[29] Montebello Report, chap. 2, p. 12.

[30] According to the Conservative analysis of core Liberals (20-25 percent of the electorate), they demanded "intelligence, an exciting personality, charisma, [and] gifted ability" in their leader. Montebello Report, chap. 2, p. 6.

leader must make certain that those who intended to vote for the Conservatives believed they were not making an error. Reluctant Tories in particular did not need to see, in Clark, a cutting, slashing debater whose forceful and argumentative personality would do little more than remind them of Trudeau. Such a posture could well have driven these voters either to abstain completely or to return to the Liberals. Since there was no guarantee that Clark could match Trudeau's aggressive debating style in any event, the safest policy was to stay clear of any attempt to project strong leadership qualities.[31]

The Tory strategists had also to decide how to deal with the NDP in the campaign. As it was known that both the Conservatives and the NDP would benefit from the strong anti-Liberal sentiment outside Quebec, the Tory strategy had to be one of minimizing the number of anti-Liberal votes that would go to the NDP in preference to the Conservatives. The plan put into effect had two basic components. The first, predictably, was to make much of the "link" that had existed between the NDP and the Liberals between 1972 and 1974, when the NDP had "propped up Trudeau" in the minority Parliament of the time.[32] On several occasions throughout the campaign, generally in the key electoral areas of the organized labor little men and women voters, Clark launched direct attacks on Ed Broadbent and the NDP. The basis for the attacks was not the NDP's celebrated connection with the Canadian Labour Congress— that might prove too costly with the "striking firemen" vote. Rather, the voters were reminded "how dangerous a vote for the NDP" could be. Broadbent's NDP was, according to Clark, no less prepared to keep Trudeau in office than David Lewis's NDP had been between 1972 and 1974. A vote for the NDP, in Clark's words, would be "worse than a wasted vote." It would merely increase the likelihood of Trudeau's surviving in a minority Parliament.[33]

The second component of Conservative plans regarding the NDP was to accord that party as little attention as possible. According to a memo from Allan Gregg to Clark, the treatment of the NDP needed to be "sympathetically inconsequential" in the hope of

[31] Interview with Allan Gregg, Ottawa, July 17, 1979. See also Richard Gwyn's column on Gregg and the Conservative strategy for the debate, *Star-Phoenix*, May 30, 1979, p. 69.

[32] The terms are those Bill Neville used in a confidential memorandum to Joe Clark shortly before the election. In the memo Neville summarized a meeting he had held with four M.P.s "with a direct interest in the subject" to plan campaign strategy toward the NDP. Memo from Neville to Clark, "Re: NDP Strategy," December 21, 1978.

[33] See, for example, reports of Clark's attacks on the NDP in St. Catherines and Timmins, Ontario, *Globe and Mail*, April 27, 1979, p. 9, and May 10, 1979, p. 9.

isolating that party from "the equation of change."[34] The NDP was to be shunted aside as a third party with no realistic chance of forming a government. Trying to ignore the NDP proved a perilous operation, as was demonstrated shortly after the campaign began when the protracted and, from the Conservatives' point of view, embarrassing negotiations over the televised debates took place. In the early stages of the election campaign, when the format for the leaders' debate was being discussed by party and television officials, no one doubted the importance to both the NDP and the Liberals of a sound performance by Broadbent in a three-leader debate. From the standpoint of the NDP, it would shore up doubtful supporters and possibly pull in new ones from the Liberals and Conservatives. So far as the Liberals were concerned, their chances of being returned to power would be improved if Broadbent came across as a strong alternative to Clark, thereby splitting the antigovernment votes. Neither the NDP nor the Liberals had anything to lose.

The Conservatives did. They stuck to their claim that the debate should feature the two major protagonists, Trudeau and Clark, with Broadbent relegated to a minor role. When it became known that the Conservatives were not prepared to participate in a debate in which all three party leaders would be on an equal footing, the Tory tactics of ignoring the NDP misfired badly. The Conservatives had made no allowance for the indignation of two calculating political opponents. The episode was seized upon by a press corps hungry for any political news that varied from their steady diet of set speeches and press releases. The picture that quickly emerged, rightly or not, was of a party afraid to put its leader over one of the hurdles of contemporary politics. Since the two other leaders might have participated in a debate of their own, the Conservatives had no choice but to reverse their position and have Clark participate in the debate. From the point of view of the public and the press, the entire exercise had been pointless. Whether it cost the party any support may never be known, but by the time the debate was held some weeks later that question scarcely mattered. For the Tory planners had before them the evidence from their polls, and it confirmed what many observers had suspected: the debate was going to make virtually no difference to the outcome of the election.[35] Sufficiently large numbers of the target groups, however reluctantly, had decided to remain with the Conservatives in the hope of defeating the government.

[34] Memo from Gregg to Clark and Neville, "Voters Research—NDP Support," December 21, 1978.

[35] See Geoffrey Stevens, "He Survived," *Globe and Mail,* May 15, 1979, p. 6; Richard Gwyn, "Debate," *Star-Phoenix,* May 15, 1979, p. 23; and Jeffrey Simpson, "The Great Debate," *Globe and Mail,* May 12, 1979, pp. 1, 2.

Capitalizing on the Mood of the Voters

The character of the Conservative campaign was exemplified by the way the top planners handled such matters as the qualities of leadership, the NDP, and the televised debate. The decisions on these and countless other campaign items were reached on the basis of the party's strategic objectives, operational plans, and opinion survey results. No political party could hope to mount a serious campaign otherwise, but certainly few could count on the coincidence of events and political skills that favored the Conservatives in 1979. For the better part of a year, Canadians outside Quebec had displayed a mood of political restlessness and dissatisfaction that expressed itself most simply in the phrase "Trudeau must go." During its last year in office, the government's inability to stem the tide of public displeasure played straight into the hands of the Conservatives. As a result, the election was fought on the Tories' terms, not on the government's.

When the election was called, the task that lay ahead of the Conservatives looked deceptively simple. It seemed that they need only exhibit the familiar portrait of the prime minister (arrogant, aloof, wasteful, dictatorial) and touch it up with the occasional brush stroke in keeping with their latest reading of the public's tastes, and victory would be theirs. Yet as the Tories had never been noted for their ability to get artists, paints, and canvas together in the same place at the same time, the task was not as simple as it looked. That they were able to come up with a piece of political art in 1979 that the audiences in the electorally critical areas of the country were willing to accept was testimony not to the ease of the job but rather to the determination and professionalism of the new Tory organizers.

The slick and carefully orchestrated campaign that the Conservatives waged was not, however, without its faults. Clark's speeches were of a curiously uneven quality, as if the flatness of some had been deliberate so as to make others seem even more brilliant than they were. Many were stilted, platitudinous, and uninformative. They did nothing more than reinforce the mechanical nature of the Conservative campaign. Some were wide of their mark, such as the speech Clark delivered on April 3 to 500 members of the Quebec Chamber of Commerce. It was an acknowledged disaster, for the Tory leader failed to address the question foremost in the minds of any Quebec audience, national unity. In marked contrast were the highly successful speeches. As a rule they tended to focus on the one theme with which Clark felt most at ease: Canada must begin to view itself as a country of many local identities ("a community of communities") rather than continue its search for a single national identity. A speech that Clark delivered early in the campaign to secondary school students in his home town of High River, Alberta, and another on April 19 to 1,300 members of the Empire Club in Toronto, were of the "visionary" type. They drew standing ovations from their audiences and universally favorable press coverage. Had he delivered more such speeches in place of the pedestrian ones, Clark might have gone a long way toward capturing the imagination of the Canadian people.

The party did little to assure Canadians that a vote *for* the Conservatives was much more than a vote *against* the Liberals. Tory candidates were not always in agreement with one another or with their leader, nor was Clark always of one mind himself, when it came to stating what the party stood for. The Liberals made much of the Tory disagreements that surfaced immediately before and during the campaign, particularly as many of them revolved around important matters of public policy: national unity and Quebec's right to self-determination; the size of the budgetary deficit implicit in the Tories' campaign promises; ministerial responsibility for wrongdoing by the Royal Canadian Mounted Police; Clark's stand on a "stimulative deficit"; and a civil service reduced by 60,000 positions. By the end of the campaign it was fair to conclude that the public could not have known with certainty what the Conservatives intended to do on these matters, for it was by no means clear that they knew themselves.

The lamentably weak condition of the Conservatives in Quebec posed problems that remained unsolved throughout the campaign. Clark could not be charged with having ignored the province since his selection as Conservative leader in 1976. He had made a special effort to become fluent in French and, in preference to relying on a Quebec lieutenant to run the party's affairs in the province, Clark had taken charge of Quebec party matters himself. He had tried to establish an effective organization in the province. He had searched for candidates whose stature in the community would reflect favorably on the party and enhance its chances of winning several seats there. Notwithstanding these efforts, it had proved impossible to break the Liberals' stranglehold on the province.

To add to their weaknesses in organization and personnel in Quebec, the Tories had to concede that Clark himself was no match for Trudeau in the prime minister's home territory. Conservative planners were at a loss to counter the commonly held view in Quebec that only Trudeau could argue the federalist case in opposition to the Parti Québécois government. They found that between 55 and 60 percent of the Quebec respondents agreed with the following statement, which was included in several of the Tory preelection polls as one of the "mood" questions used to judge public opinion: "The best way to register a protest against Lévesque is to vote for Trudeau."[36] Given that sort of widespread sentiment, an impressive Liberal victory in Quebec was the safest prediction to be made about the election.

By the time the election was called, the party's level of support in Quebec could not have been much lower. The Conservatives' polls showed that at the beginning of the campaign the party had the support of only 6 percent of the decided voters in Quebec.[37] Privately the strategists conceded that they would be lucky to add any seats to the two they already held there, but publicly they had to put a brave face on the situation. If they did not, they knew that it could cost them support elsewhere. The dilemma the Tories faced going into the election had been summed up in the Montebello Report:

> While we know that we cannot win a large majority of the [Quebec] seats, we are convinced that creating the "impression" that we have a good chance of winning Quebec seats is vital to our winning seats in metropolitan English Canada. We are therefore caught between an all out and perhaps wasteful campaign in Quebec, and waging a low key campaign in Quebec and at the same time risking seats in the province and in the rest of English Canada.[38]

Accordingly, a full slate of Conservative candidates was nominated in Quebec, financial assistance was arranged for the needy ones, and scarce organizational resources were allocated on a priority basis. On paper the Tories had a "Quebec presence," but in fact they scarcely counted. Their portion of the Quebec vote slipped to its lowest in decades, 14 percent. Not since the election at the end of World War II had such a small share of the total Conservative national vote come from the voters of Quebec (see table 5–1). In 1979, as in 1945, the Liberals had successfully defended their claim to represent best the interests of Quebec in Ottawa. But the Liberal hegemony in Quebec in 1979 was not matched, as in 1945, by enough support in the rest of Canada to enable the government to survive.

In a number of other areas, the Conservatives had a reasonably clear idea of the kinds of policies they would implement if they came to office. This was most often the case with matters relating to the role and powers of the federal government itself. The Conservatives

[36] Interview with Allan Gregg, Ottawa, July 17, 1979.
[37] Ibid.
[38] Montebello Report, chap. 2, p. 4.

had wanted to give their campaign this kind of focus on policy, for here they believed the Liberal government to be vulnerable. The Tories addressed themselves to questions on the role of government in the individual's life and in the economy, helping to reinforce some fundamental differences between the Conservatives and Liberals on matters that were of direct concern to the swing voters. This capitalized on the mood of those voters who, it was widely assumed, were moving to the right. The Tories claimed that some federal programs and constitutional powers ought to be turned over to the provinces or shared by both levels of government through new arrangements. Included in the list were lotteries, fisheries, resources, culture, and communication. Tax cuts, reducing federal spending, freedom-of-information legislation, and the sale of the crown-owned Petrocanada to private investors were also promised as part of the program of a new Conservative government. The only truly distinctive foreign policy initiative proposed by the Conservatives was a pledge to move the Canadian embassy in Israel from Tel Aviv to Jerusalem. The proposal was hotly debated, particularly in the Toronto area, where it was generally seen as a move calculated to win over the Jewish votes in several key constituencies in that city.[39]

One promise aimed at the voters most crucial to the electoral success of the Conservatives was to allow a portion of property taxes and mortgage interest to be claimed as an income-tax deduction, a proposal that had proved enormously popular at the time of the fifteen by-elections of October 1978. The strategists were sure that making it one of the key planks of the Tory platform in 1979 would reap substantial electoral benefits from the two groups from whom support was most needed: the reluctant Tories and the little men and women. Because the economic impact of the proposal was open to varying interpretations and because the plan was a good deal more generous in its benefits than anything the Liberals and the NDP were able to come up with, the scheme became the focus of sharp debate. Clark was advised by his chief of staff to make much of the proposal because it was known to have strong appeal among labor rank and file.[40] The NDP would be hurt, particularly in the heavily unionized marginal seats of southern Ontario. For the reluctant Tories who were found to be "tired of being told how bad things are," the Conservative plan had the great advantage of presenting a policy

---

[39] For Clark's pledge on this matter, made immediately before a meeting he held with a Jewish lobby group in Toronto, and Trudeau's reply, see the *Globe and Mail*, April 26, 1979, p. 9, and May 10, 1979, p. 9.

[40] Memo from Neville to Clark, "Re: NDP Strategy," December 21, 1978.

alternative to which they could easily relate. The Conservatives discovered in their surveys that the scheme was most popular with the reluctant Tories, who saw it as a positive answer to a problem that they acknowledged as real: high taxes.[41]

The exact extent to which the calculated and deliberate moves of the Tory campaign succeeded in winning the support of the various groups at which they were directed will probably never be known. A general campaign strategy aimed at winning the support of two or three key demographic groups in a country as geographically extended and socially diverse as Canada is bound to encounter some trouble spots. Although the anti-Trudeau sentiment was thought to be as strong in Manitoba as anywhere, the reluctant Tories of that province were a good deal more reluctant in 1979 than those of Ontario or British Columbia. The lack of popularity of the provincial Conservative government in Manitoba no doubt played a role in the defeat of three Conservative candidates who had been members of the last Parliament. Of the eighty-three Conservatives in Parliament at the time of dissolution who stood as candidates in 1979, all but eight were reelected. Of those eight, no fewer than five had entered Parliament between 1976 and 1978 by winning former Liberal seats in by-elections. The anti-Liberal vote that helped to elect those Tories in the first place was no longer enough to reelect them, even though that vote was substantial enough in 1979 to defeat the government. The seats may well have been lost on peculiarly local issues that worked to the disadvantage of the Conservative candidates: Ottawa civil servants unhappy with the prospects of a possible Conservative government (two seats), metropolitan ethnic and white-collar voters back in the Liberal fold by virtue of a renewed Liberal drive for votes in Toronto during the dying days of the campaign (two seats), and, in St. Boniface, redefined electoral boundaries that reduced the number of non–French Canadian voters in the riding (one seat). Given the strength of the NDP showing in the provincial election in British Columbia and that party's capacity to carry it over into the federal election, the Conservatives may have been unsuccessful in a seat or two in that province that they would otherwise have won. The strategists would spend idle moments before the next federal election counting the number of seats lost by the Conservative party for "extraneous" reasons. An unpopular Conservative government in Manitoba? By-election backlash? British Columbia

---

[41] Interview with Allan Gregg, Ottawa, July 17, 1978. By midcampaign Clark confidently asserted that any party opposing the Conservatives' mortgage deductibility scheme in Parliament would, in a future election, "be wiped out" (*Star-Phoenix*, May 10, 1979, p. 30).

TABLE 5–4

Votes and Seats: Progressive Conservative Party, 1945–1979

Year	Percentage of Votes	PC Seats	Total Seats
1945	27	67	245
1949	30	41	262
1953	31	51	265
1957	39	112	265
1958	54	208	265
1962	37	116	265
1963	33	95	265
1965	32	97	265
1968	31	72	264
1972	35	107	264
1974	35	95	264
1979	36	136	282

Sources: Thorburn, *Party Politics in Canada*, app.; and *Star-Phoenix*, May 25, 1979, pp. 34-35.

provincial NDP vote? And so on. They would, no doubt, have had little difficulty in making the case that Clark had been denied his majority by circumstances beyond their control.

On the other hand, the Conservative strategists could take a certain amount of satisfaction in the results. Their campaign strategy had worked. They had fought the election largely on their own terms and in the area of the marginal seats that had made the difference. The Conservatives had received more votes and more seats than any other party in every province save three: Quebec, New Brunswick, and Newfoundland. The final Liberal tally of 40 percent of the total vote was notably out of line with Liberals' fortunes across the country as a whole, where they placed second in four provinces and third in three. Only because of their huge Quebec vote had they earned the lead in total national popular vote. Two features, neither of them new to Canadians, were called to the public's attention by the election results. The Conservatives, with fewer votes than the Liberals, had won more seats; and the Conservative vote, only marginally better than that of 1972 and 1974, was so much more "efficiently" distributed that it enabled them to come to office (see table 5–4). The capricious Canadian electoral system was destined once again to become the subject of debate. It was doubtful, however, whether the new Conservative government would place reform of the system very high on its list of legislative priorities. The Tories felt they had made the most of the electoral system. Confident that they knew how to use it to their advantage, they were unlikely to support any claims that it should be changed. That such confidence induced in the Tory strategists a false sense of electoral security became painfully obvious with the defeat of the Clark government only nine months after it had come to office.

6

The Defeat of the Government, the Decline of the Liberal Party, and the (Temporary) Fall of Pierre Trudeau

Stephen Clarkson

The long years of Liberal ascendancy in Canada's federal politics during the twentieth century—fifty-nine years in office and only twenty-two years in opposition—have obscured how vulnerable governments can be to dramatic election reverses. Analysts of Canadian voting have established that a majority of the electorate is composed not of loyal partisans who vote for their party through thick and thin but of "flexible" and new voters who make up their minds in response to shorter-term considerations of issue or image.[1] The manner in which the Liberal party lost the 1979 election illustrates this vulnerability to voter displeasure in three dimensions. The Liberal *government* that was elected with a clear majority in 1974 proceeded to defeat itself by its indecisiveness, its incompetence, and its improprieties. The extraparliamentary Liberal *party*, whose power had waxed during the brief years of minority government, 1972–1974, saw its authority wane and its members' morale consequently fall as the Prime Minister's Office (PMO) appropriated its main functions. Finally, in the long-delayed election campaign, the efficiency of the Liberals' organization could not compensate for their strategy's lack of coherence, their policies' lack of content, and their leader's lack of conviction. This chapter argues that the Liberal party began to lose the 1979 election when it resumed office in July 1974; by the time the formal campaign was finally launched in March 1979, it could do little more than struggle to stem a tide that was flowing remorselessly against it but that would then turn again and carry it back to power the following year.

[1] Harold D. Clarke, Jane Jenson, Lawrence LeDuc, and Jon H. Pammett, *Political Choice in Canada* (Toronto: McGraw-Hill Ryerson, 1979), pp. 381, 391.

How the Government Beat Itself

Having made its comeback to majority rule in 1974 with a campaign based on the claim of strong leadership and the promise of a dozen major policy ventures, the Liberal government relapsed into inaction.[2] Pierre Trudeau, its leader, appeared devoid of the initiative and ability to launch long-range strategies. The cabinet soon showed signs of disintegration in its ranks, incompetence in its managerial functions, and malfeasance in many of its members' handling of their political responsibilities. Perhaps most damaging as far as the watching and waiting Grit loyalists [3] were concerned was the government's drift away from those moderately reformist principles the party had traditionally claimed for itself as the hallmarks of liberalism in Canada.

Whether Trudeau was rewarding himself with a long period of relaxation after the rigors of his successful election campaign, as his biographer George Radwanski hypothesized, whether his still-undisclosed marital difficulties were depressing him, as his wife's autobiography suggests, or whether he had lost interest in the problems of governing for other reasons, his failure to give leadership produced an atmosphere of indecision in Ottawa.[4] A vague Throne Speech (equivalent to the U.S. State of the Union message) in September 1974 gave the lie to the dramatic campaign promises made earlier that summer. The insubstantial achievements of the House of Commons, which did little more than deal with the backlog left over from the Twenty-ninth Parliament, perpetuated "a sense of drift not only in the expected political leadership of a triumphant majority but also in the management of the ordinary business of the House of Commons." [5]

The resignation from the government of John Turner in September 1975 left Trudeau looking not just adrift but weak. Although inside opinion generally contradicted the popular view that Turner had been a strong finance minister, the self-exile from Ottawa of this perpetual dauphin reduced the Liberals' credibility in English Canada and

[2] Stephen Clarkson, "Pierre Trudeau and the Liberal Party: The Jockey and the Horse," in Howard R. Penniman, ed., *Canada at the Polls: The General Election of 1974* (Washington, D.C.: American Enterprise Institute, 1975), pp. 57-96.

[3] "Grits" is a label that has stuck to the Canadian Liberals as Whig has to English Liberals. It derives from "clear grit," the special sand used by the stonemasons in southwest Ontario who were the base for the emerging radical Liberal party in the early nineteenth century.

[4] George Radwanski, *Trudeau* (Toronto: Macmillan, 1978), p. 291. Margaret Trudeau, *Beyond Reason* (New York: Paddington Press, 1979), p. 193.

[5] John Saywell, ed., *Canadian Annual Review of Politics and Public Affairs: 1975* (Toronto: University of Toronto Press, 1976), p. 52.

their prestige within the business world just as the government was about to introduce a dramatic if belated anti-inflation program of wage and price controls. Even in the atmosphere of crisis surrounding Quebec nationalism, Pierre Trudeau could not sustain his appeal as unchallenged champion of national unity. In the bitter months of bargaining and blackmail over bilingualism for the air-traffic controllers during the summer of 1976, Trudeau was seen as the villain both by Francophone Canadians, who felt that the cabinet had capitulated to the English-speaking majority, and by English-speaking Canadians, who saw bilingualism in the air as more evidence of creeping French power. Significantly Trudeau lost two ministers within two months over these issues—Jean Marchand (environment), who resigned over the compromise with the unilingual air-traffic controllers, and James Richardson (national defense), who resigned in protest against Trudeau's determination to see French protected in an eventual new constitution.

By the fall of 1976, according to the September Gallup poll, 36 percent of those with opinions on the nation's leadership felt that the newly chosen and still largely unknown Conservative leader, Joe Clark, would make a better prime minister, and only 28 percent felt Trudeau was still the best-qualified man. It took the momentary shock of René Lévesque's election as premier of a separatist government in the province of Quebec in November to bring Pierre Trudeau back onto the political stage with fire in his belly. In early 1977 he was able to win standing ovations before such crucial audiences as the Chamber of Commerce in Quebec City and the U.S. Congress in Washington, and respected Canadian commentators began to say again that only Trudeau could save Canada from Balkanization.

This rise in the prime minister's fortunes could not be sustained against his difficulties in managing the politicians in his cabinet. Every time another minister departed, from exhaustion or old age, attention was drawn to the continuing hemorrhage of talent: Bryce Mackasey, postmaster general, the left Liberal with as much heart as blarney (September 1976); Mitchell Sharp, president of the Privy Council, a fiscal conservative and cautious diplomat of long experience and disarming charm (September 1976); Donald S. Macdonald from finance, the successor to the dauphin, John Turner, who had been one of the first English Canadians in the party to raise the banner of Pierre Trudeau in 1967 and had loyally, even pugnaciously, defended it for a full decade. Even before Donald Macdonald's resignation in 1977, "commentators began speaking of the weakest cabinet since the sorry days of R. B. Bennett or Mackenzie Bowell." [6]

[6] Saywell, *Canadian Annual Review: 1977*, p. 3.

Disintegration in cabinet ranks bred mismanagement in the government the way stagnant pools breed algae. Despite its numerically secure position in the House, the government continually ran into difficulties when trying to push its legislative proposals through Parliament. The legislation to deracinate the Canadian editions of *Time* and *Reader's Digest* (1975), the peace and security package on gun control and electronic eavesdropping (1976), the long overdue competition bill, the revision of the Immigration Act (1977): time after time the government found itself forced to withdraw or amend its own legislation, often in response to revolts from its own backbenchers. As political mishap followed political accident, a poisonous aura of incompetence gathered over the government benches. Personal hostilities came to the surface when the minister of national defense and the minister of supply and services bickered publicly about who was to blame in the financing of a major defense contract with the scandal-struck Lockheed company. When the auditor general tabled his annual report in November 1976, he administered the funeral oration for the earthly remains of the Liberals' reputation for administrative competence: "Parliament—and indeed the Government—has lost, or is close to losing, effective control of the public purse."[7] Such a strong warning was no surprise to editorial writers, who had generally come to the conclusion that the cabinet knew neither where it was going nor how it proposed to get there.

With this air of incompetence came the stink of impropriety. Perhaps because Watergate had oversensitized the media to every hint of wrongdoing (as Liberals complained), perhaps because the cabinet had become arrogant, careless, or corrupt with majority power (as their opponents maintained), allegations of scandal plagued the government over these years, while inquiries and investigations kept the issues before the political spectators across the country. There was Harborgate, price fixing among dredging companies that implicated John Munro, minister of labor; then Sky Shops, influence peddling that implicated a Quebec Liberal bagman, Senator Giguère, and Jean Marchand, minister of transport, in an airport shop concession; Dial-a-Judge, interventions with a judge that implicated Marc Lalonde, minister of health and welfare, Bud Drury, minister for science and technology, who offered his resignation, and André Ouellet, minister for consumer and corporate affairs, who resigned when he was found in contempt of court; and Nannygate, focusing on the improper use of government aircraft by Otto Lang, minister of transport. These scandals, celebrated enough to boast their own labels, did not exhaust the list. There were also wrongdoings in the crown corporations that

---

[7] Saywell, *Canadian Annual Review: 1976*, p. 27.

were flagships for government enterprise: at Air Canada, over senior management malfeasance; at Polysar and Atomic Energy of Canada, over bribes and kickbacks to secure foreign contracts and over the uranium cartel that the government had established along with a "gag law" to prevent its disclosure to the public.

Most damaging in its extent and most corrosive of the active support within the core of the Liberal party was the seemingly endless string of revelations about wrongdoings, illegalities, and dishonesties among the ministers charged with national security and in the police force placed under their responsibility. Whether it was a blacklist of bureaucrats compiled for the solicitor general by the Royal Canadian Mounted Police (RCMP) from files stolen during the arson of the Praxis building (a center in Toronto that housed such unsubversive groups as a tenants' union and an antiexpressway coalition) or a break-in at a Montreal office to steal the list of contributors to the perfectly legitimate Parti Québécois; whether it was the surveillance of members of the NDP or the practice of mail interception, which had lasted for over a decade: the cabinet's response developed a monotonous pattern of heated denials of original allegations, followed, with the failure of the initial cover-up and the publication of further revelations, by the transfer of the investigation to the McDonald royal commission set up in October 1977 to take the political heat off the government. The Canadian Civil Liberties Association, that keeper of the nation's civil rights conscience, had turned against the government in protest not so much against the evidence of RCMP wrongdoing as against the cabinet's condoning of these illegalities.

The civil liberties association was not the only group to be disturbed by ministerial statements affirming that it was sometimes proper for the police to break the law. When Francis Fox, the solicitor general, stated on television that there was a need to change the law to permit "the commission of certain activities which normally would constitute a Criminal Code offense if brought to light,"[8] he dealt a sledgehammer blow to the wedge splitting off one of the Liberal party's most vital assets, its small-l liberal supporters. The first shock had come in October 1975 when wage and price controls were announced—just over a year after the Liberals had won their renewed mandate on the basis of a spirited attack on the very idea of controls. The establishment of the Anti-Inflation Board was worse than a mere dramatic flip-flop: it signaled the Liberals' abandonment of the popu-

---

[8] Saywell, *Canadian Annual Review: 1975*, p. 27.

list belief that an ever-expanding economic pie could continue to be divided among an ever more prospering public.[9]

Once controls were lifted in 1978, the cabinet had to grasp another economic nettle, the federal deficit. When, in August 1978, Prime Minister Trudeau returned from an economic summit meeting in Bonn and announced a dramatic cut of $2 billion from the federal budget, he not only took his own cabinet by surprise, not to mention the deputy minister of finance, but also undermined his popular support. It is doubtful whether his born-again conversion to fiscal conservatism was convincing to right-leaning Liberals; it is certain that the budget cuts confused those left-Liberal supporters who were still committed to the Liberal party as the vehicle of social reform through big government.

They were to have more reason to be baffled. In 1976 their leader had enjoyed what Richard Gwyn called his "finest parliamentary hour" with an eloquent appeal for the House of Commons to abolish the death penalty for first-degree murder.

> If penalties applied by the state against lawbreakers cannot be justified for their rehabilitative, punitive or deterrent value, they cannot be justified at all—not in a civilized society. Capital punishment fails on all three counts. To retain it in the Criminal Code of Canada would be to abandon reason in favour of vengeance; to abandon hope and confidence in favour of a despairing acceptance of our inability to cope with violent crime except with violence.[10]

Although the whips were taken off so that the M.P.s officially could vote as conscience rather than party dictated, the prime minister had had considerable pressure put on his caucus to support abolition. In September 1978, on the other hand, when the waves of conservatism blown up by Proposition 13 in the United States were sending ripples through Canadian political waters, Trudeau let his principles capsize. He stated that a referendum on hanging proposed by Otto Lang, once again minister of justice, would not be against his conscience. The abolition that the prime minister had championed in a display of leadership that was rare in 1976 he appeared ready to abandon when the political winds began blowing from the right in 1978.

Having shaken the faith of the lower-income and working-class supporters, having offended the principles of the left-leaning and the

---

[9] James Laxer and Robert Laxer, *The Liberal Idea of Canada: Pierre Trudeau and the Question of Canada's Survival* (Toronto: Lorimer, 1977), p. 76.

[10] Saywell, *Canadian Annual Review: 1976*, p. 11.

values of the right-leaning, it remained for the government to alienate its support among the professional classes. This it proceeded to do with its 1978 budget, which wiped out the corporate tax shelters previously available to such upwardly mobile professionals as dentists, lawyers, and realtors, professionals who tended to work for or at least support the government party.

It is impossible to know with certainty what damage these reversals of position on economic policy or social principle did to the loyalty of the Liberal party's own core of active workers. It stands to reason that the economic and social conservatives who were originally offended by the imposition of controls and the abolition of the death penalty would not have been entirely mollified by the budget cuts and the talk of a referendum on hanging, whereas those leaning toward economic and social reform who had been pleased by the government's actions in 1975 and 1976 would have been alienated by the reversals of 1978. Rather than winning the support of one wing of the party or the other, Trudeau and his entourage seem to have lost support from both sides by appearing so pragmatic as to be callously unprincipled. What unquestionably shocked party militants across the entire ideological spectrum was the seduction of Jack Horner.

How the Party Defeated Itself

The member of Parliament from Crowfoot, Alberta, had long led the redneck faction within the Conservative caucus that virulently opposed not just the abolition of hanging but the institution of bilingualism in the form of the Official Languages Act. When tensions that had been simmering between Horner and his party leader, Joe Clark, came to the surface over which constituency the defeated leadership candidate would represent in the next election after redistribution, a meeting was secretly arranged between the dissident Tory and the prime minister. As a result of the Liberals' blandishments, Jack Horner crossed the floor of the House on April 20, 1977, and the next day entered the Liberal cabinet after nineteen years as a Tory backbencher. This desperate attempt to buy a toehold for the Liberal party in its Alberta wasteland proved in the long term self-defeating, an act that would hang like a millstone round the Liberals' collective neck. The problem was not just that Horner's dubious conversion blurred the party's image, further confusing the general public and eventually losing votes for the Liberal party at the next election. More serious was the immediate impact that the Tory cat had among the Liberal pigeons. "When I read the news of Horner in the *Globe*," said Roy MacLaren, a rising Toronto Liberal who was planning to contest a Liberal nomination and was one of the few new candidates actually to win a seat in the 1979 election, "I wondered why I was a Liberal."[11] He was not alone in his bewilderment. Kathy Robinson, a ten-year veteran of the party elite in Ontario who was an active organizer both during the election of 1979 and throughout the long period of preelectoral preparation, felt that the Horner episode had "hurt our own people."[12] By inviting one of the most vituperative of his old-time enemies into the bosom of his own shaky government, by welcoming a Tory who had voted against that cornerstone of the prime minister's federal program, the Official Languages Act, Trudeau had indicated that his politics were now guided by sheer opportunism. As his pollster, Martin Goldfarb, confirmed, the destructive result of putting pragmatism so frequently ahead of principle was to turn off the thinking, ideologically motivated Liberals who traditionally formed the front ranks of his party workers.[13]

If the courting of Jack Horner was an immediate cause of low morale in the party core, a more basic explanation for the decline in the party's battle worthiness must be sought in a subtle but substantial shift of power away from the party's formal executive into the Prime Minister's Office. The real contents of party politics, now that an election was not contemplated for several years, were fund raising and patronage. An attempt had been made by the former party president Richard Stanbury to bring fund raising under the aegis of the party executive, but the chief bagman for English Canada, Senator John Godfrey, had persuasively and successfully insisted that a direct, personal connection between the prime minister and the fund raisers was necessary if the latter were to be motivated to meet their annual targets. Fund raising remained beyond the reach of the elected party organization or its membership. The handling of patronage appointments represented a different kind of ministerial power. On paper, decisions about the several hundred annual appointments to government boards and commissions that lay within the prime minister's purview were made collectively by the cabinet. In practice one cabinet minister was designated to handle the appointments for each province.[14] Routine culling of names was handled by a special political assistant for the minister, who would receive occasional representations from

[11] Interview with Roy MacLaren, M.P., August 15, 1979.
[12] Interview with Kathy Robinson, July 9, 1979.
[13] Interview with Martin Goldfarb, August 1979.
[14] Christina Newman, "That Big Red Machine Is the Daveymobile," *Globe and Mail* (Toronto), July 7, 1975, p. 7.

party hands or caucus members.[15] Major appointments would be discussed in full cabinet meetings, and a staff officer in the Prime Minister's Office coordinated the whole appointments process. The patronage function thus remained a prerogative of the government, not the party.

A significant indicator of the growing power of the Prime Minister's Office was the consolidation of the revamped system of geographical ministerial reporting developed during the minority government. Although this may have appeared to be ministerial politics since cabinet ministers were responsible for the political well-being of a certain number of ridings in their assigned areas, the system actually represented a considerable shift toward control of the party by the prime minister's personal bureaucracy. In the name of riding readiness, ministers' attention to their geographical partisan responsibilities was monitored by the PMO staff, and delinquents were chided by the prime minister in personal audiences if they did not visit "their" ridings and submit their reports as often as required. However understandable the rationale of maintaining the Liberal constituency associations in good repair, particularly in ridings held by the opposition, the transfer of this monitoring function from the party office to the Prime Minister's Office reinforced the shift that was quietly taking place in the nature of the Liberal party: from a cadre organization working in cooperation with the party leader and the cabinet to a personal clique in which the leader and his personal staff dominated both the cabinet and parliamentary party on the one hand and the lay party on the other. In stark contrast to the efforts of his first majority government to mobilize ideas and proposals from the country's grass roots as a counterpoint to the continuous flow of policy advice from the bureaucracy, the prime minister was now remaking the party in his technocratic style,[16] in the apparent expectation that regular visits from ministerial assistants, occasional gatherings with a minister, and intermittent form letters from himself to riding presidents would keep the party core in fighting trim. It was as if a large but inchoate body of partisan supporters spread across the 282 ridings of the country could have their loyalties and motivations kept on hold by an efficient monitoring system run by Colin Kenney, a graduate of the Dartmouth business school.

[15] Interview with Ethel Teitelbaum, August 28, 1979.
[16] Stephen Clarkson, "Democracy in the Liberal Party," in Hugh G. Thorburn, ed., *Party Politics in Canada*, 4th ed. (Scarborough, Ont.: Prentice-Hall, 1979), pp. 154-60.

Further indication of the shift in the Liberal party's command structure came in 1975 with the appointment of Jim Coutts as principal secretary in the Prime Minister's Office. For the first year after the election, the concept of lay party participation had been kept alive by the monthly meeting of a tripartite group made up of the two chief figures from each of the three power groupings of the party: the national executive—Gil Molgat, the elected president, and Blair Williams, the appointed national director; the party cadre—Keith Davey and Jim Coutts; and the PMO—Pierre O'Neill, the press secretary, and Jack Austin, the principal secretary. When alleged irregularities in Austin's previous business undertakings made him an embarrassment in the PMO (though not, apparently, in the Senate, to which he was duly elevated), Davey successfully urged Mr. Trudeau to take on Coutts, a longtime Liberal who had proved his loyalty by running for election in the Grit wasteland of Alberta in 1962 and serving as provincial campaign chairman there in 1963. He had also gained political experience as appointments secretary for Prime Minister Pearson from 1963 to 1966 and, before coming back to the aid of the party in the 1974 campaign, was said to have amassed considerable wealth as partner in a management consultancy firm where he honed skills learned at the Harvard business school. Although Coutts came to the PMO through the informal power structure of the lay party, this did not mean that he represented a victory of that party over the prime minister's entourage.

The principal secretary's master was neither the party president, whom he would see occasionally, nor the campaign cochairman, whom he would see weekly, but the prime minister, whom he saw almost hourly. Teamed with Michael Pitfield, whose job as clerk of the Privy Council was to advise the prime minister concerning government matters, Jim Coutts was charged with giving political advice. To the extent that he advised on partisan affairs—and his range of political responsibilities spread far wider than mere party concerns—his function was to bend the party to the needs of the prime minister, not the prime minister to the needs of the party, as party activists were to grumble and the press to report.

It did not take the media long to decide that the Coutts-Davey combination was doing with the Prime Minister's Office what it had done with the 1974 campaign—insulating Trudeau from the public in general and the press in particular. Calling Coutts "an honest Bob Haldeman," Allan Fotheringham maintained, with the insouciant acidity that had become his trademark, that the "remarkable plunge in popularity of Trudeau and the Liberals since their smashing majority win in 1974 is due in large part to [this] new firm of merchandisers and packagers who now wall off the PM from the world."[17] Leading members of the lay party came to share the view that, far from giving lay party members access to their leader, the PMO under Coutts was spinning a cocoon to shield the prime minister from his party. Of the many instances reported by Liberals of party opinion being filtered out before reaching Trudeau, a "perfect recent example was the 'buying' of Jack Horner in the face of the prime minister's initial distaste. It was only after the event that we discovered that the strong opposition of several key Alberta Liberals had apparently been kept from him although these views had been expressed strongly."[18] In vain did party table officers write earnest briefs urging a "true democratization of the power structure within the party so that political power is vested in elected, rather than appointed, officials."[19] The Liberal party's interest in the role of the ballot box in its internal affairs had diminished to the point where it would cut off its nose to spite its face.

Early proof of the party's declining power had come, ironically enough, when the party gathered in Ottawa in the autumn of 1975 for its biennial convention. In an unusual attempt actually to recruit a candidate for a specific office, Mr. Trudeau urged Senator Keith Davey to run for party president, so that his informal position of cochairman for the next campaign would correspond with the formal power of chief executive officer of the party. When Davey reluctantly let his candidacy for the party presidency be declared, a wave of anger swept the federal caucus and spread through the lay party elite. Expressing more frustration with the leader than personal hostility to the senator, David Collenette, an M.P. from Toronto, organized a "stop Davey" effort, swinging support to Alasdair Graham, a Nova Scotia senator who wanted the job. When it appeared he might have a difficult fight on his hands at the convention, Davey dropped out of the race, which went by acclamation to Graham. Though the press interpreted this flurry as the party summoning its courage to give the prime minister a rap on the knuckles, the delegates had in effect rejected the possibility of electing to the executive the one Liberal who enjoyed some real party power outside the prime minister's own office and could thereby have consolidated some of the cadre's waning

---

[17] Allan Fotheringham, "Davey and Coutts, Packagers of the New and Increasingly Isolated Pierre Trudeau," *Maclean's*, February 23, 1976, p. 56.

[18] Michael Webb to Christine Newman, May 24, 1979.

[19] Michael Webb, "Report of the Alberta Commissioner," mimeographed (Calgary, Alberta, 1977), p. 20. Table officers are executive officers directly elected by the party convention.

authority. Since Senator Graham's influence at the PMO was not markedly better than Senator Molgat's had been, there was little for the table officers on the national executive, for the national director's staff, or indeed for the party activists around the country to do but sit back and watch how the prime minister and his entourage performed as "their" government.

The leader-dominated party of the late 1970s left a considerable, though secondary, role to the parliamentary party. The normal power the prime minister exercised over Parliament kept his caucus generally acquiescent, although on several occasions in 1977, when the caucus developed its own consensus in revolt against the cabinet, it managed to secure changes in proposed revisions to legislation on unemployment insurance, immigration, and electronic eavesdropping.[20] In exceptional circumstances the caucus could achieve a positive success beyond these examples of reactive responses to cabinet programs. The caucus committee on industrial policy, for instance, which convened some twenty-five M.P.s for weekly meetings over a period of a year and a half, brought enough pressure to bear on the cabinet to move it in the direction of an industrial strategy for the country. The committee's proposal, a major reorganization of the economic ministries, was adopted under the umbrella title of the Board of Economic Development late in 1978.[21] Such success was exceptional. In the main M.P.s kept learning the old lesson of parliamentary politics: black sheep don't get ahead. Those independent-minded backbenchers who dared to express their own thoughts and cross swords with their leader demonstrated by their exclusion from the cabinet how the ministers of the Trudeau government had been politically castrated. Tired from being shifted too frequently to head different departments, the cabinet ministers seemed reduced to what one former national director of the party tartly called mere "salesmen of programs devised elsewhere."[22]

With its supporters' enthusiasm low, the caucus kept quiescent, and the cabinet drained of any surviving strength, the government stumbled on toward the end of its mandate, deciding its actions less by long-term strategy than by tactics devoted to short-term headlines. The national party executive had long since abandoned any pretense that it was interested in ideas or policy, while the parallel structure of the campaign committee, chaired for English Canada by Keith Davey

---

[20] Saywell, *Canadian Annual Review: 1977*, pp. 11, 12, 18.

[21] Interview with Martin O'Connell, July 1979.

[22] Blair Williams, "The Transformation of the Federal Cabinet under P. E. Trudeau" (Paper presented to the Canadian Political Science Association, May 30, 1979), mimeographed, p. 30.

and for Quebec by Marc Lalonde, held the reins of what remained of party power in its hands. Any doubt that the Liberals had become a clique dominated by its leader and his entourage was finally removed in the months leading up to the 1979 election, when the campaign committee failed to impose itself on its leader either in the planning or in the execution of the campaign.

How the Campaign Organization Failed to Save the Situation

The 1974 campaign had demonstrated how successfully this federal, binational, transcontinental party could be run by a small cadre of dedicated and experienced amateurs in conjunction with the leader and cabinet of the parliamentary wing. The 1975 party convention showed, however, that the campaign cadre was not to obtain control of the party by having the chairman of the campaign committee become chief executive officer of the party. Instead, party power shifted toward the leader with the absorption of Jim Coutts as principal secretary in the Prime Minister's Office, and the cadre became gradually more isolated from the leader.

The rising Liberal fortunes recorded by the Gallup poll brought the cadre to a significant watershed in its relationship with the leader. Conscious that Trudeau's popularity was as volatile as the Canadian dollar, knowing that his resurrection from plunging lows in 1976 had come less from long-term policies than from a chance event—the previous November's election of a separatist government in Quebec under René Lévesque, which had revalidated Trudeau's claim to stand for national unity—the reconstituted national campaign committee pressed for a fall campaign. National campaign cochairman Keith Davey was bullish by the summer of 1977, all the more since the party's pollster, Martin Goldfarb, warned that the Liberals' lead would be unlikely to last for more than six months.[23]

Although policy materials were prepared for a fall election, few in the Liberal caucus were eager to throw themselves into two months of campaigning after just three years in office. In the end it was Trudeau himself who rejected the plan for a fall campaign. That he had valid personal reasons (he had not recovered his equilibrium fol-

---

[23] The following analysis is based on several dozen interviews conducted in person and by long-distance telephone with candidates, senior members of the national campaign committee, staff officers in the Prime Minister's Office, provincial campaign committee chairmen, and personnel across the country. The interviews were conducted over the summer following the May 22 election. Requests for confidentiality dictate that precise attributions of information be dispensed with.

lowing his wife's banner-headline escapades as Canada's most famous runaway wife) is not the point here. Nor is it germane that hindsight shows this procrastination pronounced the death sentence on his government, a sentence that neither brilliant tactics by the principal secretary nor repeated gaffes by the leader of the opposition could reverse. Trudeau's rejection of his party experts' advice to call an election while his popularity was at a peak meant that the power of the cadre had waned even in campaign-strategy making, where it had enjoyed supremacy during the previous minority government. It was as if Trudeau, the champion thoroughbred, had thrown off his rider, determined to leave his jockey back in the stables along with his other attendants. The seasoned team of experts—professionals like Keith Davey, senator, and Martin Goldfarb, market researcher; volunteers like Jerry Grafstein, advertising coordinator, and Torrance Wylie, party financial agent—saw their influence diminish from this point. Their former campaign colleague Jim Coutts changed, in their words, "from one of Us to one of Them," demanding loyalty and complete faith from the campaign cadre, dismissing dissent, reducing the give-and-take of campaign committee meetings, blocking access to the prime minister so that even this inner elite felt cut off from participation in formulating strategy for the eventual campaign.

The party's table officers continued to meet as the national executive, and Coutts would occasionally attend to "stroke their egos." The campaign committee met regularly throughout the rest of 1977 and 1978, debating the pros and cons of every suggested election date. The political cabinet met regularly on Tuesday mornings. The prime minister continued to meet with the key players of his party in the ridings and the regions during his forays outside Ottawa. Yet despite the appearance of a cadre party in operation, the top members of the inner elite themselves felt that the party process, in the words of one of them, was "absolutely nil . . . the oxygen to the party leader had been cut off." Just as the cabinet committee system had led to a concentration and then constipation of policy making in the office of the prime minister, so the assumption by the leader's office of executive authority over campaign planning led to a paralysis of political strategy. The leader's professionals may have been admirably skilled in their preparation of schedules and policy material for campaigns expected first in the spring, then the fall of 1978, but they had taken over from the party cadre the command functions for which the talents of that inner party elite had been best suited.

When the writs were eventually issued for the dissolution of Parliament, the Liberal campaign showed time after time how the party's absorption by its own leader had changed what was its major asset into its chief liability. Trudeau was the first among unequals, the captain of a team with neither a seasoned first string to support him in defense nor an energetic line of rookies to give power to his offense. If few cabinet ministers shared the leader's speaking chores of the election campaign, it was because the best and the brightest of them had left in some manner, honorable or dishonorable, over the previous five years. Herb Gray and Robert Stanbury had been dropped from the cabinet shortly after the 1974 election, Tony Abbot had been demoted in 1977, and Joseph Guay had been "promoted" to the Senate. Francis Fox, John Munro, and André Ouellet had tendered their resignations under clouds of their own making. Bud Drury, Donald Macdonald, Ron Basford, Mitchell Sharp, Jean-Pierre Goyer, and Joe Greene had retired from politics during the life of the Parliament. Bryce Mackasey, John Turner, James Richardson, and Jean Marchand had resigned in protest or anger. Of the seventeen, Ouellet was brought back into the cabinet after what many felt an unduly short stay on the back benches; Gray, Abbot, and Fox stayed in the caucus to fight the next election, leaving thirteen important gaps.

Unfortunately for the new candidates, coaxed into the limelight by the party's talent scouts, the flow of public anger at Trudeau and the Liberal party was so great that, when fifteen by-elections were called for October 16, 1978 (in lieu of a general election, which the Liberals knew they would lose decisively at that time), the would-be stars, who had been billed as the party's great hope for cabinet and even leadership material, went down to ignominious defeat. In Toronto, where anti-Liberal hatred burned strongest, the rout was complete: the Liberals lost all four of the ridings they had held. Of more psychological importance was the loss of the two novice "big name" candidates, Doris Anderson, former editor of the national magazine *Chatelaine*, and John Evans, former president of the prestige-laden University of Toronto. That two strong city hall incumbents—the mayor of Scarborough, Paul Cosgrove, and the budget chief of the Toronto city council, Art Eggleton—could lose what had looked like sure seats showed how intense was the antigovernment mood in metropolitan Toronto. Across English Canada, the Liberals had lost six seats to the Conservatives, who had retained possession of four. Only in Quebec did the Liberals do well, winning Claude Wagner's vacated seat from the Conservatives, keeping Bud Drury's Westmount, and reducing the Créditiste lead in Lotbinière.

Such gains in French Canada were no help to the morale of the other candidates who had been lined up by the Grits to contest ridings held by opposition parties. The minielection of October 16,

1978, had been a crushing blow, making it evident to many an aspirant that the Liberals were engaged in an uphill if not hopeless fight. As the tacticians in the Prime Minister's Office scanned the political horizon, consulting the poll tables and watching for the perfect wave on which they could ride to one more lucky victory, many candidates abandoned the quest. Candidate after candidate stepped down, stoutly claiming they believed the Liberals would win but, alas, they had to forgo victory for reasons of professional advancement or business exigency (taking over a McDonald's franchise for the candidate in Northumberland; taking over a large American corporation for Maurice Strong, candidate in Scarborough Centre). By the spring of 1979 the Ontario farm team had been decimated by the premature resignation of fourteen of its rookie nominees.[24] As late as March 1, eighteen ridings in Ontario remained without a candidate despite the best efforts of the campaign organization.

The Campaign Structure. A federal party's campaign structure is an impressive but peculiar institution. It is informal and does not enjoy the constitutional legitimacy of the party's formal structure, to which it is a parallel, less visible, but more powerful organism. Short-lived though a campaign organization may be, it operates on an impressively large scale, spending some $4 million in the space of two months' campaigning ($3.9 million in 1979, $4.1 million in 1980)—the equivalent of a corporation with an annual turnover of $24 million. The structure of a party campaign organization is partially determined by the federal nature of the political system, partially imposed by law (for instance, the Election Expenses Act, which establishes the period for advertising and sets limits to each party's expenditures), partially established by precedents and the experience of previous campaigns, and partially improvised by the response of those in charge to the problems and crises that arise. A campaign organization is idiosyncratic: its legitimacy lasts for just eight weeks, during which it is largely autonomous and quite powerful, controlling the politicians who normally control the party and deciding the fate of hundreds of politicians front-stage and back. The decision structure is essentially authoritarian, power deriving from the party leader, who appoints the campaign cochairmen, who in turn appoint their staff. In the battlelike tension of the campaign atmosphere, in the secrecy of its strategic planning, in the war-game nature of its tactical execution, the campaign organization is like a military opera-

[24] Data derived from Office of the Prime Minister, "Ontario Riding Histories," mimeographed (March 1979, n.p.), kindly lent to the author by Colin Kenny.

tion whose purpose is to implement a battle plan and respond to daily crises.

No two campaign organizations are identical. Even if their major features are similar from one campaign to another, the peculiar chemistry of the relationship between the key players can make or break the organization's effectiveness. The Liberals' 1979 organization was considered technically excellent even by disaffected leading figures in the party who were extremely critical of the campaign.

The national campaign committee was the visible supreme body of the organization. It was chaired not by the party leader but by the campaign cochairmen, Senator Keith Davey and Marc Lalonde, minister of justice. Its membership consisted of the eleven chairmen of the provincial and territorial campaign committees together with the party's national director, president, and financial agent and Jim Coutts, the leader's principal secretary. Although it met some sixteen times over the two years leading up to the campaign and twice during the campaign itself, it was not the effective strategy-making body for the campaign. The decision-making functions had been absorbed by the PMO, which left the national campaign committee with little more than a reporting and endorsing function. During the campaign itself a smaller group, generally consisting of Coutts, Davey, and Lalonde, would meet on Sunday afternoons at the prime minister's residence to review campaign strategy and decide tactics for the week ahead. For the remaining chief players of the campaign—those in charge of planning the leader's tour, writing the speeches, making the commercials, polling the public, answering the needs of candidates, executing the campaign in each province—a feeling of alienation from the central strategy making became a major irritant. "There was no exchange, no debate, no input to be made," one complained. Below this command level the campaign structure operated on three levels: national campaign operations, binational campaign functions, and provincial campaign coordination.

National Campaign Operations. There were four principal centers of activity in the national campaign: the leader's tour, the leader's office, the national party office, and the coordination of fund raising.

The leader's tour. What turns an election campaign into an organizational nightmare is the fact that the party leader, who is de jure commander in chief, and his principal adviser, who is generally de facto commander in chief, are isolated from the party's operations centers for the bulk of the campaign, traveling by airplane, train, or bus to a demanding itinerary, yet requiring a continual flow of intelligence from headquarters and a continual supply of fresh speeches and, at the same time, having to make decisions and issue commands to the key players in the campaign in the national and provincial capitals across the country. The pressures and tensions are understandably enormous. The tour is organized primarily to generate favorable news for the national television, radio, and press as well as for the local media in each region visited by the leader. Since reporters continually comment on the quality of the leader's events—whether they were well or poorly attended, by sympathetic or hostile crowds, in interesting or boring locations—a crucial component of the leader's tour is the "advancing," the planning and organization of the events in each town visited by the leader. In 1979 three advance men prepared events in the western provinces, a team of eight to ten worked in Ontario, and two to three people "advanced" in the Atlantic provinces, Quebec events being organized independently by the Quebec campaign committee. Because the nature of campaign news reporting is determined in some degree by the capricious humor of the reporters who accompany the leader on his tour, catering to the needs of the boys on the bus is a further priority, requiring in 1979 half a dozen people to handle baggage, look after hotel accommodations, provide entertainment, and generally coddle the press following the leader. An executive assistant ministered to the leader's personal needs and maintained contact several times a day with the leader's office in Ottawa, where the advance men's work was coordinated and the speeches were drafted. Apart from Pierre Trudeau himself, the key personage on the tour was his principal secretary, Jim Coutts, who acted as master strategist, planner, and tactician. He was kept busy assessing the developing political situation, checking with Ottawa and Keith Davey as often as phone communication permitted, rewriting draft speeches that arrived a few hours before their scheduled delivery, advising the prime minister about a speech beforehand, reviewing the situation with him at the end of the day, acting as his buffer with the press in the back of the plane, reporting to the weekly strategy meeting in Ottawa on Sundays, and taking a hand in all the other major decisions that had to be made day by day. The aide-de-camp of the 1974 campaign who had become principal secretary in 1975 was, by 1979, the most powerful figure in the campaign, with more weight than both national campaign co-chairmen combined.

The leader's office. The organizational base of Coutts's power was the Prime Minister's Office, which had planned the major aspects of the campaign and now acted as the central command. It was here that the policies for the campaign had been prepared for cabinet approval and were drafted into speeches by a team of four Anglophone and two Francophone speech writers under the command of Tom Axworthy, chief policy adviser in the PMO. It was here too that the leader's tour had been planned in advance almost to the hour by Colin Kenny. The leader was to spend six days in British Columbia, five in the Prairies, ten and a half in Ontario, seven in Quebec, and five and a half in the Atlantic provinces, five and a half being allowed for travel time and fifteen days "off" to attend to government business and his children on weekends and over Easter. Working ten to fifteen days in advance of the events, Geoff O'Brian lived on the telephone, planning and coordinating events with the teams of advance men across the country.

The national party office. Dwarfed by the eighty persons in the PMO, the staff of two dozen in the office of the Liberal party of Canada handled a less glamorous job, providing material for the party's other 281 candidates. In conjunction with the caucus research bureau, it produced a "Briefing Book on Issues and Policies," a looseleaf binder that gave the candidates a compact defense of the government's record in 139 pages, a defense that did not once mention Liberalism, principle, or even, apart from the cover page, the Liberal party. The national party office circulated answers prepared by Philip Deane Gigantes in the caucus research bureau to all imaginable hostile and neutral questions. As the campaign proceeded, the communications staff sent copies of the leader's main speeches to the candidates along with a dozen "Campaign '79 Bulletins" with selected data designed to keep up candidates' morale and furnish them ammunition for their speeches and debates. A brochure defending the government's record, *Our Economy Second to None,* was produced and printed for candidates' use in the ridings. Press releases were drafted and issued to the House of Commons press gallery to keep journalists in the capital informed of the leader's movements and any ministerial engagements. Apart from producing information for candidates, the national party office received demands for information from candidates through their provincial campaign headquarters, with which the national office was linked by telex. These queries would be relayed to government departments or the caucus research bureau for answers, which would then be telexed back to the provincial office.

Fund raising. Under the aegis of the new Election Expenses Act, which was for the first time governing the raising and spending of party money in an election campaign, a Federal Liberal Agency of

Canada had been established with Torrance Wylie, former national director of the party, as chairman. In conjunction with the treasury committee, which was responsible for raising the bulk of the money from business, and the national campaign committee, which had to agree on how much money was to be spent in each province, Wylie established a campaign budget of $3.9 million—somewhat below the $4.5 million limit established by the act. Each of the four western provinces had its budget approved by Wylie and was responsible for raising its own money from business contributions and by assigning levies on the refunds with which the candidates would be reimbursed by the chief electoral officer. The Maritime provinces were also self-financed, although they did not make a levy on the candidates. For Newfoundland, Yukon, and the Northwest Territories, the national campaign contributed small amounts. The Ontario, Quebec, and national campaigns were treated as one package for budgeting purposes, thus reducing the previous financial autonomy of the Quebec campaign. The treasury committee, which was responsible for the bulk of the party's fund raising from big business in each province, met in Ottawa twice during the campaign to report on progress made and assess the problems of meeting the financial targets. Wylie himself was connected with the campaign structure formally as a member of the national campaign committee, informally by regular communication with the Prime Minister's Office.

Binational Campaign Functions. Some $2.4 million, or 62 percent of the campaign budget, was spent on advertising, an activity traditionally divided between a Francophone agency, BCP Publicité, in Montreal and an Anglophone communications group in Toronto, where an umbrella agency, Red Leaf Communications, under party activist Jerry Grafstein made the commercials and prepared the free-time broadcasting allowed by the various radio and television national networks (see table 6–1). Provincial campaign chairmen and local candidates were free to do their own advertising if they could afford it from their own budgets. Those who were unhappy with the national English-language advertising campaign did just that. In Alberta, for instance, where the word "Liberal" is almost obscene, the provincial campaign committee placed a series of full-page ads headed "And now a good word from the 'bad guys' in this election." The Manitoba committee also developed a provincial advertising campaign to exploit the growing hostility towards the Conservative government of Sterling Lyon.

In contrast to the English-language advertising, which was centrally prepared in Toronto for the whole of English Canada independ-

171

TABLE 6–1

DISTRIBUTION OF LIBERAL ADVERTISING DOLLARS, 1979 CAMPAIGN

| Medium | Paid by National Campaign | | Paid by Provinces | Total |
	Quebec	Rest of Canada		
Television	282,000	932,000	81,000	1,295,000
Radio	125,000	369,000	69,000	563,000
Print	240,000	93,000	243,000	576,000
Total	647,000	1,394,000	393,000	2,434,000

SOURCE: Torrance Wylie, Federal Liberal Agency of Canada.

ently of the provincial campaign committees, the French-language advertising was created as an integral part of the Quebec campaign committee's operation. In further contrast to the uphill struggle in English Canada, Quebec Liberals knew they were running a winning campaign. From 51 percent of the votes and 84 percent of the seats in 1974, they were gaining ground. By May 22 they had 60 percent of the vote and 89 percent of the seats. Their slogan, "Parle fort Québec avec Trudeau et tout le Canada" [Speak up, Quebec, with Trudeau and the whole of Canada], expressed the self-confidence of the Quebec Liberals. The advertising, created as usual by Jacques Bouchard, emphasized the theme of national unity and the positive accomplishments on Trudeau's balance sheet after eleven years in power—themes that could be used for the French-speaking ridings of New Brunswick and the English-speaking ridings of Montreal where Trudeau and the Liberals were still unqualified electoral assets.

Provincial Campaign Coordination. The organizational framework for the Quebec campaign was bicephalous. Marc Lalonde, the national cochairman, was chairman of the Quebec campaign committee responsible for overall strategy, while André Ouellet acted as chief organizer in charge of the nuts-and-bolts operation of this superb electoral machine. In the Liberal party of Canada's Quebec office, eight to ten people looked after public relations while others coordinated ministerial visits to marginal ridings. A policy committee of six to eight volunteers met every evening and drafted material that a full-time staff person sent out daily to the candidates. For the few visits to Quebec of the prime minister, the Montreal office provided the advance work.

With ten provincial and territorial campaigns to coordinate, the function of the English national cochairman, Keith Davey, was both more complex and more demanding. From his office in the Senate, he maintained daily phone contact with each provincial campaign. The Newfoundland Liberals were struggling to hold onto their four of the province's seven seats against an upsurge of the NDP. In Nova Scotia, where the Liberals held but two of the eleven seats, the NDP was also threatening to deprive them of any gains. The Liberals' situation in New Brunswick was stronger: they held six of the ten seats and had a fourteen-percentage-point lead over the Conservatives that they were trying to maintain. In Prince Edward Island, on the other hand, they were in danger of losing the one seat they held. The island federal Liberals' predicament was worsened by the sudden call of a provincial election campaign by the local Liberal government, which proceeded to lose, thus wiping the Liberal party off the country's provincial government map.

In the West the Liberals were the second party in each province in the 1974 election and third in the Yukon and Northwest Territories. By election day they had been displaced by the NDP in British Columbia, where they managed to hold but one seat with a margin of fifteen votes after a campaign marked by considerable tension within the provincial campaign committee; in Saskatchewan they fell by nine percentage points and lost their three seats; in Manitoba they held two seats but fell by four percentage points in the popular vote. Only in Alberta did they hold second place ahead of the NDP—little cause for satisfaction since this represented but 22 percent of the vote and zero seats once again.

In Ontario, where the Liberals had won fifty-five of the eighty-eight seats in 1974 with a ten-percentage-point lead in the vote, they were now in danger of losing twenty-five to thirty seats since they were ten percentage points behind in the polls. It was understandable that Keith Davey devoted a disproportionate amount of his time to liaison with the Ontario campaign committee. His choice of a campaign chairman had been controversial. Not only had Royce Frith not been actively involved in politics for many years; he was paid in advance for his services by being appointed to the Senate before undertaking the job, a fact that raised as many party eyebrows as did his old-fashioned managerial style. As in the 1974 campaign, Davey attended the weekly meetings of the crucial Ontario committee. More controversial still was the relationship between the PMO and the Ontario committee. The leader had ten and a half days of campaigning scheduled for this pivotal province, and Colin Kenny, the officer in the PMO responsible for Ontario, was determined that the prime minister's Ontario events should work flawlessly. Back in 1977, a year and a half before the actual event, Kenny had decided that the campaign should open in Earlton, Ontario. He knew, in the words of a colleague in the Prime Minister's Office, that they could "close down the whole town" for Trudeau. Though it was a small place, known to the rest of Canada mainly because its temperatures were forecast daily on Environment Canada's weather reports, Kenny could be sure of a "big event." Ensuring that the prime minister always had big events with the appropriate school bands, enthusiastic handmade signs waved by normal-looking youngsters, and hecklers muted by well-drilled, soft-arm ushers was Colin Kenny's main function. Kenny, the "advance man's advance man," as insiders admiringly called him, had been recruiting his eleven blitz captains and his 300 volunteers for two years. He had selected sites and chosen ridings that could perform according to his criteria; that is, provide good television coverage for the prime minister and give him three, four, or five stages every day to use as platforms for his policy message. Once selected, the ridings had been conditioned: campaign colleges were held and candidates impressed with the poll data showing that the prime minister was more popular than the party and the party more popular than the candidates. For most candidates Trudeau's visit to their ridings offered the sole chance of the campaign to get their pictures and names on the front page of the local papers. Ridings were played off against each other, being encouraged to bid for a prime ministerial visit: if one constituency could promise two bands and a turnout of 400 bodies while another could marshal three bands and 600, Trudeau would go to the latter. No matter if the Liberal loyalists in the former riding were left angry and shaken, many days of organization suddenly came to naught. The ever-present crowds in the background of the television screen on the nightly news were a tribute to the organizational power of Kenny and the advance men. As one provincial campaign chairman complained, the PMO was more interested in sticking to its schedule than in winning votes.

On details of scheduling, the PMO ran roughshod over the local campaign committees, often changing at the last minute plans that had been devotedly and laboriously made. The message was always the same: the party people were lucky to have the prime minister grace their city or riding with his presence. The Ontario blitz bus that brought a squad of youth into an auditorium before Trudeau spoke to fill up the front-row seats and form a buffer between the prime minister and the potential hecklers symbolized the campaign's compulsion for organizational perfection and its domination by the leader's clique.

Tension between the Prime Minister's Office and the Ontario ridings was but one of the problems resulting from this complex organization with its enormous communications problems. Overlapping authority was bound to create conflicts. When Jerry Grafstein requested another hour of the leader's time to film commercials after one shooting had failed, he was refused: Kenny's schedule took precedence over the production of the ads. Grafstein was a member of the national campaign committee, but the Prime Minister's Office had control of his master's voice. There was tension between the Quebec campaign and the Prime Minister's Office since Quebec's strategy called for Trudeau to spend his time working in marginal seats. The poor crowds that turned out at his Quebec meetings contrasted with the thousands who were organized for his events in English Canada. As reported in the national media, Trudeau's apparently poor reception in Quebec contradicted the Liberals' image of superiority in that province. The Prime Minister's Office was not amused. When it arbitrarily canceled the leader's appearance on a popular Winnipeg talk show, an event that Lloyd Axworthy had spent many days setting up, Axworthy was furious. As the star candidate in Manitoba and chairman of the campaign committee, he was able to use his weight, threatening to resign if Trudeau did not appear. In this case, the Prime Minister's Office backed down, and the talk show went on the air with the prime minister. Considering the communications difficulties, the decision bottlenecks, and the personality conflicts that are endemic to such an ungainly, crisis-centered organization, most Liberal insiders felt the campaign organization to have been technically excellent. Three, four, or five stages surrounded by applauding partisans were made available to the leader every day. But when the leader's message was delivered, it turned out day after day to be intellectually bankrupt.

For those who had observed the shift of power from the party's cadre to the prime ministerial clique, it came as no surprise that deciding policy for the campaign had not come under the aegis of Keith Davey, as it had in 1974, but had become part of the speech-making functions of the PMO. While it was not startling that the policy function should also have been absorbed by the party leader's office, opponents, observers, and supporters alike were surprised when Trudeau's campaign turned out to be so empty of coherent content. At the press conference with which he launched his campaign, Trudeau mentioned a "decade of development" for Canada, as if this slogan would be the framework for a series of policies to be announced as the campaign progressed; the phrase was not to be heard of again. Energy formed the major issue of Trudeau's first two weeks on the hustings, but even with news reports of lines forming at California gas stations and with Petrocanada's successes in the energy field confounding the Conservatives' commitment to its abolition, Trudeau had difficulty establishing in his speeches that only the retention of a federal Liberal government would save the country from a fuel crisis. The Liberals' defense of a strong central government as a crucial component of federalism was different from the Conservatives' position, but the theme of national unity was not presented to the public in a meaningful way. Although the Liberals had used policy announcements to excellent effect in 1974, Mr. Trudeau's use of policy announcements was ineffective in 1979. In Nova Scotia Trudeau proposed an employee stock-ownership incentive plan, but this hesitant gesture in the direction of capitalist democracy in the work place was left to dangle as nothing more than a bizarre memory. An Agriculture Export Corporation was announced hurriedly in Vancouver on April 23 by the prime minister and the minister of agriculture, who had been rushed out to British Columbia to give the notion some weight and to divert press attention from Trudeau's indiscretion the previous week about clinging to power even if defeated. As for actual promises that the voter could associate with a new Liberal government, there was little beyond a pledge to reform the pension system. The promised changes won the approval of pension fund experts but would need provincial agreement after prolonged negotiation and in any case went over the heads of most observers. In her form letter sent to citizens who requested copies of the Liberals' platform, Audrey Gill, the communications coordinator in the Liberal party's federal office, wrote:

> As you may have noticed by now, Mr. Trudeau is not conducting a campaign of "promises" in the traditional sense of promising to spend the taxpayers' money on big government programs. He is, on the contrary, talking about the larger issues that face the country at this time, and how the Liberal government would deal with them. Enclosed are copies of the "announcements" he has made. They are, in some cases, expansions or further details on existing programs; in other cases they are new programs or proposals for action where the provinces are involved (e.g. pensions). They could not, taken together, be called a "platform."[25]

[25] Audrey Gill, "Memorandum," mimeographed, May 8, 1979.

It is true that the Liberals had failed to keep the promises made in the 1974 campaign and that they knew the press corps was wary of being manipulated again into uncritical reporting of government party announcements. It is also true that Trudeau felt his options limited by his impulsive promise of August 1978 to cut $2 billion from the federal budget to reduce the alarming growth of the government's deficit. Nevertheless it is remarkable that this seasoned campaigner could not manage to establish a consistent mood for his appeal to the public—if only a mood of restraint, as the one responsible position to take at a time when the growth of big government had to be contained in order to grapple with inflation.

During the previous five years, the prime minister and the team he had chosen to work for him had been responsible for seriously confusing the public image of the Liberal government (attacking, then imposing, wage and price controls; fighting for, then questioning, the abolition of capital punishment; expanding, then constraining, government expenditures). Now the same team whose modus operandi in government had approached a state of policy paralysis was caught in the contradictions of its own making. These contradictions jumped from the page of the campaign cochairman's strategy document. On the one hand, the prime minister was to talk growth: "He will describe new economic policies which will strengthen the country by strengthening the regional economies; projects which will stimulate the economy." On the other hand, he was to talk retrenchment: "Canadians want responsible government which will end the free rides and give Canadians their money's worth for their tax dollars—more bang for their tax buck." Even in the subliminal question of the campaign's mood, Trudeau was caught in the skeins of his own contradictions. His primary appeal was pitched to the need for strong leadership to preserve national unity. This meant "Prime Minister Trudeau will reassure Canadians about our future together, and about our potential for economic growth." Boosting the country's confidence was to be the mood message. "If at the end of sixty days Canadians are more optimistic than pessimistic about the country's prospects . . . the government will be returned. Ours must be a campaign that builds confidence." At the same time Trudeau had to reinforce Canadians' fear of separatism since his issue of national unity was primarily the fight against Quebec's independence. "Because Canadians worry more about the economy than about unity it is important that we consistently point out that the growth in the Canadian economy is inextricably linked with the uncertainty about separation. The threat of Quebec separating is harmful both spiritually and economically to all Caadians." [26] If the Trudeau campaign aimed simultaneously to build confidence and to increase insecurity, it is not surprising that it failed to generate a coherent message that could correct the confused image of the outgoing government.

The apparent exception to this record of ambivalence was the Liberal party's refusal to adopt as its own the Conservatives' promise to allow property taxes and mortgage interest to be deducted from taxable income. Again there were sound reasons for this stand. The minister of finance, whose credibility had been shaken by the cutbacks of the previous August, refused to accept the idea; his officials feared its impact on the government deficit and on the value of the Canadian dollar. Many among the progressives in the party opposed the plan because of its regressive bias in favor of the well-to-do who already owned homes and had relatively comfortable incomes. Party conventions had regularly repulsed efforts to pass resolutions calling for the deductibility of mortgage interest. On the other hand, the weight of the party cadre favored some satisfactory response. The caucus had pressed for an alternative scheme that was not regressive but included relief for tenants. Martin Goldfarb, the party pollster, insisted that the government had to counter the strong appeal that the Conservatives' policy had for middle-class voters. The campaign cochairman and his intimates felt that a Liberal shelter plan was crucial to their meager chances for success. Once again the cadre lost out to the leader. The Liberal response was to be a "nonresponse." [27] The party would have to sink with its leader just as firmly—and just as temporarily—opposed to the Conservatives' major policy as he had been in 1974. It is small wonder that, when Trudeau shouted at his huge audience in Maple Leaf Gardens, "We are the party with the policies," he did not manage to bring even these enthusiastic listeners to their feet.

"It will be imperative for all of us—the Prime Minister, Ministers, candidates, and every last worker to say the same thing, in the same way, at the same time. This is how we maximize impact. Timing will be an essential ingredient of our campaign. Please follow the Prime Minister's lead." Thus spoke the Davey strategy document to the candidates. Though they were instructed to follow their leader, the candidates received few cues to guide their own campaigns. Since election legislation prohibited advertising until the last four weeks of the campaign, candidates had to rely on the news media to pro-

[26] Keith Davey, "Memorandum to All Liberal Candidates," mimeographed, March 29, 1979.

[27] "Nonresponse" was the word used by Pierre Trudeau in an interview with the author, July 21, 1979.

vide their party's national campaign message to their ridings. As Trudeau's campaign was based on the premise that his feistiness —rather than a concrete platform—would create the news, the message received by Liberal candidates in the ridings was more likely to be the news of an insult that Trudeau had hurled at a heckler than the report of an attractive program that the Liberals were offering. "What campaign?" responded one successful Liberal candidate in Newfoundland when asked about the impact in his riding of the national campaign. "I felt stark naked," said another successful new candidate from metropolitan Toronto who, not knowing what to say when asked at all-candidates meetings about Liberal policies, made up his own version on the spot. The federal party office mailed out documents to candidates every week to give them the basic outline of Trudeau's major announcements, but Ontario candidates' requests to the provincial campaign headquarters in Toronto for information indicated, according to the Ontario policy chairman, that "obviously the public asks questions about our policy announcements well before our candidates get any information. Although Audrey Gill is doing a good job of getting information out, still many of the calls indicate that our candidates are being left behind in the information flow. (What happened to the Great Plans for Telex?)"[28] Telex messages were indeed sent to candidates from the national party office, but the speed of their transmission was not an index of the importance of their contents.

> *Item.* May 12 from Keith Davey: "I spent the morning with the Prime Minister. He is in great shape. We are going to win."
>
> *Item.* May 16 from Keith Davey: "Our campaign is cresting at exactly the right moment."
>
> *Item.* May 20 Mini Bulletin: "Heard this one? Question: What do you do if Clark throws a pin at you? Answer: Run, because he's got a grenade in his mouth."

Joe Clark jokes, selected quotations from the press, laundered poll data, anti-Tory items: such vapid material was hardly the kind of communication to help the party's 281 candidates follow the prime minister's lead and "say the same thing, in the same way, at the same time." An exception to this treatment of the candidates as sad sheep was the Ontario policy committee, which sent out thirteen policy bulletins of its own with substantial analysis and data on such subjects as labor force statistics, youth unemployment, abortion law, the dollar, energy, and small business policy. Many of

[28] Lorna Marsden, "Memorandum," mimeographed, week of May 12, 1979.

these were written by Fred Lazar, a qualified economist. Even the best mailings to the candidates could do little to close the large gap that separated the leader from his candidates in the ridings. The lucky ones received a personal boost from a prime ministerial visit, an anointing, as it were, with the momentary presence of the leader. Apart from such fleeting contact, for which the candidate was expected to provide that "best event" platform for a prime ministerial clip on the national news, the candidates had no effective contact with their leader. Even on such an important question as the Tory promise to move the Canadian embassy in Israel from Tel Aviv to Jerusalem, the Toronto candidates who were directly affected by this move found Trudeau indifferent to their concerns and inaccessible to their pleas. They approached Jim Coutts, but Coutts reported back that Trudeau would neither budge nor listen to their case any more. The leader kept himself shielded from his party to the end. The advertising teams had nothing to use but Trudeau playing strong leader, ads that may have reinforced his image as the better leader but may equally have reinforced the public's anti-Trudeau feelings, as many party insiders feared. The lack of inspiring and unequivocal appeal from their leader left party activists confused. Party workers did not go door-to-door in their polls believing strongly in their leader, their party, and their policies. Old stalwarts were apparently no longer sure just why they were Liberal. The traditional Liberal voters had been given no reminder of the Liberal tradition to bring them back to the fold. The independent-minded who thought before they voted had been given no clear diagnosis of Canada's problems or blueprint that the Liberals undertook to implement if elected; nor had they gained a sense that a team of candidates was there ready to take office and govern competently. Only in one major respect had the Liberal campaign been successful. It had managed to make and keep Trudeau as the burning issue of the campaign.

"This election is about Canada, Prime Minister Trudeau and leadership—specifically which leader, the Prime Minister or Joe Clark, has the experience and ability necessary to make the tough decisions the times require—tough decisions to keep Canada together, strong and free."[29] Thus spoke the opening sentence of the strategy paper. Candidates reading Davey's strategy document learned that Trudeau was going to "reassure Canadians about our future together" and "describe new economic policies which will strengthen the country." In short the Liberal party would be relying on Pierre Trudeau, the brilliant campaigner of 1974, to save the bacon that he himself had

[29] Davey, "Memorandum," p. 1.

already burned. In 1974 Trudeau had been closely managed by his campaign team; although the 1979 command group comprised the same people for the most part, it was not at all the same body it had been in the heady days of the 1974 election—and not just because sideburns were grayer and scalps were balder. The relationships of personality and power had changed subtly but crucially. Jim Coutts, who had traveled with the leader in 1974 as second in command to Keith Davey, the campaign strategist, was now the more powerful of the two. As "political tactician," Coutts now had far more direct control over the campaign than Davey, the nominal campaign cochairman.[30] The chief strategist of 1974 was restricted to a secondary position in 1979 as coordinator with the provinces because of his less frequent access to the leader. Because there was nobody in the command structure who had both the perspective and the authority to impose a battle plan geared to the political realities outside Ottawa, Trudeau could repeat the error of his first majority government campaign in 1972. In 1979, as in 1972, he imposed his style as the strategy itself, his approach subject to modification in detail but not to alteration in principle by the entourage of political technicians who had learned over the previous years in office under his thrall to put tactics before strategy and intelligent obedience before independent judgment. Because the boys in the Prime Minister's Office knew they could catch the opposition leader off guard by calling the election a bit earlier than expected and because the Quebec caucus was putting pressure on Trudeau to issue the writs soon, lest Fabien Roy, the hastily anointed Créditiste leader, produce spontaneous combustion in the Beauce, the decision was made "to go" early. This decision was made even though Trudeau had promised his candidates they would not have to campaign in the slush of late winter and even though Keith Davey and his Toronto experts wanted to wait for a summer election, when the mood of the country could be expected to improve and the Liberals could have produced a shelter plan to answer the Tories' proposal of mortgage-interest deductibility. The truth was that there was no coherent strategy for the leader's approach to campaigning. The strategy document was the product of an uneasy compromise between the actual dictates of the man and the apparent needs of the campaign.

"Canadians associate leadership with toughness and intelligence —qualities which even the Prime Minister's critics acknowledge as his principal characteristics," read the Davey strategy memo on one

[30] "Political tactician" was the phrase Pierre Trudeau used in describing Jim Coutts to the author in an interview, July 21, 1979.

page, while on the next it forecast that "this campaign will demonstrate the Prime Minister's compassion and concern for ordinary Canadians."[31] The campaign actually demonstrated that Pierre Trudeau was a brilliant but erratic political performer who could alienate the public with harsh responses to hecklers (charging in Quebec that farmers were grumblers and shouting in British Columbia that those protesting unemployment should "get off their ass") just as easily as he could entrance an audience (in Vancouver) with his vision of Canada or impress a high school (in Toronto) with his clear command of the most delicate questions of public policy.

To overcome the press corps's longstanding suspicions and resentment of Trudeau, an open press policy had been decided on. In making Trudeau available to journalists, the strategy intended to contrast the seasoned incumbent prime minister, who could address a crowd without a note, face down hecklers with his own wit, and respond to unscreened questions without counsel, with Joe Clark, the closely controlled and carefully scripted aspirant. Although this bold campaign approach did point out the difference between the party leaders, it left Pierre Trudeau as the player prone to errors while Joe Clark managed not to make a serious political blunder. In the first week of the campaign, Trudeau fired a salvo at the provincial premiers to make his pitch for a strong federal government. But he did not restrict his attack to Premier Peter Lougheed, scapegoat of Canada's fuel price problem, whose Alberta held no prospective seats for the Liberals. In Ontario's capital city he included Premier William Davis in the ranks of the threats to national unity, thereby turning a previously neutral Conservative into one of the most effective campaigners at Joe Clark's side. Davis often received warmer responses at political meetings in Ontario than the federal party chief. During the fourth week of the campaign, in an informal conversation with television reporter Mark Phillips of the Canadian Broadcasting Corporation, Trudeau allowed himself to speculate that he might hold onto power as head of a minority government even if he lost by a few seats to Conservatives, thereby giving Clark the chance to tell his listeners that in the past Trudeau had ignored their views; now he was going to ignore their votes. For months and months Keith Davey and Jim Coutts had been keeping up morale among Liberal candidates by insisting that, however low the polls might show the party, Trudeau could save them because he was an unrivaled campaigner. Although undoubtedly no other politician could deliver such speeches without a note, Davey and Coutts had not considered in their calculations

[31] Davey, "Memorandum," pp. 3, 4.

the impact of personal stress on their leader. An intensely private politician who could not tolerate reports about the details of his family life, he was now subjected almost every day to excerpts in the press from his estranged wife's tastelessly revealing autobiography, *Beyond Reason*, or fragments from the still more outrageous elaborations that Margaret Trudeau was giving to interviewers as she promoted the newly released book in the United States. Election campaigns have always focused on the words and deeds of party leaders. This phenomenon has been reinforced by the concentration of television news on the personal and the colorful, so that the newsworthiness of chance comments by leaders in campaigns has been greatly magnified.[32] The Trudeau campaign further emphasized the newsworthiness of his rapier-sharp tongue when honed by his irritation and tension.

Because Trudeau *was* the Liberal campaign, national attention was given to his offhand remark on an open-line show that those who didn't consider national unity a crucial issue were "almost treasonous." No attempt was made to build up the image of Trudeau's team of experienced ministers or incoming new candidates, many of whom were of considerable stature. No efforts were made in the party's free broadcast time or its commercial advertising to appeal to the specifically Liberal identification of that strong plurality of Canadian voters who habitually supported the Grits but whose loyalty had been shaken by Trudeau's own performance. Instead the free-time programs replayed for half an hour at a time videotapes of Trudeau's public addresses in front of huge crowds, speeches that showed him shouting at the thousands in Maple Leaf Gardens, doing nothing to convey the impression that he was a politician with "compassion and concern for ordinary Canadians." The commercials showed Trudeau with Israeli Prime Minister Begin or on campaign platforms and never failed to close with the slogan to end all tautologies, "A Leader Must Be a Leader." "We must ask Canadians," the strategy paper urged, reviving John Turner's by then tired line from 1974, "to compare the Prime Minister not to the Almighty, but rather to the alternative." Apart from the televised debate among the three main party leaders—an event that gave a noticeable fillip to the Liberal campaign because viewers could directly contrast the verbal rigidity of Clark with the dramatic intellectual presence of Trudeau—the prime ministerial campaign managed less to invite comparisons with the opposition leader than to focus attention on the head of government. Trudeau was the issue of the campaign.

[32] Clarke et al., *Political Choice in Canada*, p. 280.

The fact that Maple Leaf Gardens was filled to the rafters two hours before Trudeau appeared for his rally there did not mean that the Liberals were winning Toronto. "Only one man could draw 10,000 people to the Toronto–Dominion Centre plaza," reported Michael Valpy in the clipped dramatic tones of CBC radio's "Sunday Morning." Trudeau was spontaneous, exciting, alive. Only he could "switch on Disco Toronto."[33] He was Canada's great political star, and voters turned out by the thousands to see him, even if their silent message was what an airplane trailed through the sky above the same rally: "GOOD-BYE PIERRE."

Through most of the campaign, Trudeau behaved almost as though he believed he was making his farewell to the public. He knew that the Conservatives had entered the campaign with such a lead in English Canada that only a disastrous performance by Clark or a flawless campaign by the Liberals could save him. He knew he was the party's chief asset, the one who could get candidates onto the front page of the regional newspapers, but he knew also that he was the Liberals' chief liability, the personification of the problems the public associated with the government, the symbol of "French power," the scapegoat for the angers and frustrations of the average Canadian. He was a tragic figure alone on stage after stage, talking to his audience as if he was himself scripting the lines for his approaching downfall. Never one to enjoy being managed by lesser minds, he set aside the texts that had been prepared for his introductory and concluding remarks in the three-leader debate, discarded the speech that his office had produced for his climactic appearance at Maple Leaf Gardens, and insisted that the last two weeks of the campaign be spent talking about the patriation of the constitution. Party polls might show that "national unity" was far down the list of issues thought crucial by the public outside his Quebec stronghold, but Pierre Elliott Trudeau wanted to be defeated—if defeat was unavoidable—on his issue, not that of his advisers.[34] In the last eight days of the campaign, provoked perhaps by his triumph in the direct encounter with Clark during the leaders' debate in the television studio, he seemed at last to want to win the campaign. He delivered passionate lectures on the national shame of Canada's not being able to amend its own constitution without approval from Westminster. He warned the public that "this is not the time to bring on the second string." While the Conservatives coasted for

---

[33] Michael Valpy, "Sunday Morning," CBC radio, May 20, 1979.

[34] "Vote for Trudeau, Support the Amending Formula," was the slogan proposed in despairing jest by one member of the Liberals' advertising group.

the last week secure in their lead, Trudeau, ever the political athlete, turned on a final spurt in the homestretch, racing to the last minute. On the evening of May 21, just hours before campaigning legally had to end, Pierre Trudeau appeared in the stands to watch the Montreal Canadiens win the Stanley Cup. Millions of viewers of Hockey Night in Canada saw the crowd at the Forum come to its feet in applause. To no avail. "When politicians," Christopher Lasch has written, "have no other aim than to sell their leadership to the public, they deprive themselves of intelligible standards by which to define the goals of specific policies or to evaluate success or failure."[35] Whether he was talking about the tired issue of the constitution or returning again and again to the need for strong central government, Trudeau appeared to have no idea to sell other than leadership as a blank check that he would himself fill in as he wished upon reelection. The leader no longer knew how to inspire his troops or command his public's loyalty. He had failed to convince the nation that this was indeed a historic campaign that would decide the future of the country.

Conclusion

On May 22, 1979, the Liberal party of Canada received 62 percent of the vote in Quebec and took sixty-seven of the province's seventy-five seats while the Conservatives fell from second to third place with 14 percent of the vote and two seats. Simultaneously, in the English-speaking provinces, Trudeau's support fell from 40 percent of the vote and 43 percent of the seats (eighty-one M.P.s) to 32 percent of the vote and 23 percent of the seats (forty-seven members). A large part of the public had expressed its hostility to or disappointment with the Liberal government. Surveys during the campaign had shown the Liberal vote to have softened. A poll conducted by Carleton University and the CBC in midcampaign showed that of those who had voted Liberal in 1974, only 57 percent remained faithful, 14 percent switching to the Conservatives and 6 percent to the NDP and 21 percent becoming undecided.[36] In metropolitan Toronto on the eve of the election, 23 percent of the 1974 Liberal voters had switched to the Conservatives, 9 percent to the NDP.[37] Surveyed by Gallup after the election, 37 percent of the citizenry felt that the May 22

---

[35] Christopher Lasch, *The Culture of Narcissism: American Life in an Age of Diminishing Expectations* (New York: Norton, 1978), p. 78.

[36] *Toronto Star*, April 24, 1979, p. A6. The n for this survey was 2,286.

[37] Michael J. Adams, "Metro Favors Liberals," *Sunday Sun* (Toronto), May 20, 1979, p. 41.

vote had meant it was time for a change, that the voters wanted something new and wanted to get rid of the Liberals; 16 percent felt it had been an anti-Trudeau vote, more personal than party.[38] Evidently the public had not felt that Canada was in such delicate shape that it could not afford to dismiss its government.

While the Liberals had, in the words of one insider, run a Tory campaign with Tory results, the Conservatives had run a Liberal-like campaign making substantial, newsworthy promises for every region. Their advertising had been strong, vitriolic, and effective. The mistakes they had made had not hurt them. In riding after riding they benefited from a flood of volunteers fervently working to throw out the Liberals, while their Grit counterparts were starved of workers. Difficult though it is to measure the impact of the Conservatives' campaign in general and their individual promises in particular, it is nevertheless striking that in those Ontario ridings where the proportion of homeowners with mortgages was 50 percent or more of the total households, the Liberal party lost 100 percent of its seats to the Conservatives; where the proportion of mortgage holders was 40 to 49 percent, they lost 69 percent of their seats to the Conservatives; in ridings with 30 to 39 percent homeowners with mortgages, they lost 42 percent of their seats; and in ridings with under 30 percent of homeowners with mortgages, they lost 26 percent of their seats to the Conservatives. Not only had the Conservatives' policy of allowing a proportion of interest paid on mortgages to be deductible from income tax been a highly salient issue; it had been clearly identified with the Conservatives. Although the NDP had finally advanced a scheme of its own to ease the impact of high mortgage payments, the Liberals had not managed to blunt the appeal of this Tory proposal to the broad middle class of English Canada. While Trudeau's technical knockout of Clark in the debate and his strong last week of campaigning may have denied the Conservatives a majority victory, the powerful impact of the mortgage plan may well have been the decisive factor in preventing the Liberals from salvaging a minority government position. Whatever the might-have-beens of the campaign, the Liberal party emerged on May 23 as the third party throughout the western provinces and the second party in Ontario and half of Atlantic Canada.

"The election was a defeat," conceded a member of Pierre Trudeau's staff. "But," he continued with the self-confidence that characterizes his party, "it was not a catastrophe." A sign on the wall of the PMO read "We'll Be Back" when Joe Clark's assistants moved into their new quarters in June. That line, which sounded like

[38] *Toronto Star*, July 7, 1979.

the arrogant overconfidence so long a hallmark of the Liberal government, was to prove prophetic. Only 273 days after May 22, the Liberals had defeated the vacillating government of Joe Clark, had recalled Pierre Trudeau from his attempted retirement as party leader, and had mounted a winning campaign with a clearly articulated and carefully executed strategy, so that by February 18, 1980, they were again in power with a majority.

Back in mid-1979 most observers had wondered whether several years in opposition would be enough for the Liberal party to renew itself—its leadership, its structures, and its grass-roots support. Some pundits quickly declared that the Liberal party was finished. When, after a mere nine months out of office, the man who had been its albatross brought it back to power, commentators presumed that the fourth Trudeau government would be a spent force with the same old leadership, the same old lack of purpose, and the same old passive rank and file. By the summer of 1981 Pierre Elliott Trudeau had confounded his most skeptical critics. Far from being rendered ineffectual by his promise to retire before another election, he had turned his government into an energetic and clearly directed regime. The prime minister himself had decided to take the lead in the international summitry concerning the North-South dialogue and had moved—after the Parti Québécois's failure to win its referendum on a mandate for sovereignty-association—to cut the Gordian knot of federal-provincial negotiations over the constitution by "patriating" the British North America Act regardless of provincial opposition. Furthermore, a new, more nationally conscious direction had been taken in other important policy domains. His energy minister and Quebec lieutenant, Marc Lalonde, launched a dramatic National Energy Program designed to "Canadianize" the vital oil and gas industries, which were still controlled by foreign, mainly American, corporations. Meanwhile his minister for industry, trade, and commerce, Herb Gray, was preparing an industrial strategy, long deemed the crucial prerequisite for restructuring Canada's troubled branch-plant economy according to a more self-sufficient and balanced model less dependent on the export of raw material staples. While the success of these initiatives remained to be proved by time, the new government showed enough resolve that commentators ready to write Pierre Trudeau's political obituary scrapped their gloomy assessments of the 1970s and waited to see what these new developments would bring.[39]

[39] One reassessment of Pierre Trudeau's significance in the light of his new nationalism can be found in James Laxer, *Canada's Economic Strategy* (Toronto: McClelland and Stewart, 1981).

The fact that these moves had been decided on in the Prime Minister's Office and the cabinet with no discernible input from its volunteer, extraparliamentary wing was significant for the Liberal party as an institution. It is true that a "platform committee" had been hastily assembled when the Clark government was defeated, and Trudeau's strategists felt they must make a symbolic gesture to indicate that the lay party was being involved in drafting policy material for the leader's campaign speeches. In the end, the hand-picked participants experienced considerable frustration when they discovered that they were not really being invited to participate in drafting an election platform but merely allowed to proffer advice for consideration by the strategy committee. The truth is that the volunteer wing had not blossomed during the party's months in the political wilderness.

Analysts of the Liberal party have observed "a cyclical pattern of decay and renewal; the decay coming after a number of years in power and the renewal prompted by electoral defeat . . . [when the] extra-parliamentary wing has subsequently become the source of new ideas and fresh faces."[40] Implicit is the questionable proposition that Roberto Michels's "iron law of oligarchy" is an accurate description of the Liberal organization's internal dynamic;[41] also, that there is an active, democratically motivated base to the party, a rank and file whose participatory energies are constrained by the oligarchs at the summit of the party structure. The reenergizing of the Liberals' old leadership and its success at finding a progressive direction for itself without going through a period of grass-roots resuscitation suggests that any resemblance between the Liberals and a European-style mass party is deceptive. This federal party can apparently transform itself without paying heed to the theory of cyclical, two-party democracy.

Seen in this perspective the 1979 campaign was the first phase of a two-round engagement. In the first round, Pierre Trudeau had tried to defend himself on his exposed right but had gone down to a technical knockout in the face of Joe Clark's dogged attack. When Clark tripped himself up, weaving around the political canvas with one policy change after another, and when the Liberals managed, by defeating the minority government, to precipitate a second electoral encounter, Trudeau was able to fight a cautious round, relying on his more comfortable left jab to dispatch an opponent who had already defeated himself in the eyes of the citizen referees.

[40] Joseph Wearing, *The L-Shaped Party: The Liberal Party of Canada, 1958-1980* (Toronto: McGraw-Hill, 1981), p. 235.
[41] Ibid., p. 249.

By February 18, 1980, it was obvious that the Liberal party of Canada was still the Liberal party of Pierre Trudeau. A year later, it was clear that the Liberal government of Pierre Trudeau would bear little resemblance to his previous administration. More from a change of heart of its leadership than from a change of role of its membership, the Liberal government entered the new decade challenging the gospel of neoconservatism, asserting the need for a strengthened federal state, and directing the economy away from its continental drift. The Progressive Conservative party, through its errors, had not held onto power long enough to renew itself. The Liberal party, in its cunning, had regained power to renew itself in office.

7

The New Democratic Party in the 1979 Federal General Election

Walter D. Young

The disappointment of the New Democratic party (NDP) campaign organizers with the 1979 election results is easily understood. In comparison with other NDP election campaigns, and even in comparison with the Liberal and Conservative campaigns, the party campaign was a model of its kind. The press and television coverage were all that could have been desired; the leader performed flawlessly, and his tours seemed to go without a hitch. The Canadian Labour Congress (CLC), for the first time ever, put its weight behind the party in a campaign of unprecedented breadth and thoroughness. The result was only a modest growth in party support—more or less back to 1972 levels.

At the conclusion of the campaign, party workers assuaged their disappointment by suggesting that the residual effect of what had been a monumental electoral effort by the NDP and the CLC would be felt in subsequent contests. The validity of that view was tested sooner than expected. The 1980 election nudged the NDP share of the popular vote up to 19.8 percent and gave the party five additional seats in the House. It was hardly a dramatic surge forward. The results were cold comfort for the party leader and his advisers, who, once again, had to settle for the same slow growth.

Because of the intellectual debt Canadian socialism owes to the English Fabians, it is somehow particularly appropriate that the progress of the socialist party in Canada should be so well characterized by Beatrice Webb's aphorism, "the inevitability of gradualness." Electorally, the New Democratic party has advanced slowly, suffering setbacks from time to time but always getting back on its feet and moving a bit further ahead.

In 1972, led by David Lewis, the national party found itself the makeweight in a minority government situation. The thirty-one NDP members kept the Liberal government in office for eighteen months. In the same year the NDP came to power in British Columbia, the third provincial government to fall to the left. Two years later the national party suffered a severe setback in the general election. Its share of the popular vote dropped from 17.7 percent to 15.4 percent, and it lost fifteen seats. In two years it had gone from its highest to its lowest point, measured by seats in the House of Commons.

It was hoped that the election in 1979 would demonstrate the party's capacity not only to get back on its feet but also to move beyond its position in 1972. A number of factors provided some justification for optimism. One was the presence of a new leader. Admittedly neither a fluent orator nor a folksy genius like his two predecessors, Ed Broadbent was the first leader of the New Democratic party who had not come from the founding dynasty of the Cooperative Commonwealth Federation (CCF). Both David Lewis and Tommy Douglas had their roots in the Regina Manifesto[1] and the "dirty thirties." Broadbent symbolized the new aspect of the party: its ties with labor and its more open pragmatism. Under Broadbent the party seemed to have put aside a good deal of its evangelical heritage.

A second factor expected to make a difference in 1979 was the Election Expenses Act, which for the first time made it possible for the NDP to compete with the Liberal and Conservative parties on a more equal basis.[2] The party was able to mount the most elaborate media campaign in its history, plan a more extensive itinerary for the party leader, and, for the latter part of the campaign, charter a jet aircraft for the leader and his press entourage.

A third factor was the active and extensive involvement of the Canadian Labour Congress in the election on behalf of the NDP. The NDP had been founded in 1961 on the twin piers of the Cooperative Commonwealth Federation and the Canadian Labour Congress, with a modest infusion of "other liberal-minded Canadians." Despite the declared partnership, the Canadian Labour Congress as such had never been an active partner in election campaigns. Trade-union involvement was usually a matter for individual affiliates of the

---

[1] The Regina Manifesto was the statement of fundamental principles drafted by the founders of the Cooperative Commonwealth Federation (CCF) in 1933. It remained formally in effect until 1956. For left-wing social democrats it is still an article of faith. The NDP was formed in 1961 as the result of the joint effort of the CCF and the Canadian Labour Congress.

[2] Khayyam Z. Paltiel, "Campaign Financing in Canada and Its Reform," in Howard R. Penniman, ed., *Canada at the Polls: The General Election of 1974* (Washington, D.C.: American Enterprise Institute, 1975), esp. pp. 201ff.

Canadian Labour Congress, but principally at the level of the provincial labor federations and union locals. There had never been a nationally coordinated Canadian Labour Congress effort on behalf of the NDP, although the congress had raised funds for the NDP from its affiliates from 1965. In 1979 there was such an effort.

The federal by-elections in the autumn of 1978 indicated a growing antigovernment sentiment in the country. For the NDP the fact that the party held its seat in Toronto Broadview was satisfying. The fact that it won Humber–St. George's–St. Barbe in Newfoundland was cause for jubilation and optimism. The success of Fonse Faour and the members of the Canadian Paperworkers Union in turning the 1974 election's 4 percent of the vote to the by-election's 43.5 percent was astonishing. The constituencies of the Atlantic provinces, with one or two exceptions, were dry wells for the NDP. The by-election victory was seen as a positive augury.

The appointment by the queen of Edward Schreyer as governor general of Canada in 1978 probably had no measurable effect on the outcome of the 1979 election.[3] It did, however, establish both the respectability and the acceptability of the New Democratic party as a Canadian political institution, because at the time of his appointment Schreyer was a former premier of Manitoba, leader of the official opposition in the province's legislature, and, of course, leader of the Manitoba NDP.

These positive indicators came late in the 1970s. The first few years of Ed Broadbent's leadership had been less promising. On assuming the leadership, Broadbent set his sights on major party status, aiming at sixty seats in the next general election.[4] This emphasis was characteristic of Broadbent's leadership campaign. He, of all the candidates, laid most emphasis on organizing the party toward winning seats in the next election. He offered the delegates a pragmatic and politically oriented leadership that was in some contrast to the approach of the other candidates, most notably his chief rival, Rosemary Brown.

The leadership campaign was run in a manner that could be fairly described as typically NDP. It was designed to be scrupulously fair for all candidates, predictably boring—partly as a result of the determined fairness—and frankly pedagogical: the other parties

---

[3] The governor general is the monarch's representative in Canada and, as such, is the formal head of state. Governors general are appointed for a six-year term by the queen on the advice of the prime minister. The functions of the office are almost entirely ceremonial and, beyond the act of appointment, the relationship with the sovereign is purely nominal.

[4] *Globe and Mail* (Toronto), July 8, 1975, p. 8.

should look and learn how a truly democratic leadership contest is run. Strict limits were placed on the expenditures of candidates, and the party gave each a $1,000 subsidy. A group tour of the candidates to specially convened meetings in all the major centers was arranged so that delegates could see all the candidates together. These meetings were not well attended, and the lesson of this aspect of the campaign was that it was not a good way to generate interest and enthusiasm.

Of the five final candidates, only four were serious contenders. Broadbent was clearly the favorite. He was endorsed by T. C. Douglas, the former leader and party folk hero, as well as by six other members of the parliamentary caucus and all three NDP provincial premiers. The only other M.P. in the contest was Lorne Nystrom, who had no supporters from among his colleagues in the House of Commons. The other two candidates were John Harney, a university professor from Toronto who had been an M.P. from 1972 to 1974, and Rosemary Brown, a member of the British Columbia legislature.

In the balloting Harney was the first to be dropped. Although he had the support of three M.P.s and was fluently bilingual, he was regarded as something of an intellectual dilettante and had, after all, been defeated in 1974. Lorne Nystrom was the next to fall, leaving the field to Brown and Broadbent.

Broadbent led on every ballot and at the third count was 200 votes in front of Brown. Brown was attractive to many delegates because she was an excellent speaker and, as a black woman, had proved an effective champion of the rights of women and minorities. She presented herself as the candidate of the ideological purists in the party—those who still yearned for the exciting days when the Waffle Movement[5] brought so much heat, if little light, to convention debate. According to Stephen Lewis, then leader of the Ontario NDP, the Brown campaign was a "mixture of fundamentalism and feminism . . . a very potent brew."[6]

When Nystrom's 413 supporters cast their ballots on the fourth run, 254 went to Broadbent, and he became the third national leader of the party. There would have been much less of a contest at the convention if organized labor had sent all the delegates the affiliated

[5] The Waffle Movement was a group of radical activists in the NDP whose objective was to move party policy to the left, closer to the principles of the Regina Manifesto. The name came from a statement of Ed Broadbent's, made before he was party leader, when he said that if the party was going to waffle about its socialism he would rather "waffle to the left than waffle to the right." First organized in 1969, the Waffle Movement was dissolved in 1972.

[6] *Globe and Mail*, July 7, 1975, p. 1.

unions were entitled to, since most would have supported Broadbent. Instead of 1,086 delegates from the party's labor wing, only 384 actually attended—24 percent of the registered delegates. This surprising lack of labor interest in the leadership convention of the official party of labor was an indication of the shallowness of labor support and, accordingly, of NDP vulnerability.

The press reaction to the convention was summed up by Geoffrey Stevens of the *Globe and Mail*, who commented that, while there was the expected talk of the workers and the poor, "the rhetoric is a muted ritual, the policy resolutions are pablum, and the sense of outrage that once inspired socialists has given way to something that approaches complacency."[7] There was, nevertheless, an impression that the party had, if anything, moved slightly leftward. Lacking any evidence other than convention resolutions and the debate they occasion, the apparent leftward move of the party at its conventions is understandable. There is a sense in which the biennial conventions of the party are best seen as exercises in ideological narcissism, with the delegates principally interested in how the party looks to them and how they look to each other. Conventions focus attention inward. The usual explanation of this characteristic is the distance of the party from power. More to the point, however, is the suggestion that the existence of a definite ideological core serves to invite debate on issues that will be more relevant to delegates than to observers and the public at large.

Because it was a leadership convention, the 1975 convention attracted extensive coverage on national television and in the major newspapers. Much less attention was paid to the 1977 gathering. There was no indication that major changes in the party's position on the principal issues were either being undertaken or in the offing. The party militants moved to have the party endorse the notion of a separate Quebec, but the attempt was beaten back. The convention did approve a resolution the gist of which was to ensure that Quebec stayed in Canada. It included a restatement of the party position on unemployment, the elimination of regional disparity, and the need for tax reform to ensure a more equitable distribution of income. The inclusion of these elements in the resolution dealing with Quebec presaged the position the party took in the 1979 campaign: the issue of national unity was, by itself, of no greater significance than jobs, regional equity, and fair shares. And, as in 1975, labor left many of its seats vacant.

[7] Ibid., p. 6.

Broadbent led his party in Parliament with consistency and determination. The advent in 1978 of television coverage of debates in the House of Commons enabled him to display his skills as a debater to greater advantage. He emerged from this exposure as a tough and persistent opponent of the prime minister. He lacked the easy wit of Tommy Douglas and the fluency of David Lewis, but his understanding of the issues shone through his often dogged attacks.

The consistent theme of the NDP in Parliament in the period between the elections was its attack on the government's failure to deal with unemployment. The choice of the theme was in some measure determined by the deliberations of the party election planning committee, which had begun meeting regularly in 1976.[8] In 1977 Broadbent announced a four-point program designed to create more jobs through tax cuts and government spending on housing, urban transit, and grants for small business. In September 1978 he unveiled an economic package that would, in his view, create upwards of 400,000 jobs in two years. The principal features of this plan were a cut in the manufacturing sales tax, a tax credit for low-income earners, and a negative-income-tax plan that would inject $3 billion into the economy. There were also several references to the NDP industrial strategy for Canada, a vague concept that had been mentioned at both the national conventions in the late 1970s but had never surfaced in any detail. Clearly in these pronouncements the NDP was methodically staking out its ground for the coming general election.

The period between the elections was not a time during which the fortunes of the party steadily improved. Provincially they seemed to be in some difficulty. The NDP government of Dave Barrett in British Columbia perished after three years in office, replaced by a refurbished but no less antisocialist Social Credit party. Allan Blakeney's government in Saskatchewan held on to power in 1975, but his share of the popular vote fell fifteen points. The villain of this piece was not the provincial Liberal party but a rejuvenated Conservative party. A year later the NDP government of Edward Schreyer, the least socialist of all the NDP premiers, was defeated by the Manitoba Conservative party, led by the stridently right-wing Sterling Lyon. Those pundits who were proclaiming an international shift to the right whooped with satisfaction at this Canadian demonstration of their prognostic accuracy.

[8] Interview by the author with Dean Terry Grier, chairman of the election planning committee, October 1979.

The period was not without its successes, however. In 1975 the Ontario party found itself in the role of official opposition, winning thirty-eight seats to the Liberals' thirty-one and the Tory government's fifty-one. Two years later, however, the opposition roles were again reversed when the Liberals emerged with thirty-four seats and the NDP with thirty-three, though in both cases there was relatively little slippage in the share of the popular vote. In the fall of 1978 the Saskatchewan voters again went to the polls, this time returning the NDP with an increased majority. It was taken as a clear indication that, in the West at any rate, prospects were starting to improve.

The relationship between the federal and the provincial wings of Canada's political parties varies from province to province and from party to party. With the possible exception of the NDP, the fortunes of a provincial party do not necessarily foretell the results for that party in a federal election. In British Columbia and Alberta, for example, federal Liberals collect more votes than their provincial counterparts. In fact the provincial Liberal party is moribund in both provinces. In the case of the NDP, loyalty to party is stronger and electoral consistency somewhat higher. Moreover, the organizations overlap and, although there are occasions of tension between federal and provincial party headquarters, the common cause is normally triumphant.

This characteristic of the NDP was nicely illustrated in British Columbia in 1979 when, except for the last twelve days, the federal and provincial campaigns overlapped. The NDP turned the coincidence to some advantage. Broadbent appeared frequently with Barrett, canvassers distributed two leaflets, one federal and one provincial, and the ubiquitous NDP lawn signs were designed to be quickly converted from provincial to federal candidates. By contrast, the provincial Conservative party and its leader, Vic Stephens, were either studiously ignored or kept strictly at arm's length by the federal party, much to Stephens's chagrin, since the advantages of any association would have been entirely in his favor. Prominent federal Conservatives more often than not supported Social Credit candidates. In Stephens's own riding, which he lost to Social Credit, the provincial Social Credit organization was a major component of the Victoria federal Conservative riding association.[9]

The federal New Democratic party started planning for the election in August 1976. The election planning committee, chaired by Terry Grier (dean of arts at Ryerson Polytechnic Institute in Toronto,

[9] *Victoria Times*, April 11, 1979, p. 1; April 14, 1979, p. 13; April 16, 1979, p. 4.

former M.P., and former national secretary of the party), met regularly from then on and provided a rolling review of election strategy and issue selection. The committee was a functional rather than a representative committee. In previous election campaigns, the principal agency had been an election campaign committee that included representatives from all the provinces.[10] The effectiveness of this body had been minimal, and the campaign had been run largely on a province-by-province basis, with such coordination as was needed for the leader's tour handled by a small group around the leader. It had not been effective.

In contrast, the election planning committee for the 1979 election ran the national campaign from Ottawa and consisted of individuals whose presence was more a reflection of their abilities than of their particular provincial origin. Its core was drawn from full-time party professionals in Ottawa, including Robin Sears, the party secretary, Marc Eliesen, research director for the caucus, and Pat Kerwin, political education director for the Canadian Labour Congress. The process of continuous analysis was expensive, for, as material was regularly prepared in anticipation of an election, the passage of time and the changing character of national politics would render it obsolete.

In 1978 the committee focused attention on unemployment. By the autumn of that year it was their judgment that jobs were a less prominent issue than inflation, and accordingly the research and media preparation moved in that direction. From the spring of 1978, the party was on an election footing. All the activities of the party and its leader were planned and coordinated in the context of an election campaign and under the direction of the election planning committee. The approach taken by the committee, once the issues had been identified, was to develop the principal themes within the issues and to provide detailed and carefully researched background papers on the issues. The NDP policy on industrial strategy for Canada and on the sectoral economic programs, for example, was fully researched. All the documentary material was made available to the representatives of the media well in advance. It is the view of the committee chairman that the serious attention paid to the NDP campaign and to Broadbent's statements during the campaign was in large measure the product of the careful preparation and research that provided the foundation for the campaign statements.

[10] See Jo Surich, "Purists and Pragmatists: Canadian Democratic Socialism at the Crossroads," in Penniman, *Canada at the Polls, 1974*, p. 135. Subsequent details about the NDP election planning committee are from an interview with Terry Grier, campaign chairman, October 1979.

Throughout the campaign the steering committee of the election planning committee met weekly to assess the effect of the campaign, to adjust the leader's itinerary, and to revise press releases in the light of information received from an elaborate network of contacts across the country—in particular, in the fifty-five constituencies the committee had designated as priority ridings. These constituencies were identified before the election as those that the party already held, those in which the hold on the seat was marginal, or those in which the potential of victory was relatively high. Each Sunday the steering committee would meet to review videotapes of news coverage of the campaign as well as press coverage in the major dailies and reports from the constituencies. The itinerary of the leader was then adjusted if necessary to meet the needs of any priority riding or provincial campaign committee. By midcampaign the machinery was running so smoothly that, according to Grier, debates in the steering committee were usually over the nuances of the campaign rather than principal strategy. There were no major shifts in either strategy or tactics.

In the judgment of the election planning committee, the care with which the campaign was planned and managed contributed to the willingness of the reporters to accord the NDP national campaign virtually the same coverage as the Liberal and Conservative campaigns. The fact that the leaders' debate was a three-way affair contributed to this significantly. The format of the debate and the equal place given to Broadbent in it were a result of particularly effective negotiations conducted by Robin Sears, the national secretary of the party, with the network representatives and the two other parties.

This was, of course, the first national campaign for the NDP in which money was not a major problem. The election planning committee did not have any responsibility for raising funds for the national campaign, as previous NDP and CCF election organizations had had. That responsibility was assigned to an election finance committee. The election planning committee took the money allocated and remained within its budget. The net campaign expenditure of the committee was in the neighborhood of $1.2 million. Including the federal and media rebates under the Election Expenses Act, the gross expenditure was close to $1.9 million.[11]

From the perspective of the steering committee and the election planning committee, the Broadbent campaign—the national NDP campaign—was technically perfect. What the committee could not contend with was the anti-Trudeau issue. At the beginning of the

[11] Interview with Terry Grier.

campaign, party polls in Ontario indicated that there was some slippage of NDP provincial voters toward the Conservatives to defeat Trudeau. There was little the party could do to counteract this mood specifically beyond mounting the kind of general campaign it did. The results on election day indicated that the party had regained the slippage but had not moved much beyond that, especially in southwestern Ontario. The Conservative rallying cry that a vote for Broadbent was as good as a vote for Trudeau was difficult to counter. The NDP campaign directors regard the failure to capture their share of the anti-Trudeau vote as a flaw in a campaign that many observers considered almost flawless.

In a manner unprecedented in socialist electoral politics, the national campaign in 1979 focused on the leader. This strengthened the impression given by media coverage that there were three party leaders to choose from. The campaign was further arranged to ensure that, as Broadbent enunciated each aspect of the party's policy, he would do so in an appropriate setting. Not only was each policy based on careful research, but the presentation of each issue was designed as a media event. Careful design of the leader's itinerary made the regular news coverage of his daily activities a staged piece of political propaganda. All parties endeavored to prepare their television advertising to look like newscast footage; the NDP alone managed to use regular newscasts as television advertising.

In preparing its own television advertising, the NDP had retained the services of Lawrence Wolf, an advertising executive whose success in marketing a number of commodities—shoe polish among them—was legendary among the Toronto practitioners of that gray art. There were some in the party who found a trifle discomfiting the blatant adoption of the very tactics the NDP had vigorously disparaged in the years when it could not afford them. For most members of the party, however, it was reassuring to see their party and their leader moving in the big league along with the prime minister and the leader of the opposition.

The policies that Broadbent elaborated throughout the campaign turned on eight main concerns: food prices, industrial strategy, Medicare, resource development, a Canadian merchant marine, tax reform, homeownership, and women's rights. The food prices issue centered on the NDP proposal for a Fair Prices Commission with power to investigate price increases and order price reductions. Broadbent named three supermarket chains as responsible for excessive price increases, accusing them of "ripping off" the consumer. Later in the campaign he announced a program of food subsidies to bring down prices to consumers and maintain producers' incomes. He was particularly concerned about the rise in milk and flour prices that resulted from the lifting of federal subsidies.

The industrial strategy was the least specific of the NDP planks, involving a reiteration of the social democratic argument for public ownership of the "commanding heights" of industry but not total ownership. Broadbent cited Premier Blakeney's handling of the potash industry in Saskatchewan as an example of this approach. Equally important was the restoration to Canadian ownership of resource industries. His theme, which he used throughout the campaign and in his opening statement of the three-leader debate, was to "bring Canadian resources home to Canadians." [12] His resources policy reflected the current concern with domestic oil supplies and prices. Broadbent's solution was a freeze on domestic oil prices and a more effective use of Petrocanada. The latter agency should, he argued, assume full responsibility for all oil imports and distribution and should take over the Canadian division of Exxon, Imperial Oil.

The proposal to establish a Canadian merchant marine was unique, a question addressed only by the NDP. The objectives, as Broadbent described them, were to create jobs, reduce foreign spending, and increase federal tax revenues. This would be achieved by repatriating Canadian-owned but foreign-registered vessels, restricting the nationality of ships carrying Canadian goods in Canadian waters, and providing a stimulus to the shipbuilding industry.[13] A committee endorsed the policy wholeheartedly and ran a series of large advertisements urging voters in the Maritime provinces to support the only party concerned with maritime prosperity.

Broadbent announced his party's alternative to the popular Tory proposal for mortgage-interest deductibility at a press conference in the financial heart of Toronto. The NDP proposal would provide a monthly refund of up to $83.33 for families with an income below $30,000 per year. The program would cost the treasury $330 million in the first year, but the cost would decline because an NDP government would enforce a lowering of interest rates. The objective was to contrast the NDP effectively with the Tory scheme, which would benefit middle- and upper-income brackets and do very little for the lower-income homeowners.[14]

The Medicare issue was one that Broadbent alone created. It was a timely issue and one that was given added emphasis by well-

---

[12] *Globe and Mail*, May 17, 1979, p. 7; *Victoria Times*, April 18, 1979, p. 12. The slogan, according to Grier, was devised after the campaign had begun.

[13] *Globe and Mail*, April 3, 1979, p. 90.

[14] Ibid., April 26, 1979, p. 9.

publicized decisions of doctors in several provinces to opt out of the provincially controlled Medicare schemes on the ground that their incomes were not keeping pace with inflation. Broadbent's proposal was a simple one: return to the fifty-fifty cost-sharing formula that had been abandoned by the Trudeau government. By placing funding almost entirely in provincial control, the federal government had surrendered any effective influence on the delivery of medical services. Provincial fiscal restraint programs led to unwillingness to accept higher fee scales for physicians, and this, in turn, led the doctors to begin to move out of the Medicare scheme, either by refusing patients on the scheme or by "extra billing" their patients for the amount of their fee not covered by it.[15]

The tax-reform proposal was simply a variant of the negative income tax. The party proposed a cost-of-living tax credit. The lower the individual's income, the higher the tax credit granted. It was estimated that the scheme would cost about $1.8 billion. There were also various regional pledges made by the NDP leader, including one to keep Prairie branch rail lines open.[16]

The women's rights plank was an important one for the party ideologically and strategically. Broadbent's principal opponent for the leadership had demonstrated, through the support she attracted and the favorable press commentary her campaign generated, the importance of this issue for the party. It was recognized by the election planners that no breakthrough was possible unless the party could crack the union households that did not vote NDP or in which only the husband voted NDP. The plank was based on a four-point program involving an affirmative action hiring scheme for the federal civil service and for private sector companies with government contracts. Job training and counseling programs for women that had been cut back by the Liberals would be reinstated, and matching grants would be given to the provinces to establish day-care centers, emergency hostels, and rape relief centers.

On the question of national unity, Broadbent simply asserted that it was not an issue in the campaign, since all three leaders were federalists. It was his view that the national unity debate served only to mask the really pressing issues of Medicare, energy, inflation, unemployment, and the need for an industrial strategy.[17]

The party platform and the strategic elaboration of the issues selected by the election planning committee showed Broadbent to

---

15 *Victoria Times*, April 19, 1979, p. 32.
16 Ibid., April 21, 1979, p. 30.
17 *Globe and Mail*, April 2, 1979, p. 9.

good advantage. He projected the image of a responsible political leader, but clearly a social democrat of the kind for whom the mixed economy is an article of faith. Broadbent did not rant. His manner was confident and positive. In British Columbia he attracted headlines by praising the province's largest corporation as "an example of a corporate citizen doing a good job." He was not trying to bury the radicalism of the NDP, he told one reporter, he was simply trying to stake out a "relevant left" position.[18] It was the view of this reporter, the Ottawa columnist of the *Globe and Mail*, that Broadbent "consistently outperformed both Mr. Trudeau and Mr. Clark." [19]

This view was shared by other journalists [20] and most notably by the publisher of the *Toronto Star*, the largest-circulation daily in the country. Two weeks before election day, the *Star* published an editorial endorsing the NDP as the best of the three alternatives because, as the editorial put it, "Ed Broadbent strikes us as a reasonable, intelligent person. We disagree strongly with certain of his policies but respect the way in which he has conducted his campaign and faced up to the fundamental economic problems facing the country." [21] The newspaper was not under any illusion that the NDP could form the next government; it was opting for a minority government with a strong NDP presence. In subsequent editorials it singled out the NDP platform on taxes, home purchase grants, industrial strategy, Petrocanada, and Quebec—as Broadbent discussed it in the television debate—and concluded on election eve that "the NDP needs a strong presence in the next Parliament to speak up for the needs and interests of all those Canadians who are being ignored by the Liberals and Tories." [22] This first-ever endorsement of the NDP (or the CCF for that matter) by a major newspaper raised party morale and justified the careful planning and structuring of the campaign. It was not, however, an unexpected act by the newspaper. Broadbent had met with publisher Beland Honderich and discussed the NDP program in some detail.[23] Undoubtedly the other parties had done the same. The endorsement was thus a major coup for Broadbent.

More difficult to assess is the effect of the Canadian Labour Congress involvement in the campaign. For the first time in the

[18] Ibid., May 17, 1979, p. 7.

[19] Ibid., p. 7. See also *Victoria Times*, April 12, 1979, p. 5, and *Saturday Night*, July-August 1979, p. 15.

[20] See Richard Gwyn, *Victoria Times*, April 18, 1979, p. 4, and April 12, 1979, p. 5.

[21] *Toronto Star*, May 9, 1979, p. A8.

[22] Ibid., May 12, 15, 16, 17, 18, 21, 1979.

[23] Terry Grier interview, October 1979.

eighteen-year history of the NDP, the congress undertook a large-scale parallel campaign on behalf of the party. The president of the congress, Dennis McDermott, was more forthright and determined in his commitment to the party than any of his predecessors had been, although all certainly endorsed the political party their congress had helped create. It was McDermott's view that "collective bargaining is not enough. We have to become a part of the political process." [24] He nailed the colors of the 2.3 million members of the affiliated unions to the mast by stating at the start of the campaign that, if the backing of the Canadian Labour Congress did not pay off in increased strength for the NDP in the House of Commons, the political clout of the CLC would disappear. [25] In fact there was not much clout for the Canadian Labour Congress to lose. Successive Liberal governments had paid little attention to the congress. It was conceivable that their success in turning out the union vote for the NDP would make them more effective in their dealing with either a Liberal or a Conservative government. Failing to do so would simply leave them where they had been when it all started.

The Canadian Labour Congress ran a separate campaign, although it was closely linked to the NDP campaign. Michael Lewis, seconded by the Ontario NDP to work with the congress, and Patrick Kerwin, director of political education for the congress, were both members of the election planning committee. Both the congress and the party recognized that there was an untapped reservoir of union support; according to their own data, less than 25 percent of trade unionists voted NDP. It made sense to approach the other 75 percent through their unions.

The Canadian Labour Congress strategy was straightforward. Dennis McDermott visited most of the major cities in most of the provinces and urged union members to get out and work for the NDP. Ranking officers in the affiliated unions urged their staffs and the shop stewards at the local level to stimulate interest in the issues and in the policies of the NDP. The key to this aspect of the campaign was the distribution of close to a million and a quarter leaflets to workers in the plants. The strategy was shop-floor campaigning using full-time union officers. In previous election campaigns union involvement was almost entirely through the provincial labor federations. This continued in 1979 but with the added impetus of direction from the Canadian Labour Congress and the head offices of the affiliated unions. In some constituencies telephone campaigns were

[24] *Saturday Night,* June 1979, p. 6.
[25] *Victoria Times,* April 9, 1979.

mounted to ensure that every union member was informed of the NDP position and the union's endorsement of the party. The campaign, following the pattern set by the NDP election planning committee, was also focused on the fifty or so priority ridings.[26]

How successful the campaign was depends on whether a short- or long-run view is taken. From the Canadian Labour Congress's perspective, it was a successful beginning. The congress executive council was sufficiently satisfied to decide to continue the effort to inform union members of political issues on a direct, plant-floor contact basis, and the implication would seem to be that in the next election there would be the same extensive CLC presence on the side of the NDP. According to Kerwin, the feedback from the campaign within the union movement was overwhelmingly favorable. In the 1980 campaign CLC support for the NDP was every bit as visible as it had been in 1979, but it was difficult to prove that Labour's involvement had been decisive. All of the five seats the party lost in 1980 were in heavily unionized ridings; but then, of the ten additional seats the party won, at least six were from the same sort of constituency. And the share of the popular vote did increase in every province except Newfoundland.

Short-run analysis suggests that most of the 75 percent of trade union members who did not vote NDP in 1974 did not do so in 1979 or 1980. On the other hand, Canadian Labour Congress officials point to the fact that every priority seat in Manitoba was won and that in that province both the telephone canvass and leaflet distribution went smoothly and well. This may have been due in part to the reaction of the Manitoba trade unionists to the antilabor policies of the provincial Conservative government. But the same judgment was made about British Columbia and about the Atlantic provinces. In the latter, the NDP share of the vote in 1979 increased significantly, and the party held the Newfoundland seat very comfortably; certainly in that case it was very much a trade-union effort in both the by-election and the general election. The 1980 result in that province suggests, however, that the remarkable surge from 9.3 percent in 1974 to 29.7 percent in 1979 was abnormal and that the 16.7 percent result in 1980 was more consistent with the steady growth that appears to be the case in the rest of the country.

On the other hand, as one student of Canadian labor has pointed out, the NDP fared worst in the industrial heartland of Canada, southwestern Ontario. Here, despite the effect of some of the stronger

[26] Information about the Canadian Labour Congress campaign was drawn from an interview with Pat Kerwin, CLC director of political education, October 1979.

unions like the United Automobile Workers and the steelworkers, "Canadian workers could not be budged from their traditional voting habits."[27] Many of the best candidates who were defeated were trade unionists, while there are few union members among the successful candidates. The Canadian Labour Congress election slogan, "The Perfect Union: Me and the NDP," did not rouse the sleeping giant of Canadian labor, although preliminary intelligence from the CLC indicated that the attempt to awaken it would be made again when the next election was called. And when the Clark government was defeated, the CLC election machinery was started up a second time.

The left in Canada and in the NDP considered the apparent failure of the Canadian Labour Congress the result of the pursuit of the middle-class vote by the party and the congress, thereby ignoring the postal workers and the "militant strikers of Sudbury."[28] What is interesting about this analysis is that the strikers of Sudbury were so militant that they returned the sitting member, Commons Speaker and Liberal James Jerome, by an almost two-to-one majority over his NDP rival. As the former CCF leader, M. J. Coldwell, never tired of pointing out, the workers in Canada are fundamentally conservative and see themselves as middle class. The astigmatic left as reflected in the pages of *Canadian Dimension* is of little account in the internal workings of the NDP. What is doubtless of more concern is the weight the apparent failure may give to the arguments of those within the councils of the Canadian Labour Congress who would prefer the relationship with the NDP to be at an extended arm's length. As long as McDermott is in the chair, that is not likely to occur, but his successor may have a different, less activist perspective. If Irving Abella is correct and "most workers see their unions as solely economic agencies which have no business meddling in politics,"[29] there will be some interesting debates in the affiliated unions before the next federal election.

Drawing conclusions from the results and the share of the vote the NDP achieved is a little awkward, since the boundaries of the constituencies were redrawn after the 1974 general election. In general, however, it is clear that the party did win back the ground that it lost in 1974. Then the party's popular vote in Ontario, for example, slipped two percentage points. In 1979 it was back to 21 percent, a mere one-half of one percentage point below the 1972 level. It was

---

27 Irving Abella, "The Imperfect Union," *Canadian Forum* (September 1979), p. 8.
28 *Canadian Dimension* (July-August 1979), p. 8.
29 Ibid., p. 8.

back to within two points of the 1972 level in British Columbia, at 32 percent. In Manitoba, on the other hand, as in the Atlantic provinces, the NDP popular vote rose sharply. In Manitoba it stood at 33 percent, six points higher than 1972, nine higher than 1974. In the Atlantic provinces the growth was striking. In Newfoundland the popular vote climbed from 4.7 percent in 1972 to 29.7 in 1979. In Nova Scotia it was 11 percent in 1974, down one point from 1972, and in 1979 it reached 18.7 percent. The increase in New Brunswick was no less spectacular. The growth was steadily upward, from 5.7 percent in 1972 to 8.6 in 1974 and 15.3 percent in 1979.

These data were undoubtedly the basis for some enthusiasm in the New Democratic party's Ottawa office, for they demonstrated that the party was effectively establishing a national base. Quebec remained almost static, however; the party attracted 162,080 voters in 1974 and 163,492 in 1979. Of course, that is almost as many as it attracted in Manitoba and almost three times the votes it won in Newfoundland, but the vagaries of the electoral system effectively deny the party even one Quebec voice in its caucus. But the triumph of the campaign for the NDP must remain the fact that in the Atlantic provinces it tripled its share of the popular vote and increased its actual vote across the four provinces by a factor of eleven.

It remains the case, however, that even two swallows from the east do not a political summer make. Nationally the party remains at the 20 percent barrier. This can be readily accounted for: Quebec and Alberta. It is possible that the prospects for breaking this barrier may improve, however, and largely as the result of the credibility accorded the party and its leader during the campaign. In 1980, with a smaller turnout in both provinces, the NDP share of the popular vote was up four percentage points in Quebec and just less than half a point in Alberta. For the NDP, progress must be seen as any kind of movement forward. As has been suggested above, this can be attributed both to the way Broadbent conducted his personal campaign and to the way the party campaign was organized and managed by the election planning committee. It is possible that the virtual disappearance of the Social Credit party will increase the attention paid to the NDP and that this could further enhance the party's general standing in the country.

Two general elections in twelve months left the NDP in a relatively healthy position, with more seats in the House of Commons than it had ever had before, virtually 20 percent of the voters supporting it, and a new sense of the importance of electoral collaboration with organized labor. The party leader remained the only leader in the Commons who was not either publicly committed to resigning or facing a most uncertain future through thinly disguised disaffection in his own ranks. There were no complaints about Broadbent's conduct in either campaign. After the 1980 election the party could look forward to at least four election-free years for consolidation. As it faced the 1980s, the New Democratic party was best described as secure but not yet within striking distance, a familiar position for politicians on the left in Canada.

8
Quebec

Vincent Lemieux and Jean Crête

For many observers federal and provincial election results in Quebec seem paradoxical. Take, for example, the results of the provincial election in November 1976 and those of the federal election in May 1979. In 1976 the Liberal party suffered a loss of about twenty percentage points (it received 34 percent, down from 55 percent in 1973) and was replaced by the Parti Québécois, which took command of the Quebec provincial government. But less than three years later, in the May 1979 federal election, the Liberal party achieved its best performance since the 1950s: it received 62 percent of the vote and sixty-seven of seventy-five seats.

The Liberal party is not the same at the federal and the provincial levels of Quebec politics. More generally the party system is not the same at these two levels, just as the political stakes differ greatly from one level to another. We shall first explore these differences to give a context to Quebec politics, before studying the campaign and the results of the 1979 federal election.

The Federal Party System

In 1867, when Quebec entered the Canadian federal system of government, there were two major political parties in the province as elsewhere in Canada: the Conservative party and the Liberal party. The Conservatives were more favorable to the federation than the Liberals and thus dominated Quebec federal politics for about twenty years. This domination ended in 1896, when Wilfrid Laurier, a French Canadian, led the Liberal party to a sizable victory in the federal election, capturing thirty-four of the sixty-five seats in Quebec. From that time on the Liberals have continually won more seats than the Conservatives in Quebec, the only exception being 1958, when the Conservatives, led by John Diefenbaker, got fifty of the seventy-five seats.[1]

In the opinion of the French Canadian voters of Quebec (who constitute 80 percent of the electorate), the Conservatives have had several serious drawbacks. First, they have never had a French Canadian leader, in contrast to the Liberal party, where a French Canadian normally alternates with an English Canadian leader. (Laurier, St. Laurent, and Trudeau were selected in this way.) Second, since the end of the last century, the Conservative party has been associated with certain measures contrary to the interests of the French Canadians: Louis Riel, a rebel leader of partially French Canadian origin, was hanged under a Conservative government in 1885; French Canadian schools in the province of Manitoba were denied their constitutional rights in the 1890s; and during World War I a conscription law was enacted by the Conservatives though opposed by the great majority of French Canadian leaders and voters. In the 1921 election, the first to be held after the war, the Conservatives received only 18 percent of the vote and no seats at all in Quebec. They have never recovered from this disaster, except for their 1958 upsurge.

As a result, the Liberal party has dominated federal politics in Quebec, winning twenty-three of the twenty-four electoral competitions since 1896. Most of the Quebec Francophone voters consider it the only party able to protect their interests in federal politics and government. Therefore the Liberal party is an ethnic party in federal politics, just as the Parti Québécois is a Francophone-based party in provincial politics. When a French Canadian leads the Liberals, the party is unbeatable in Quebec, as the federal elections from 1957 to 1968 demonstrate. In 1957 the Liberal party suffered great unpopularity everywhere outside Quebec, losing so many seats that it was pushed out of the government by the Conservatives, led by John Diefenbaker. But in Quebec the Liberals lost only three percentage points (dropping from 61 in 1953 to 58 percent) and four seats (from sixty-six to sixty-two, out of seventy-five). The main reason was that Louis St. Laurent, a French Canadian, was still the leader of the Liberal party. In the 1958 election, St. Laurent was replaced by Lester Pearson, and consequently the Liberals did not do so well: the Conservatives captured fifty seats and got 50 percent of the vote in Quebec.

[1] On this period, see Peter Regenstreif, *The Diefenbaker Interlude* (Toronto: Longmans, 1965).

TABLE 8–1

FEDERAL ELECTION RESULTS, QUEBEC, 1949–1979

(percent of the vote and number of seats)

Year	Total Seats	Liberal Party		Conservative Party		Social Credit		Other[a]	
		Vote	Seats	Vote	Seats	Vote	Seats	Vote	Seats
1949	73	60	68	25	2	—	—	15	3
1953	75	61	66	29	4	—	—	10	5
1957	75	58	62	31	9	—	—	11	4
1958	75	46	25	50	50	—	—	4	0
1962	75	40	35	30	14	26	26	4	0
1963	75	46	47	20	8	27	20	7	0
1965	75	46	56	21	8	18	9	15	2
1968	74	53	56	21	4	16	14	10	0
1972	74	49	56	17	2	24	15	10	1
1974	74	54	60	21	3	17	11	8	0
1979	75	62	67	14	2	16	6	8	0

Dash (—): Not applicable.

NOTE: Vote figures are percentages of valid votes.

[a] All the "others" elected were independent candidates. Although the New Democratic party has won most of the votes in this column since the 1960s, it has never won a seat in Quebec.

SOURCE: Canada, Ministry of Supply and Services, *Report of the Chief Electoral Officer*, Ottawa, appropriate years.

The Conservative government was a great disappointment, more in Quebec than in the rest of Canada. This disappointment combined with some important transformations in Quebec society and politics (including the defeat of the conservative Union Nationale government in 1960 after sixteen years in office) to bring about the sudden upsurge of Social Credit, a populist party.[2] Led by Réal Caouette, this new party secured twenty-six and twenty seats respectively in the 1962 and 1963 elections, second to the Liberals, who captured thirty-five and then forty-seven seats; the Conservatives were reduced to fourteen seats in 1962 and only eight in 1963. The 1965 electoral results

[2] On the Social Credit party in Quebec, see Michael B. Stein, *The Dynamics of Right-Wing Protest: A Political Analysis of Social Credit in Quebec* (Toronto: University of Toronto Press, 1973), and Maurice Pinard, *The Rise of a Third Party: A Study in Crisis Politics*, enlarged ed. (Montreal and London, Ont.: McGill and Queen's University Press, 1975).

FIGURE 8–1

Social Credit, Conservative, Liberal, and Minor Parties' Shares of Valid Votes in Quebec, General Elections, 1963–1979

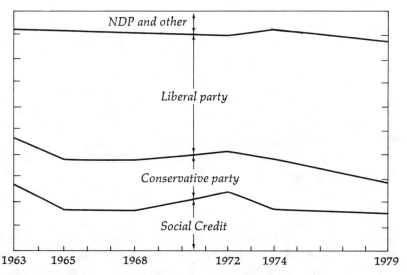

SOURCE: Reports of the chief electoral officer for relevant years.

in Quebec were almost the same as those of 1963. But in 1968 and after, the Liberal party, now led by Pierre Trudeau, succeeded in climbing up again to 50 percent of the votes, a level that had not been attained since 1957. The Conservatives and the Créditistes together never captured more than eighteen of seventy-four or seventy-five seats (see table 8–1).

The Liberal party remains a dominant actor in the federal party system of Quebec, the Conservative party and Social Credit holding minor positions (see figure 8–1). Neither of them has obtained more than 25 percent of the vote since 1965. The New Democratic party, a very minor player, has never attained more than 10 percent of the vote since 1965.

The provincial party system in Quebec, on the other hand, looks much more competitive and is composed of different parties with different stakes and issues.

The Provincial Party System

In 1867 the provincial party system in Quebec was very similar to the federal one. There were two parties, the Conservative party and the Liberal party, corresponding to their federal counterparts, with electoral results determined for the most part by the political game at the federal level.

At the end of the last century, the provincial party system became much less competitive, following the trend of the federal party system. The Liberal party captured the provincial government in 1897, one year after the Liberal victory at the federal level, and Liberal government in Quebec lasted thirty-nine years. It was defeated in 1936 by a new party, the Union Nationale, a coalition of the Conservative party and the Action Libérale Nationale, the creation of some dissident young Liberals. The leader of this coalition, Maurice Duplessis, a former Conservative, was to become one of the most famous prime ministers of Quebec history.

From that time on, the provincial party system has remained truly different from the federal one. The Union Nationale was defeated by the Liberal party in 1939, only to come back to power in 1944 and stay there until 1960, even though concurrently the Liberal party was dominant at the federal level. The provincial Liberal party was at its best at the beginning of the 1960s, while its federal counterpart, led at that time by Lester Pearson, had difficulty in Quebec with the Conservative party and the Social Credit party. Then the Liberal government was defeated in Quebec in 1966, just as the federal party had begun to perform better against its rivals. In 1964 the provincial Liberal party opted to resign from the provincial section of the federal Liberal party, becoming an autonomous party within the Liberal political family. At about the same time some independentist parties emerged in Quebec provincial politics, a development without an equivalent in federal politics that exemplifies clearly the divergence between the two levels of Quebec politics.

The big changes underlying this ever-growing separation were related to the actions of the Quebec provincial government. Until midcentury this government had remained fairly inactive; its budget was relatively small, and its parliamentary sessions did not last very long. At the end of the 1950s and above all at the beginning of the 1960s, however, with the election of the Liberal party, the Quebec government became much more active in educational matters, in social affairs, in the development of public enterprises, in the building of highways, etc. This development of the public sector and the quasi-public sector (schools, universities, public enterprises, etc.) of the economy and society came in response to a demand for well-paid jobs by the increasingly numerous young graduates of the Quebec universities. (French Canadians did not have much control over the

Quebec economy, and the private sector did not provide for them well.) To perform these new tasks the Quebec government had to get more resources and powers from the central government. Some of them were obtained at the beginning of the 1960s, and local positive feedback induced the government to demand more of the same. After 1965, however, it had less success. After the accession of Pierre Trudeau as federal prime minister, it became clear that more concessions to Quebec would impede the existence of a strong national government, to which he was committed.

The increasing intervention of the Quebec government in society, coupled with the strong nationalist tendencies of many young Quebecers, who were very sensitive to their minority position in Canada and North America, promoted the emergence of independentist parties. These parties intended to work through the provincial government to change society in conformity with their own views. In 1966 two small independentist parties together captured roughly 10 percent of the vote. In 1970 the Parti Québécois, which had succeeded in bringing together the various independentist tendencies, obtained 23 percent of the vote, but only 7 of 108 seats. In 1973 the Parti Québécois captured 30 percent of the vote (but only 6 of 110 seats) in a landslide victory for the Liberals, led by Robert Bourassa, who got 55 percent of the vote and 102 seats.

This landslide victory was deceptive. Unable to cope effectively with many problems, the Bourassa government steadily declined in public opinion from 1974 to 1976. In a two-party system, there is only one alternative for dissatisfied voters: the other party. So the Parti Québécois was elected on November 15, 1976, with only 41 percent of the vote and 70 of 110 seats. The Liberal party got 34 percent of the vote and 27 seats, while the Union Nationale captured 18 percent of the vote and 11 seats. Two very minor parties divided the two remaining seats (see table 8–2).[3]

The Quebec Political Context after 1976

The election of an independentist party has caused turmoil in Canada and in some sectors of Quebec society. This is not the place, however, to analyze the many aspects of this important phenomenon. Let us sort out only those features of Quebec politics since 1976 that are

[3] On the provincial party system in Quebec until the Parti Québécois victory in 1976, see Vincent Lemieux, "Québec: Heaven Is Blue and Hell Is Red," in Martin Robin, ed., *Canadian Provincial Politics*, 2d ed. (Scarborough, Ont.: Prentice-Hall, 1978), pp. 248–82. On the 1976 provincial election, see André Bernard, *Québec: Elections 1976* (Montreal: Hurtubise HMH, 1976).

TABLE 8–2

PROVINCIAL ELECTION RESULTS, QUEBEC, 1948–1976
(percent of the vote and number of seats)

Year	Total Seats	Liberal Party Vote	Liberal Party Seats	Union Nationale Vote	Union Nationale Seats	Independentist Parties[a] Vote	Independentist Parties[a] Seats	Other[b] Vote	Other[b] Seats
1948	92	36	8	51	82	—	—	13	2
1952	92	46	23	51	68	—	—	3	1
1956	93	45	20	52	72	—	—	3	1
1960	95	52	51	47	43	—	—	1	1
1962	95	57	63	42	31	—	—	1	1
1966	108	47	50	41	56	10	0	2	2
1970	108	45	72	20	17	23	7	12	12
1973	110	55	102	5	0	30	6	10	2
1976	110	34	27	18	11	41	70	7	2

Dash (—): Not applicable.

NOTE: Vote figures are percentages of valid votes.

[a] In 1966 two small independentist parties, the Rassemblement pour l'Indépendance Nationale (RIN) and the Ralliement National (RN), competed in the election. Since 1970 the Parti Québécois has been the only independentist party.

[b] In 1948 the Union des Electeurs, a Créditiste party, got 9 percent of the vote but no seats. From 1970 to 1976, most of the votes and seats won by "others" were captured by Créditiste parties.

SOURCE: Report of the président des élections, appropriate years.

relevant for a good understanding of the 1979 federal election campaign and results in Quebec.

During the 1976 electoral campaign, the Parti Québécois leaders made it clear that their victory would not mean the separation of Quebec from the rest of Canada. The election, they said, gave the voters an opportunity to defeat a bad government and replace it with a good government led by the Parti Québécois. Afterward, this new government would devote itself to organizing a referendum on the constitutional future of Quebec. Then the Quebec voters would have the opportunity to make a decision on Quebec political independence.

There was a commitment to hold the referendum before the next provincial election, but the timing was left rather vague, partly because the Parti Québécois leaders did not want to interfere with the federal election that was supposed to be held in 1978. For many reasons, the federal election was delayed until 1979, forcing the Parti Québécois to postpone its referendum to the beginning of 1980. In such a context it was not surprising that the federal election in Quebec should be presented by some leaders of the federalist option as a kind of prereferendum on this option.

It looked advantageous to the federal Liberal party to present it in this way. The polls had consistently indicated through the years that the Liberals remained very popular in Quebec, while the other parties trailed far behind. Moreover, the Liberals could rely on the support of the provincial Liberal party, whose new leader, Claude Ryan, formerly a well-known editor of the influential newspaper *Le Devoir*, seemed more congenial to Pierre Trudeau than Robert Bourassa was. Under Ryan's leadership the Liberal party had made some progress in the voters' opinion, as revealed by the polls. Within the party there was a rejuvenated will to win the battle against the Parti Québécois separatist option.

Moreover, the emergence of the Parti Québécois and the development of the independentist ideology since the beginning of the 1970s have tended to reinforce the links between the two Liberal parties, the federal and the provincial. The electoral support of the federal party remains more important and more constant, for the reasons already given. The polls reveal that some 20 to 30 percent of the voters supporting the Parti Québécois also support the federal Liberal party, the more "nationalist" party in Quebec federal politics. Most of the voters are nationalists. They want more power for Quebec *within* the federal system. Neither the federal Liberal party nor the Parti Québécois adequately represents their point of view.

On the eve of a federal election, the Parti Québécois leaders are in an uneasy position, since there is no equivalent to the Parti Québécois on the federal level of Quebec politics. In the 1972 and 1974 federal elections, the Parti Québécois indicated to its supporters that they would do better to abstain. This suggestion was disregarded by a great number of voters, and many observers have noted that it favored the victory of the federal Liberal party. In 1979 some independentists within and around the Parti Québécois formed an independentist party, the Union Populaire, to compete in the federal election, with disastrous results. René Lévesque, the Quebec premier, did not favor such a venture, preferring the Social Credit party, whose new leader, Fabien Roy, was a former member of the Quebec Parliament and a rather strong nationalist. Lévesque considered Social Credit a genuine Quebec party, apt to be supported by nationalist Quebecers.

In the 1976 provincial election, the Union Nationale did better than in 1973, capturing 18 percent of the vote and 11 out of 110 seats. After 1976, however, the strong polarization between the Parti Québécois and the Liberal party on constitutional matters reduced the Union Nationale significantly. On the eve of the federal election, polls revealed that less than 10 percent of the Quebec voters intended to support the Union Nationale. This support was located in only a few regions. In the other Quebec regions, the Union Nationale organization could not be of any great help to the Conservative party, though in the past such assistance had been quite important. Almost all the election organizers of the Conservative party in Quebec were members of the Union Nationale, and the federal party got its best results in Quebec when the Union Nationale organization was working hard for the Conservatives. The 1958 victory over the Liberals, for example, can be explained to a certain degree by the active support of the Union Nationale, led by Maurice Duplessis. In 1979 a declining Union Nationale failed to draw such support for the Conservative party.

The 1979 Federal Campaign

The idea that campaigns change votes substantially is not sustained by the literature on elections and probably has never been strongly held by party activists. Furthermore, when party is clearly more significant than candidate, as it has been shown to be in the previous section, one may quite reasonably ask with Butler and King why, if campaigns do not decide elections, "so much energy is put into them by politicians and why observers think it worth while to chronicle them in detail."[4]

One reason is that, though campaigns may not substantially change the distribution of votes among parties, they do change some votes, which may be the decisive ones in a constituency where the election is closely contested. (As we will see, however, there were very few such constituencies in the 1979 federal election in Quebec. Most, to borrow from an American author, were safe at any margin.)[5] But besides their immediate impact on voters' preferences, political campaigns have many other functions, one of which is of the utmost importance in Quebec federal politics: to "Canadianize" the

[4] David E. Butler and Anthony King, *The British General Election of 1966* (London: Macmillan, 1966), p. 95.

[5] Thomas E. Mann, *Unsafe at Any Margin: Interpreting Congressional Elections* (Washington, D.C.: American Enterprise Institute, 1978).

Francophone population, who consider the federal government less important than the provincial government.

In such circumstances, federal politicians have to build credibility not only for their own party but also for the federal system of government. A federal election gives them the opportunity to boost the importance of federal politics, to detail the beneficial intervention of the federal government, to underline the importance of the French-speaking politicians (the French power) in the process of government. This last theme recurs in most speeches by Liberal candidates, while the Conservatives implore the Québécois to vote Conservative if they want to keep their say in Ottawa when the Liberals are out.

The Parties. The campaign began poorly for the Conservatives. First they were not able to find outstanding candidates. In addition, the main point of their platform, to give homeowners tax and mortgage-interest relief, did not have much impact in Quebec, where an unusually large proportion of householders are tenants and where the price of houses is generally lower than in English Canada. The situation worsened as the leader of the Conservatives declared that a Tory government's position on the coming Quebec referendum would be a firm "Quebec cannot vote its way out of Canada." This last declaration was interpreted as intended to reassure the Canadian "rednecks" in Ontario that a Conservative government would handle the "belle province" firmly.

It was equally claimed that such a declaration, after months of fuddling, was a clear sign that the Conservative party had given up the idea of gaining seats in Quebec. From then on, the strategy of the Conservative party in Quebec was perceived as intended to win votes in the English part of Canada.

Since the election of 1962, the main opposition to the Liberal hegemony in Quebec had come from the populist Social Credit. This party was leaderless at the beginning of the 1979 campaign, and its first task was to find a leader. The man it finally chose, Fabien Roy, was a member of the Quebec National Assembly, elected under the banner of the Parti National Populaire. When Roy resigned from the National Assembly to become leader of the Social Credit party, he received the blessing of the Quebec premier but not the full support of the Parti Québécois electoral machine. Lacking funds and a platform, the Créditiste campaign was clearly unprepared. Each candidate ran his own campaign without much help from the central organization.

Another party, the Union Populaire, formed specifically for the 1979 election, also sought the support of the Parti Québécois. They were rebuffed by the Parti Québécois officials, who had no intention of getting openly involved in the federal election.

A third party based in Quebec, the Rhinoceros party, entered the race. The members of this party, who have been referred to by the incumbent prime minister as anarchists, can more aptly be described as humorists. Their party platform was entitled: "Everything You Don't Need to Know about a Federal Political Party—Just Like the Others." They succeeded in some sections in making a joke of the federal election. Four other parties, all pan-Canadian, had candidates in Quebec: the New Democratic party, the Communist party, the Marxist-Leninist party, and the Libertarians. None of them was locally important. When the NDP attracted media attention, it was on the question of how it would behave outside Quebec.

The number of political parties in this election was higher in Quebec than in the other provinces. On the average, the voter in Quebec had a choice of seven candidates, while in the neighboring province, Ontario, the average figure was below five. The proportion of women candidates in Quebec was similar to that in Ontario, 16 percent. For the most part, though, their prospect of election appeared very weak because they were not candidates of the Liberal party.

The Slogans. A federal campaign in Quebec relies mostly on the media, and one of the few surprises of the campaign was the Conservative advertisements on television. During the first weeks of the campaign, the Conservatives went on television with an advertisement spot stronger than their usual fare. The ad started with the traditional coverage of inflation, unemployment, and how badly hurt the voters had been. Then the image of Prime Minister Trudeau appeared, seated in what appeared to be a witness-box. Superimposed on this image was the label "Guilty." In fact, the setting was the House of Commons with the prime minister seated at his desk. The image had been borrowed from tapes that are used to broadcast the debates of the House.

The idea of a frontal attack on Prime Minister Trudeau instead of a campaign against the government or the Liberal party had been fiercely discussed by Tory activists. Some considered it poor strategy to attack in Quebec a prime minister who happened to be a Francophone. On an all-Canada basis, however, the idea was not bad. Any such attack by the main spokesmen for the Conservatives, who were mostly English speaking, might appear bigoted or racist. The series of "Guilty" spots made by Francophones and televised in French was intended to free the Tories of any such criticism.

For their part, the Liberals put forward a nationalistic slogan: "Speak Up, Quebec!" The slogan was especially surprising since Quebec's Liberals had an ideological commitment to equal rights for individuals all across Canada rather than to equal rights for communities. Their slogan clearly appealed to the local community only. As for the other parties, their resources did not allow them to be present in the electronic media during the campaign.

Reporting the events of the campaign, the newspapers provided balanced coverage. The French newspapers, if they took a position in leading articles, tended to favor the Liberals while the English newspapers preferred the Conservatives. Oddly enough, there was no exaggerated gossiping about the prime minister's matrimonial problems. This was particularly remarkable in the English newspapers, known for their detailed interest in these subjects. Dull and without momentum, the campaign failed even to rate front-page headlines.

The Outcome of the Federal Election

In an election where 518 candidates dispute 75 seats, one may expect a rough game. The outcome of the 1979 federal election in Quebec, however, had always been predictable. Indeed, since 1896 the Liberals had, with one exception, repeatedly won a majority of the seats in Quebec. So on election night the observer focuses his attention not on the distribution of seats in Quebec but on more specific questions. What happened in the constituency where, in the media, the contest was reported to be closest? How did the minor parties fare? What were the turnout figures? the rejected votes?

The answer to these questions comes when the overall results are known (see table 8–3). While turnout was high, minor parties did not score well. The Union Populaire, a party that had tried to attract the nationalist vote, failed badly. As for the other parties, Communist, Marxist-Leninist, Libertarian, and Rhinoceros, they received, in total, less than 3 percent of the votes. The New Democratic party continued its slow move downhill. The two other opposition parties, the Conservatives and Social Credit, although they do not normally receive a very large share of the vote, manage to get parliamentary representation because their votes tend to be concentrated in a few regions (which is why it is important to look not only at the overall results but also at detailed results at the constituency level). The Tories won two seats, but the Liberals were not very far behind in either constituency; both constituencies were strongholds not so much of the Tory party as of local candidates who had survived their party's misfortunes in the past.

TABLE 8–3

ELECTION RESULTS IN QUEBEC, 1979

Party	Percentage of Eligible Voters
Liberal	46.1
Social Credit	12.0
Conservative	10.1
New Democrat	3.8
Rhinoceros	1.5
Union Populaire	0.5
Marxist-Leninist	0.2
Communist	0.1
Other and independent	0.7
Invalid votes	1.1
Abstention	24.0
Total	100.1[a]

[a] Rounding error.

SOURCE: *Report of the Chief Electoral Officer, 1979*, tables 4 and 5.

Social Credit has a social basis that goes far beyond the attractiveness of the local candidates even if some candidates, like the leader Fabien Roy, have personal followings.[6] As time goes on, however, a given percentage of votes does not bring as many M.P.s as it used to. This is because the party now receives more votes in constituencies where it is weak and fewer in those where it used to be strong. Social Credit's average percentage of votes in Quebec may be constant or may grow, but in an electoral system that is a zero-sum game in each constituency, the party tends to lose. Overall the results of the 1979 federal election in Quebec caused no surprise.

While the results caused no surprise, they stressed again the apparent paradox of electoral results in Quebec. Indeed, it has often been remarked that electors in Quebec vote for the Liberals in federal elections but against them in provincial elections. This so-called paradox has been labeled "blue" in Quebec and "red" in Ottawa and has remained a lasting subject of debate among students of Quebec politics. A theory that explains this shift in electoral support has recently received attention.[7] According to this theory, the fact that

[6] Vincent Lemieux, "Les dimensions sociologiques du vote créditiste au Québec," *Recherches sociographiques*, vol. 6 (1965), pp. 181-82; and Pinard, *Rise of a Third Party*.

[7] Pierre Drouilly, *Le paradoxe canadien* [The Canadian paradox] (Montreal: Les Editions Parti Pris, 1978).

FIGURE 8–2

THE LIBERAL VOTE IN QUEBEC, FEDERAL AND PROVINCIAL ELECTIONS,
1930–1979

Percentage of registered voters

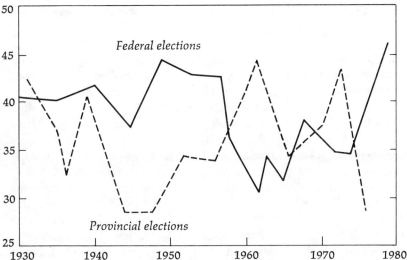

SOURCE: Reports of the chief electoral officer for relevant years.

turnout is generally lower in federal than in provincial elections means that the same number of Liberals voting at the two elections may give a strong majority for the Liberal party when turnout is low and a smaller proportion of votes when turnout is high, as in provincial elections. Comparison of the elections held in the late 1960s and early 1970s substantiates this thesis. At the provincial elections of 1966 and 1970, the Liberals received 34 and 37 percent of the votes; at the federal elections of 1968 and 1972, they got 38 and 35 percent. Furthermore, it is argued that since Canadian politics interests the Québécois much less than Quebec politics, only the hard-core Liberal voters vote at federal elections, and other voters who are not as attracted to the federal Liberal party may abstain. If the thesis is correct, one would expect to find most of the time a lower percentage of voters for the federal Liberal party than for the provincial one, since the federal party is supposed to get its support from hard-core Liberals only. As shown in figure 8–2, for elections from the late 1930s to 1960, the federal party got more votes, not the provincial party. From 1960 to 1973, however, the provincial party gathered more votes than the federal one. Lately, the two parties have switched again, placing the federal party in the lead. Therefore this part of the thesis must be discarded.

221

The available evidence suggests that while the strong partisans of each party, federal and provincial, support the other, the long-term strength of each is slightly different, and variations from election to election can best be explained by variables specific to each party system.[8]

The Leadership. In the first section of this chapter, we argued that the leadership of the Liberal party was, in the federal system, a strong determinant of the variations in Liberal federal votes in Quebec; we present here further evidence to support the hypothesis. The variations in the vote can be measured as the difference between actual results and the support the Liberals would have received if the long-term partisan force ("normal vote") had been the only factor at work. The measure of the long-term strength of the Liberal party is taken as the average of the vote that the party has won over the six preceding elections. The difference between this moving average and the actual results gives that part of the vote to be explained by short-term factors. The only short-term factor considered here is the leadership of the party. If the leader of the party is a Francophone, the Liberals should get more votes; if he is an Anglophone, the party should get fewer votes. To measure the effect of leadership on Liberal success in Quebec federal elections, data from fifteen general elections covering nearly fifty years (1930–1979) of electoral activities are used to estimate the single linear regression equation

$$y = a + bx + E$$

where $y = V_i - L_i^6$; $V_i =$ percentage of votes the Liberals got at the federal election i; $L_i^6 =$ the average percentage of votes the Liberals got at the six elections before i; $X = 1$ if the leader is a Francophone, 0 otherwise; and $E =$ other short-term forces not explicitly taken into account. The results:

$$y = -6.13 + 8.80X$$
$$R^2 = 0.67$$

This simple model fits well and with relatively strong effects. An Anglophone leader costs the Liberal party 6 percentage points in Quebec while a Francophone leader is worth, on average, an extra 2.7 percentage points. With a determination coefficient of 0.67,[9] there

---

[8] Vincent Lemieux and François Renaud, "Les partis dans la région de Québec" [The political parties in the Quebec region], mimeographed (Quebec: Département de Science Politique, Université Laval, 1970), p. 127.

[9] Four-fifths of the residual sum of squares comes from the 1979 election, when the Liberals won 46.4 percent of the votes despite the model's prediction of 35.7 percent.

is still room for other variables, some of which, like economic dissatisfaction, may be pertinent to both the provincial and the federal systems. The evidence shown above, however, stresses the importance of specific characteristics of the federal system and tends to support the hypothesis that many Québécois do cross the party line when they switch from Canadian politics to Quebec politics.

The Quebec Electorate on the Eve of the Referendum

A month after the federal election, an important opinion poll was conducted under the sponsorship of the Quebec Ministry of Intergovernmental Affairs to measure the perceptions of the Quebec electorate on constitutional matters. The poll data were released in September 1979, seven or eight months before the Quebec referendum to be held in the spring of 1980.[10]

First, there was a series of questions on the results of the May 22, 1979, federal election. A majority of Quebecers were not satisfied with the results, understandably enough, considering that the Liberals got an overwhelming majority of votes and seats in Quebec but did not win the contest at the national level.

The Quebec voters were very skeptical about the effect of the Conservatives' victory on the future of Quebec and the possibility of renewing Canadian federalism: 47 percent of them doubted that it would be easy to renew Canadian federalism with a new Conservative government in Ottawa. Only 31 percent of them agreed with the statement that it would be easy.

Moreover, 37 percent of the voters considered that the results of the May 22 federal election would increase the chances of a Parti Québécois victory in the referendum, and 28 percent held the contrary view. One can explain this result by a loss of identity with the federal government after the Conservative victory. The great majority of Quebec voters, as we have shown, do not identify themselves with the Conservative party, which they consider inimical to the French Canadians in Quebec and elsewhere in Canada. So with a Conservative government in Ottawa, in which the ministers from Quebec are not very numerous, the Quebec government appears more important to the Quebec voters.

In response to questions regarding the existence of two governments, a large majority of Quebecers (69 percent, against 25 percent)

[10] Quebec Ministry of Intergovernmental Affairs, *Sondage sur la perception des problèmes constitutionnels par la population du Québec* [Research into the Quebec population's perception of constitutional problems], September 1979.

feel that it is beneficial to have two governments, one federal and the other provincial. But to the question, "When you think of *your* government, which government comes to mind first: the government of Quebec or the government of Canada?" 47 percent answered "Quebec," and 35 percent answered "Canada." In addition, a majority think that the government in Quebec is more competent than the government in Ottawa.

What about the referendum? In the polls and in some debates about the constitutional problem, a distinction is usually made between four options: the status quo, a renewed federalism, sovereignty-association (that is, political sovereignty for Quebec coupled with an economic association with the rest of Canada), and complete political independence. In the poll on the constitutional problem, as in the other polls conducted in Quebec since 1976, 10 percent of the voters favor political independence, about 15 percent the status quo, about 20 percent sovereignty-association, and about 40 percent a new federalism. So a federal solution (the status quo or a new federalism) has greater support than a nonfederal solution (political independence or sovereignty-association).

There is also a net majority in favor of nonradical constitutional change. To arrive at this, negotiations would have to be handled by the two governments. This is the opinion of a majority of Quebecers, who are ready, accordingly, to give their provincial government a mandate to negotiate sovereignty-association. It is hoped, however, that this will be only a first position in the negotiation process. To the question, "Personally, what would your preference be, that sovereignty-association be a *negotiation position* from which the government could make a compromise or be a *firm position* from which the government should not yield?" 54 percent of the people chose a negotiation position, and 27 percent preferred a firm position.

Current thought is that Quebec is now involved in a large negotiation process on constitutional matters. Indeed, the 1979 federal election and the 1980 Quebec referendum are only two steps in this enduring process, initiated by Quebec's "quiet revolution."

Conclusion

If one considers the secular trend of federal politics and elections in Quebec, there is no surprise in the results of the 1979 general election. Under the leadership of a French Canadian, Pierre Trudeau, the Liberal party obtained, as usual, a large share of votes and a tremendous majority of seats in Quebec. But some features peculiar to the current state of Canadian society and politics give these results a particular significance.

First, although the Liberal party improved its position in Quebec, the Conservatives won, with majorities, in seven of the ten provinces and also in the Yukon and the Northwest Territories. Some observers have spoken of an ethnic vote: French-speaking areas in Quebec and elsewhere chose Trudeau, while he was rejected outside this milieu. The defeats of several Liberal ministers in Ontario and elsewhere seem to indicate that it was less the prime minister as a French Canadian who lost popularity than the government he led. In Quebec, opposition to the Trudeau government from the outside may have had the effect of increasing the number of Liberals. In any case they seemed strong, largely because of the weakness of their opponents. Fabien Roy strayed into the area of nationalist demands, while the Social Credit party, as its name indicates, was a party of social demands. As for the Conservative party, it made the mistake of believing that it would benefit automatically from the Conservative surge outside Quebec without having to find an original style and an original position for itself.

Second, the Conservative party's victory at the federal level coupled with its bad performance in Quebec produced a federal government with only two ministers elected in Quebec, in addition to two others coming from the Senate. This was a major difference from the Trudeau government, in which so many of the most important ministers were Quebecers that observers often used the phrase "French power" to describe the federal government. The Conservative federal government was less able to elicit a feeling of identification from the Quebec people; on the other hand, the new prime minister, Joe Clark, seemed less aggressive toward the Quebec government than former Prime Minister Trudeau. He had a pragmatic view of constitutional matters and intended to play a low-key role in the referendum campaign.

The Conservative government had too short a life to have an effect on the constitutional debate between Quebec and Ottawa. It was replaced in February 1980 by a Liberal government led again by Pierre Trudeau, the "favorite son" of Quebec voters. Then in May, Trudeau played a major role in the defeat of the independentist option in the Quebec constitutional referendum. Joe Clark was rather absent in the debate, where the Conservatives, once again, seemed to be a party estranged from Quebec.

9

Party Finance, the Election Expenses Act, and Campaign Spending in 1979 and 1980

F. Leslie Seidle and Khayyam Zev Paltiel

Cabinet government, Parliament, the single-member-district first-past-the-post electoral system, and federalism together constitute the institutional framework of Canadian politics. Each element has had a profound impact on Canadian parties, influencing their structure, organization, articulation, and leadership. The cabinet and the parliamentary system have combined to produce disciplined parties with power concentrated at the center, most notably in the hands of the party leader. Federalism, on the other hand, has tended to attenuate this authority by creating rival power centers in the shape of provincial legislatures, governments, and party organizations. In Canada, regionally based ethnic and economic cleavages contribute to social and political fragmentation, magnifying the centrifugal tendencies inherent in the constitutional system.

The Traditional Pattern of Party Finance and Electoral Law

Canadian party and election financing since the foundation of the state in 1867 has reflected both these fissiparous characteristics and

The authors would like to express their gratitude to the following people, who provided a great deal of information in interviews, letters, and telephone conversations: Jean-Marc Hamel, the chief electoral officer, and members of his staff, especially R. G. Dubé (director, Election Financing Branch) and J. O. Gorman (commissioner of Canada elections); Torrance J. Wylie (chairman, Federal Liberal Agency); John Guthrie (executive director, PC Canada Fund); Paul Curley (former national director, Progressive Conservative party of Canada); and Robin V. Sears (federal secretary, New Democratic party). Leslie Seidle would also like to thank the party officials and activists, official agents, journalists, M.P.s, and senators who granted him some fifty interviews between 1979 and 1981. A vast amount of information was gained from these personal contacts, and it would be impossible to acknowledge every source in an article of this sort. It is hoped that these people will recognize their contributions in the following pages.

the efforts of political leaders to overcome these difficulties.[1] Party leaders since Confederation have attempted to overcome through financing the problems created by the absence of cohesive parliamentary factions and extraparliamentary organizations. They were faced with the task of raising and allocating funds to finance campaigns as well as to weld together a loyal and disciplined legislative following. As a result, they were inevitably vulnerable to the temptation of fund-raising abuses and to their subsequent exposure. The Pacific scandal of 1872 led to the defeat of Canada's first prime minister after disclosure of his dealings with the promoters of the Pacific Railway in the search for Conservative party election funds. The following decades were to witness repeated examples of improper fund raising by both the Liberal and the Conservative parties. Canadian electoral history has been regularly punctuated by scandals associated with the activities of fund raisers like Thomas McGreevy and Israel Tarte, culminating in Andrew Haydon and the notorious Beauharnois affair of 1930–1931, which involved the Liberal leader, William Lyon Mackenzie King. Party leaders have gradually learned to dissociate themselves from the more sordid and potentially dangerous aspects of fund raising by assigning these tasks to specialists and "bagmen."

The two major parties, the Liberals and the Conservatives, have tended to follow a similar pattern in fund raising during the postwar period. The principal source of funds for both parties has been the corporate business community centered in Toronto and Montreal, increasingly supplemented in recent years by the regional financial centers of western Canada and the headquarters or branch offices of multinational corporations operating in Canada. The collection mechanisms in both parties have generally been autonomous and separate from the formal party organizations.[2] The traditional fund-raising structure has been a finance committee headed by a chairman named by the party leader. Recruited by co-option or appointed to their positions by older members of their families or law firms, these solicitors most often have neither held nor sought elective office.

[1] The most complete descriptions of the financing of Canadian political parties are provided in Committee on Election Expenses, *Report of the Committee on Election Expenses* (Ottawa: Queen's Printer, 1966); *Studies in Canadian Party Finance* (Ottawa: Queen's Printer, 1966); and Khayyam Z. Paltiel, *Political Party Financing in Canada* (Toronto: McGraw-Hill, 1970).

[2] This development in the Liberal party is described in detail by Reginald Whitaker, *The Government Party: Organizing and Financing the Liberal Party of Canada, 1930-58* (Toronto: University of Toronto Press, 1977). Some comments on the operation of the Liberal party's national Treasury Committee in recent years are contained in Joseph Wearing, *The L-Shaped Party: The Liberal Party of Canada, 1958-1980* (Toronto: McGraw-Hill Ryerson, 1981), pp. 59-60, 173-80.

The usual reward for such service has been a government appointment, most notably to the Senate.

In contrast to the major-party pattern have been the efforts of the smaller third parties, a regular feature of the Canadian political scene since the 1920s, to raise money at the grass-roots level. Indeed, protest against the dependence of the old parties on the business community has been a repeated refrain of the United Farmers, the Progressives, Social Credit and the Créditistes, the Cooperative Commonwealth Federation (CCF), and its successor, the New Democratic party (NDP). More or less successful attempts at popular fund raising were made by these groups, and the tradition lingers on in the NDP, although this party has become increasingly dependent on support from the organized labor movement, including dues collected regularly from members of affiliated trade unions.

Interest in the reform of Canadian party and election finance down to the 1960s was at best fitful, intermittent rather than systematic, in reaction to rather than in anticipation of scandal and corruption. Thus the Pacific scandal produced the first reforms with the introduction in 1874 of the doctrine of agency, fixing responsibility for election funds in a single agent, and the requirement that candidates and their agents file a statement of campaign expenditure. Useful as these innovations were, they fell short of meeting the problem and did nothing to prevent the improprieties they were purportedly designed to correct. Disclosure of the source of funds was not required; the quid pro quo involved in the scandal would thus have remained undetected. More important, the 1874 act, by placing the onus on individual candidates, ignored the existence of parties and failed to address the central role they and their leaders were beginning to play in Canadian politics and the electoral process. Furthermore, no attempt was made to provide for the verification of the required reports and the enforcement of adequate sanctions for violations of the law.[3]

The McGreevy scandal of 1891, again concerning a government contract to a railway company, led to an amendment to the Dominion Elections Act making it illegal for anyone to assist a candidate in return for a "valuable consideration" or a promise of appointment to public office. The inadequacy of this reform was shown a genera-

---

[3] For example, in the last four elections before the proclamation of the Election Expenses Act (1965, 1968, 1972, and 1974), on average 25.5 percent of candidates did not file returns of expenses. Although members of Parliament could not legally take their seats in the House of Commons until they had submitted these returns and virtually all elected members complied with the law, there were still some who failed to submit reports of election expenses.

tion later by its uselessness in the Beauharnois affair, which involved the granting of the concession for an important hydroelectric plant in Quebec. The Progressive era in the United States spilled over into Canada with the introduction in 1908 of a series of reforms designed to strengthen the doctrine of agency and to prohibit corporate contributions to candidates and parties. These reforms proved unable, however, to eliminate the parties' dependence on the business community. No prosecutions were ever made under this section of the act, and paradoxically it served only to prevent trade unions from participating financially in election campaigns. The clause prohibiting corporate donations was eliminated from the Dominion Elections Act in 1930, on the very eve of the disclosure of the Beauharnois wrongdoings, on a motion of J. S. Woodsworth, M.P., the future leader of the socialist CCF.

Repeated scandal did not move politicians to amend the basic weakness of the original 1874 legislation, and even the Beauharnois affair failed to stimulate action. In 1938 C. G. Power, a longtime Liberal organizer in Quebec, introduced a bill attempting to regulate both the amounts to be spent and the persons entitled to spend them. Although the bill succeeded in reaching committee stage, it failed because the members could not agree on what constituted reasonable limits. A watered-down version was reintroduced by Power in 1949, but it too did not succeed. Subsequently, private members and leading members of the CCF attempted to limit expenditures and introduce controls on the monetary aspects of the electoral process.

Background to the Passage of the Election Expenses Act

By the early 1960s, the conjunction of several factors stimulated a reexamination of federal electoral law. Financial difficulties arose from the rapid succession of five elections between 1957 and 1965, and, although the major parties usually gathered sufficient funds for election campaigns, each election seemed costlier than the last—a process accelerated by the use of television advertising beginning in 1957. Scandal had not disappeared, as was shown by the revelations of the Rivard affair and by allegations of acceptance of political funds from the underworld. A spirit of reform began to emerge.[4] A demand for major changes in the law rose in Quebec after the defeat of

[4] For a discussion of the emergence of the Quebec amendments, see Harold M. Angell, "The Evolution and Application of Quebec Election Expenses Legislation," in Committee on Election Expenses, *Report*, pp. 279-319. The beginnings of reform within the federal Liberal party are described in Wearing, *The L-Shaped Party*, pp. 60-64.

Maurice Duplessis's Union Nationale government by the Liberals in 1960. Debate within the Quebec Liberal party led in 1963 to sweeping amendments to the Quebec Elections Act. Discussion of changes in methods of fund raising had begun in the federal Liberal party during its period in opposition (1957–1963). This and other events meant that the time was ripe for a serious study of election spending and party finance.

On October 27, 1964, the Canadian secretary of state, Maurice Lamontagne, named a five-member Committee on Election Expenses "to advise on the best practicable way to set enforceable limits to expenditures in election campaigns." The committee carried out the most extensive study of election costs, party finance, and electoral law ever undertaken in Canada. The Barbeau committee (as it came to be called, after its chairman, Alphonse Barbeau) was critical both of the cost of elections and of the way political parties had traditionally been financed. Its recommendations were strongly influenced by the 1963 amendments to electoral law in Quebec, which introduced candidate and party spending limits, government reimbursement of candidates, and a mechanism for the legal recognition of parties.[5] The Barbeau committee went further than the Quebec plan by suggesting a limit to the amount of advertising time available to parties on the electronic media and a scheme for public subsidization of the cost of that advertising. The committee also hoped to stimulate popular fund raising through a system of tax credits for contributors to party and campaign funds.

When the Committee on Election Expenses submitted its *Report* on October 11, 1966, it was clear that its members were recommending reforms that could bring about major changes in election spending and party finance but would also be acceptable to M.P.s and party activists. The Barbeau committee's recommendations can be briefly summarized as follows:

• Political parties should be recognized in law and, through the doctrine of agency and a system of party registration, be made legally responsible for their financial activities.

• A "degree of financial equality" should be established among candidates and among political parties by a free mailing for candidates, a reimbursement of part of candidates' media advertising costs, and the provision of a total of six hours of radio and television time with no charge to the political parties.

[5] The influence of the Quebec amendments on the Barbeau committee's work is reviewed in Norman Ward, "Money and Politics: The Costs of Democracy in Canada," *Canadian Journal of Political Science*, vol. 5 (1972), p. 340.

• The costs of elections should be reduced by prohibiting advertising on radio, television, and in the print media except during the last four weeks before polling day; candidates should be prohibited from spending more than ten cents per elector on such advertising.

• Public confidence in political financing should be strengthened by requiring parties and candidates to disclose their income and expenditure.

• Public participation in politics should be increased and the base of party finance widened through tax concessions to donors.[6]

For several years very little was heard of the recommendations of the Barbeau committee. But in the early 1970s, when the federal government finally began to take steps to reform the law, the general pattern of the 1966 *Report* was followed. In June 1971 a Special Committee on Election Expenses recommended to the House of Commons a series of amendments to the Canada Elections Act. In May 1972, at the tail end of the Twenty-eighth Parliament, Bill C-211 was introduced. Among other things, that bill contained a limited form of disclosure for candidates and parties and a statutory limit on candidates' and parties' advertising expenditure. Bill C-211 did not reach second reading before the House of Commons was dissolved for the October 30 general election.[7]

The Election Expenses Act

A minority Liberal government was returned on October 30, 1972, and after several months of drafting and consultations, Bill C-203 (which eventually became the Election Expenses Act) was introduced in the House of Commons on June 22, 1973. A number of factors influenced both the content of the bill and its timing.[8] Allegations about questionable forms of fund raising, at both the provincial and the federal levels, continued to arouse public opinion. Nova Scotia, Manitoba, and Saskatchewan had reformed their electoral laws to bring in spending controls and related measures. In December 1972, after rumors arose about the connection between Progressive Conservative fund raisers and property developers doing business with

---

[6] Committee on Election Expenses, *Report*, p. 37.

[7] The *Report* of the Special Committee on Election Expenses and Bills C-211 and C-203 are discussed in detail in F. Leslie Seidle, "Electoral Law and Its Effects on Election Expenditure and Party Finance in Great Britain and Canada" (D.Phil. thesis, Oxford University, May 1980), chap. 5.

[8] Ibid.; and Khayyam Z. Paltiel, "Campaign Financing in Canada and Its Reform," in Howard R. Penniman, ed., *Canada at the Polls: The General Election of 1974* (Washington, D.C.: American Enterprise Institute, 1975), pp. 200-201.

the Ontario government, Ontario Premier William Davis asked the Ontario Commission on the Legislature to study the questions of political finance and the reform of electoral law.

Public discussion of party finance and election spending had become much more widespread in Canada and was further stimulated by the Watergate revelations, which began to excite public opinion on both sides of the American border. It is difficult to estimate how much events in the United States influenced the Canadian government, but it is clear that there was a desire to act before public suspicion about party financial activities was heightened even further. More important for the final shape of Bill C-203 was the fact that the Liberal government from 1972 to 1974 depended on the New Democratic party to stay in office. Members of the NDP, most especially its leader, David Lewis, were consulted extensively both before Bill C-203 was introduced and during its passage. The NDP influenced the details of the bill in several ways, notably in weighting the tax credit more toward small contributions and in lowering the threshold for reimbursements to candidates. Bill C-203 introduced a far more comprehensive set of reforms than had been advocated by the Barbeau committee and in several details, such as the definition of "election expenses" and the disclosure requirements, went much further than the earlier Bill C-211. Amendments to Canadian electoral law had been encouraged by events a decade earlier, but the existence of a minority government helped ensure that the actual reforms were both more detailed and more fundamental than had earlier been advocated.

The Election Expenses Act, which came into effect on August 1, 1974, took the form of a series of amendments to the Canada Elections Act, the Broadcasting Act, and the Income Tax Act. Its major provisions are summarized under the following headings.

Party Registration and Agency. Under the Canada Elections Act, political parties are now fully recognized as legal entities.[9] Through the concept of agency, the parties are publicly accountable and can be prosecuted and fined up to $25,000 for an infraction of the act. The system of party registration began in 1970, when the Canada Elections Act was amended to allow party labels to be placed on the ballot papers after the candidates' names.[10] During the 1972 and

[9] The relevant part of the Canada Elections Act, covering party registration, agency, spending limits, and penalties is sections 13-13.8.

[10] For a thorough review of this change and other developments that led to the legal recognition of parties at the federal level, see John C. Courtney, "Recognition of Canadian Political Parties in Parliament and in Law," *Canadian Journal of Political Science*, vol. 11 (1978), pp. 33-60.

1974 elections, six parties were registered (Liberal, Progressive Conservative, New Democratic, Social Credit, Communist, and Marxist-Leninist). All had to meet the following criteria: they had to have been represented in the House of Commons in the outgoing Parliament by twelve or more members, or they had to have nominated fifty candidates by the thirtieth day before polling day of the current campaign. The 1974 act required that parties appoint a chief agent and an auditor whose names, as well as those of party officers, must be registered with the chief electoral officer. "New" parties were obliged to supply similar information. Since 1977, when Bill C-5 was passed, each new party applying for registration must supply the names, addresses, occupations, and signatures of 100 electors who are members of the party.[11] A party cannot be registered for the election at hand if its application is received later than sixty days before the issue of writs for that election. When an election is called, a new party must confirm that the information on file about it is up to date, and also, as a result of the 1977 amendments, its registration can come into effect only when it has nominated fifty candidates. The changes introduced by Bill C-5 tightened up the registration provisions, largely because of fears that the generous tax credit provisions were attracting too many parties with less than serious intentions.

Spending Limits. At a general election, each registered party can spend up to thirty cents for each elector whose name appears on the preliminary list of electors in all the electoral districts in which the party presents official candidates. The act defines "election expenses" to include most conceivable items; but some expenditures, such as parties' grants to candidates, are not included. A further specific limit applies to the amount of advertising time on the electronic media available for purchase by the political parties. A total of six and one-half hours of time on all broadcast outlets is set by law and is divided among the registered parties in a way that approximately reflects their previous popular vote.

Candidates' spending is also subject to a ceiling.[12] In nearly all constituencies, the limit follows a statutory formula: one dollar for each of the first 15,000 names on the constituency's preliminary list of electors, plus fifty cents for each of the next 10,000, plus twenty-five cents for each elector in excess of 25,000. This limitation was altered

---

[11] The bill was given royal assent on December 20, 1977 (*Statutes of Canada 1977-1978*, chap. 3).

[12] The relevant part of the Canada Elections Act for candidates' election activities is sections 61.1-63.1.

slightly by the 1977 amendments: in an electoral district where the number of names on the preliminary list of electors is less than the average number of names on the preliminary lists for all electoral districts, the number of names for that electoral district is deemed to be increased by one-half of the difference between that number of names and the average number of names on the list for all electoral districts.

Candidate and party spending is also restricted by the fact that the Canada Elections Act now prohibits advertising outside a four-week period beginning on the twenty-ninth day before polling day and ending at midnight on the day immediately preceding polling day.

Reimbursements. Provided that they comply with the requirements concerning the filing of a return of election expenses, registered parties can be reimbursed for one-half the costs incurred in the purchase of permitted radio and television advertising time. This is the only form of direct public funding available to political parties, although they are assisted in fund raising by the tax credit for contributions. All candidates who receive 15 percent of the votes within a constituency and who comply with the requirements for submitting their return of election expenses can be reimbursed for part of their campaign costs. Candidates receive an amount that is the lesser of their election expenses and the aggregate of the following items: the cost of sending one mailing by first class to each person on the preliminary list of electors in the electoral district, eight cents for each of the first 25,000 electors on the list, and six cents for each name in excess of 25,000. In electoral districts where the number of names on the list is less than the average of all electoral districts, the amount of the reimbursement is adjusted upward in a way similar to the provisions for the candidates' spending limit.

Disclosure. Now that parties are legally recognized, party funds are no longer considered their private business, and expenses and the amount and sources of contributions must be disclosed. Six months after the end of the party's fiscal year, a return must be submitted. This return must be audited and must contain a detailed statement of the party's contributions and operating expenses. Contributions must be itemized under a number of categories, and the name of anyone who donated more than $100 during the fiscal year must also be disclosed. In addition, within six months after a general election, a statement of the party's election expenses must be submitted. After each general election or by-election, candidates are required to file detailed audited returns as well. These returns must be received by the returning officer in the constituency within four months of polling day. Vouchers for any expense greater than $25 must be included, and the name of anyone who donated more than $100 to the candidate's campaign must be provided. A copy of the candidate's return must be sent to the chief electoral officer. This return is a public document, as are the parties' annual and election returns.

Tax Credits. One of the major advantages afforded registered parties is that they can issue receipts that allow contributors to claim income-tax credits. The same privilege is allowed candidates during election campaigns. Any taxpayer may subtract from his federal tax payable the following amount: 75 percent of the amount contributed if it is less than $100, $75 plus 50 percent of the amount exceeding $100 but less than $550, $300 plus one-third of the amount by which the total contributed exceeds $550. The maximum amount that can be claimed as a tax credit is $500, which is reached with a total contribution of $1,150.

The 1974 Election Expenses Act introduced potentially revolutionary changes into federal electoral law. It focused on controlling election spending by means of statutory limits on candidates' and parties' campaign costs. The introduction of various forms of public funding was intended to help candidates and parties meet some of their election costs. It was also argued at the time that the imposition of limits and the introduction of reimbursements would help to equalize chances among parties and candidates. In addition, political contributions would be encouraged by the generous tax credit provisions, weighted especially in favor of small donations. Finally, the disclosure of parties' yearly financial activities and of parties' and candidates' election activities was intended to open up the process of fund raising and election spending to public scrutiny. It was hoped that the disclosure provisions and the related innovations would induce greater public confidence in the political and election process.

Party Finance 1974–1979

Although the Election Expenses Act focused primarily on controls at election time, it had numerous implications for party finance on a year-to-year basis. The parts of the act that most affected parties' yearly activities were the extension of the concept of agency to political parties, the disclosure requirements, and the income-tax credit. Before discussing the 1979 and 1980 elections, we must briefly review how the parties reacted to these changes.

The 1974 act required each party to name a chief agent. The parties vary in the way in which they have complied with this innovation, but one requirement is common to all of them: each party's chief agent has to submit an annual report of party contributions and expenses, called a fiscal period return, to the chief electoral officer. The spending of the party and donations to it must be broken down into categories. Furthermore, the return must include the name of any person or body giving more than $100 to the party during the fiscal year. Because the chief agent must maintain financial control and as a result of the disclosure requirements, parties have adopted far more detailed record-keeping practices than ever before in Canadian politics. Since 1974 all major parties have computerized a great deal of their operations in this area. Some party officials complained at first about the overly detailed and strict requirements put on them by the law, but most would agree that party activists have by now adapted to the changes in procedure. An indirect consequence of the changes is that those in charge of party finances are much more aware of what is happening at the various levels of the party. As one party official put it, one of the major effects of the new legislation was "to open up the fund-raising operations of the party to the party itself."

The tax credit provisions gave the parties the potential of expanding their base among individual contributors and, in the case of the two older parties, lessening their dependence on major corporate donors. The tax credit is strongly weighted toward small donations—a contribution of $100 costs the taxpayer only $25. Since the maximum amount to which a tax credit applies is $1,150, a much smaller incentive is given to the large corporations that traditionally provided most of the two largest parties' funds. The tax credit promised a great boon to the political parties, but, as will be seen, they reacted to this possibility in different ways, and their ultimate success has varied markedly.

Liberal Finances since 1974. The Liberals appointed as their first chief agent Senator Paul Lafond, a former secretary general of the National Liberal Federation. By the beginning of 1976, they had adopted a corporate form of agency, something the Progressive Conservatives had done as soon as the Election Expenses Act came into force. The introduction of this new body, the Federal Liberal Agency, did not mean that additional powers were assumed by Liberal national headquarters. The party's national office has never played a dominant role in the Liberal party and has had to compete with relatively strong provincial associations and with other centers of power in

Ottawa.[13] The Federal Liberal Agency was given an essentially reporting function: all contributions to the party are channeled through it, the receipts required for income-tax purposes are issued by it, and the agency disburses the money it handles upon instructions from the party's national officers. The Federal Liberal Agency was a new structure grafted onto the party's national organization, but one that assumed limited powers.

Shortly after the passage of the Election Expenses Act, the Liberals made a couple of important decisions that affected fund raising in subsequent years. The first was that the constituency would be used as the major organizational basis of fund raising. Although some party activists, both in 1972 and after the passage of the act, had pressed for the introduction of direct-mail solicitation of donations, this was strongly opposed because of uncertain returns and because it was thought that it would not accord with the party's structure. More important, leading Liberals argued that nothing could surpass the face-to-face approach in seeking donations at the local level. Accordingly, a formula for apportioning revenues obtained by such solicitation was devised: 50 percent of what is raised in the constituencies is placed in a constituency election "trust fund," 25 percent is returned to the constituencies for ongoing expenses, and 25 percent is allocated to the provincial association. The national office continued to be funded by annual grants from the Treasury Committee, the party's select body of leading fund raisers chosen for their close connections with the business community in Canada.

The Liberals also decided that an upper limit should be placed on corporate contributions. Traditionally, the Treasury Committee had raised most of its money during election years. Since the 1960s it has often gathered sufficient funds to pay off the national office's overdraft and fund it for a year, in addition to paying for the election costs at the national level. Election-year contributions sometimes were as high as $100,000 from a single source. After the proclamation of the Election Expenses Act, it was decided that a ceiling of $25,000 would be placed on a single donation; that ceiling is raised to $50,000 in an election year.[14] As part of the party's reassessment of its fund-raising procedures, it was planned that the canvassing of

---

[13] Stephen Clarkson, "Pierre Trudeau and the Liberal Party: The Jockey and the Horse," in Penniman, *Canada at the Polls, 1974*, p. 72. Wearing refers to the national office of the Liberal party as "an apex without real levers of power" (*The L-Shaped Party*, p. 144).

[14] This was apparently Pierre Trudeau's idea, and he has been quoted as saying: "We don't want to be indebted to any small number of large corporations." See Ian Urquhart, "The Bucks Start Here," *Maclean's*, May 15, 1978, p. 44p.

major donors would become more systematic and would be done annually.

The pattern of Liberal party finance from August 1, 1974, to the end of 1979 is shown in table 9–1. (Because the fiscal periods of the three major parties did not coincide until 1977, the figures in tables 9–1, 9–2, and 9–3 up to the end of 1976 have been totaled, to allow for comparisons among parties.) Although table 9–1 is basically self-explanatory, a couple of points should be made. First, although the Liberals managed to obtain about half their funds from individuals in the first three years after the passage of the Election Expenses Act, by 1977 the effects of the decision to canvass major corporations annually began to be seen. Corporate contributions rose further in 1978, when an election was expected, and climbed to $3.9 million in 1979 (74 percent of Liberal party contributions).[15] A preliminary analysis of the 1980 figures for party contributions shows that the proportion of Liberal party funds coming from public and private corporations dropped to 60 percent of total donations to the Liberal party of $6,217,795.

It should be noted that even though corporate contributions continue to account for the largest portion of Liberal party funds, the Treasury Committee met some difficulty in the years just after the act was passed in encouraging its traditional sources to give annual contributions.[16] Some companies felt the Liberal party should raise more money from individuals, but their reluctance can be explained more completely by the new disclosure requirements and changes in American political finance laws after Watergate. Although the Canadian federal law places no restrictions on the source or size of a political contribution, party bagmen found it difficult to convince the executives of multinational companies of the major contrasts between the Canadian and American laws.

---

[15] Ten large corporations, including the five major banks, each gave $50,000 or slightly more to the Liberals in 1979: Alcan, Inco, Northern Telecom, Gulf Canada, Power Corporation, the Royal Bank, the Bank of Montreal, the Canadian Imperial Bank of Commerce, the Bank of Nova Scotia, and the Toronto-Dominion Bank. An article critical of the Liberals' reliance on corporate donations is "La démocratie politique: une farce," *La Presse*, December 6, 1980; see also "Parties Richer, but Democratic Dreams Fading," *Globe and Mail* (Toronto), November 29, 1980.

[16] Wearing points out that in the first fiscal year after the Election Expenses Act came into effect, only seventeen corporations gave $10,000 or more to the Liberal party. Traditional donors such as Canadian Pacific and Inco "at first refused to give anything and the fund raisers of both the older parties feared an organized boycott by some of the big corporations" (*The L-Shaped Party*, p. 226). See also Urquhart, "The Bucks Start Here."

As the Liberals' source of funds shifted more toward the corporate sector in 1978 and 1979, the share of party contributions received from individuals dropped markedly. In 1977 over 21,000 people gave to the Liberal party; this figure rose slightly in 1978 but fell to 13,025 in 1979, when individual contributions amounted to only 23 percent of total contributions to the party.[17] Leading Liberals expressed dissatisfaction with the earlier decision to rely on constituencies for the major source of party funds. Many constituency associations have little incentive to raise large amounts of money between elections, especially if there is a sitting Liberal M.P. At election time, local activists are oriented virtually exclusively to the constituency campaign, and it is thus no wonder that individual contributions to the party as a whole dropped off significantly in 1979. In mid-1979 Liberal party finances were in very bad shape, and a party committee under Gordon Dryden, the national treasurer, was set up to investigate the possible introduction of direct-mail fund raising. The Liberals improved over 1979 in their solicitation from individuals: in 1980, 17,670 people contributed nearly $2.3 million, or 37 percent of total Liberal party contributions. Nevertheless, the Liberals could not deny the clear success of the Conservatives' venture in this area, and despite some opposition from within the party, direct mail began to be used at the national level in early 1981.

Progressive Conservative Finances since 1974. Whereas the Liberals' fund raising since mid-1974 shows a somewhat mixed record, that of Progressive Conservatives flourished. Dissatisfaction with the government party no doubt encouraged contributions to Conservative coffers in the 1978–1979 period, but the most credit must be given to the system of direct-mail fund raising that they introduced and used extensively. The Progressive Conservatives' financial situation was far from rosy when the Election Expenses Act came into effect. A deficit of nearly $1 million remained from the 1972 and 1974 elections, in addition to a long-term debt. Constituency organization had been neglected during the Diefenbaker era and, according to George Perlin, did not improve very much during Robert Stanfield's tenure as leader.[18] It was thus not surprising that major changes in

[17] It is interesting to contrast this with the financial base of the Liberal party of Quebec. The Quebec act to govern the financing of political parties of 1977 allows for donations only from individuals. In 1979 the Liberal party of Quebec received $2.59 million from 124,439 contributors. See *Rapport annuel 1979-1980, Directeur général du financement des partis politiques* (Quebec: Editeur Officiel, 1980), p. 39.

[18] George C. Perlin, *The Tory Syndrome* (Montreal: McGill-Queen's University Press, 1980), pp. 20-22.

TABLE 9-1

FINANCIAL ACTIVITIES OF THE LIBERAL PARTY, AUGUST 1, 1974–DECEMBER 31, 1979

	August 1, 1974–December 31, 1976	1977	1978	1979
Income and expenses (dollars)				
Contributions	7,748,155	4,423,566	4,779,694	5,220,520
Other income	291,452	163,040	237,817	1,081,513
Total income	8,039,607	4,586,606	5,017,511	6,302,033
Operating expenses	3,428,123	2,363,712	3,391,406	2,758,789
By-election expenses	—	83,063	29,016	4,700
Transfers to party associations	3,236,490	1,739,933	1,862,604	7,134
Other expenditures	4,739	—	—	—
Total expenditures	6,669,352	4,186,708	5,283,026	2,770,623

Details of contributions	No.	$	No.	$	No.	$	No.	$
Individuals	35,752	4,060,162	21,063	1,983,687	22,350	2,101,716	13,025	1,184,755
Public corporations	519	1,403,370	376	864,349	435	1,054,838	321	1,799,516
Private corporations	7,049	2,164,343	5,296	1,427,206	4,586	1,433,176	3,415	2,076,051

Governments	5	653	—	—	—	—	—	—
Trade unions	7	1,295	3	1,154	1	400	2	1,663
Corporations without share capital	35	4,651	13	6,453	5	559	1	300
Unincorporated organizations	359	113,681	455	140,717	713	189,005	462	158,235
Total	43,726	7,748,155	27,206	4,423,566	28,090	4,779,694	17,226	5,220,520

Details of operating expenses (dollars)

Salaries, wages, and benefits	1,364,765	908,510	1,150,906	1,001,375
Traveling expenses	312,097	186,169	396,660	128,160
Party conventions and meetings	402,152	240,525	385,861	213,453
Rent, light, heat, and power	159,656	94,773	102,217	120,626
Advertising	136,529	159,483	208,852	215,969
Broadcasting	4,461	652	3,435	1,756
Printing and stationery	349,457	227,176	272,919	217,772
Telephone and telegraph	170,784	124,260	142,233	131,242
Legal and audit fees	106,716	43,213	53,476	109,010
Miscellaneous expenses	421,506	378,951	674,847	619,426
Total	3,428,123	2,363,712	3,391,406	2,758,789

Dash (—): None.
SOURCE: Registered party fiscal period returns submitted to the chief electoral officer.

the party's financial organization were seen as necessary, and those who accepted these changes were delighted when they began to reap significant rewards for the party.

The Progressive Conservatives used a corporate agent, the PC Canada Fund, from August 1, 1974, but, unlike the Liberals, they planned from the beginning that it would be a good deal more than a reporting agency. In addition to fulfilling the requirements of agency (record keeping, reporting, issuing tax credit receipts), the fund was intended to provide "better financial management and new fund-raising potential." [19] There was some opposition to this new structure, notably from M.P.s, but given the Progressive Conservatives' past financial record, it was difficult to object to a move that would benefit the party as a whole.

The PC Canada Fund has been responsible for coordinating all forms of fund raising within the party, but its most notable success has been in the area of direct-mail solicitation. This method of political fund raising, which was widely used in the United States by the early 1970s, relies heavily on computers. Not long after the establishment of the PC Canada Fund, David McMillan, the fund's national coordinator until mid-1979, visited Republican party offices in the United States. He was subsequently responsible for adapting the American direct-mail efforts to the needs of the Progressive Conservative party. Lists of potential contributors are purchased from newspaper and magazine publishers. Tens of thousands of letters are dispatched at a time, and those who reply with a contribution can be approached over and over again. The initial costs of direct mail were high, but after extensive "prospecting," the Progressive Conservatives began to get a return on their outlay. Extensive research allowed the party to determine which sorts of lists would provide the most prospective donors. The tax credit provides a direct incentive for political contributions, and this is emphasized in the letters sent out. An additional advantage of direct mail is that many people who might not normally give to political parties or who might not normally be approached by local canvassers can be asked for a donation.

Direct-mail fund raising did not, however, replace more traditional methods. Like the Liberals, the Progressive Conservatives established a formula, albeit a different one, for the allocation of funds raised by constituency associations: 75 percent of the amount collected by the local association is returned to it, and 25 percent is retained by the national party. This formula provided a strong incentive to the local associations but did not starve the national party,

[19] Letter from David McMillan to Leslie Seidle, January 24, 1978.

which kept all the funds raised through direct-mail solicitation. The National Finance Committee continued to solicit donations from the corporate sector, but its previously dominant role in party fund raising was greatly diminished.[20] The board of directors of the PC Canada Fund became the effective financial committee of the party.

Table 9–2 provides a summary of the Conservatives' financial activities since the passage of the Election Expenses Act. Although the Liberals received more donations in the period August 1, 1974, to December 31, 1976, the Progressive Conservatives began to improve their finances significantly during that time. A party bulletin noted that in the fiscal year August 1, 1974, to July 31, 1975, the number of contributors to the party increased by 400 percent.[21] In early 1976 the party was able to retire in full the balance it owed after the 1974 election. The Liberals continued to gather more funds in 1977, but during the 1978 fiscal year, contributions to the Conservatives edged ahead (compare the first lines in tables 9–1 and 9–2). During 1979 the Conservatives collected nearly $8.4 million, compared with $5.2 million for the Liberals.[22] Total contributions to the Progressive Conservative party increased fivefold between the first fiscal year after the passage of the Election Expenses Act (1974–1975) and the 1979 fiscal year. Also impressive is the fact that the number of individuals giving to the party increased more than fivefold during the same period (from 6,423 in 1974–1975 to 34,952 in 1979). In 1980, the number of individuals contributing to Progressive Conservative coffers dropped slightly to 32,720; they donated $3 million (40 percent of the total of $7,564,120 contributed to the party). Donations from business continued to provide a significant proportion of Conservative party funds.[23] Contributions from private and public cor-

---

[20] Traditionally, the National Finance Committee has occupied a position in the Progressive Conservative party roughly analogous to that of the national Treasury Committee in the Liberal Party. Its chairman is appointed by the Progressive Conservative leader, and the committee itself is separate from the party's extraparliamentary organization, the Progressive Conservative Association of Canada.

[21] Progressive Conservative Party of Canada, *Report to our Supporters*, February 1, 1976.

[22] According to David McMillan, $6.4 million of the party's total contributions for 1979 ($8.4 million) had been channeled through the office of the PC Canada Fund by the end of June 1979 (interview with Leslie Seidle, August 31, 1979).

[23] The traditional pattern of large corporations giving virtually identical contributions to the two older parties still seems to hold: all ten of the large corporations and banks that gave $50,000 or slightly more to the Liberals in 1979 also gave $50,000 or slightly more to the Progressive Conservatives, with the exception of Gulf Canada, which gave $53,324 to the Liberals and $36,400 to the Conservatives.

TABLE 9–2

FINANCIAL ACTIVITIES OF THE PROGRESSIVE CONSERVATIVE PARTY, AUGUST 1, 1974–DECEMBER 31, 1979

	August 1, 1974–December 31, 1976		1977		1978		1979	
Income and expenses (dollars)								
Contributions	6,700,513		3,545,446		5,363,536		8,375,716	
Other income	307,893		229,002		100,974		—	
Total income	7,008,406		3,774,448		5,464,510		8,375,716	
Operating expenses	3,688,408		2,921,103		3,617,030		3,664,661	
By-election expenses	18,293		55,645		129,479		23,578	
Transfers to party associations	1,586,628		1,256,624		1,723,321		1,395,111	
Other expenditures	689,820		—		—		—	
Total expenditures	5,983,149		4,233,372		5,469,830		5,083,350	
Details of contributions	No.	$	No.	$	No.	$	No.	$
Individuals	36,426	3,190,610	20,339	1,742,964	35,615	2,661,175	34,952	3,182,897
Public corporations	494	1,572,145	205	740,235	220	879,669	278	1,732,801
Private corporations	8,561	1,802,555	4,165	983,704	7,820	1,745,672	7,413	3,287,484

Governments	17	2,270	2	170	—	—	—	1
Trade unions	—	—	2	432	—	—	1	1,190
Corporations without share capital	36	3,769	131	11,521	65	9,771	61	27,215
Unincorporated organizations	556	129,164	333	66,420	225	67,249	243	144,129
Total	46,090	6,700,513	25,177	3,545,446	43,945	5,363,536	42,948	8,375,716

Details of operating expenses (dollars)

Salaries, wages, and benefits	1,085,173	931,648	1,063,349	1,126,899
Traveling expenses	465,824	378,651	545,355	551,966
Party conventions and meetings	892,169	429,012	50,105	176,649
Rent, light, heat, and power	200,609	98,663	151,648	316,703
Advertising	5,016	—	535,287	106,986
Broadcasting	—	—	—	—
Printing and stationery	238,129	401,546	660,157	870,675
Telephone and telegraph	208,722	108,056	183,265	201,385
Legal and audit fees	33,325	38,050	40,884	58,697
Miscellaneous	559,441	535,477	386,980	254,701
Total	3,688,408	2,921,103	3,617,030	3,664,661

Dash (—): None.
SOURCE: As for table 9-1.

porations accounted for 49 percent of all donations in 1978. This proportion rose to 60 percent in 1979, the highest for any fiscal period since mid-1974 but still significantly lower than the comparable figure for the Liberals during that year. In 1980, corporate contributions amounted to 58 percent of total donations to the Progressive Conservative party.

NDP Finances since 1974. One of the assumptions behind the Election Expenses Act was that there should be a greater equality in the financial resources available to candidates and registered parties. By the time of the 1979 election, it was clear that the New Democratic party and a large number of its candidates no longer suffered poverty, at least relative to the two older parties. A certain equalization of resources had begun long before the first election held under the 1974 amendments. In many people's view, the NDP has benefited more than any other party from those amendments.

The NDP (like its predecessor the CCF) has traditionally relied on large numbers of fairly small contributions for its year-to-year finances. Leading NDP activists were conscious of this, and during the negotiations leading to the introduction of Bill C-203 in 1973, David Lewis was able to get agreement to a tax credit formula that benefited small contributors more than did the earlier proposals. It was not difficult to predict that NDP finances would be given a significant boost by this part of the Election Expenses Act.

Even though the tax credit gave a probable advantage to the NDP, one characteristic of the party's structure could have created major difficulties. In several ways, the NDP has been a fairly decentralized party, relying strongly on the success of the provincial parties in its areas of strength (chiefly in the West, except for Alberta, and in Ontario). Before 1974, the NDP federal headquarters was maintained largely by membership fees and contributions funneled through the provincial offices. The federal activities of the NDP depended on the same party members who were the backbone of provincial riding associations and provincial executives.[24] It has been a fact of the party's history that the federal NDP has suffered more than the provincial organizations as a result of these divided loyalties.

The Election Expenses Act required more central control, at least in the financial area, than the NDP had ever had before. At the same time, Ed Broadbent campaigned for the federal leadership (which he won in 1975) on a platform of a more powerful federal

[24] Jo Surich, "Purists and Pragmatists: Canadian Democratic Socialism at the Crossroads," in Penniman, *Canada at the Polls, 1974*, p. 136.

presence for the NDP.[25] According to the NDP federal secretary, Robin Sears, the party made a fairly smooth transition after the passage of the 1974 act. He pointed out that the party has maintained an extensive professional and volunteer staff at all levels. Party activists were trained in the year-to-year implications of the law, and by 1976 the party was already holding schools to acquaint people in local organizations with the rules that applied to elections.

The NDP was able to fit the financial provisions of the 1974 changes into its party structure by deciding to use the tax credit for both federal and provincial purposes. In this way, party members whose primary loyalty was to the provincial organization could raise funds, with the tax credit's incentive, and help both the provincial and the federal levels of the party. A decision made when the legislation came into effect was that 15 percent of all money raised, anywhere in the party, would go to the federal office. The remaining 85 percent is returned to the appropriate province and divided among the provincial office and the federal and provincial ridings from which it originated. The formulas vary from province to province, but it is fair to say that over half of what is returned to the province goes, at least initially, to the provincial party office or the appropriate provincial riding.

Although the other parties have used the tax credit scheme to benefit some of their provincial operations, the division of revenues in the NDP is weighted fairly strongly in favor of the provincial organizations. It is widely felt that the NDP's decision to use the federal tax credit for provincial purposes encouraged the passage of the Election Finances Reform Act in Ontario in 1975. That act, with its emphasis on controls on contributions, prohibits transfers from a federal party to a provincial party, candidate, or constituency association, except for relatively small amounts during a provincial election. Similar prohibitions have been introduced in Alberta and New Brunswick.

The details of NDP finances since mid-1974 are presented in table 9–3. In the period from August 1, 1974, to December 31, 1976, the NDP's total revenues were somewhat lower than those of the two older parties, but it received contributions from nearly four times as many people as the Liberals or the Progressive Conservatives. This strong reliance on individual donations has continued at the level of over 60,000 contributors each year. Nearly twice as many people gave to the NDP in 1979 as to the Conservatives and

[25] Desmond Morton, *Social Democracy in Canada* (Toronto: Hakkert and Co., 1977), pp. 171, 176.

TABLE 9–3

Financial Activities of the New Democratic Party, August 1, 1974–December 31, 1979

	August 1, 1974– December 31, 1976		1977		1978		1979	
Income and expenses (dollars)								
Contributions		6,223,685		2,860,838		3,259,347		4,597,112
Other income		75,031		145,295		141,223		144,169
Total income		6,298,716		3,006,133		3,400,570		4,741,281
Operating expenses		4,638,763		2,848,181		3,008,952		3,365,009
By-election expenses		6,610		8,926		19,105		14,100
Transfers to party associations		1,575,090		247,773		486,077		1,298,727
Other expenditure		—		—		—		—
Total expenditure		6,220,463		3,104,880		3,514,134		4,677,836
Details of contributions	No.	$	No.	$	No.	$	No.	$
Individuals	142,941	5,125,887	60,169	2,209,500	67,133	2,552,866	63,655	2,720,675
Public corporations	30	48,107	13	38,080	2	6,045	2	1,100
Private corporations	444	201,800	299	151,830	483	200,601	294	169,298

Governments	—	—	1	16,079	1	3,014	—	—
Trade unions	2,100	838,530	750	436,214	757	490,359	1,046	1,701,616
Corporations without share capital	1	220	—	—	6	725	—	—
Unincorporated organizations	20	9,141	50	9,135	27	5,737	32	4,423
Total	145,536	6,223,685	61,282	2,860,838	68,409	3,259,347	65,029	4,597,112

Details of operating expenses (dollars)

Salaries, wages, and benefits	1,952,773	1,253,360	1,550,523	1,536,081
Traveling expenses	638,461	383,306	413,859	408,366
Party conventions and meetings	323,460	247,340	56,951	347,844
Rent, light, heat, and power	176,320	104,189	133,520	119,203
Advertising	521,292	174,717	311,721	268,934
Broadcasting	176,083	220,130	—	—
Printing and stationery	454,282	226,812	264,652	339,160
Telephone and telegraph	98,543	66,986	79,611	90,856
Legal and audit fees	77,421	50,533	43,827	68,077
Miscellaneous	220,128	120,808	154,288	186,488
Total	4,638,763	2,848,181	3,008,952	3,365,009

Dash (—): None.
SOURCE: As for table 9-1.

five times as many to the NDP as to the Liberals. The NDP received only a very small proportion of its revenues from business sources (just over $170,000 in 1979). Trade union contributions accounted for a small portion of NDP funds up to the 1979 election year. In 1978, for example, trade union donations amounted to only 15 percent of total party contributions. In 1979 this proportion rose to 37 percent; the comparable figure for 1980 is 35 percent of total contributions of $4,920,447.

It is clear that NDP finances have been greatly improved since 1974. The tax credit and other parts of the Election Expenses Act have helped give the federal office of the party greater "political muscle." One result is that the number of people employed in the NDP federal office has trebled, from seven in 1973–1974 to twenty-two in late 1979. In short, the NDP at the federal level is no longer just a "creature" of the provincial parties, as some used to describe it. The federal office has assumed a major role in party organization and fund raising and in recent years has been attempting an even greater redistribution of resources among the various levels and geographical divisions of the party.

Party Spending and Campaign Finance in 1979 and 1980

The year-to-year aspects of the Election Expenses Act had major consequences for the fund-raising methods of the three major parties and for the general state of their finances. But the 1974 act was directed mostly at election spending. It was meant to control the escalating costs of elections, especially media advertising, and it was hoped that placing a limit on all parties' spending would somewhat reduce the disparities in their financial capacities. Similar principles lay behind the limits on candidates' spending.

All parties faced a common constraint: their spending could not exceed the limit prescribed by the Canada Elections Act, and appropriate steps had to be taken to ensure that control was kept at the various levels of the party. Each party's chief agent is legally responsible for seeing that the limit is not exceeded and must submit a return of expenses within six months of the election. A contravention of the provisions of the Canada Elections Act relating to party spending can result in fines of up to $25,000 for the party. These strict provisions of the Election Expenses Act no doubt helped party managers to convince people throughout each party of the importance of adhering to the limits. They were much discussed at the time, and in the following years all parties made serious efforts to educate activists at all levels in the new rules. Nearly five years elapsed before they were put into practice in the election of 1979.

For the first time, in 1979, parties had to plan their election budgets within well-known limits. Before, the effective limit was how much the parties' financial committees could raise. The Liberals had in general been the most successful at this, and for the 1974 general election, their national Treasury Committee raised some $6.2 million, well ahead of the $5.5 million spent by the national campaign committee.[26] For the Conservatives, the temptation to keep up with the Liberals' spending accounted at least in part for the $1 million deficit which they accumulated during the 1972 and 1974 elections. Under the new statutory limits, the parties could no longer spend in unlimited fashion, and carefully planned budgets were necessary. The result was that in 1979 and 1980 reported election expenses by the two major parties were lower than they had been in 1974, even making no allowance for inflation during the intervening period. The NDP spent several times more than in 1974.

The 1979 and 1980 Liberal Campaigns. In recent Liberal campaigns, the national campaign committee has been headed by two cochairmen, one Anglophone and one Francophone. Even though provincial campaign committees also existed, the national committee assumed by far the most important functions for all of English Canada. The Quebec committee has maintained a large degree of independence and has controlled the media advertising in that province, both in French and in English. National campaign spending was financed almost entirely from corporate donations solicited by the national Treasury Committee. Within each province, the campaign committee spent the funds it raised through a treasury committee in that province (assisted in some cases by grants from the national level) with no reference to a budget for the Liberal party as a whole.

In the months preceding the 1979 election, the provincial committees submitted budgets to the national campaign committee, and major decisions were made about the share of legally permitted spending that would be allocated to the national and provincial committees. The three key people in these decisions were the campaign cochairmen, Senator Keith Davey and Marc Lalonde, and the chairman of the Federal Liberal Agency, Torrance Wylie. After these allocations were made, proportions were allotted to various forms of spending: media and other forms of advertising, travel, and so on. Within each provincial campaign organization, a member of the Federal Liberal Agency was responsible for monitoring and controlling the plans that had been drawn up. The Federal Liberal Agency

[26] Paltiel, "Campaign Financing in Canada," p. 190.

TABLE 9–4

ELECTION EXPENSES REPORTED BY POLITICAL PARTIES,
1979 GENERAL ELECTION
(dollars)

Category	Progressive Conservative	Liberal	NDP	Social Credit
Advertising	267,209	576,168	314,613	28,006
Broadcasting				
Radio	939,272	563,029	247,616	7,580
Television	1,539,020	1,295,208	770,851	10,141
Hire of premises	12,644	53,996	21,153	3,116
Salaries and wages	116,897	145,942	413,065	230
Professional services	231,409	231,146	0	26,367
Travel	632,321	691,019	233,073	24,540
Administration	106,445	356,318	187,262	9,422
Miscellaneous	0	0	2,460	0
Total election expenses	3,845,217	3,912,826	2,190,093	109,402
Expense limits	4,459,249	4,459,249	4,459,249	1,700,701
Media advertising reimbursement	793,967	718,020	496,350	7,769

NOTE: Total spending by other registered parties was as follows: Marxist-Leninist $31,118, Communist $3,999, Libertarian $13,329, Rhinoceros $8,634, Union Populaire 0.

SOURCE: *Report of the Chief Electoral Officer Respecting Election Expenses, Thirty-first General Election, 1979* (Ottawa: Minister of Supply and Services Canada, 1980).

had final responsibility for keeping records and for reporting on the party's spending after the election.

The Liberals' reported spending in 1979 is shown in table 9–4.[27] The total of just over $3.9 million represents 88 percent of what was allowed by law. The $1.86 million spent on media advertising accounted for 47 percent of this total. In addition to the party's reported election expenses, $249,000 was allocated to candidates for local campaigns—down dramatically from the $2.6 million distributed to candidates in the 1974 election. These figures do not include any spending in the long run-up to the election. All parties spent significant amounts in this prewrit period on, for example, polling and

[27] Information on Liberal party spending and election finances, apart from what is publicly available from the party's election return, was supplied to the authors by Torrance J. Wylie.

election preparation, but it would be virtually impossible to place a monetary value on these activities. In the case of the Liberals, the advantages of incumbency must also be mentioned. Many members of the prime minister's staff and cabinet ministers' assistants devoted a substantial part of their time during the campaign to election-related activities. It should thus be remembered that the parties' reported spending includes only what the act refers to as "election expenses" and for that reason provides a somewhat incomplete view of what each party actually spent to fight an election campaign.

After the 1979 election, several leading Liberals admitted that the statutory controls were not a stringent restraint. These people stated that they doubted if the Liberals would have spent more without the limits. In Senator Davey's words, the limits were "a procedural rather than a real restraint." [28] Even though the long-term prospects for the Liberal party's finances did not seem bright in mid-1979, there was no lack of funds for the election itself. The party's longstanding objective of finishing each election with a surplus had been met—according to one party official, $1 million remained in bank accounts across the country.

The funds for the Liberal party campaign in 1979 came from three principal sources. The national Treasury Committee provided just over $2.3 million. This money, raised almost entirely from corporations in Ontario, Quebec, and to a lesser extent Alberta, accounted for over half the money required for the 1979 campaign. Not all this money was actually raised in 1979—a substantial proportion had been held in reserve by the Treasury Committee. The second major source of funds was the media reimbursement, which amounted to $718,020. It should be noted that the media reimbursement does not cover production costs, and so the figures on the bottom lines of tables 9–4 and 9–5 are not equal to 50 percent of what the parties reported having spent on television and radio advertising.

The third major source of Liberal party revenues in 1979 deserves some additional comment. In the months before the 1979 election, the national campaign committee devised a plan by which candidates would channel part of their reimbursements back to the national campaign committee. Candidates were subsequently asked to sign a pledge form that was sent to the chief electoral officer. After the election, when each candidate's return had been submitted and verified in the office of the chief electoral officer, part of the reimbursement was sent to the candidate and part to the Liberal party national office. Nearly all candidates in Ontario and Quebec signed

[28] Interview with Leslie Seidle, August 21, 1979.

TABLE 9–5

ELECTION EXPENSES REPORTED BY POLITICAL PARTIES,
1980 GENERAL ELECTION
(dollars)

Category	Progressive Conservative	Liberal	NDP	Social Credit
Advertising	578,246	402,504	425,943	12,409
Broadcasting				
Radio	651,541	578,597	233,105	3,586
Television	1,876,284	1,612,532	1,167,232	1,974
Hire of premises	27,532	15,514	24,547	2,800
Salaries and wages	57,543	155,254	591,743	0
Professional services	100,827	373,928	63,722	32,304
Travel	639,448	420,914	378,122	35,566
Administration	470,928	284,377	197,474	4,928
Miscellaneous	4,858	2,603	4,288	3,943
Total election expenses	4,407,207	3,846,223	3,086,176	97,510
Expense limits	4,546,192	4,546,192	4,531,562	1,371,016
Media advertising reimbursement	977,835	909,923	677,481	1,749

NOTE: Total spending by other registered parties was as follows: Marxist-Leninist $68,365, Communist $2,872, Libertarian $15,344, Rhinoceros $9,167, Union Populaire $7,434.

SOURCE: *Report of the Chief Electoral Officer Respecting Election Expenses, Thirty-second General Election, 1980* (Ottawa: Minister of Supply and Services Canada, 1981).

the necessary "pledge forms"; in Quebec candidates handed over half their reimbursements, and in Ontario the usual amount was one-third. In other provinces a small number of candidates were asked to return some money to the provincial committee, although the pattern varied widely. The amount gained at the national level from candidates in Ontario and Quebec was $830,000, over one-fifth of the Liberal party's reported expenses.

In the 1980 election, the pattern of Liberal party spending did not change very much. The party spent somewhat less than in 1979 (see table 9–5), but the amount allotted to media advertising rose to $2.19 million, representing 57 percent of total reported expenses. (Total media spending by all parties rose in 1980, partly as a reflection of a significant rise in the cost of buying television time in the period between the two elections.) The Treasury Committee contributed some $1.9 million to the 1980 campaign at the national level, and the party received $909,923 from public funds through the media reimbursement. Again, candidates were asked to return part of their reimbursement to the national party, and the amount returned accounted for about $1 million of the funds required for the 1980 election.

The transfer of part of candidates' reimbursements to the national party was criticized by some M.P.s and defeated candidates after the 1980 election. The national officials had worked on the assumption that many candidates, who had accumulated large "trust funds" before 1979 with the help of the tax credit, would have large surpluses in their election accounts. This was indeed the case, especially since the reimbursements usually covered half the total allowable expenses of a candidate.[29] No portion of funds raised locally in the 1974–1979 period was skimmed off by the national office, as it had been in both the NDP and the Progressive Conservative parties. The subject was raised during the Liberal party's national convention in July 1980 and, according to one press report, M.P.s and party workers claimed that the scheme had been "imposed from on high." They complained that candidates who opposed the plan to transfer part of their reimbursement to the national organization were told they might lose their endorsement as official Liberal candidates.[30] In interviews, leading Liberals involved in the 1979 and 1980 campaigns did not deny that pressure was applied to candidates who appeared unwilling to agree to this plan.

This highlights one of the difficulties the parties have faced in the past several years under the new election expenses and tax credit regime. Many local associations have grown rich through dedicated fund raising and the surplus that can accumulate from campaigns assisted by public funds. The national party organizations have access to some of the public funding provisions, but, as shown above, they have varied in the way they approached the advantages of the tax credit. Party officials have commented over and over again that the parties are rich at the local level and starved at the center. The Liberals succeeded in 1979 and 1980 in recapturing some of the surplus funds from candidates' campaigns, but it remains to be seen if such a scheme could be implemented for another general election.

[29] For example, in Ontario in the 1979 election, 65 of the 190 candidates for the Liberals and Progressive Conservatives raised more money before reimbursement than the limits would allow them to spend.

[30] In order for the name of the candidate's party to appear on the ballot paper, a written endorsement from the party leader must be filed at the time of nomination (Canada Elections Act, sections 23[2][h], 23[4]). See *Globe and Mail*, July 7, 1980.

The 1979 and 1980 Progressive Conservative Campaigns. The Progressive Conservative party faced the 1979 election with much healthier finances than in 1972 and 1974. The innovations in fund raising discussed above had begun to pay off significantly by 1978, when an election was generally expected. The improved state of Progressive Conservative finances went hand in hand with a systematic approach to campaign planning. The somewhat fragmented nature of past campaigns, with a good deal of expertise being provided by activists in Toronto in addition to the campaign organizers at the national level, was not repeated. Joe Clark appointed Lowell Murray as campaign chairman in 1977, and it was clear from then on that the next campaign would be run from Ottawa, though with a decentralized structure based on campaign committees in the provinces. As John Courtney points out in chapter 5 in this volume, the Ottawa group headed by Murray had the "power to determine the ultimate course of the national campaign," even though the provincial committees were to play a significant role in adapting that campaign to their province and overseeing the functioning of the constituency campaigns.[31]

The legal training of party activists and candidates' agents began even before the campaign committees were formed. The Progressive Conservatives organized a three-level system of legal services: "constituency counsel," "regional counsel" (at the provincial level), and, at the national level, the legal services division of the party's national headquarters. The party published a comprehensive *Legal Counsel Reference Guide,* and the legal services division conducted training sessions for lawyers and official agents throughout the country. The process of training party personnel began in 1977, and by 1978 the entire legal service was organized and prepared for an election.

Financial planning for the election was carried out over a fairly long period of time, and the provincial campaign chairmen were invited to Ottawa on successive occasions. The national and provincial organizers agreed on financial activities to cover election costs. Several plans were drawn up, because of the delay in calling the election. The board of directors of the PC Canada Fund was required to approve each plan, and it was consulted on the anticipated fund-raising activities. The board did not, however, say yes or no to particular programs or items of expenditure. In early March 1979 the campaign committee submitted a budget for the election period to the board of the PC Canada Fund. This budget was approved, and

31 "Campaign Strategy and Electoral Victory: The Progressive Conservatives and the 1979 Election," chap. 5 in this volume.

the campaign committee was told that the fund could meet the obligations outlined in the budget.

During the 1979 campaign, many people felt that Conservative spending would come very close to the statutory limit. As table 9–4 shows, the party reported a total election expenditure of over $3.8 million, or 86 percent of the permitted limit. Of this amount, some $2.5 million was spent on radio and television advertising—nearly two-thirds of the party's reported spending. The reported election expenses do not include grants to candidates, but, like the Liberals, the Progressive Conservatives spent much less in this area than in previous elections. In 1974 about $1.7 million of a total national expenditure of $4.5 million was allocated to candidates.[32] In 1979 about $450,000 was spent on assistance to candidates. Most constituency associations outside Quebec had accumulated large reserves in the 1974–1979 period and thus could finance their own campaigns (and often end up with a surplus) with very little help from the national campaign committee.

Progressive Conservative party officials have been unable to say exactly how the 1979 campaign was financed. All the money raised by the party, at any level, is received by the PC Canada Fund. This includes money raised in the constituencies outside an election period, by the National Finance Committee, and through direct mail. The National Finance Committee was quite active in early 1979, as the increase in contributions from private and public corporations between 1978 and 1979 clearly shows (see table 9–2). The National Finance Committee did not of course occupy the preeminent position in financial planning and fund raising that it had previously done, for by 1979 the board of directors of the PC Canada Fund had effectively replaced it as the major party financial organ. But direct mail was used to reach only rather small businesses, and the job of approaching leading executives in the financial and business world was left to the members of the National Finance Committee, some of whom sit on the board of the PC Canada Fund. From the available figures, it seems reasonable to estimate that half the 1979 campaign was paid for by donations from corporations, both public and private. The party received 7,413 donations from private corporations in 1979, and so it is reasonable to conclude that these smaller businesses, which contributed over $3.2 million, accounted for a significantly larger portion of funds allocated to the 1979 election than the funds given by large public corporations.

[32] Paltiel, "Campaign Financing in Canada," p. 195.

The Progressive Conservatives received $793,967 in reimbursement for their television and radio advertising expenses. This meant that $1.59 million of the total expenditure for radio and television broadcasting ($2.48 million) was actually spent on the purchase of air time. The balance was accounted for by production costs—a significant proportion of total Progressive Conservative expenditure and well ahead of what the Liberals spent in that area.

The pattern of Progressive Conservative spending in 1980 did not change much, except that the Progressive Conservatives' reported election expenditure jumped ahead of that of the Liberals by some $500,000. Their total declared spending of $4.4 million amounted to 97 percent of the limit allowed by the Canada Elections Act. The Conservatives were, of course, still in fine financial shape (note the surplus in party funds of over $3 million indicated in table 9–2). Unlike the Liberals, they reduced somewhat from its 1979 level the proportion of their budget devoted to advertising on television and radio (to 57 percent of total reported spending). The total amount granted to candidates did not exceed $400,000. Money did not buy political success, however, and after the 1980 defeat contributions to the party fell significantly.[33] Nevertheless, at the end of 1980 the Progressive Conservative party owed no money, even after fighting two elections in less than a year.

The 1979 and 1980 NDP Campaigns. The 1979 NDP campaign presents a strong contrast to the party's efforts in previous federal elections. First of all, a much more centralized campaign was organized and executed. In previous elections, the party had relied strongly on the provincial parties for much of the preparation for the leader's tour, the organization of party meetings, and even a good deal of the advertising. Jo Surich in his article on the 1974 campaign wrote: "No specific point of national control over an NDP campaign can be identified, since many decisions are made at the local level."[34]

Greater control at the center was now necessary because the federal level of the party, through the chief agent, had to ensure that the limit was observed and provide an accounting of the party's spending after the election. But the requirements of the law provided only part of the reason for a more centrally controlled campaign. The

[33] As a result, the Progressive Conservatives organized a telephone canvass for donations—another innovation in national party fund-raising techniques. Fifteen students were hired to ask for contributions from those who had given to the Progressive Conservatives in the 1976-1979 period, and in two weeks some $450,000 was raised.

[34] Surich, "Purists and Pragmatists," p. 136.

party's leader, Ed Broadbent, had argued strongly for a party with "muscle and resources" at the federal level; even during his bid for the NDP leadership, he had advocated a new approach to election organization. After the 1975 convention, he kept his promise, and a federal Election Planning Committee began its work early in 1976. It was composed of about twenty people representing various branches and functions of the party: the leader's office, fund raising, research, party organization. The Election Planning Committee was responsible for drawing up an election budget, which was approved by the finance committee of the party's national executive. The Election Planning Committee had to justify the expenditure, but responsibility for obtaining the necessary funds remained with the finance committee.

A second, more visible, contrast with previous elections was evident in the style and cost of the 1979 campaign. NDP finances had improved markedly with the introduction of the tax credit, and although the party's resources were still not equal to those of the two older parties, the disparity had been narrowed significantly. The NDP's healthier financial condition allowed it to conduct a far more lavish campaign than ever before—the party laid out more than four times the $475,000 it had spent in 1974. Just over a million dollars was channeled into radio and television advertising, an expenditure made easier by the media reimbursement. All these changes led Jeffrey Simpson of the *Globe and Mail* to comment that "the election expenses act, in its first national election, is a dream come true for the NDP."[35]

NDP spending, as reported in the party's postelection return, is itemized in table 9–4. The party spent just under half the limit prescribed by the Canada Elections Act. The expenditure on radio and television advertising placed it well behind the Liberals and the Progressive Conservatives. But it must be remembered that the NDP concentrates its efforts in those parts of the country where its past record is strong or where it feels it might soon make a breakthrough. Its list of sixty "concentration ridings" is a closely guarded campaign tool, but it is well known that the vast majority of these were in British Columbia, Manitoba, Saskatchewan, and Ontario. Candidates in these ridings received some additional funding from the national level, and the NDP spent far more on advertising there than in provinces where its organization is comparatively weak. In metropolitan Toronto, for example, it virtually matched the other two parties in its media expenditure. Ed Broadbent, the party's leader, traveled

[35] *Globe and Mail*, March 26, 1979.

on a chartered jet for the whole campaign—a marked contrast to his predecessor, David Lewis, who in 1972 and 1974 toured the country in a rented propeller airplane. The NDP recouped some $150,000 in travel fees from the corps of journalists who traveled with Broadbent.

The NDP was able to negotiate various allocations of funds from the lower levels of the party to help cover the cost of the election.[36] In recognition of the help the federal tax credit had given many of the provincial parties, they were asked to contribute a quota to the federal campaign. About $450,000 was raised in this way. A further $300,000 was raised from a plan called "media co-op," whereby candidates' organizations in about 175 constituencies contributed toward increased spending on media advertising in their areas. Trade union contributions accounted for the largest single source of funds for the 1979 election.[37] Some $450,000 was received in cash contributions and about $650,000 in goods and services provided through the "parallel campaign" organized by labor. Finally, the reimbursement for media advertising expenditure amounted to $496,350, nearly one-quarter of the NDP's total spending in 1979.

The NDP's spending in 1980 followed a fairly similar pattern. It is important to note (see table 9–5) that the gap between NDP spending and that of the two older parties narrowed even further in 1980. NDP reported that spending rose by more than 40 percent, to within $800,000 of that of the Liberals. The NDP allocated 45 percent of the reported amount to radio and television advertising, down very slightly from 1979; it spent $425,943 on other forms of advertising, putting it ahead of the Liberals in that category. In media advertising, the NDP allocated its resources even more selectively in 1980 than in 1979, especially toward the end of the campaign. The Conservatives claimed that the NDP spent more money on television advertising in metropolitan Toronto in 1980 than either of the two older parties.

The sources of NDP funds in 1980 did not change much from 1979. The provincial quotas amounted to $350,000, and $400,000 was received from the media co-op. Cash contributions from the trade unions amounted to some $370,000, and the goods and services provided by labor were valued at $950,000, up by nearly 50 percent from 1979. Just before the defeat of the Clark government, the NDP sent out what turned out to be a very successful mailing. The party had

[36] Information on the sources of funds for the 1979 and 1980 NDP campaigns was provided by Robin V. Sears.

[37] The federal party has sole access to the national offices of the party's trade union affiliates for funds to finance federal election campaigns. See Paltiel, *Political Party Financing*, pp. 56-61.

used direct mail since 1977, though on a much smaller scale than the Progessive Conservatives, using it as a tool of political communication, as well as to appeal for funds. The mailing that went out in November 1979 concerned Petrocanada and attacked the Clark government's proposal to dismantle the public corporation. The message it contained proved very timely when the government fell, and the response to the mailing astonished party officials. After deducting administrative costs, $80,000 was raised by this mailing and allocated to the 1980 campaign. The NDP's media reimbursement in 1980 was $677,481—a significant contribution from public funds toward its campaign, though down slightly as a proportion of overall spending from 1979.

Other Registered Parties. During the 1979 election, nine parties qualified as registered parties under the Canada Elections Act. All six parties registered during the 1974 election remained registered in 1979,[38] and three new parties, the Libertarians, the Union Populaire, and the Rhinoceros party, were able to meet the requirements of the law, the strictest of which is to find fifty candidates to run under the party banner. The election spending of the six parties not discussed in detail is shown in tables 9–4 and 9–5. The Social Credit party, once an important minor party at the federal level (in the 1962 and 1963 elections it elected more M.P.s than the NDP), was on the decline in the 1970s: in 1979 only six Social Credit M.P.s were returned, and in 1980 not one was elected. In both those elections, the Social Credit party spent only a small amount. None of the fringe parties' spending represented anything more than a token effort.

Although some people felt that the 1974 amendments, notably the tax credit and other public funding provisions, would result in a proliferation of parties, this has not happened. The much stricter party registration rules passed in 1977 were partly responsible for limiting the number of parties registered for the 1979 and 1980 elections. Within three months of the passage of Bill C-5, twelve "parties," ranging from the Nude Garden party to the United Free Enterprise party, were deleted from the registry maintained by the chief electoral officer. Three others that managed to remain registered were deleted after the 1979 election had been called.[39]

---

[38] Since the Election Expenses Act came into effect, all these parties have had to submit annual fiscal period returns. Except for 1974-1975, Social Credit contributions and expenses ranged between $200,000 and $400,000 annually. The figures for the Communist and Marxist-Leninist parties are much lower.

[39] Information on the deletions of parties from the registry was provided by Andrée Lortie, administrative assistant to the chief electoral officer.

No new parties qualified for registration by the time of the 1980 election, and the nine parties registered for that election will remain registered until the next election, provided they continue to comply with the ongoing registration requirements of the act. All these parties thus have the privilege of issuing income-tax credits for donations to their coffers, but it appears highly unlikely that this will allow any of the newer ones to make a breakthrough at the federal level. The Election Expenses Act has benefited the Liberals, the Progressive Conservatives, and the NDP but has given no significant boost to any other party.[40] In some people's view, the act and the 1977 amendments place severe barriers in the way of an emerging party and have contributed to the further institutionalization of the existing federal party system.

Constituency Campaigns and Candidates' Spending

The introduction of limits on candidates' election expenses posed a potentially more difficult problem than the limit on national parties' spending. Local campaigns, run almost entirely by volunteers, could have proved difficult to control. A new regime in election procedures had begun, but thousands of people had to be educated about the new rules of the game—rules that were far from simple and called for a vast amount of paperwork and record keeping. From all accounts, however, the changes were fairly well accepted, and throughout the country in the 1979 and 1980 elections the law was generally understood and respected. The political parties and the office of the chief electoral officer played an important role in instructing party activists about the election expenses provisions, and this process deserves some comment.

The sections of the Canada Elections Act containing the restrictions on candidates' spending are detailed, as was necessary if effective control was to be kept over local campaigns. But even though the necessary changes were spelled out at some length, everything could not be covered by the act or contained in schedules to it; several forms are referred to, for example, that were not included in the legislation. Other changes in election procedures, especially in the role of the official agent, were not completely outlined. This difficulty was

---

[40] The institutionalization of the party system and the effect of some of the registration rules on minor or new parties is discussed in Courtney, "Recognition of Canadian Political Parties," pp. 58-60, and in Khayyam Z. Paltiel, "The Impact of Election Expenses Legislation in Canada, Western Europe, and Israel," in Herbert E. Alexander, ed., *Political Finance* (Beverly Hills, Calif.: Sage Publications, 1979), pp. 20-26.

resolved through the development of an all-party committee, composed of representatives of the registered parties with members in the House of Commons.[41] The "ad hoc committee," as it came to be called, acquired the status necessary to ensure agreement among the major parties about the intention of the law and the way its provisions can be enforced and obeyed.

The ad hoc committee began meeting early in 1974 and carried on extensive discussions about the new law and its implications. The party representatives began to clarify some points of contention, but several shortcomings soon became evident. By April 1975 thirty-eight amendments to the election expenses provisions had been suggested. These amendments became the basis of the major part of Bill C-5. More important perhaps, the parties were able to agree on an elaborate set of guidelines for candidates and their agents. These guidelines were later published by the chief electoral officer, with a note in the introduction that they had been specifically approved by the party representatives on the ad hoc committee.[42]

The new election expenses regime led to the establishment of a new branch in the office of the chief electoral officer. The director of election expenses (now known as the director of the Election Financing Branch) was instrumental in bringing about interparty agreement on the guidelines and in designing the forms candidates and agents later used to comply with the election expense controls. The director also played a significant role in educating party and election activists in the new law. In 1976 and 1977 he conducted seminars in several constituencies where by-elections were held. During 1978 and early 1979, a comprehensive series of seminars was held throughout the country; approximately 2,500 party officials, candidates, official agents, and auditors attended. The efforts of the director of election financing were reinforced by the extensive training given by leading officials in the major political parties. From several accounts, candidates and agents were strongly encouraged to respect the spirit of the Election Expenses Act in every way. In most cases, those who carried out this training emphasized strongly the penalties contained in the Canada Elections Act and the potential embarrassment to a political

---

[41] The committee contained up to three representatives from each of the political parties represented in the House of Commons. Usually, each party sent two officials and an M.P. The first meeting was held on February 8, 1974, after the chief electoral officer sent a letter to each of the four political parties. By the end of 1976, the Social Credit party no longer sent anyone to the committee's meetings, and since then the committee has been effectively composed of Liberal, Progressive Conservative, and NDP members.

[42] *Guidelines and Procedures Respecting Election Expenses* (Ottawa: Chief electoral officer, 1980).

party if one of its candidates was found guilty of an infringement of it. This argument was reiterated in manuals the parties distributed to candidates and official agents in every constituency.[43]

The imposition of spending limits greatly altered the way in which constituency campaigns were organized and executed. Because of the variations in party strength throughout the country, it is impossible to make generalizations that apply to all candidates. Clearly the limits did not mean as much to a Progressive Conservative candidate in Quebec or an NDP candidate in Alberta as they did to candidates in metropolitan Toronto. But a couple of basic points can be made. First, it was evident that constituency campaigns were much more carefully planned than before. Traditionally, the limit on a candidate's spending was the amount of money that could be raised. If money kept coming in, ways were found of spending it. Donations of goods and services were freely accepted. In the 1979 election, candidates had to plan how they would allocate the amount they were permitted to spend by law. Serious decisions had to be taken about the cost-effectiveness of various sorts of expenditure. Television and radio advertising were often avoided almost entirely, especially in urban areas, because they would have taken up too large a portion of the budget. The largest proportion of candidates' advertising budgets went for brochures and signs and, to a lesser extent, print advertising. Pamphlets were often delivered by hand rather than sent through the mails. Fewer workers could be paid than previously,[44] and donations of goods and services were sometimes refused because there was now an obligation to count them against the limit.

Another major difference from earlier local campaigns was that very tight financial control had to be maintained. This was the principal job of the official agent, who had to submit a return after the election and could be punished for infractions of the relevant parts of the Canada Elections Act. Most campaign organizations planned for a safety margin (often 10 percent) to allow for unforeseen expenses. The detailed record keeping the law required was often criticized. For example, the agent had to include with the return of election expenses a voucher for any expense over $25. But it is clear from a wide variety of accounts that most of the agents in the three largest parties took their jobs very seriously. They had been

[43] *Legal Counsel Reference Guide* (Progressive Conservative party legal services); *Financial Management Guide* (Liberal party of Canada); *Official Agent* (New Democratic party).

[44] The payment of campaign and election workers is a familiar part of Canadian election practices and is not prohibited by law. Such payments count against a candidate's spending limits.

told over and over how important it was to respect the law, and by and large they were able to convince party workers that the new procedures were necessary and had to be respected.[45]

During the 1979 and 1980 elections, many people pointed out how restrictive the constituency limits were in a large proportion of cases.[46] In 1979 the average permitted expenditure was $26,924. In more populous constituencies, chiefly in large cities, the limits were higher, but it was rare for a candidate's limit to exceed $30,000. The Liberal government had tried to index the limits to inflation in Bill C-5, but they were forced to withdraw that clause when it emerged in the House of Commons that the ad hoc committee had been opposed to raising the limits. The limits were thus the same as they had been in Bill C-203. If they had kept pace with inflation, the average limit of $26,924 referred to would have had to be raised to $43,078.[47] After both the 1979 and the 1980 campaigns, there was much talk about the restrictiveness of the limits, and it was widely agreed that they would have to be raised before the next general election.[48] But the principle of a spending limit for candidates is now firmly accepted, and no one argues seriously for a return to the old system.

The details of candidates' spending in 1979 and 1980 are provided in tables 9–6 and 9–7. Although these are aggregate figures for

[45] After the 1979 election, charges were laid against two candidates, alleging that they had exceeded the spending limits. George Kirby, the Progressive Conservative candidate in Argenteuil electoral district in Quebec was found guilty and fined $200. Armand Lefebvre, the Progressive Conservative candidate in Verchères electoral district in Quebec, and his official agent have also been charged with exceeding the limits and submitting a false election-expenses return, but at the time of writing the trial had not yet been held. After the 1980 election, Georges Lebreque, the Progressive Conservative candidate in Montmorency electoral district, Quebec, was also charged, although his return showed that he had exceeded the limit. This trial also had not been held at the time of writing.

[46] This was widely discussed in political circles after the two elections and was repeated by several official agents who were interviewed. Two thorough articles evaluating the impact of the limits on candidates' campaigns are "Money Squeeze on Candidates," Globe and Mail, March 30, 1979, and "Le plafond aux dépenses électorales: les agents des partis crient famine!" Le Devoir, April 27, 1979.

[47] Based on the change in the consumer price index from January 1974 to May 1979. It is acknowledged that the CPI provides only an approximate guide to the rises in costs of those goods and services purchased by candidates and political parties.

[48] After the 1979 general election, a questionnaire was sent by the chief electoral officer to the official agents for candidates of the four parties then represented in the House of Commons. The response rate to this questionnaire was 56 percent; 76 percent of the respondents replied that the spending limits should be adjusted for increased costs in campaigning.

265

TABLE 9–6
Contributions to Candidates and Expenses of Candidates, 1979
(dollars)

Category	Progressive Conservative		Liberal		NDP		Social Credit	
	Number	Amount	Number	Amount	Number	Amount	Number	Amount
Contributions								
Individuals	27,597	2,642,884	18,525	1,758,424	13,765	812,550	3,958	167,006
Public corporations	850	317,636	584	195,865	56	5,997	69	11,045
Private corporations	8,636	1,743,531	6,417	1,257,902	229	27,835	333	42,499
Governments	56	15,742	12	1,850	2	117	0	0
Trade unions	7	280	1	100	722	420,186	1	50
Corporations without share capital	29	13,932	27	3,326	11	2,563	9	635
Unincorporated organizations	328	53,639	467	86,229	96	28,455	41	4,119
Political organizations	227	470,015	178	465,841	208	421,183	13	3,770
Registered parties	249	776,431	320	2,700,669	331	553,312	13	8,127
Proceeds from fund-raising functions	—	52,391	—	88,059	—	34,832	—	4,148
Total contributions	37,979	6,086,481	26,531	6,558,265	15,420	2,307,030	4,437	241,399

Expenses							
Advertising							
Radio/television	—	639,474	—	579,309	—	164,728	—	92,846
Other	—	2,980,496	—	2,934,345	—	1,313,500	—	208,231
Salaries	—	531,067	—	711,490	—	498,261	—	82,992
Office	—	992,763	—	1,030,904	—	473,609	—	80,169
Travel	—	285,985	—	329,217	—	82,119	—	68,052
Other	—	585,988	—	600,438	—	133,070	—	66,835
Total expenses	—	6,015,773	—	6,185,703	—	2,665,287	—	599,125
Total allowable expenditure	—	7,751,445	—	7,751,445	—	7,751,445	—	2,867,663

Dash (—): Not applicable.
SOURCE: As for table 9-4.

TABLE 9–7

Contributions to Candidates and Expenses of Candidates, 1980
(dollars)

Category	Progressive Conservative		Liberal		NDP		Social Credit	
	Number	Amount	Number	Amount	Number	Amount	Number	Amount
Contributions								
Individuals	23,489	2,220,137	25,823	2,180,404	16,778	1,020,806	1,573	125,637
Public corporations	766	304,030	832	241,259	175	15,094	14	3,985
Private corporations	7,361	1,532,037	8,009	1,531,886	233	29,680	240	32,281
Governments	67	11,086	2	350	2	68	0	0
Trade unions	2	515	2	1,000	739	468,769	0	0
Corporations without share capital	10	1,700	26	6,005	8	5,867	1	100
Unincorporated organizations	333	58,749	478	80,583	109	20,255	10	1,380
Political organizations	234	755,742	195	667,142	183	403,933	7	7,633
Registered parties	239	969,768	363	1,545,858	278	654,783	9	12,585
Proceeds from fund-raising functions	—	34,600	—	38,157	—	55,160	—	6,072
Total contributions	32,501	5,888,364	35,730	6,292,644	18,505	2,674,415	1,854	189,673

Expenses

Advertising

Radio/television	—	755,450	—	794,052	—	373,157	—	67,013
Other	—	2,768,302	—	2,611,634	—	1,305,258	—	92,309
Salaries	—	395,015	—	696,367	—	544,446	—	71,568
Office	—	1,036,179	—	1,068,604	—	540,186	—	31,499
Travel	—	260,663	—	346,022	—	97,524	—	23,680
Other	—	464,749	—	556,925	—	126,770	—	24,425
Total expenses	—	5,680,358	—	6,073,604	—	2,987,341	—	310,494
Total allowable expenditure	—	7,840,987	—	7,840,987	—	7,787,729	—	2,301,028

Dash (—): Not applicable.
SOURCE: As for table 9-5.

the country as a whole, some general points can be made about the pattern of candidates' expenses. The emphasis on forms of advertising other than radio and television is clear (Progressive Conservative and Liberal candidates spent just under half their total on "other advertising").[49] The average expenditure for Liberal and Progressive Conservative candidates in 1979 was nearly the same: $21,333 for Progressive Conservative candidates and $21,935 for their Liberal counterparts. Average spending by NDP candidates was less than half what the Liberals and Progressive Conservatives spent: the comparable figure for the NDP in 1979 was $9,451. The pattern was very similar in 1980, although total spending by Progressive Conservative candidates dropped slightly and that of the NDP candidates rose by some $300,000.

Although it is not possible here to provide figures for candidates' spending province by province, some idea of the variation in candidates' spending can be seen in table 9–8. This table shows, by province, the average percentage of the limit spent by candidates of the three largest parties in 1979. It is interesting to note that even though the total spending of Liberal candidates exceeded the total spending of Progressive Conservative candidates, the former spent on average a larger percentage of the limit than the Progressive Conservatives in only three provinces and the northern territories. Liberal candidates spent freely in Quebec (on average 87 percent of the limit), and this helped to bring the Liberal candidates' national total above that of the Tories.

Spending near to the limit did not guarantee success for a candidate, but a recent article has provided some interesting statistics on spending by winners and losers. Seymour Isenberg[50] has shown that in the 1979 election, 57 percent of the candidates who spent most in a constituency were elected; 38 percent of those who spent the second most were elected. On average, those who spent second most and won came within 8 percent of what the highest spender laid out on the election. Those who spent most and won expended on average $23,954; the comparable figure for those who spent second most and won was $22,024. These figures are informative but must be qualified by pointing out that candidates did not necessarily spend in what might be called a "rational" manner: the case of the Liberals in Quebec has already been mentioned, and in a Conservative

---

[49] On average, candidates spent 9.5 percent of their total on radio and television advertising and 49 percent on "other advertising." See Seymour Isenberg, "Can You Spend Your Way into the House of Commons?" *Optimum*, vol 11, no. 1 (1980), p. 33.

[50] Ibid., pp. 34-35.

TABLE 9-8

Average Percentage of the Limit Spent by Liberal,
Progressive Conservative, and NDP Candidates, by Province,
1979 General Election

	Liberal	Progressive Conservative	NDP
Ontario	80	84	48
Quebec	87	65	4
Nova Scotia	85	86	36
New Brunswick	90	84	9
Manitoba	66	79	50
British Columbia	74	83	67
Prince Edward Island	86	94	10
Saskatchewan	75	88	81
Alberta	65	79	9
Newfoundland	79	58	53
Territories	74	66	45
Canada	80	78	35

Source: Calculated from information contained in the chief electoral officer's *Special Report to the Speaker of the House of Commons Respecting Election Expenses of Registered Parties and Candidates for the Thirty-first General Election, May 22, 1979* (Ottawa: Minister of Supply and Services Canada, 1980).

"safe" area like Alberta, Progressive Conservative candidates also spent close to the limit.

NDP candidates' spending varied widely from province to province and was highest in the provinces where the party's "concentration ridings" were situated. It is not possible to obtain an accurate list of the NDP's "concentration ridings," but some idea of the significance of this strategy can be obtained from calculating the average spent by incumbent M.P.s. All twelve NDP M.P.s who ran in 1979 certainly benefited from concentration, and the average NDP expenditure in their electoral districts was 78 percent of the limit— almost equal to the national average for Liberal and Progressive Conservative candidates.

Tables 9–6 and 9–7 also provide a summary of the sources of contributions to candidates' campaigns in 1979 and 1980. In 1979 contributions to Liberal candidates exceeded total contributions to their Progressive Conservative counterparts, but this was due to large transfers from the trust funds in which 50 percent of the money raised by constituency associations since August 1, 1974, had been kept. Progressive Conservative candidates did far better than Liberal candidates in soliciting from individuals in 1979: 43 percent of the money given to Progressive Conservative candidates came from individuals, compared with 27 percent for the Liberals. NDP candidates received just over one-third of their total contributions from individuals. Trade union donations are mostly channeled to the national level of the NDP, and candidates received only 18 percent of their total funds from this source.

The pattern of candidates' contributions did not change significantly in 1980, although Liberal candidates pulled ahead of Progressive Conservative candidates in the number of donations from individuals. A large proportion of Progressive Conservative and Liberal constituency associations had surpluses after the 1979 election, and this is reflected in the rise in donations from "political organizations" (this category in the returns includes principally local party associations). Contributions to NDP candidates rose slightly in 1980, but the distribution among the various sources was virtually unchanged.

The reimbursement to candidates introduced by the Election Expenses Act proved a most significant source of funds. Although the reimbursement had been intended to equal about one-third of the spending limit of any candidate, its potential value rose to close to one-half the limit in the period between 1974 and 1979. The reimbursement is calculated on the basis of a formula, part of which is the cost of sending one first-class mailing to each elector in the constituency. First-class postage had risen from eight cents in 1974 to seventeen cents by the time of the 1979 election, making the reimbursements more generous than originally planned. If Progressive Conservative candidates in Quebec are excluded, virtually all Liberal and Progressive Conservative candidates were able to obtain the required 15 percent of the vote, as table 9–9 clearly indicates. Just over half the NDP candidates qualified for reimbursement in 1979, along with twenty-nine Social Credit candidates and two independents. Similar proportions of each party's candidates qualified in 1980, although only eight Social Credit candidates qualified in that election.

The total value of the reimbursement to each party's candidates is also shown in table 9–9. When these figures are compared with the total spending by each party's candidates, it becomes clear that total public funding for candidates was equal to over half their total expenses in the 1979 and 1980 elections. In 1979 the total value of reimbursements to Liberal, Progressive Conservative, NDP, and Social Credit candidates amounted to 55 percent of what the candidates in

TABLE 9-9

Reimbursements to Candidates, 1979 and 1980 General Elections

	Progressive Conservative	Liberal	NDP	Social Credit	Other Parties	Independents and No Affiliation	Total
1979							
Number of candidates	282	282	282	103	406	69	1,424
Number of candidates eligible for reimbursement	219	273	147	29	0	2	670
Percentage of candidates eligible for reimbursement	78	97	52	28	0	3	47
Total of reimbursements (dollars)	2,867,691	3,594,244	1,670,601	359,273	0	25,972	8,517,781
1980							
Number of candidates	282	282	280	81	461	111	1,497
Number of candidates eligible for reimbursement	215	275	152	8	0	0	650
Percentage of candidates eligible for reimbursement	76	98	54	10	0	0	43
Total of reimbursements (dollars)	2,871,029	3,656,074	1,884,863	111,802	0	0	8,523,768

Sources: As for tables 9-4 and 9-5; and the chief electoral officer's *Statutory Report 1980* (Ottawa: Minister of Supply and Services Canada, 1980).

those four parties spent. This proportion rose marginally, to 57 percent, in 1980.

The large amounts of money returned to candidates from reimbursements meant that after both elections many candidates had huge surpluses in their election accounts. With the incentive provided by the tax credit, many of them raised far more money than they were allowed to spend. Many local associations had gathered quite a reserve in the 1974–1979 period, and along with the reimbursement it was not unusual for a candidate to have twice as much money as the law would allow him or her to spend. The Liberals, as shown above, managed to "tax back" a share of the reimbursement for the national campaign committee in both 1979 and 1980. During 1980 the Progressive Conservatives began to make efforts to get constituency associations to share some of their surplus funds with the national party. At a meeting of his own constituency association in late 1980, the Progressive Conservative leader, Joe Clark, commented that there was something like $2½ million "salted away in constituency funds across the country." He mentioned one constituency in Ontario where the constituency association had $100,000 in the bank after the 1980 election. He thanked the Yellowhead Progressive Conservative Association for agreeing to give $8,000 to the national party and suggested that "we should . . . be giving serious concern, as a national Party, to whether or not there should not be a greater contribution by local associations to national funds."[51]

It is thus clear that after two general elections and nearly six years' experience with the income tax credit, local associations had been handsomely enriched. One of the intentions of the framers of the Election Expenses Act was to ensure that financial barriers would not prevent qualified people from running for office. Certainly, most local associations, at least in the two largest parties, will have more than enough money to sponsor a candidate in the next election. But many party officials have become worried about these surpluses in local hands. They feel that the large sums put away in bank accounts will weaken the enthusiasm of local activists for year-to-year fund raising. In the Progressive Conservative and New Democratic parties, part of what is raised locally outside the election period is given to the national level of the party. Diminished fund-raising activity at the local level thus has implications for the party's finances at the national

---

[51] "Text of remarks by the Rt. Hon. Joe Clark at the Yellowhead PC Association Annual Meeting in Barrhead, Alberta, November 16, 1980," pp. 1-3. Mrs. Jean Piggott, a prominent Progressive Conservative M.P. defeated in 1979, gave $30,000 from her campaign surplus to the national party on condition that it hire a director of women's affairs. See *Globe and Mail*, December 29, 1980.

level. Others fear the surpluses could create a "chain of feudal fiefdoms"[52] whose associations and candidates will have much less need for the national headquarters of the party. This is certainly a problem the parties must try to resolve in the next few years, but it is generally agreed that the parties should try to correct this imbalance themselves and not look to changes in the law.

Public Funding since 1974

The preceding discussion of party finance and election spending in 1979 and 1980 has given some indication of the major role public funding has assumed since the passage of the Election Expenses Act. The tax credit benefits parties and local associations on a year-to-year basis; at election time candidates can also issue tax credit receipts. At elections all registered parties can be reimbursed for half their advertising expenses on radio and television, and any candidate who receives 15 percent of the vote in a constituency qualifies for a reimbursement equal to about half his election expenses.

In the period leading up to the 1979 election, all parties benefited from the tax credit, although their success in encouraging donations, especially from individuals, varied a good deal. The incentive provided by the tax credit led greater numbers of individuals to contribute to parties, and by the end of 1979 the value of this form of subsidization of the political process since August 1, 1974, amounted to over $22 million. Table 9–10 provides a breakdown of the value of tax credits taken by individuals and corporations since the passage of the Election Expenses Act. The 1979 figures show the impact of the candidates' use of the tax credit. The tax credit has become an important part of the financing of politics at the federal level in Canada and has without doubt encouraged more people to contribute to parties and candidates.[53]

In order to judge the total impact of the public funding provisions introduced in 1974, it is necessary to include the reimbursements paid at two general elections. Reimbursements to the parties totaled $4,583,505 in the 1979 and 1980 elections. Candidates' reimbursements were nearly four times that amount—$17,015,577 in the two elections. The public funding provided as a result of the

---

[52] "Parties Find Money Rolling In, Control of Ridings Trickling Out," *Globe and Mail*, November 29, 1980.

[53] It is, of course, impossible to make any form of comparison with the pre-1974 period. It should be noted, however, that the number of people contributing to parties and candidates in 1978 and 1979 is only 1 percent of the adult Canadian population.

TABLE 9-10

VALUE OF THE INCOME-TAX CREDIT FOR POLITICAL CONTRIBUTIONS,
AUGUST 1, 1974–DECEMBER 31, 1979

Year	Individuals Claiming Tax Credits	Value of Tax Credits to Individuals (dollars)	Value of Tax Credits to Corporations (dollars)
1974	19,584	1,273,000	—[a]
1975	36,227	2,394,000	—[a]
1976	48,313	2,800,000	465,000
1977	48,027	3,114,000	504,000
1978	64,547	3,901,000	653,000
1979	92,353	6,111,000	1,213,000

[a] The value of the tax credit to corporations is not available for taxation years 1974 and 1975.

SOURCE: Information supplied by an official of Revenue Canada.

passage of the Election Expenses Act thus amounted to just over $44 million by the end of the 1980 election, not including tax credits that will be claimed for the 1980 taxation year.

Conclusion

This chapter has provided a relatively detailed description of recent Canadian party finance and campaign spending in the 1979 and 1980 federal elections. A central theme has been the introduction by the 1974 Election Expenses Act of a new set of rules to regulate not only election spending but also various aspects of parties' year-to-year financial activities. That act ushered in a new regime characterized by detailed controls on the gathering and use of political money at the federal level in Canada. How effective have the new rules been? Have the objectives of the Election Expenses Act been met, and how fully? Have the 1974 changes had unintended consequences, and what is their significance?

The most notable objective of the Election Expenses Act was to limit the cost of federal elections. It is clear that the imposition of statutory spending limits for both parties and candidates made a big difference in the way the election campaigns were planned and executed. Working within a limit has obliged parties and candidates to assess the potential usefulness of certain expenditures and has undoubtedly helped control frivolous spending that used to occur as long as funds did not run out. The local limits were far more restrictive than the national ones in the 1979 and 1980 elections. Nevertheless, the cost of elections to the national parties has been substantially reduced, partly as a result of the media reimbursement, but also because party grants to candidates in 1979 and 1980 were only a fraction of what they had been in other recent elections.

Parties and candidates are limited in a specific way by the statutory restriction on the amount and timing of media advertising. The limit of six and one-half hours on electronic media advertising was not very significant because the parties could not afford to purchase their total allocation. The restriction of all forms of advertising to a four-week period had the obvious effect of compressing such spending into the last half of the campaign. An indirect consequence of the reimbursement to parties for time purchased on the electronic media was that the national campaign committees were encouraged to spend a greater proportion of their budget than ever before on this form of advertising. "Fifty-cent dollars" are hard to resist, and parties were given an incentive that accentuated the long-term trend in Canadian election campaigns away from the use of the print media to the heightened use of radio and especially television advertising. Issues and substance have been almost completely replaced by the image makers' vacuous slogans and symbols of the appropriate sort of leadership. This tendency has combined with television's ever greater role as a medium of information to the voters, leading Jeffrey Simpson to characterize the 1979 and 1980 campaigns, quite aptly, as "the apotheosis of telepolitics in Canada."[54]

Another purpose of the 1974 amendments was to open up the process of party and election financing to public scrutiny. The legal recognition of parties and the annual disclosure requirements have had a most salutary effect: no longer is party finance seen as a private affair, clouded by suspicion, rumor, and innuendo. We know who finances the parties and how much is given. Unfortunately, the vast amount of information now available has been very little used. Apart from the odd newspaper article, often focusing on the large corporate donations, no one has seriously examined in detail the sources of donations to parties and how these may have changed since 1974. The disclosure of candidates' spending and contributions has helped introduce a sense of regularity and probity into local election campaigns but again has received only limited attention.

A third general objective of the 1974 reforms was to involve more people in the financing of elections and political parties. Clearly,

[54] Jeffrey Simpson, *The Discipline of Power* (Toronto: Personal Library, 1980), p. 285.

the tax credit has been a highly successful innovation, and parties and candidates have been able to exploit it effectively. Registered parties received some 115,000 contributions from individuals in 1979, and in the 1980 election candidates from across the country obtained more than 92,000 donations from individuals. The attractions of the tax credit, combined with the reimbursements, enabled many candidates to accumulate large surpluses, something that has helped create rich local party associations. This phenomenon was certainly not expected when the Election Expenses Act was passed, and what many see as a potentially dangerous imbalance will no doubt occupy the minds of party officials in coming years. The parties themselves varied in their success in seeking and attracting individual donations, even with the incentive of the tax credit. The introduction of direct-mail fund raising provided a great boost to Progressive Conservative finances in the late 1970s, pushing that party well ahead of the Liberals. The NDP was generally successful, for different reasons, in attracting a large number of individual contributors in the post-1974 period. But neither of the two older parties transformed itself into a mass party, financed from a large number of small contributions gathered at the local level. Although a somewhat healthier balance may have been struck between the various sources of funds, the Progressive Conservatives and Liberals still rely fairly strongly on donations from the business world, especially at elections.

A final objective of the Election Expenses Act was to make the financial capacities of parties and candidates more nearly equal. As with many programs aimed at a certain equalization of resources, the poorest have benefited the most: of the three leading federal parties, the NDP (and many of its candidates) enjoyed the largest boost in financial fortunes. By the 1980 election, the NDP was spending only $800,000 less than the Liberals at the national level, and in both elections it used electronic media advertising in large areas of the country nearly as extensively as the two older parties. The tax credit certainly helped most candidates of the three major parties to gather sufficient funds to wage a local campaign, and the vast majority of them could rely on the reimbursement to cover about half their permitted expenses.

Through a combination of provisions, the most notable of which are the spending limits and the various forms of public funding, the process of party and election finance has changed in several significant ways since the passage of the 1974 amendments. These changes produced some difficulties for political parties and candidates, notably in the detailed requirements for disclosure and the tendency toward a somewhat bureaucratic approach to many financial activities.[55] But few would deny that the major benefits to the parties and the federal political system have outweighed the disadvantages. It is important to note, however, that the financial advantages resulting from the 1974 amendments have accrued almost entirely to the Liberals, the Progressive Conservatives, and the NDP. For example, of the total amount of reimbursement given to parties and candidates in the 1979 and 1980 elections, 98 percent went to the three leading parties and their candidates. New parties have not been seriously encouraged by the public funding provisions; on the contrary, additional barriers were put in their way as a result of the 1977 amendments. Through the mechanism of the ad hoc committee, the three major parties have the power to set rules that not only work to their own financial advantage but also could lead to an even greater institutionalization of the federal party system and to potential rigidities in the structure of Canadian politics. Many healthy changes have been brought about, but a critical stance must be kept so that a spirit of openness and participation can truly develop and flourish in this area of Canadian politics.

[55] As Dalton Camp has put it: "A rush of affluence . . . has produced a new world of modalities, structures, systems, print-outs, flow-charts and cash at hand." See Camp, *Points of Departure* (Ottawa: Deneau and Greenberg, 1979), p. 141.

10
Playing the Game: The Mass Media and the 1979 Campaign

Frederick J. Fletcher

More than any previous campaign, the 1979 federal election campaign was run for the news media, especially television. The party leaders crisscrossed the country speaking not so much to local audiences as to the television crews they brought with them. Speech writers labored daily to come up with brief inserts and one-liners to be added to set speeches to provide a ninety-second clip for the nightly news and a new lead for the forty or more reporters traveling with each leader. Campaign organizers often informed television journalists of the timing of the new segments so they would not waste film or video tape (though they expended an estimated one million or more feet in any case). The three major parties, moreover—the incumbent Liberals, the Progressive Conservatives, and the New Democratic party (NDP)—each had staff units monitoring the media and preparing daily summaries. Daily and weekly strategy sessions often began with viewing a digest of television coverage from the previous night or week. Campaign tactics were adjusted according to how well they were going down with the media, as well as on the basis of continual

This study was made possible by the cooperation of many journalists who agreed to be interviewed and of network officials at CBC, CTV, and Global who provided in-house data and memos. I am also grateful to the University of Windsor group—E. Donald Briggs, Walter I. Romanow, Walter C. Soderlund, and Ronald H. Wagenberg—who provided me with preliminary data from their extensive content analysis of the 1979 coverage, and to William O. Gilsdorf of Concordia University for access to his comprehensive material on the media's role in the campaign. My thanks also to my research assistants at York University: Richard Bédard, Joan Boase, Mustafa Chowdhury, and especially Lucinda Flavelle. Clive Cocking kindly shared with me the insights he had gained while following the reporters on the campaign trail. Since many of the interviews were confidential, not all ideas are attributed. In any event, the interpretations and misinterpretations are my own. It should be noted that some of these ideas were presented in a background paper for the Conference on Politics and the Media at Erindale College, University of Toronto, Mississauga, Ontario, June 12-13, 1980.

polling.[1] The deference accorded the media by party personnel made the orientation very clear. For example, camera crews and reporters got the best vantage points at most rallies, often to the annoyance of audiences.

Although the 1979 coverage was marked by an unprecedented commitment of resources by the media and Canada's first true television debate among party leaders, the coverage patterns and party-media relations tended to be extensions of trends observed in 1974.[2] The television orientation, the tendency to focus on party leaders, the concern with image and style, the obsession with polls, and the use of media consultants by the parties had all been present in 1974 but were even more in evidence in 1979.

For many purposes, it is useful to view an election campaign as a series of contests. In the process of competing for votes, the parties and leaders are engaged in a contest to get media attention and to determine the issues around which the campaign will revolve. Other things being equal, the party that wins these contests can expect to win the competition for the allegiance of the uncommitted voters and, perhaps, the election.[3] In another sense, the parties compete with the news organizations to determine who will set the campaign agenda. And reporters and news organizations compete among themselves for "scoops" and, more important, for prestige. For political reporters, elections are "the Olympics of news coverage."[4]

The outcome of these contests determines in large part the information available to voters. Despite the fact that most Canadian news organizations are privately owned, with the notable exception of the Canadian Broadcasting Corporation (CBC), they generally acknowledge a public duty to cover election campaigns. This consideration, along with concern for prestige, accounts for the substantial financial commitment to coverage of the campaign made by many news organizations in 1979, a commitment that produced little in the way of direct financial returns. The feeling among journalists that

---

[1] William O. Gilsdorf, "Getting the Message Across: The Communication Strategy of the Federal Liberal Party with 1979 and 1980 Canadian Federal Elections" (Paper presented at the Founding Meeting of the Canadian Communications Association, Montreal, June 1980), p. 23.

[2] See Frederick J. Fletcher, "The Mass Media in the 1974 Canadian Election," in Howard R. Penniman, ed., *Canada at the Polls: The General Election of 1974* (Washington, D.C.: American Enterprise Institute, 1975), pp. 243-89.

[3] For a discussion of voter choice in Canada, see Harold D. Clarke, Jane Jenson, Lawrence LeDuc, and Jon H. Pammett, *Political Choice in Canada* (Toronto: McGraw-Hill Ryerson, 1979), esp. chaps. 9-12.

[4] Trina McQueen, executive producer of CBC English television national news, in an interview in Toronto, December 5, 1979.

elections must be covered was strong enough to cause several key people to threaten to quit until Ontario's recently established Global network, in financial difficulties, authorized funds for coverage.[5]

Given the central role of the media in modern democratic elections, then, it is appropriate to assess coverage in terms of such questions as: How well were the informational needs of the voters served? Were the parties given a reasonable opportunity to communicate their policies and perspectives? Were the important questions raised?

The Canadian Campaign Communication System

Between 1974 and 1979, there were important changes in the Canadian system of campaign communication. Although the essential features—free-time broadcasts, paid advertising, and leader tours aimed at obtaining favorable news coverage—remained unchanged, the interelection period saw significant amendments to the electoral laws and substantial alterations in the media system, as well as changes in party communication strategies.

The new campaign regulations were designed to provide registered political parties with a reasonable opportunity to communicate their appeals directly to the public. The new rules restrict paid advertisements to the final half of the eight-week campaign, regulate the allocation of paid and free time, and provide for reimbursement from the federal treasury of half the costs of radio and television commercials purchased by registered parties.[6] All broadcasters, including the CBC radio services, which are normally noncommercial, are required to sell prime-time[7] spots at normal rates to the parties up to a total of six and one-half hours, divided among the parties according to a formula based on seats held in the House of Commons when the election was called and number of seats contested in the election. Free time is allocated on the same basis. For advertisements, the 1979 formula permitted the Liberals to buy up to 153 minutes on each station or network, the Conservatives, 132, the NDP, 63, Social

[5] Peter Trueman, *Smoke and Mirrors: The Inside Story of Television News in Canada* (Toronto: McClelland and Stewart, 1980), p. 211.

[6] The regulations are outlined in Canadian Radio-television and Telecommunications Commission (CRTC) public notices of February 27, 1979, and May 8, 1979, and circular no. 245 of March 21, 1979. See also the chapter by F. Leslie Seidle and Khayyam Zev Paltiel in this volume. The estimates of the value of the allotted time were made by advertising agency officials.

[7] Prime time is defined in section 99.4(b) of the Canada Elections Act as: radio, 6:00 to 9:00 A.M., noon to 2 P.M., 4:00 to 7:00 P.M.; television, 6:00 P.M. to midnight.

Credit, 22, the Marxist-Leninists and Communists, 8 each, and the Rhinoceros party (a satiric party), 4. Since the total time available would have cost $20 to $25 million, only a fraction of the allocated time was taken. A total of seventeen hours of free time, four hours on radio networks and the remainder on the three national television networks—CBC English, CBC French, and the privately owned CTV (English)—and on TVA (French), a private Quebec network, was provided in 1979.

The new rules permitted the parties to reach a substantial number of voters without risk of journalistic distortion. The free-time broadcasts on CBC English television, for example, had an average audience of 620,000, quite similar to the figure for 1974. While not rivaling Hockey Night in Canada, these programs did reach many voters. The party advertisements, not surprisingly, reached a much larger audience: 77 percent of respondents in a national survey reported having seen or heard a party spot during the campaign.[8]

In addition, the rules helped to equalize access to the airwaves. While the two largest parties continued to have a decided advantage, accounting for 78.6 percent of all advertising expenditure (down from 91.1 percent in 1974), the third party, the NDP, was able to increase its share of the expenditure threefold, from 6.8 to 20.3 percent. Indeed, by careful targeting, the NDP was able to compete on even terms in key areas where it had a chance to win.

Given the essentially propagandistic nature of the party broadcasts, however, voters continued in 1979 to depend on news organizations, especially the national media, for information. In fact, the national media, loosely defined as the prestige papers—such as the Toronto *Globe and Mail*, *Le Devoir* (Montreal), the *Toronto Star*, the Montreal *Gazette*—and the major television networks, as well as the Canadian Press (CP, a cooperative news service owned by most of the country's 121 daily newspapers), the Southam News Service (SNS, which provides specialized news, analysis, and commentary to the fourteen member papers of the Southam chain), and a few syndicated columnists, tended to set the tone for election coverage.

On a day-to-day basis, the key style setters were the senior members of the parliamentary press gallery, which is made up of some 225 journalists (an increase of 100 since 1974) who specialize in national politics. Their dominant role in campaign reporting ensured knowledgeable coverage but also permitted long-established attitudes

---

[8] The audience figure is from *CBC Research Report*, TOR/79/31. The poll data are from a Carleton University School of Journalism poll conducted for CBC, April 30 to May 10, 1979, unpublished summary (hereafter cited as Carleton-CBC poll).

and common opinions, influenced by the views of a few high-prestige correspondents, to affect coverage. The longstanding hostility to Prime Minister Pierre Trudeau (Liberal), based in part on his ill-disguised contempt for journalists,[9] and the doubts about the competence of the Progressive Conservative opposition leader, Joe Clark, are two such common opinions that influenced coverage in 1979. The key role of the Ottawa-based gallery and the very small number (seven) of correspondents representing outlets from outside Ontario and Quebec tend to give political coverage a central Canadian bias. News media in the other eight provinces often take their coverage from CP and, increasingly, from chain-operated services like the SNS and its newly established counterpart for FP Publications, Canada's other chain of major dailies. The Ottawa bureaus of the two chains serve newspapers accounting for nearly half the country's daily newspaper circulation. It has been suggested that the national media assume "that it is central Canada where things happen, not on the periphery."[10]

Although there was some improvement between 1974 and 1979, the burden of maintaining a national flow of news about public affairs continued to fall on relatively few organizations: CP, assisted by more efficient transmission facilities; CBC television, assisted by expanded network facilities (both French and English) and longer national newscasts; CTV, which also lengthened its newscast; *Maclean's,* which emerged as a weekly newsmagazine;[11] CBC radio, which has increased its attention to public affairs; and a few others. While the *Globe and Mail* has doubled its circulation outside Ontario since 1974 to 12,000, it is not yet a national newspaper. However, the *Globe* and several other news organizations have created networks of regional correspondents, some of whom contributed effectively in 1979 to broadening the geographical focus of election coverage. Nevertheless, despite efforts at improvement, the major discontinuity in news flow, that between French and English, remained substantial.[12]

[9] For a discussion of the press gallery and the roots of this hostility, see Fletcher, "Mass Media," pp. 251-53.

[10] John Sawatsky, quoted in Clive Cocking, *Following the Leaders: A Media Watcher's Diary of Campaign '79* (Toronto: Doubleday, 1980), p. 14. Sawatsky is a former Vancouver *Sun* correspondent in Ottawa.

[11] The transformation of *Maclean's* was a result of federal legislation that withdrew tax deductions for advertisements by Canadian business for Canadian audiences in foreign-owned publications, such as *Time.* The new law led *Time* to discontinue its Canadian edition, which had been a condensed version of the U.S. edition with a few pages of Canadian news at the front, opening the way for *Maclean's.*

[12] The linguistic barrier to information flow was well documented in Committee

The relative weakness of national coverage is well illustrated in television news. In terms of audience, the local supper-hour newscasts outdraw the three late evening national newscasts by more than two to one (about 8 million to 3.5 million). And the local newscasts are generally longer than the national ones, which range from sixteen (CTV) to twenty-five (CBC) minutes. Further, the majority of local news viewers watch the private stations, which are generally very parochial in content, as they seek to maximize audiences at minimum cost.[13] This local orientation is offset somewhat by the fact that both CBC and CTV operate syndication services that provide the local stations with most of their national political coverage. As with newspapers, however, local editors are free to select whatever they wish from the material provided by the national services, thereby influencing the campaign agendas in their regions.

Television was even more dominant than in earlier elections as a source of campaign information. A clear majority of voters (52 percent) reported getting most of their campaign information from television in 1979; 30 percent mentioned newspapers and 11 percent radio.[14] Newspapers continued, of course, to be the most complete sources of information and to influence broadcast news, but the radio and television news organizations became increasingly autonomous in their news judgments during the 1970s and devoted more resources to public affairs. They were assisted in covering the federal Parliament by the introduction of the "electronic Hansard" in 1977. Television cameras were installed in the House of Commons, under the control of the Speaker, to tape all proceedings and to make available a live feed to any cable company wishing to carry it. Live coverage is not yet widely available, and the major effect has been to provide clips for newscasts and weekly programs on events in the House.[15]

In an important sense, the culmination of the campaign was "Encounter '79," a series of televised debates among the three major

of Inquiry into the National Broadcasting Service, Canadian Radio-television and Telecommunications Commission, *Report* (Ottawa, 1977). Efforts have been made to improve the situation by several major news organizations since the report, but the flow is still restricted.

[13] These estimates are from Trueman, *Smoke and Mirrors*, pp. 14-15; Peter Raymont, "History on the Run," a film study of the 1979 campaign; and data provided by CFTO-TV, Toronto.

[14] Carleton-CBC poll.

[15] Audiences for full coverage would remain small even if it were widely available. See Richard D. Price and Harold D. Clarke, "Television and the House of Commons," in Harold D. Clarke, Colin Campbell, F. Q. Quo, and Arthur Goddard, eds., *Parliament, Policy and Representation* (Toronto: Methuen, 1980), pp. 58-83.

party leaders.[16] The program was important not only in its own right—with a total audience of nearly 7.5 million, half the English-speaking population—but also as a heavily covered political event, perhaps the ultimate media event in a television campaign. It dominated the news for the next twenty-four hours and was examined in depth by political analysts right up to polling day nine days later.

The two major English television networks—CBC and CTV—which had failed to gain party agreement to a leaders' debate in 1974, were joined in the effort in 1979 by Global. The network representatives agreed on four principles for the proposed program: (1) the leaders must relate directly to one another; (2) the content must be of real substance, not simply campaign rhetoric; (3) the pace must be fast enough to hold audience interest for two hours; and (4) production quality must be high. The networks proposed that a nonpartisan moderator (the principal of McGill University) and a panel of journalists (the chief political correspondent from each network) be used to keep things focused and moving. They also proposed that the fourth national party, Social Credit, not be represented.[17]

After lengthy negotiations and considerable foot dragging by the front-running Conservatives, the three party leaders finally agreed to participate. The Conservatives apparently concluded that accusations that Clark was afraid to debate were too damaging. In the negotiations, the networks agreed to a Liberal demand that there be no "instant analysis," rejected a Conservative demand that the NDP be excluded because it had no chance to form a government, but agreed to a round-robin format and the inclusion of brief opening and closing statements by the leaders. Each debate lasted thirty minutes, and the luck of the draw made it Clark versus Ed Broadbent, leader of the NDP, in the first debate, Broadbent versus Trudeau in the second, and Clark versus Trudeau in the third.

In the event, the program proved in the eyes of many to be excellent television, holding most of its very large audience for the entire two hours. The networks retained control of the program and used five cameras to cover it like a sports event. The format and studio design have excited considerable interest among broadcasters in other countries. Certainly, it increased interest in the election and provided another basis for assessing the men who might be prime

---

[16] The information on "Encounter '79" is drawn from interviews and network documents.

[17] Fabien Roy, the Social Credit leader, was given time on the French networks. All the Social Credit seats were in predominantly French constituencies, and Roy speaks English poorly. The problems of presenting such debates in both official languages have yet to be resolved.

minister. Some observers complained, however, about reporters inter-
rupting the leaders to change the topic, as did many voters, according
to party surveys. Although a plurality of respondents (47 percent)
found the debate informative and enjoyable, many made disparaging
comments (42 percent).[18] Its impact was limited somewhat by the fact
that it was entirely in English.

The 1979 Campaign: Parties

Party strategists and news executives both consulted McLuhan's
"rearview mirror" as they planned the 1979 campaign, seeking to
avoid the mistakes of 1974. The Conservatives tried to avoid what
they viewed as their major error in 1974, when they were on the
defensive with their wage and price control proposal, by stressing
attacks on the Liberal economic record and promising benefits, such
as an income-tax deduction for mortgage interest and property tax to
selected groups. The Liberals, apparently feeling that a repeat of their
carefully orchestrated 1974 campaign[19] would generate too much
hostility among the media, chose to run a more open campaign featuring Trudeau. This had somewhat disastrous results when, apparently
upset by the antics of his estranged wife, he put down hecklers rather
sharply early in the campaign.[20] His pungent retorts tended to reinforce his image of arrogance and touchiness and to provide the
perspective from which many reporters approached the campaign.[21]
The Liberal strategy was to contrast Trudeau with Clark as a leader
and to stress national unity and energy policy as issues. The NDP
maintained its usual stress on economic issues, especially unemployment, inflation, and foreign ownership, but ran a more leader-oriented
and media-oriented campaign than in 1974. Its greater access to funds
under the new election rules helped. NDP planners felt they had not
done enough "selling" in 1974.[22]

[18] Jon H. Pammett, Harold Clarke, Jane Jenson, and Lawrence LeDuc, "Change in
the Garden: The 1979 Federal Election" (Paper presented at the Annual Meeting
of the Canadian Political Science Association, Montreal, June 2, 1980), p. 16 and
table 6.

[19] Fletcher, "Mass Media," pp. 253-54.

[20] The release of Margaret Trudeau's memoirs, *Beyond Reason*, as the campaign began appeared to have a greater effect on the prime minister than on the
campaign. The "Margaret factor" was handled with restraint by the media and
political opponents.

[21] Gilsdorf, "Getting the Message Across," pp. 11-12.

[22] I am indebted for some of these observations to William O. Gilsdorf, "The
Liberal Party and the Media in the 1979 Federal Election," unpublished working
paper, and Pammett et al., "Change," pp. 6-11.

The leaders' campaigns had a major impact on the style as well as the substance of the coverage.[23] For example, the prime minister helped to ensure that news stories would often focus on his attacks on Clark by using a single basic speech but freshening it with quips about the leader of the opposition. Because reporters had soon exhausted the contents of the speech, his references to Clark as a "tumbleweed" (a reference to apparent shifts in Conservative positions), a "headwaiter" (serving the interests of provincial governments out to weaken Ottawa), and the "7 billion dollar man" (the Liberal estimate of the cost of Clark's campaign promises) tended to provide the lead items in the coverage. Clark's attacks on Trudeau were also featured, giving the impression of a slanging match. Broadbent, in contrast, made effective use of "theme days" in which visuals were provided to match the policy announcement for the day. A proposal for a new fisheries policy, for example, would be made after a tour of a fishing harbor. Clark also used this tactic, but to a lesser extent. It promoted issue coverage, though often at a superficial level.

At the personal level, only Broadbent mixed with journalists in a spontaneous way. Trudeau's aloofness (despite a reasonable degree of formal access in press conferences) and Clark's personal awkwardness tended to preclude such relationships. In addition, formal access to Clark declined sharply after reporters seized on some ill-advised comments he made early in the campaign. It was the contention of Conservative strategists that reporters were predisposed to look for errors by Clark (an issue discussed below).

As table 10–1 shows, the parties were far from content to rely on free time and news coverage to reach uncommitted voters. Television and radio were the preferred advertising media, most spots running only thirty seconds on television and sixty on radio. Not surprisingly, they tended to be aimed more at image making than informing, though some (especially from the NDP) did have significant content. The target audience for the spots was, of course, voters not committed to a party after the first four weeks of the campaign, estimated at about 10 percent of the electorate, mainly voters with little interest in or knowledge of politics.[24] The advertisements were, therefore, run on popular general-interest programs, especially sports.[25]

[23] This paragraph draws on Gilsdorf, "Getting the Message Across," pp. 8-9, and scattered references in Cocking, *Following the Leaders.*

[24] This perspective is derived from the comments of party strategists at the Conference on Politics and the Media at Erindale College, June 12-13, 1980, and is confirmed in general terms in Clarke et al., *Political Choice,* chaps. 9-12, though that study also identifies a substantial issue-oriented category of voters.

[25] Global was the only network to carry partisan spots on its newscasts. Other

TABLE 10–1

ADVERTISING EXPENDITURES, BY MEDIUM AND PARTY, 1979

Medium	Conservative	Liberal	NDP	Other	Total Spent on Advertising	
					%	$
Print	10	24	24	70	18	1,202,858
Radio	34	23	19	14	27	1,758,612
Television	56	53	58	16	55	3,615,220
Total	100	100	101	100	100	
Total spent on advertising ($)	2,745,501	2,434,405	1,333,080	63,704		6,576,690
Percentage of total reported expenditures	71	62	61	65	65	

SOURCE: Calculated from data reported in Chief Electoral Officer, *Special Report to the Speaker of the House of Commons Respecting Election Expenses of Registered Parties and Candidates for the Thirty-first General Election, May 22, 1979* (Ottawa: Ministry of Supply and Services, 1980).

The Conservative advertisements came in two waves. The initial wave focused on the failures of the Trudeau government, reminding voters not only of scandals and unsuccessful policies but also of Trudeau's controversial statements. A typical spot featured a clip of Trudeau standing in the House of Commons while a voice intoned quotations (often out of context) attributed to him over his years in office. Others were attacks on specific policies backed by slick visuals, such as one in which the narrator accused Trudeau of having damaged Canada's world standing, illustrated by a Canadian flag being lowered (conveniently overlooking Conservative opposition to the adoption of the flag in the 1960s). The second phase began with spots featuring the Conservative "team" (leading candidates for Cabinet posts) and then shifted to clips presenting Clark in a positive light or setting out party policy. The essential theme was "time for a change" or, in the words of the slogan that ended every spot, "Give the Future a Chance."

---

networks refused, to avoid confusing audiences, since many advertisements used news clip formats. The material on advertisements in the following paragraphs is drawn from Cocking, *Following the Leaders*, pp. 259-62; Gilsdorf, "Getting the Message Across," pp. 21, 41; and personal interviews.

The Liberal campaign focused on Trudeau, stressing his strength as a leader in contrast to Clark's inexperience. The spots generally used clips from early campaign speeches, often with Trudeau attacking Clark's "fuzziness" on key issues. A typical spot used film clips of Trudeau with world leaders, stressing his stature and experience. The focus was on Trudeau throughout, with contrasting references to Clark. The closing slogan for the spots was "A Leader Must Be a Leader."

The NDP advertisements, in the party's first major venture into television advertising, all featured Broadbent talking directly to the voters about party positions on key issues, often in a visually appropriate setting. For example, he would be shown discussing rising food prices in a supermarket. The strategy, developed by a high-powered advertising agency specializing in marketing new products, was to present Broadbent as an alternative leader and to underline his moderate stance (as an antidote to the NDP's radical image). The most effective spot, according to experts, was a response to polls showing Broadbent's personal appeal growing in relation to that of the other leaders. It was an all-print message, featuring an announcer reading a script as it rolled up the screen:

> A lot of Liberals and Conservatives believe that Ed Broadbent would make the best Prime Minister. They say, if Ed Broadbent were the leader of their party, he'd win the biggest landslide in Canadian history. People don't have the same kind of nagging doubts about Ed Broadbent they have about Trudeau and Clark. Maybe it's time to put aside the old Liberal and Conservative myths and simply vote for the best man. If enough people did that, Ed Broadbent would be the next Prime Minister of Canada.[26]

Though more issue-oriented than those of the other two parties, the NDP commercials also had as their primary purpose the selling of the leader.

Although television has made Canadian campaigns increasingly national, party strategists continue to run separate campaigns in French and English. The Liberal advertisements were much more positive in French, focusing on Trudeau, the favorite son, and the accomplishments of his government. In contrast, the Conservative spots were primarily scorching attacks on Trudeau. One, showing Trudeau in the House of Commons as a backdrop, presented the election as a trial in which the prime minister was declared "coupable" (guilty) of various "crimes" taken from the record of his

[26] Cocking, *Following the Leaders*, p. 262.

government, punctuated by the sound of a jail door slamming. An Anglophone Quebec journalist described it as "the most insulting and politically stupid advertising that has ever gone out over Quebec airwaves."[27] The Conservatives were also criticized for offering much less information on their policies in French than in English.[28] Certainly, attacking Trudeau so directly in his home province was an act of desperation. The NDP's modest effort in Quebec was a replica of its campaign in English.

Many observers objected to the negative tone and manipulative style of the spots, arguing that they contributed little to voters' information. As Anthony Westell put it: "They are appeals to ignorance and prejudice, and I don't see why we should put up with them in future campaigns."[29] Another leading political commentator, Geoffrey Stevens of the *Globe*, also called for a ban on commercials, suggesting that partisan broadcast advertising be banned and replaced by free time to be made available in segments no shorter than five minutes:

> This might force the parties and the leaders to talk to the voters intelligently, to address themselves to issues and policies, rather than . . . fill the air with slick, superficial 30 or 60 second spots, which tell us nothing about what's right about the party sponsoring the commercial, but a great deal about what's . . . alleged to be wrong with the other fellows.[30]

The free-time broadcasts, however, often expanded versions or sets of the spots, were only marginally more informative, though one could get a general idea of party positions on certain key issues from them.

The 1979 Campaign: Media

One of the most striking features of the 1979 coverage was the extent to which it reflected the experience of 1974. Despite considerable turnover of key news personnel, the "lessons" of 1974 had a major influence on planning for 1979. Some features of the coverage were extrapolations of 1974 patterns—for example, the overwhelming emphasis of party strategists on television news—while others were reactions to the widespread view that the Liberals had effectively

---

[27] Ian MacDonald in the Montreal *Gazette*, May 16, 1979.

[28] Dalton Camp, *Points of Departure* (Ottawa: Deneau and Greenberg, 1979), p. 230.

[29] *Toronto Star*, May 12, 1979.

[30] Geoffrey Stevens, "A Case of Image over Reality," *Globe and Mail* (Toronto), February 23, 1980.

manipulated the coverage in 1974. The Liberals had controlled access to the prime minister and timed the release of complex policy statements so that reporters had little choice but to report the proposals without analysis.[31] The media planners responded in four major ways: (1) tough-minded, experienced reporters were assigned to the Trudeau tour (and to cover Clark as well); (2) reporters were encouraged to report on the tactics of the parties and to comment on the purposes underlying media events; (3) most major news organizations assigned teams of reporters and researchers to prepare analyses of campaign issues, independent of partisan sources; and (4) attempts were made to get beyond the parties and to report on public reactions to the campaign and on key local issues in regional reports. As one television news executive put it, "Most Canadian journalists were very annoyed in 1974 by the way the media had beem manipulated. This time we went out with our guards up and saw ourselves as a kind of truth squad."[32]

These developments accentuated a trend in Canada toward more judgmental journalism. Most reporters on the planes with the leaders agreed with a veteran television journalist that reporters had to be interpretive and, on occasion, critical of the style and objectives of the campaigns. Indeed, the television networks and some major newspapers encouraged a more judgmental approach, which often went beyond putting events in context to editorializing. Combined with the focus on tactics, this resulted in reports from the leaders' tours stressing campaign style and the prospects for victory. Whatever substance there was in the leaders' campaigns often got lost in the shuffle, especially for the two major parties. Reports came to resemble sports writing or theater reviews.

This trend was, however, compensated for in part by the major increase in issue-oriented and regional reports by some of the national media. The CP Ottawa bureau, for example, established a twenty-four-hour election desk and assigned specialist reporters to check out major proposals and claims made by party leaders. CBC English television established an issues team, backed up by researchers and detailed election fact books, to prepare special issues reports. The issues team was also assisted by elaborate systems for retrieving past party positions and relevant film clips. The national news devoted about 14 percent of its campaign coverage to issues (more than an hour of air time during the course of the campaign) and another 7 percent (about thirty minutes) to commentary. The *Toronto Star* also had a perma-

---

[31] Fletcher, "Mass Media," pp. 253-56.
[32] Interview with a senior CBC producer in Ottawa.

nent issues team of three veteran Ottawa reporters and assigned two reporters to each leader, with one on the plane, covering the leader, and the other off the plane, writing analytic pieces in alternate weeks. The detailed issue analyses, often based on interviews with independent experts, were supplemented by a weekly digest of the campaign and a weekly scorecard of party stands on key issues. The *Globe* carried similar summaries, but the *Star* issue coverage was generally judged the best in the country. CTV, however, made little effort in this direction, devoting only about forty-five minutes during the campaign to issues and analyses, and many dailies used only a few of the issue analyses provided by CP and SNS. Regional mood pieces were quite widely used, however, providing some flow of information across provincial boundaries.

As in 1974, approaches to campaign coverage differed by region. In the West, most outlets relied on syndicated copy for national coverage and focused their own resources on local issues. In Alberta, where a Conservative sweep was inevitable, the campaign was treated as an event of marginal interest, perhaps because the only real contests had already been covered—at the Conservative nomination meetings.[33] Despite some lively contests in Saskatchewan and Manitoba, news media there also stressed local and regional matters. In Manitoba, disastrous spring floods got more attention than the campaign, and one daily did not assign a single staff member exclusively to the campaign. In British Columbia the two major dailies, the Vancouver *Sun* and the *Province*, were on strike, and the remaining outlets gave their primary attention to the provincial election and seemed too exhausted after it was over on May 10 to catch up on the federal campaign, despite the crucial role the Vancouver area ridings were expected to play in the outcome. The coverage gave a sense that the key events were taking place elsewhere.

In contrast, the Quebec media—both French and English— devoted substantial resources to the coverage, despite the fact that real contests in the province were few. Although the popular press did not provide much, *Le Devoir* provided its usual highly analytic coverage, and *La Presse* devoted unprecedented resources (twenty-five reporters, two editors) to the campaign. By the last two weeks of the campaign, *La Presse* was filling four pages daily with leader coverage, issue analysis, regional mood pieces from across Canada, and riding profiles. CBC French radio and television also provided extensive cross-Canada coverage, and CP filed regularly in French.

---

33 Pointed out by William Gold, publisher of the Calgary *Herald*, at the Conference on Politics and the Media at Erindale College, June 12-13, 1980.

This commitment of resources may have reflected the high political interest generated by the imminent referendum on sovereignty-association for Quebec and the central role in the election of favorite son Pierre Trudeau. Certainly it contrasted sharply with the very inward-looking coverage in 1974.[34] The English media also devoted substantial resources to campaign coverage.

Despite the distraction of three recent provincial elections (and one expected), including one in Prince Edward Island on April 23, the federal campaign got considerable attention in the Atlantic provinces. This was mainly the result of the Halifax *Chronicle-Herald*'s decision to cover the leaders' tours and to examine local contests and issues in all four provinces. It devoted a third of its staff to the coverage. ATV, the regional CTV affiliate, also sent its own correspondents to cover the leaders, and the CBC services offered regional coverage to supplement network reports.

In Ontario, where the election was expected to be decided, coverage was extensive, especially in Toronto and Ottawa. Some smaller outlets, like the London *Free Press* (circulation 135,000), provided exemplary coverage, supplementing leader coverage by their own reporters with issue analysis and detailed examinations of the campaign across the country.[35] Others were extremely parochial, using only a fraction of the issue and regional materials provided by CP and services like SNS.

At the national level, the 1979 coverage was extensive and modestly innovative, though it could be faulted for excessive attention to the style of the leaders' campaigns. Coverage in the regions was highly variable and appeared to depend as much on the personal preferences of media executives as on the competitiveness of the contests or the presence of other important news.

Despite regional differences and the introduction of regional reports, there remained a distinct central Canadian bias in the coverage. Fully 60 percent of the front-page campaign stories located in the newspaper analysis originated in Ontario, and it was the dominant source in all regions except the West, even when Ottawa items are subtracted. Only 12 percent of the front-page election stories in Ontario newspapers came from outside the province. The next most inward-looking region was the West, where half the items originated outside the region.

---

[34] Fletcher, "Mass Media," pp. 261ff.
[35] Cocking, *Following the Leaders*, pp. 130-31.

Focus of Coverage: The Race

Despite the impression of most observers that the media had a leader fixation,[36] the attention paid to the party leaders was probably less than in 1974. In the daily newspapers, 54 percent of all front-page campaign headlines mentioned a party leader (more than twice as many as mentioned a party), down from 59 percent in 1974. On television newscasts, party leaders were featured in from 28 percent (Global) to 43 percent (CTV) of all election items.[37] Aside from leader interviews, of which there were several, public affairs shows often gave less attention to leaders than did newscasts. A deliberate attempt had been made by the major news organizations to broaden the coverage, but the impression left with audiences was of a constant preoccupation with the campaign performance of the leaders.

This impression of a leadership focus was fed by several factors. First, leadership was a major issue throughout the campaign. Second, the leaders appeared day after day on newspaper front pages and in the main items on television and radio newscasts. Third, the broadened coverage dealt with issues and public reactions, not alternative party spokesmen, however appropriate that might be in a parliamentary system. Fourth, the media did seem obsessed with the "horse race" element of the campaign, and many reports that did not deal directly with the leaders referred to their campaigns and vote-getting prospects.

This focus on the electoral contest was reflected in and reinforced by the proliferation of public opinion polls.[38] From the first flutter-ings of election butterflies in early 1978 until voting day itself, polls were a central feature of the coverage. During the long run-up to the election, the polls were closely examined to assess the likelihood that the prime minister would call an election. A sense of the fluctuation in national popularity between elections can be gleaned from table 10–2. Throughout 1978 the polls showed the Liberals trailing the Conservatives outside Quebec. The Gallup polls showed

---

[36] Murray Goldblatt, "Media Had a Leader Fixation," *Globe and Mail*, May 23, 1979. Professor Goldblatt wrote a useful four-part series for the *Globe* on media coverage of the campaign.

[37] The figures for CBC were: French, 35 percent; English, 32 percent. E. D. Briggs, W. I. Romanow, W. C. Soderlund, and R. H. Wagenberg, "Television News and the 1979 Canadian Federal Election" (Paper presented at the Founding Meeting of the Canadian Communications Association, Montreal, June 1980), table 5.

[38] For an excellent discussion of election polling in Canada, see Lawrence LeDuc, "The Measurement of Public Opinion," in Penniman, *Canada at the Polls, 1974*, pp. 209-42.

TABLE 10–2

PARTY PREFERENCES IN SELECTED GALLUP POLLS, 1975–1979
(percent)

Date	Liberal	Conservative	NDP	Other
Actual vote, July 8, 1974	43	35	15	6
Date of poll				
February 1975	47	30	17	6
February 1976	38	37	19	6
March 1976	34	43	17	6
February 1977	41	37	17	4
February 1978	43	36	17	4
April 1978	41	41	14	4
June 1978	43	37	16	4
August 1978	45	35	15	4
September 1978	41	38	17	4
October 1978	37	42	17	4
November 1978	35	45	18	2
December 1978	38	40	18	4
March 1979	41	41	15	3
April 1979	43	38	17	2
May 3–5, 1979	39	38	16	7
May 15–16, 1979	37.5	37.5	19	6
Actual vote, May 22, 1979	40	36	18	6

SURVEY QUESTION: "If a federal election were held today, which party's candidate do you think you would favor?"
NOTE: Undecided respondents have been omitted.
SOURCES: Kielty et al., *Canadians Speak Out*, p. 11; and Gallup reports.

that two-thirds of the voters were dissatisfied with the direction of the country and a substantial number believed the Conservatives would do a better job of managing the economy.[39] At midcampaign a CBC poll showed the voting intentions of decided voters outside Quebec as: Conservative, 48 percent; Liberal, 32; NDP, 19. In the same poll 57 percent of respondents reported dissatisfaction with the record of the Liberal government.[40] Poll findings such as these and the long Liberal delay in calling the election made it clear that the governing party was entering the campaign as an underdog. This was

[39] Trudeau even slipped behind Clark briefly, in November 1978, in personal popularity. See Frank Kielty, Clara Hatton, and Peter Munsche, eds., *Canadians Speak Out: The Canadian Gallup Polls* (Toronto: McNamara Press, 1980), pp. 2–5.
[40] Carleton-CBC poll.

sometimes obscured by the huge Liberal vote in Quebec, which gave the party the overall lead in many polls, but a lead that could not be translated into a plurality of seats in the House of Commons. The expectation of a Liberal defeat and the possibility of a Liberal resurgence colored much of the coverage.

During the campaign itself, there were eight national published polls: three Gallup polls, one *Toronto Star* poll (conducted by the Canadian Institute of Public Opinion, the Gallup organization in Canada), two surveys by the Carleton University School of Journalism for CBC, and two CTV polls, carried out by a private firm. In addition, there were a few provincial polls and uncounted local and riding polls, conducted with varying degrees of professionalism. The national polls were generally of a reasonable technical standard, though secondary reports of poll results were often misleading, especially on radio. Aside from failure to provide adequate information on such matters as sampling techniques, sample size, and question wording, the most common flaw in poll reports was to exaggerate the importance of small differences or changes from one poll to another. One consequence of this was to create the impression that the various polls were in contradiction when in fact they were in broad agreement. This pattern can be traced not only to ignorance but also to the desire of the media to present the election as a dramatic contest. In fact, the polls suggest that only minor shifts of voting intention took place during the campaign.

The exaggeration of differences for dramatic effect is part of a general tendency to focus on the party and leader preference questions with a view to predicting the outcome and explaining it in terms of leader appeal. Yet many of the surveys went beyond these questions to explore the issues perceived as most important, the reasons given for the party and leader preference, the party thought best able to deal with specific issues, interest in the campaign, qualities sought in a party leader, and numerous other matters of interest. These data, however, were usually to be found on inside pages or in brief references on television specials. Analysis was generally confined to a few simple variables, like region. As one pollster ruefully put it:

> Newspapers are obsessed by the horse race aspect of the monthly party preference figures. There tends to be very little discussion of the figures and what they do not tell—for example, the strength of voting commitment, the nature of the undecided vote, the relationship between voting preferences and attitudes towards leaders and issues.[41]

[41] Alan Frizzell, "The Student as Political Pollster," *Carleton Journalism Review*, vol. 2, no. 3 (Autumn 1979), pp. 10-11.

TABLE 10–3

National Poll Forecasts, Election Result, and Difference, 1979
(percent and percentage points)

Party	Gallup May 15–16	Carleton-CBC April 30–May 10	CTV May 11–14	Election Result May 22
Liberal	37.5 (2.5)	40 (0)	40 (0)	40
Conservative	37.5 (1.5)	41 (5)	40 (4)	36
NDP	19 (1)	15 (3)	17 (1)	18
Other	6 (0)	5 (1)	3 (3)	6
Total	100	101	100	100
N	(2,037)	(2,300)	(1,000)	(11,541,000)
Expected confidence interval (at 0.95)[a]	±3	±3	±4	—
Total deviation from actual election result	5	9	8	—

Note: Deviation from actual result shown in parentheses.

[a] For a discussion of confidence intervals, see Lawrence LeDuc, "The Measurement of Public Opinion," in Penniman, *Canada at the Polls, 1974*, p. 216.

Source: Adapted from data provided by Alan Frizzell, School of Journalism, Carleton University, Ottawa.

Although some local polls, such as one in the *Toronto Sun* that forecast a Liberal sweep of metropolitan Toronto,[42] were wildly inaccurate, the major polls were reasonably accurate in 1979. The final forecasts from the three major polls are shown in table 10–3. In only one case was the result for a party beyond the expected error range. Perhaps it is the failure of the news media to report polls in terms of estimates and ranges that prompts politicians and others to criticize them as inaccurate and misleading.

It is true, however, that the Liberal stranglehold on Quebec made the national totals misleading as far as the probable outcome was concerned. The pollsters, however, made unprecedented efforts in 1979 to provide data broken down by region, even in some cases when sample sizes were too small for reasonable accuracy. Nevertheless, some of the polls provided regional breakdowns that were very useful in forecasting the outcome, particularly those revealing

[42] Research notes provided by Alan Frizzell.

the Conservative lead in southern Ontario. These findings had a major influence on the reporting of the campaign, and the Liberals tried to reduce the demoralizing effect of the negative expectations created by hinting that their own polls showed them gaining. In fact, it has become common practice for parties to try to discredit polls that show them trailing in key areas.

A number of other poll results also influenced the coverage. For example, the polls reinforced reporters in their belief that economic issues and not national unity were most important outside Quebec. The overwhelming popularity of the Conservative proposal for a tax deduction for mortgage interest and property taxes, despite expert criticism, reinforced expectations of Conservative gains in the suburbs. The fact that the Liberals appeared to be losing ground during the campaign, especially in Ontario, helped create a sense of the inevitability of a change of government. On the other hand, Trudeau's continued dominance as the preferred leader in virtually all polls helped to reinforce doubts about Clark's electoral appeal. A typical poll showed Trudeau the preferred leader of 44 percent of respondents, with Clark at 19 and Broadbent at 8.[43] The poll results no doubt both reflected and reinforced media perceptions.

Though news items based directly on polls accounted for only about 5 percent of reports on the campaign,[44] their influence on the coverage was pervasive. Journalists are for the most part avid consumers of surveys, and poll results were used regularly as context items for reports on party tactics and prospects. Commentators used them as a basis for forecasts, as did regional reports. In addition, they received good play in most weekly campaign summaries and the preelection wrap-ups and, of course, CBC and CTV had news specials on their polls. Their prominence reinforced the focus on party leaders because the results were often presented as measures of how the leaders' campaigns were going.

Media Attention to the Campaign

In purely quantitative terms, the substantial resources devoted to campaign coverage in 1979 did result in increased election content, especially on radio and television. This attention, however, was more on the inside pages of newspapers, in special reports on newscasts,

---

[43] The question asked respondents, "Which man do you think would make the best prime minister?" Kielty et al., *Canadians Speak Out*, p. 16.

[44] According to one study, the percentage of campaign news items dealing with polls ranged from 6.4 on Global to 2.7 on CTV. See Briggs et al., "Television News," table 1. The figures for newspaper front pages were similar.

and in radio public affairs programming than in high-profile news items. The coverage, therefore, provided more information to voters but did not necessarily signal to them that the election was unusually significant or exciting, though the special reports and election pages might have conveyed that message to the politically attentive audience. Gallup poll data do, however, show a slightly higher level of voter interest in the campaign in 1979 than in 1974.[45]

Looking at tables 10–4 and 10–5, we find that front-page and editorial-page attention in a sample of dailies[46] remained roughly stable from 1974 to 1979 but that broadcast coverage increased considerably, especially on the English networks. In fact, the broadcast figures understate the increase because they do not include all public affairs programs. The CBC English service increased its overall coverage from 530 minutes in 1974 to 843 minutes in 1979, a result primarily of increased time on national newscasts. Time devoted to news specials was actually down 30 minutes. (It also provided 2,638 minutes of local and regional news and public affairs coverage.) CTV devoted increased time to the campaign on news and public affairs shows. "Canada AM," for example, provided nearly eleven hours of campaign items, a significant increase over 1974. Although CBC English and CTV devoted more time on their national newscasts to election news in 1979 (ten and seven minutes on the average), the average share of each newscast (41 percent for CBC and 45 for CTV) taken up by campaign news was unchanged from 1974.[47] The French networks did not match these increases, perhaps because they had in 1974 already devoted the maximum possible resources and air time to the campaign.[48]

[45] In 1974, 35 percent of Gallup poll respondents reported being very interested in the campaign; in 1979, the figure was 41 percent. Kielty et al., *Canadians Speak Out*, p. 18.

[46] The daily newspapers in the 1979 sample were: West: Victoria *Colonist* (m), circulation 40,579, owner, FP Publications; *Edmonton Journal* (e), 159,730, Southam; Regina *Leader-Post* (e), 62,595, Sifton; Winnipeg *Free Press* (e), 135,143, FP; Ontario: Ottawa *Citizen* (e), 115,165, Southam; *Toronto Star* (e), 481,286, independent; Toronto *Globe and Mail* (m), 266,439, FP; Quebec: *La Presse* (Montreal) (e), 142,358, Trans-Canada/Power Corp.; *Le Devoir* (Montreal) (m), 49,532, independent; *Le Soleil* (Quebec City) (e), 113,862, Uni-media; *Montreal Star* (e), 166,056, FP; East: St. John's *Telegram* (e), 32,598, Thomson; St. John *Telegraph-Journal* (m), 32,348, Irving; Halifax *Chronicle-Herald* (m), 71,544, independent. The sample contains a mix of morning (m) and evening (e) papers and represents both major chains. A random sample of twelve dates was chosen for analysis. For the 1974 sample, see Fletcher, "Mass Media," pp. 257-59.

[47] I am indebted to the networks and to David Balcon of the CRTC for these figures. Journalists at both CTV and CBC English tried without success to obtain lengthened newscasts and time allocations for a special election package for part of the campaign period.

[48] See Fletcher, "Mass Media," p. 257.

In broad terms, the regional and linguistic differences shown in tables 10–4 and 10–5 were paralleled by some fragmentary data on local radio and television coverage. In a general way, they reflect the difference in resources allocated to campaign coverage by the news organizations in different regions.

TABLE 10–4

ATTENTION GIVEN TO THE CANADIAN GENERAL ELECTIONS
IN FOURTEEN DAILY NEWSPAPERS, 1974 AND 1979

	Front-Page Stories on Election				No. of Days Election Was Main News Item on Front Page		No. of Days at Least One Election Editorial Appeared	
	1974		1979					
Newspaper	%	No.	%	No.	1974	1979	1974	1979
West								
Sun (Vancouver) and Colonist (Victoria)[a]	14	13	12	10	3	4	5	6
Edmonton Journal	14	10	9	4	2	0	5	10
Leader-Post (Regina)	33	25	33	7	5	5	5	5
Free Press (Winnipeg)	13	20	9	6	3	2	6	6
Ontario								
Citizen (Ottawa)	18	14	13	7	3	3	9	3
Toronto Star	26	27	18	10	5	2	4	9
Globe and Mail (Toronto)	21	17	24	10	1	0	6	16
Quebec								
La Presse (Montreal)	28	17	49	25	3	2	7	2
Le Devoir (Montreal)	27	22	31	19	4	3	7	6

(Table continues)

TABLE 10–4 (continued)

Newspaper	Front-Page Stories on Election				No. of Days Election Was Main News Item on Front Page		No. of Days at Least One Election Editorial Appeared	
	1974		1979					
	%	No.	%	No.	1974	1979	1974	1979
Le Soleil (Quebec)	19	12	31	19	3	2	5	n.a.
Montreal Star	6	5	28	17	5	5	9	8
East Chronicle- Herald (Halifax)	29	28	27	32	3	4	1	3
Telegram (St. John's) [b]	—	—	8	15	—	2	—	3
Telegraph- Journal (St. John) [b]	—	—	19	16	—	4	—	4
Average	21	18	22	14	3.3	2.7	5.75	6.2

NOTE: n.a. = not available.

[a] The Vancouver *Sun* was not publishing during the 1979 campaign and was replaced by the *Colonist* in the sample.

[b] The St. John's and St. John dailies were not included in the 1974 study.

SOURCE: In both 1974 and 1979, a random sample of twelve issues of each newspaper was surveyed. The 1974 data are from Fletcher, "Mass Media," table 9-3.

The Contest for Media Attention

The contest for media attention involves not only the amount of attention but also the tone of the coverage and the issues stressed. The first challenge for party strategists, however, is to get media coverage, though this is now more or less automatic for the two major parties and increasingly also for the NDP. Despite the policy of most major news outlets to ensure a degree of balance among the three major parties, news values continue to play a role, and media attention remains an indicator to the public of which candidates to take seriously.

TABLE 10–5

Time Devoted to the Campaigns on Major National Newscasts, 1974 and 1979
(minutes)

	1974	1979
CBC television (English)	198	445
CBC television (French)	535	564
CTV	147	277
Global television	—[a]	345
CBC radio (English)	596	1,313[b]
CBC radio (French)	1,364	1,380[c]

Note: Because different coding methods may have been used, comparisons between networks cannot be made with confidence.
[a] Global was founded after the 1974 election.
[b] Includes some programs not counted in 1974.
[c] Estimated.
Sources: Fletcher, "Mass Media," table 9-3; Briggs et al., "Television News," table 2; and materials provided by the authors; data provided by the networks.

The quantitative results of the contest for attention in 1974 and 1979 are set out in tables 10–6 and 10–7. Despite their quasi-underdog status, the Liberals were able by and large to preserve the traditional incumbent advantage, though their share of coverage slipped slightly in the press. The slippage probably resulted primarily from the rather ineffective Trudeau campaign. Data from CBC English radio suggest that the Liberal advantage in 1979 was based more on stories about the Liberals than on reports of statements by Trudeau or other party spokesmen. In fact, Broadbent, probably because of his greater accessibility, received more CBC radio air time than either Trudeau (who ranked third) or Clark, though there were more actual items about Trudeau.[49] The likelihood is that many of the Liberal items were unfavorable. On television, however, Trudeau received most attention (except on CTV).

As far as the national media are concerned, it appears that there was no clear winner of the contest for media attention in 1979. The Liberals maintained a modest incumbent advantage, but much of the coverage was unfavorable.

[49] Michael McEwen, "Federal Election Logging—CBC Radio," CBC internal memo, 1979.

303

TABLE 10–6

ATTENTION GIVEN TO PARTIES AND LEADERS ON THE FRONT PAGES OF A
SAMPLE OF DAILY NEWSPAPERS, 1974 AND 1979

(percent)

	Stories		Headlines	
	1974	1979	1974	1979
Party				
Liberal	41	39	52	45
Conservative	29	36	32	23
NDP	23	24	12	27
Other	6	1	5	5
N	(192)	(189)	(60)	(44)
Leader				
Trudeau	50	48	43	51
Stanfield/Clark	29	33	35	27
Lewis/Broadbent	17	18	20	20
Other	4	1	2	3
N	(192)	(189)	(113)	(102)

SOURCES: The 1974 figures are adopted from Fletcher, "Mass Media," table 9-4.
The 1979 figures are from a content analysis done for this study. See table 10-4
for the list of newspapers.

Editorial Endorsements

For the past decade, the tide of editorial endorsements has been
running against Trudeau and the Liberals. In 1972 and 1974, a
number of traditionally Liberal dailies defected to the Conservatives,
including the *Toronto Star,* Vancouver *Sun,* and *Edmonton Journal,*
and most of the dailies that had abandoned the Conservatives in the
1960s—such as the *Globe and Mail*—returned to the fold.[50] In 1979
there were several more defections, including the traditionally Liberal
Ottawa *Citizen,* which moved from lukewarm Liberal to reluctant
Conservative, and the *Montreal Star,* which endorsed the Conservatives for only the second time in forty-nine years. The *Toronto Star*
abandoned its flirtation with the Conservatives in the two previous
elections and caused a minor sensation by endorsing (cautiously) the
NDP, becoming the second daily newspaper ever to endorse that party
in a federal election. In the end, only the Winnipeg *Free Press* and
La Presse (Montreal) held firm among the traditionally Liberal major

[50] For details, see Fletcher, "Mass Media," pp. 271-72.

TABLE 10-7

Attention Given to the Three Major Parties on Network News Broadcasts, 1974 and 1979

(percent)

Party	CBC TV (French)		CBC TV (English)		CTV		Global[a]	CBC Radio (French)		CBC Radio (English)	
	1974	1979	1974	1979	1974	1979	1979	1974	1979	1974	1979
Liberal	43	43	42	40	37	38	42	39	43	37	39
Conservative	34	35	35	32	34	36	35	35	34	35	34
NDP	23	22	24	28	29	26	23	26	23	28	27
N[b]	(405)	(387)[c]	(184)	(278)	(147)	(277)	(345)[c]	(1,035)	(263)[c]	(571)	(12,369)

NOTE: Some calculations are based on a count of news items rather than of broadcast time. Except for CBC Radio (English), the figures show news and news specials only. The figures for CBC Radio (English), which proved impossible to disaggregate, include all coverage.

[a] Global was not in operation in 1974.

[b] Minutes unless otherwise noted.

[c] Items.

SOURCES: Same as for table 10-5; and Fletcher, "Mass Media," table 9-5.

dailies and the Winnipeg paper did so halfheartedly. The dailies in the Atlantic provinces continued their longstanding tradition of Conservative-leaning neutrality.

The 1979 editorial endorsements were similar to those in 1974 in one essential element: they were grudging. Editorial writers across Canada seemed to agree that the Trudeau government was worn out, that it suffered from hardening of the arteries, and, more specifically, that its economic policies were bankrupt. There were also elements of opposition to Trudeau's leadership style and a general feeling that it was time for a change. Few went so far as the Calgary *Herald*, which took the view that "a majority Trudeau government would be a national tragedy," but the general sentiment was there. Most editorialists, however, expressed profound misgivings about Clark's leadership qualities and the confusion surrounding some of his policies. Overall, the tone was much more anti-Trudeau than pro-Clark. In the rare cases when Broadbent was mentioned, the general line was that he was a good man in a radical party, with no chance to form a government.

The *Toronto Star's* decision to endorse the NDP, after considerable internal dissension, reflected both its disenchantment with the two older parties and its recognition that its editorial positions on key economic issues, such as Petrocanada, economic nationalism, and the need for an industrial strategy, were represented best by the NDP. Nevertheless, despite the old saw that the *Star* has always been NDP between elections anyway, publisher Beland Honderich, who wrote the editorial himself, felt it necessary to point out that Broadbent is a "reasonable intelligent person" whose policies are "far removed from the doctrinaire socialist policies the party once advocated." It appears that he expected—or at least hoped for—a Liberal minority government in which the NDP would be able to promote its economic policies in a balance-of-power role. The endorsement concluded: "We endorse the NDP hoping it will have a strong presence in the next Parliament so it can give voice to the needs of Canadians who find no other party speaking for them." [51] The endorsement of the NDP brought a strong and mainly negative reaction from subscribers and boosted NDP morale.

The Tone of the Coverage

Survey evidence suggests that more than one-third of the voters cast their ballots in the 1979 election on the basis of the general images

[51] For an interesting discussion of the endorsement and the *Star's* long flirtation with social reform, see Cocking, *Following the Leaders*, pp. 228-29.

TABLE 10–8

ELECTION CAMPAIGN STORIES REFLECTING POSITIVELY AND
NEGATIVELY ON MAJOR PARTIES, BY TELEVISION NETWORK, 1979
(percent)

Party	CBC French Positive	CBC French Negative	CBC English Positive	CBC English Negative	Global Positive	Global Negative	CTV Positive	CTV Negative
Liberal	4.7	14.0	5.9	17.3	6.4	14.9	8.8	12.0
Conservative	1.5	9.0	7.9	11.4	8.4	10.2	7.3	11.7
NDP	1.9	1.2	6.9	4.0	4.4	3.2	6.6	3.1
Other	0.9	1.5	1.0	2.9	0.0	5.5	0.8	2.4
N	(322)		(306)		(345)		(259)	

SOURCE: Adapted from Briggs et al., "Television News," table 6.

of the parties (22 percent) or of the party leaders (17 percent).[52]
While direct evidence of the impact of the campaign is difficult to
find, the 1979 data do show that changes in the images of both
parties and leaders took place during the run-up to the election and the
campaign itself. It is therefore important to assess the tone of the
coverage of parties and leaders in an effort to trace its influence.
Despite the fact that bias is often in the eye (or ear) of the beholder,
careful analysis of items clearly favorable or unfavorable to a party
or leader can be revealing.

A group of researchers at the University of Windsor has examined
the positive and negative references to parties and leaders in the 1979
coverage, and their findings for the television networks—the primary
image setters—are set out in tables 10–8 and 10–9. These data support the impressions of observers that both older parties tended to be
treated negatively while the NDP received generally positive treatment. In fact, the NDP emerged as the "good guys" of the campaign
while the Liberals were treated most negatively on two networks and
the Conservatives got the worst press on the other two, including the
CBC French service. The French radio network, however, was harder
on the Liberals than on the Conservatives.[53]

Most of the newspaper stories with a clear slant dealt with the
Liberals, and these were as often positive as negative. Reports of

[52] Pammett et al., "Change," p. 34.
[53] Nearly half the coverage was neutral or balanced, about 45 percent on the
English networks and 65 percent on CBC French. See Briggs et al., "Television
News," table 3.

TABLE 10–9

Election Campaign Stories Reflecting Positively and Negatively on Party Leaders, by Television Network, 1979

(percent)

Leader	CBC French			CBC English			Global			CTV		
	Positive	Negative	N	Positive	Negative	N	Positive	Negative	N	Positive	Negative	N
Trudeau	19	68	(53)	22	79	(40)	28	50	(46)	27	55	(40)
Clark	16	72	(26)	23	74	(34)	17	79	(33)	8	70	(47)
Broadbent	20	40	(10)	24	43	(11)	47	9	(11)	51	30	(17)
Total	18	66	(89)	23	72	(85)	26	56	(90)	22	58	(104)

Source: Calculated from Briggs et al., "Television News," table 5.

attacks by Trudeau on Conservative policies and Clark's leadership capacities were given considerable prominence, as were attacks by private groups on certain key Conservative policies.[54]

As far as leader image is concerned, the data in table 10–9 show that a majority of references to both Trudeau and Clark on television newscasts were negative, with Clark generally getting the worst treatment. Broadbent also had a net unfavorable balance on the two CBC networks—perhaps reflecting a generally adversarial approach—but was treated positively on the two private networks. Analysis of newspaper columns produced a similar pattern.

These coverage patterns are reflected in the public perceptions reported in the 1979 national election study, but only in a general way. Comparing the 1974 and 1979 postelection surveys, the study found that while the Conservatives and NDP had gained at the expense of the Liberals, Trudeau remained the most popular leader. Trudeau's popularity had declined between 1974 and 1979, however, while both Clark and Broadbent scored slightly higher than their predecessors. Nevertheless, Trudeau's continued high standing, especially among new voters, may well have prevented the Conservatives from achieving a majority. The study suggests that his personal appeal helped keep a significant number of Liberals in the fold as well as attracting a disproportionate share of new voters. In fact, the Liberals got the votes of 65 percent of those who reported voting primarily on the basis of the leaders' personal qualities.[55]

Party image, in contrast, benefited the Conservatives. The Liberals tended to be presented in the press as a party that was worn out, while the NDP was unable to shake its radical image or the equally damaging perception that it was controlled by trade unions. In addition, the Conservatives had some success in saddling it with the image of a party that could not win but might put the Liberals back in power. This perception was important because a significant proportion of voters who switched to the Conservatives in 1979 did so because they thought it was time for a change.[56] Broadbent was able to overcome this somewhat by his personal appeal and did bring some votes to his party, though not as many as Trudeau. Clark ran behind his party.[57]

[54] Only about 15 percent of front-page campaign stories contained direct positive or negative comment on the parties, but 20 percent were accounts of partisan attacks on another party, and a significant proportion of nonpartisan items contained nonparty critiques of party positions. The selection and play of these items appeared biased in the direction of the editorial endorsement in some dailies.

[55] Pammett et al., "Change," p. 18.

[56] Carleton-CBC poll.

[57] Pammett et al., "Change," pp. 11-19.

Lacking the image capital built up by Trudeau since 1968, Clark seems to have suffered most from the negative treatment accorded the two major party leaders. In fact, his negative image was established before the 1979 campaign and can be traced in large part to a disastrous world tour early in the year, which had been dreamed up by party strategists to help overcome Clark's relative lack of international experience. The tour was also intended to attract press attention during the interminable wait for Trudeau to call an election. Given little of substance to write about, reporters under pressure to justify the cost of their trips focused on gaffes, foul-ups, and Clark's personal idiosyncrasies, including physical awkwardness (recalling the way the press treated Gerald Ford) and a circumlocutory way of speaking ("What is the totality of your acreage?"). When reporters filed accounts of both his policy pronouncements and his misadventures, as many did, editors invariably chose to feature the latter. In the end, his slight awkwardness and mild pomposity were greatly exaggerated by the media, some of the less genteel columnists calling him a "nerd" or "wimp." The coverage appears to have created public doubts about his competence and to have given reporters their angle for the campaign: Would Clark make the "one big mistake" that would permit the shopworn Liberals to return to power? In fact, he did make several major policy-related errors, but these were not pounced upon by reporters, who were apparently looking for something more tangible, like a fall down stairs.[58]

Conservative insider-turned-pundit Dalton Camp explains the media's tendency to "put down" Clark in generational terms. For most reporters, "he was of their age and too much one of them."[59] They saw in him all the campus politicians they had viewed with contempt from the editorial offices of campus newspapers. In addition, most had no role model for the prime ministership other than Trudeau and found it difficult to see Clark in the role.

Trudeau for his part suffered an even more hostile press than in 1974. If Clark was portrayed as weak, indecisive, and inexperienced (as a survey of political columns revealed), Trudeau was presented as arrogant, bored, cynical, and weary. This image was reinforced by the prime minister's ill-advised comment that he would attempt to form a government with NDP support if the Conservatives won only a small plurality in the House. Despite the fact that this would be

[58] Jeffrey Simpson, "Leadership Still an Issue As Campaign Closes," *Globe and Mail*, May 19, 1979. For a general discussion of Clark's trip and its media coverage, see Cocking, *Following the Leaders*, pp. 94-95, 106-7.

[59] Camp, *Points of Departure*, p. 172.

appropriate behavior in a parliamentary system, the speculation was reported as an intention to cling to power and damaged both the Liberal and the NDP efforts. The CBC and some other national media examined the precedents in later reports, but the initial reports had much more impact.

Although Trudeau's personal popularity remained higher than the other leaders', he also excited more personal hostility. A CBC poll found that Trudeau was thought to exemplify the best (28 percent) and the worst (27 percent) qualities of a political leader.[60] In 1979 he was unable to win back enough of the swing voters to stave off defeat. Tough treatment by reporters, especially on television, may have been a factor. Reporters perceived him as losing and no longer combined awe with their hostility.

The leaders' campaign culminated in "Encounter '79," the debates among the three party leaders. While the substance of the debates was often informative, the attention of the media was focused on the question who had won. Although the vehemently anti-Trudeau *Toronto Sun* declared Clark the winner, the journalistic consensus was that his performance had been poor, as expected, and that both Trudeau and Broadbent had done well. For novelist Mordecai Richler, it had been "a debate between two men and a boy [Clark] with the most hollow laugh in the world."[61] The assessment by the media apparently had an influence: two days after the debate, when the pundits had weighed in, a greater proportion of respondents thought Clark had lost than in a poll immediately following the debate. In addition, respondents who had not seen the debate were more likely than those who had to believe Clark had lost.[62] Looking back on it after the election, two voters identified Clark as the loser for every voter who thought he had won. Two thought Trudeau had won for each who saw him as the loser. But the overall victor was Broadbent, for whom the winner-loser ratio was three to one.[63] Although the media had created low expectations for Clark, his nervous mannerisms clearly hurt his image.

It is plausible to argue that Clark's inability to use the debates to overcome his media image cost him a majority in 1979. In Dalton Camp's words: "The televised debate . . . hurt the Conservatives more than they realized, or would admit; after that, they nervously

---

[60] Carleton-CBC poll.

[61] Quoted in Cocking, *Following the Leaders*, p. 250.

[62] Richard Gwyn in the *Toronto Star*, May 18, 1979; and John Marshall, "Ed, Pierre and Joe," *Content* (Toronto), August 1979, pp. 16-17.

[63] Pammett et al., "Change," p. 16 and table 6.

sat on their lead, even while it was melting."[64] In fact, the polls suggest that it was potential rather than committed Conservative votes that were lost.

Perhaps the most striking finding regarding the tone of the coverage is the unfavorable treatment of the two older parties. This negative coverage no doubt reflects the emergence of an adversarial style of reporting in Ottawa, especially among television reporters, and the media backlash against the 1974 campaign. In addition, the strongly negative campaigns waged against one another by Trudeau and Clark (with the NDP coming in for less frequent attack) and the positive campaign of the NDP, with Broadbent much more accessible than the other leaders, also probably influenced the coverage. In fact, many observers felt that the media were "soft" on Broadbent, not subjecting his style and policies to the same scrutiny as the other leaders. It has been suggested that working reporters, hostile to Trudeau and unimpressed by Clark, latched on to Broadbent as a source of positive copy. It is also true that the national media put their tougher reporters on the two major leaders and gave NDP policy less scrutiny because of the low probability that it would form a government.

The poll data give clear support to the view that public perceptions of Broadbent and, to a lesser extent, the NDP were changed by the campaign. Broadbent entered the campaign trailing the other two leaders in popularity but was running even with or ahead of Clark by the end. In a postelection Gallup poll, more respondents (35 percent) thought Broadbent had run the best campaign than thought that for his rivals: Trudeau, 28 percent; Clark, 17. Fully one-quarter of respondents said their opinion of the NDP had gone up as a result of the campaign; the figures for the Conservatives (14 percent) and Liberals (8 percent) were much lower.[65]

Covering the Issues

Nearly half of all voters in the 1979 election cited issues as the primary basis for their voting choice, according to the national election study.[66] Not surprisingly, the parties tried to fight the election on their own issues, while the better news organizations attempted to subject party policies to critical scrutiny and to raise neglected issues, a function performed effectively by only a few outlets.

[64] Dalton Camp, preface to Warner Troyer, *200 Days: Joe Clark in Power* (Toronto: Personal Library, 1980), p. 8.

[65] Kielty et al., *Canadians Speak Out*, pp. 9-10.

[66] Pammett et al., "Change," p. 20.

To influence an election, an issue must (1) be regarded as important by a substantial proportion of voters, (2) divide voters so that one side has substantially more support than the others, and (3) be identified by the public—or at least those who consider it important—with one political party.[67] Issues thought to be unimportant, upon which voters are evenly divided, or upon which all parties are perceived to agree are unlikely to have much electoral payoff. News coverage helps to determine which issues are regarded as important and is crucial in communicating party positions.

Though there was no one overriding issue in 1979, there were several that met these conditions. Confederation issues—national unity, Quebec's place in Canada, language policy—were helpful to the Liberals, the national election study found. Social service issues were marginally Liberal but relatively unimportant. General economic issues were Conservative issues, while the NDP had significant support among voters who thought unemployment important. More specific issues had impact in particular regions. The Conservatives' mortgage-interest proposal helped them in Ontario, for example. Leadership was, as we have seen, basically a Liberal issue, though neutral in its impact in the West.[68]

In the contest to control the media agenda, the Liberals scored a modest overall victory. Confederation and leadership taken together obtained more coverage than economic issues, as table 10–10 shows, but economic issues did tend to predominate in the English media, to the benefit of the Conservatives. In particular, economic issues emerged as dominant in western Canada, where Trudeau had no edge on the leadership issue (see tables 10–11 and 10–12), and a series of more specific issues—such as the mortgage tax scheme—got good play in southern Ontario. The Conservatives' regional successes proved the more important to the outcome of the election, however.

In general, the parties were able to communicate their issues through the media. The Confederation issues were probably not covered as extensively as the prime minister would have liked, however, especially in the West. And many Conservatives felt that the Liberal economic record received inadequate scrutiny. Both the NDP and its opponents seem to have believed that NDP proposals were not taken seriously enough.

On the whole, in fact, the media permitted the parties to set the campaign agenda. Issues neglected by the parties, ranging from

[67] This is a simplified version of an elegant formulation in Pammett et al., "Change," p. 20.

[68] Ibid., pp. 26–29.

TABLE 10-10

Issues Emphasized by the Media, 1979 Campaign

Issue	Daily Newspapers				CBC TV (French)		CBC TV (English)		Global		CTV		CBC Radio (French)		Voters Mentioning as Important (percent)
	Front page		Editorials												
	No.	%	No.	%	No.	%	No.	%	No.	%	No.	%	No.	%	
Confederation[a]	89	38	49	33	54	17	46	15	30	9	38	15	39	15	38
Economic issues[b]	69	30	44	30	38	12	54	18	40	12	43	17	25	9	70
Energy[c]	18	8	11	7	9	3	12	4	9	3	7	3	8	3	13
Leaders[d]	44	19	23	16	27	8	23	8	22	6	28	11	18	7	18

NOTE: "Number" refers to news items, "percent" to percentage of all campaign-related news items.

[a] Includes references to national unity, bilingualism, Quebec, and federal-provincial relations.

[b] Includes references to the economy in general, inflation, unemployment, tax reform, and government spending.

[c] Includes references to energy and Petrocanada.

[d] Includes references to leadership and the party leaders.

SOURCES: For newspapers, as for table 10-4. For television data, Briggs et al., "Television News," table 3. For voters, Pammett et al., "Change," table 8.

TABLE 10–11
Issues Emphasized in Daily Newspaper Front-Page Coverage, by Region, 1979 Campaign

Issue	West No.	West %	Ontario No.	Ontario %	Quebec No.	Quebec %	East No.	East %	Canada No.	Canada %
Confederation	8	24	4	22	37	51	39	36	88	38
National unity	3	9	1	6	14	19	12	11	30	13
Quebec/bilingualism	1	3	1	6	13	18	4	4	19	8
Federal-provincial relations	4	12	2	11	10	14	23	21	39	17
Economic issues	14	42	4	22	15	21	28	26	61	26
Inflation	7	21	3	17	6	8	4	4	20	9
Unemployment	3	9	1	6	2	3	7	6	13	6
Other	4	12	—	—	7	10	17	16	28	12
Leaders	2	6	4	22	10	14	13	12	29	13
Energy	4	12	3	17	2	3	9	8	18	8
Total number of stories	(33)		(18)		(73)		(108)		(232)	

NOTE: "Number" refers to number of front-page stories in which the issue is given significant attention, "percent" to percentage of all front-page election stories. Subcategories are included in the totals for the issue beneath which they are listed.

SOURCE: As for table 10-4.

TABLE 10-12
Issues Emphasized in Daily Newspaper Editorials, by Region, 1979 Campaign

Issue	West No.	West %	Ontario No.	Ontario %	Quebec No.	Quebec %	East No.	East %	Canada No.	Canada %
Confederation	6	18	15	44	23	43	5	19	49	33
National unity	2	6	5	15	10	19	3	11	20	14
Quebec	1	3	1	3	5	9	1	4	8	5
Federal-provincial relations	3	9	9	26	8	15	1	4	21	14
Economic issues	15	44	8	24	14	26	7	26	44	30
Inflation	5	15	5	15	6	11	4	15	20	14
Unemployment	0	0	1	3	3	6	3	11	7	5
Other	10	29	2	6	5	9	0	0	17	11
Leaders	6	18	1	3	11	21	5	19	23	16
Energy	2	6	5	15	2	4	2	7	11	7
Total number of election editorials	(34)		(34)		(53)		(27)		(148)	

NOTE: "Number" refers to number of editorials dealing primarily with the issue, "percent" to percentage of editorials on election. Subcategories are included in the totals for the issue beneath which they are listed.
SOURCES: As for table 10-4.

capital punishment to civil liberties, were not given adequate attention by most outlets. Indeed, with a few notable exceptions, news organizations failed to get behind the campaign rhetoric to examine party positions in terms of past party practice or of their significance for the average voter. Party positions on specific regional issues— such as the problems of the grain transport system—were more often examined for their likely influence on the vote than for their effectiveness as public policy. Few if any attempts were made outside Quebec to pin the parties down on constitutional issues or to explain the local relevance of the crisis. In permitting the parties not only to set the agenda but to get away with slogans or vague promises in important policy areas, the news organizations largely abandoned their own responsibility to clarify party positions and to identify key issues for their audiences.[69]

It should be noted, however, that a number of news organizations did attempt to deal effectively with issues.[70] CBC radio and television, especially on the English side, broke new ground in broadcast news with substantial issue coverage, though the inherent limitations of their media permitted only the major points of any issue to be dealt with. *Le Devoir* and the *Globe and Mail* provided good analytical materials, though only on selected issues. *La Presse* and the *Toronto Star* provided the most comprehensive coverage. They treated most major issues in clear and readable prose. Smaller dailies, such as the London *Free Press*, the *Winnipeg Tribune,* and the Montreal *Gazette* also provided extensive issue analysis, and the Halifax *Chronicle-Herald* covered the Atlantic provinces and relevant regional issues with unprecedented thoroughness. *Maclean's* magazine attempted a weekly synthesis but provided little not available in the better dailies.

As in 1974, there emerged a fairly clear national agenda, with only modest regional differences, at least in the major daily newspapers and on network television. Overall, in fact, regional differences had declined since 1974. For television, the University of Windsor group found that the agendas of the three English networks (defined according to the frequency with which they covered major issues) were very similar. The CBC's French service had elements of a distinct agenda but shared in a national agenda as well, with substantial similarities to the coverage on CBC English and CTV. CBC French and Global were least similar, perhaps because each found its

[69] For a useful discussion of this issue, see Cocking, *Following the Leaders,* pp. 295-96.
[70] Ibid., pp. 286-87, 292ff.

primary audience in a single province (Quebec and Ontario, respectively).[71] The distinctive elements of the French agenda were greater emphasis on the Confederation issues and a focus on economic development rather than rising prices among the economic issues.

As tables 10–10 and 10–11 show, the newspaper pattern was not greatly different from that for television. Differences in news and editorial priorities tended to reflect specific regional interests, such as Quebec's focus on Confederation issues, the concern about federal-provincial relations in both East and West, or Ontario's worries about energy costs.

The existence of a national agenda is not a new phenomenon, but the apparent decline in regional differences over recent campaigns may reflect the growing influence of national television and the gate-keeping role of central Canadian newsrooms at CP, the networks, and the pooled services of Southam and FP. The extent of regional variations is probably greater, however, on the crucial local supper-hour telecasts and on the inside pages of newspapers.

Concluding Comments

Although the Liberals appeared to have won the contest for media attention in 1979 by a slight margin, they lost the election. The most plausible explanation is that their chances of winning were slight when the campaign began and that, despite the very effective Conservative advertising campaign, the Liberals gained enough from the negative media coverage of Clark to stave off a Conservative majority. It seems clear that Clark was the victim of a rather harsh process of stereotyping, resulting from coverage of his world trip, and that he suffered from the disdain of the working press. In addition, the media lens tended to magnify his weaknesses—awkwardness, pomposity, hollow laugh—and miss his strengths: self-discipline, personal warmth, a capacity to listen. Negative assessments of his performance in the debates reflected these factors as well as some policy errors.

The new electoral regulations contributed little to the level of voter information, except to the extent that they permitted the NDP, which clearly benefited from the subsidy, to make its case more effectively. The party's greater access to advertising time, which it used effectively to promote its leader and preferred issues, seemed also

---

[71] The Spearman rank-order coefficients of correlation were: CBC English-CTV, + .839; CBC English-Global, + .776; CBC French-CBC English, + .654; CBC French-CTV, + .531; CBC French-Global, + .332. See Briggs et al., "Television News," p. 7.

to help persuade the news organizations to give it more attention. Certainly the exposure helped to improve the party's public standing. In the longer run, the influence of the contest for media attention on the outcome of any particular election is less important than its impact on the political process itself. As practiced in 1979, the coverage misrepresented the political system, narrowed the focus of public debate, and denigrated political leaders and institutions.

Although the media, especially television, must cover the leaders and transmit their arguments, excessive attention to them is misleading. Overemphasis on rating the leaders' campaign performances draws attention away from their other strengths and weaknesses, the influence of potential cabinet ministers, and their policy commitments. While most journalists concentrated on the foul-ups during Clark's ill-fated trip, a few were examining the implications of his policy statements.[72] Despite the fact that the media were ostensibly helping citizens decide how to vote, not a single article on the functions of the member of Parliament, the cabinet, or the prime minister cropped up in our survey. And attempts to measure the leaders against the characteristics necessary for a good prime minister were few.

Although the focus of election coverage in 1979 was visibly broader than in 1974, complex problems, such as inflation, unemployment, federal-provincial relations, constitutional change, and the medical care system, were examined by only a few outlets.[73] Little was written on the internal politics of the parties, the links of parties to external interests, or the process of cabinet selection. More important, perhaps, much of the coverage failed to involve the citizen, to explain the relevance of abstract issues to the individual. As Clive Cocking has put it, "The media did not (with the exception of some coverage, notably in the *Toronto Star*) generally approach this election from the standpoint of the problems facing ordinary Canadians or the major challenges facing the country."[74]

Although politicians must share the blame for the state of public debate, it is true that the most effective means for party leaders to reach the voters is to play by the media rules. In the television era, these rules inhibit thoughtful exposition of policies and promote simple and flashy promises and one-line put-downs of the opposition. Even when policies are effectively set out, the quips often grab the headlines. The sugar coating swallows up the pill. As long as print journalists focus on the leaders' tours, which are essentially television

---

[72] See, for example, Cocking, *Following the Leaders*, pp. 219-20.
[73] Goldblatt, "Media."
[74] Cocking, *Following the Leaders*, p. 295.

campaigns, they will find themselves with little to write about and little time to think about what they do write, given television's demands.

The defensive strategy adopted by journalists in 1979 to avoid manipulation by politicians—to include commentary in most reports on leaders' statements and to focus attention on party tactics—combined with the natural cynicism of the press gallery and the negative campaigns of the two major parties to give much of the coverage a nasty tone. This was reinforced by hostility to the incumbent government and the "culture" of journalists. As Cocking puts it,

> the normal journalistic reaction is not to praise but to criticize. There is a tacit understanding among journalists that to write favorably about events or people is, if not perverse, at least gutless and certain to harm one's career. Criticisms, charges and accusations produce the most jolts on television news and the biggest headlines in the papers.[75]

Coverage, therefore, tends to be not discriminating but rather capriciously negative, tending to bring the entire system into disrepute for no well-worked-out reasons. This tendency has begun to worry thoughtful journalists.

Brief note should also be made of the potentially negative effects on political integration of the inordinate influence of Ontario on the national political agenda. This pattern could easily fuel a sense of alienation in other parts of the country. Quebec news organizations, however, have become less inward looking since 1974.

Despite the clear improvement in scope and volume of coverage ver 1974, thoughtful observers were concerned about the 1979 campaign, particularly about the dominance of television, with its emphasis on glibness and cosmetics. Marcel Adam of *La Presse* called upon the broadcast media to alter the rules of the game to make campaigns less a circus and more a grand political debate.[76] The clash of ideas has always had more currency in the French than in the English press. For television, which seldom has the undivided attention of its audience, abstract ideas are difficult to handle unless they can be personified. A campaign communication system that institutionalized the leaders' debates (in both official languages) and added a series of debates with party spokesmen on specific issues might be a step forward. Other suggestions include prohibiting advertising and providing free time in blocks of at least five minutes to promote

---

[75] Ibid., p. 111.

[76] "Les campagnes électorales et le rôle de la presse" [Electoral campaigns and the role of the press], *La Presse*, May 22, 1979.

presentation of policy-related material, deemphasizing polls—or at least reporting them more appropriately—and shortening the campaign.[77] Certainly a system that relies heavily on thirty- and sixty-second spot commercials and the reports of exhausted correspondents on a two-month round of television events to communicate essential information to voters could stand improvement.

Although reform is likely to be slow, change is inevitable. New technologies and new tactics are on the horizon. Increasingly, parties will communicate directly with voters through phone-in shows, which allow ordinary voters to set the agenda, computerized direct mail with messages tailored to specific groups, and instant polls using two-way television systems.[78] Nevertheless, the informed journalist will still be needed to expose misrepresentations and to tell voters what it all means.

[77] Some of these ideas are from Stevens, "A Case of Image."
[78] Marshall, "Ed, Pierre and Joe," p. 17.

11

The More Things Change . . . Women in the 1979 Federal Campaign

M. Janine Brodie and Jill Vickers

There is considerable evidence in the literature on the characteristics of legislators in Western democracies that subtle social and political practices discriminate against the participation of significant groups in decision making. Principal among these groups are the working class, marginal ethnic and religious groups, and women. While the disparity between ethnic and class distributions in the general population and in legislative representation varies considerably from one polity to another, statistically women (who are everywhere about half the population) remain the most underrepresented group in elected assemblies today.[1] Canada is no exception to this general condition, and the 1979 election did nothing to reduce the disparity.

Canadian women gained the right to vote and hold office in federal politics in 1921.[2] The extension of the same rights to women in provincial politics, however, was achieved only after a long and complex history.[3] In the provinces west of Ontario, for example, full political emancipation was granted to women as early as 1917. In contrast, women's right to hold provincial office was withheld in New Brunswick until 1934 and in Quebec until 1940. In some Canadian cities property qualifications for municipal enfranchisement

---

[1] Robert Putnam, *The Comparative Study of Political Elites* (Englewood Cliffs, N.J.: Prentice-Hall, 1976), p. 32.

[2] Women who were the wives, daughters, or widows of soldiers were granted the right to vote in the 1917 federal election under the Wartime Elections Act. This was surrogate voting rather than the political emancipation of women.

[3] M. Janine Brodie, "The Recruitment of Canadian Women Provincial Legislators, 1950-1975," *Atlantis*, vol. 2 (Spring 1977), pp. 6-17.

excluded many women (as well as some men) from local office until as late as 1970.[4]

In the fifty-eight years since women's political emancipation, their integration into mainstream Canadian politics has been only partial. Although they now read about elections, discuss politics, vote, and attend political meetings almost as often as men, few women yet hold political office.[5] Elected women become rarer, moreover, as one moves up the hierarchy from municipal office to federal. In the period between 1950 and 1975, for example, 505 women contested municipal office in a sample of twenty-four Canadian cities. When one moves from the largely nonpartisan municipal sphere to provincial and federal politics, where party constituency organizations intervene in the selection process, however, women candidates are much less common. During this same period only 283 and 337 women, respectively, contested their first election at the provincial and federal levels.[6] Of those women who ran, few were elected: between 1921, when the first woman was elected to the federal House of Commons, and 1979, only thirty-two women became federal legislators, and from 1950 to 1975 fifty-four were elected to provincial legislatures. This is clearly a small proportion of the total number of politicians elected since women's political emancipation. Indeed, the Royal Commission on the Status of Women has reported that between 1917 and 1970 less than 1 percent of all members of the federal and provincial legislatures were women.[7] Although increasing numbers of women compete for federal office, the proportion of women in the Canadian House of Commons remains lower than in the legislatures of most liberal democracies.[8] Despite predictions that women would find their place beside men in elected assemblies

[4] Montreal was the last Canadian city with a population exceeding 100,000 to eliminate property qualifications for municipal voting and office holding. It did so in 1970. See Donald J. H. Higgens, *Urban Canada: Its Government and Politics* (Toronto: Macmillan, 1977), p. 195.

[5] Mike Burke, Harold D. Clarke, and Lawrence LeDuc, "Federal and Provincial Participation in Canada: Some Methodological and Substantive Considerations," *Canadian Review of Sociology and Anthropology*, vol. 15 (February 1978), pp. 61-75; and Jerome Black and Nancy McGlen, "Male-Female Political Involvement Differentials in Canada, 1965-1974," *Canadian Journal of Political Science*, vol. 12 (September 1973), pp. 471-98.

[6] See Jill McCalla Vickers, "Where Are the Women in Canadian Politics?" *Atlantis*, vol. 3 (Spring 1978), pp. 40-51.

[7] Canada, *Report of the Royal Commission on the Status of Women* (Ottawa: Information Canada, 1970), p. 343.

[8] Jill McCalla Vickers and June Adam, *But Can You Type?* (Toronto: Clarke, Irwin and Co., 1977), p. 90.

TABLE 11–1

Women Candidates and M.P.s in Canadian General Elections, 1921–1979

(percent)

Year	Candidates	M.P.s
1921–1967	2.4 [a]	0.8 [a]
1968	3.5	0.4
1972	6.4	1.8
1974	9.4	3.4
1979	13.8	3.6

Note: By-elections are not included; small-party candidates and independents are included.

[a] Average for general elections between 1921 and 1967.

Sources: 1921-1968, Canada, *Report of the Royal Commission*; 1972-1979, calculated from the *Report of the Chief Electoral Officer of Canada* (Ottawa: Information Canada, 1972, 1974).

as time passed, Canadian women remain conspicuously absent from Canadian legislatures.

Although the rate of election of women to the House of Commons has increased in the last decade, the number of women contesting federal office has risen substantially (see table 11–1). In the forty-six years between 1921 and 1967, the proportion of women among federal candidates remained below 3 percent, while it more than doubled between 1972 and 1979, moving from 6.4 percent to 13.8 percent. The proportion of women elected to the federal legislature increased at a parallel rate until the 1974 election, but the trend did not continue in 1979. The 1979 general election can be summed up in a few words in relation to women: though many women offered themselves for office in 1979, few were chosen. The obvious question is, Why are Canadian women rarely *selected* for political office when they regularly *choose* to participate in politics? [9]

It is often argued that the paucity of women legislators reflects the fact that there are fewer women candidates than men. In Canada, however, at least in the 1970s, an examination of the success rates of the women and men who run for federal office (always a tiny propor-

[9] For a discussion of the distinction between voluntary participation and selection, see J. Stiehm and R. Scott, "Female and Male: Voluntary and Chosen Participation" (Paper presented at the Annual Meeting of the American Political Science Association, Chicago, 1974).

TABLE 11–2
MEN AND WOMEN CANDIDATES ELECTED, GENERAL ELECTIONS, 1972–1979

	Women		Men	
Year	No.	%	No.	%
1972	5	7.6	259	25.6
1974	9	7.2	255	20.4
1979	10	5.1	272	22.1

NOTE: By-elections are not included; small-party candidates and independents are included.
SOURCE: Calculated from the *Report of the Chief Electoral Officer of Canada* (1972, 1974, 1979).

tion of the electorate) shows the inadequacy of this explanation. The success rates of men and women exhibit considerable stability—and inequality (see table 11–2). In the three elections of this decade, approximately one of every five male candidates won election. In contrast, far fewer than one in ten of their female counterparts were elected to the House of Commons. While cultural and sex-role explanations of the failure of women to offer themselves as candidates as frequently as men may be important, a more detailed explanation of the obstacles facing women candidates might throw some light on the remarkable imbalance of the results.[10]

Party Recruitment of Women Candidates

Canadian political science has largely ignored the study of women in politics and the ways they are recruited to run for office. The general literature on recruitment, however, outlines a number of factors that are important to an understanding of the reason some people achieve elected office while so many others do not. Among these are intensive political socialization, high socioeconomic status, membership in "brokerage" occupations or occupations that are seen as convergent with politics, and prior participation in political parties or voluntary groups. The tendency of the literature has been to regard recruitment as dependent solely on the personal characteristics of candidates or

[10] See, for example, M. Janine Brodie, "Voluntary Groups and the Recruitment of Women in Canada: Some Preliminary Survey Findings" (Paper presented at the Annual Meeting of the Canadian Political Science Association, Saskatoon, 1979).

legislators and to ignore the mediation of political structures. The political party is such a structure, serving as a critical bridge between the political aspirant and elective office. Its role in the recruitment process is rarely explored, even though in Canada the local constituency organizations of the parties largely determine who the candidates for federal office will be.[11] There are few countries for which James D. Barber's observation about candidate selection is more appropriate than it is for Canada:

> However strong his motives, however ready he stands to serve, the potential candidate remains on the sidelines until and unless some practical opportunity presents itself. . . . The role of the political recruiter is central, whether he seeks out candidates for nomination or merely selects from those who appear.[12]

Parties are the hidden but often the most influential forces in the recruitment of both men and women. In fact, the electoral strength of the party that selects a candidate, male or female, is more important in explaining the candidate's eventual success or failure than any personal characteristics of the candidate.[13]

There is considerable evidence to suggest that Canada's major political parties have been reluctant to select women as candidates in constituencies where they have a chance of winning. The Royal Commission on the Status of Women concluded, after extensive interviews with elected women, that winning the party's nomination was their most formidable task, and the 1979 election showed no break in this pattern.[14] In fact, a close examination of the party affiliation of women who ran in 1979 reveals that the increased number of women candidates actually reflects two trends, neither of which is particularly conducive to the election of women (see table 11–3). First, there was a greater willingness on the part of the three major parties than in the past to permit women to run as candidates, but, as will be seen, they ran primarily in "lost-cause" ridings.

[11] Three exceptions to this observation are M. Janine Brodie and Jill McCalla Vickers, "Gates, Gatekeepers and Women Legislative Candidates in Canada" (Paper presented at the Annual Meeting of the Canadian Political Science Association, London, Ontario, 1978); Allan Kornberg, Joel Smith, and Harold D. Clarke, Citizen Politicians—Canada (Durham, N.C.: Carolina Academic Press, 1979); and M. Janine Brodie, "The Recruitment of Men and Women Party Activists in Ontario" (M.A. thesis, University of Windsor, 1975).

[12] James D. Barber, The Lawmakers (New Haven, Conn.: Yale University Press, 1965), p. 237.

[13] Brodie and Vickers, "Gates, Gatekeepers."

[14] Report of the Royal Commission, p. 349.

TABLE 11–3
Candidates, by Sex and Party, 1979

Party	Female	Male	Percent Female
Liberal	21	261	7.5
Progressive Conservative	14	268	5.0
NDP	47	235	16.7
Social Credit	7	96	6.8
Marxist-Leninist	48	96	33.3
Communist	19	52	26.8
Other (independent, Libertarian, Rhinoceros)	39	221	15.0

Source: Chief Electoral Officer of Canada, *1979 General Election: Preliminary Statistics*, June 15, 1979.

Second, there was a substantial increase in the number of women contesting election as independents, or more often as candidates for fringe parties such as the Marxist-Leninist, Libertarian, and Communist parties. This tendency began in the 1974 general election, when 73 of the 125 women candidates ran as independents or fringe-party candidates and as such had no realistic hope of winning. In 1979, as table 11–3 indicates, 106 of the 195 women candidates were not mainstream party representatives.

Women candidates can be seen as belonging to at least three distinct categories. First, there are the *hopefuls,* incumbent women M.P.s or those few women who are candidates for the major parties in constituencies where they have some chance of success. Second are the *standard-bearers,* women who are candidates for the major parties but in constituencies where their parties are weak. Finally, there are the *zealots,* who are independents or candidates for fringe parties and who, like the standard-bearers, have little chance of election. It is evident that the few women who contest election do so for a variety of reasons and with varying expectations of the rewards of candidacy. A survey of a sample of federal women candidates from 1950 to 1974 confirms that hopefuls, standard-bearers, and zealots had different motives for running for political office. Zealots defined their motives solely as educating the electorate or bringing specific issues to its attention. The standard-bearers and hopefuls, in contrast, had a variety of motives. In addition to educating the electorate and drawing issues to the fore, they cited defeating the opposition, building a personal career in politics, and gaining political experience as reasons for running for Parliament.[15]

The experiences of the zealots in the 1979 campaign will not be considered further here. It should be noted briefly, however, that the feminist movement appears to have indirectly stimulated the large increase in the zealot category. Their numbers first mushroomed in the 1974 election, reflecting a reaction against the traditional party system or a more general antiparty bias. The campaign literature of many of these candidates included a condemnation of the mainstream parties for failing to deal with the question of women's status in Canadian society. As fringe-party candidates, however, with limited resources and credibility among the electorate, they have been largely unable to bring this issue into the dominant political debate. The recent foundation of the Feminist party of Canada may make it possible for feminists to appear more cohesive and visible in the federal elections of the 1980s.

As will be seen, issues affecting women as a social category (especially their unemployment) did emerge in the Thirtieth Parliament and were discussed in varying degrees by the three major parties during the 1979 campaign. It is perhaps surprising, then, given the growing awareness of women's status in Canada, that so few women were actually recruited by the three major parties in this campaign. Only the NDP showed an increase in the candidacies of women between 1974 and 1979. Approximately 12 percent of the NDP candidates had been women in 1974; 17 percent were women in 1979. The proportion of women among Liberal and Conservative party candidates remained stable for the two election years, approximately 7 percent and 5 percent respectively. Most of the seats in the House of Commons are held by Liberal and Conservative males; so these parties, recruiting their incumbent M.P.s first, have fewer nominations available for women. Fewer opportunities for women to gain nomination by these parties in winnable ridings could be expected unless a conscious effort were made to recruit them. Thirty-four sitting members of the Thirtieth Parliament chose not to seek reelection in 1979—thereby creating vacancies in safe ridings that could have been offered to women—but in only five instances were women nominated to succeed them.

The general practice of the three major parties has been to recruit women in regions or constituencies where the parties' popularity is lowest, and the results of the 1979 election show no departure from

[15] These data were derived from a mail questionnaire survey conducted by Brodie and Vickers of municipal, provincial, and federal women candidates who ran for election in the 1950-1979 period.

TABLE 11–4

Women Candidates of the Major Parties, by Region, 1979

Party	Atlantic	Quebec	Ontario	Prairies	British Columbia	Total
Liberal	2	6	8	2	3	21
Progressive Conservative	1	3	7	1	2	14
NDP	2	19	15	5	6	47
Total	5	28	30	8	11	82

Source: Chief Electoral Officer, *1979 General Election*, table 6.

this tendency.[16] The NDP, for example, ran nineteen of its forty-seven women candidates in Quebec, where the party is little more than a paper organization and its candidates are simply standard-bearers (see table 11–4). Similarly, the Progressive Conservatives ran three of their fourteen women candidates in Quebec, where the party's fortunes have been dismal since the turn of the century (except for the brief "Diefenbaker interlude"). In the center of their electoral strength, the Prairies, they offered only one woman candidate. Only the willingness of the Liberal party to permit a small number of women to run in safe seats within its bastion of electoral strength —Quebec—prevented the number of women in the Thirty-first Parliament from dropping dramatically. This policy of the Liberal party also accounts for much of the increase in the number of women elected in 1974.

The tendency of the Liberal party to place women in its strong constituencies and the opposite practice of the NDP and Conservative party are more clearly demonstrated in table 11–5. When the kinds of constituencies for which women are recruited are examined, the relationship between party strength at the constituency level and women's recruitment is apparent. Although the boundaries of most constituencies were substantially altered for the 1979 election, a poll-by-poll reconstruction of the parties' strength in the new ridings from the 1974 results shows that, except in the case of the Liberal party, few women were nominated to priority ridings—those where their party had been strongest in 1974. In fact, only two Conservative women and two NDP women were nominated in priority ridings. All four of these women were elected, indicating that running women

16 Brodie and Vickers, "Gates, Gatekeepers."

TABLE 11–5

WOMEN CANDIDATES RUNNING IN PRIORITY CONSTITUENCIES,
BY MAJOR PARTY, 1979

(percent)

Party's Strength, 1974	Liberal	Progressive Conservative	NDP
Strongest in constituency	61.8	14.2	4.2
N	(13)	(2)	(2)
Not strongest in constituency	38.2	85.8	95.8
N	(8)	(12)	(45)

SOURCES: Calculated from Chief Electoral Officer of Canada, *List of New Electoral District Names: 1976 Redistribution;* and Chief Electoral Officer, *1979 General Election.*

in winnable ridings does make a difference. The Liberals nominated more women in favorable ridings, although their 1979 success rate for candidates in general was lower than that of the other two parties. The proportion of safe Liberal seats may be exaggerated, however, by the fact that the Liberals won a strong majority in 1974. The Liberals also ran women as standard-bearers in 1979 in hopeless races, nominating women to run against the leaders of both the NDP and the Conservative party.

Most women candidates in 1979 were standard-bearers or zealots —and with the fortunes of the Liberal party falling, many hopefuls went down to defeat. Three incumbent Liberal women (Iona Campagnola, Coline Campbell, and Simma Holt), as well as one Progressive Conservative (Jean Piggott) elected in a 1976 by-election, were defeated. Despite these defeats, the number of women in the House of Commons rose to ten, one more than before the election was called. The four incumbent Liberal women and one incumbent Conservative were joined by another Conservative, two more Liberals from Quebec, and two NDP women, one of whom had sat as a Liberal M.P. in the House a decade earlier. Although the number of women in the House rose, the proportion barely improved, because the number of federal seats was increased from 265 in 1974 to 282 in 1979. The change of government also meant that only two women sat on the government benches in the new House.

Who Is Selected and Who Wins?

Although the biographical information on women candidates in the 1979 election is scanty, we are able to construct a tentative profile that can be compared with the profiles constructed from a study of federal women candidates for the period 1950–1974 conducted by the authors.[17] Canadian women candidates do not differ dramatically from their male counterparts or from political women in other liberal democracies (see table 11–6). Like most candidates and legislators, they tend to be married, have children, be middle-aged, and be professionally trained and highly educated. Surprisingly few, however, in comparison with women candidates in other countries, are homemakers by occupation.[18] Only two of the 1979 candidates whose biographies were available to us were essentially homemakers. The sample of federal women candidates of the 1950–1975 period, by contrast, indicates that approximately 34 percent were primarily homemakers when they sought election. This undoubtedly reflects the increase in women's participation in the paid work force and perhaps also the tendency observed elsewhere for political women to be drawn increasingly from the ranks of upper-middle-class career women.[19]

The profiles of the women elected in 1979 differ from those of defeated female candidates in several respects. For example, the mean age of women elected was forty-eight, but that of female candidates was only forty-four; six of the ten were married. Like their male counterparts, women elected at the federal level are not representative of the Canadian population in occupation and education; six of the ten women had university degrees, and at least four had advanced degrees. Only one was primarily a housewife, and only two had been trained as secretaries. While the others were drawn from high-status occupations, they were not drawn from professions or occupations commonly considered convergent with legislative careers (for example, law or business). While there is a higher proportion of graduate degrees among female legislators than among male, a substantially greater number of male legislators held law degrees and were practicing lawyers when nominated to run for federal office. A study of legislators in the Twenty-eighth Parliament (1972) indicates that a full 33 percent of federal legislators held law

[17] This is part of the larger sample of women candidates described in footnote 15.
[18] See, for example, Jeane J. Kirkpatrick, *Political Woman* (New York: Basic Books, 1974), a study of state legislators in the United States, p. 61.
[19] Jeane J. Kirkpatrick, *The New Presidential Elite* (New York: Sage Publications, 1976), p. 472.

TABLE 11–6
Characteristics of Women Candidates and Elected Members,
1950–1979

Characteristic	Major-Party Women Candidates, 1979 (N = 50)	Sample of Women Candidates, 1950–75 (N = 56)	Women Elected, 1979 (N = 10)
Family status			
Married	27	41	6
With children	25	39	5
Mean age	43.7	45.5	48
Occupation			
Professional	24	21	7
Homemaker	2	19	1
Other	16	16	2
Not ascertained	8	—	—
Education			
No university degree	10	9	4
B.A.	16	16	2
Graduate degree	12	9	4
Not ascertained	12	22	—

Dash (—): Not applicable.
Sources: Biographies of 1979 political party candidates were provided by party organizations; 1950-1975 study of women candidates was conducted by the authors.

degrees. Another 75 percent were professionals, business proprietors, or executives when they first entered Parliament.[20] The women elected in 1979, while professionals, do not belong to the same categories. None of them had a law degree, three were associated with higher education, another three had backgrounds in journalism or public relations, and two others were involved in social work.

Overall, then, while Canadian women legislators are predominantly recruited from the professions, their career patterns reflect the sexual division of labor in Canadian society in general. Women

[20] Allan Kornberg and William Mischler, *Influence in Parliament* (Durham, N.C.: Duke University Press, 1977).

legislators are drawn from the upper ranks of typically "feminine" sectors of the professional labor force, such as teaching, journalism, and social work, while men tend to enter elected office from the male preserves of law and business.

Women and the Issues

Issues of particular concern to women came to the fore during the life of the Thirtieth Parliament—well before the 1979 election was called. The emergence of these issues in the legislature was largely the result of reactions against numerous government austerity measures that appeared to most women's groups and to some members of opposition parties to have more negative consequences for women than for men. As early as 1975, for example, union leaders and, to some extent, the NDP criticized the government's wage and price control policy because they feared it would freeze women in their already inferior position in the labor market. In fact, the legislation and regulations introduced by the Liberal government included exemptions allowing women's wages to catch up to the levels of their male counterparts. In the implementation of wage and price controls, however, previous suspicions proved well founded as the Anti-Inflation Board rolled back numerous negotiated settlements that had provided catch-up remuneration for primarily female bargaining units. The discussion concerning women's status intensified in the following two years in response to the Liberal government's frequent, but unfounded, assertions that Canada's escalating unemployment could be attributed to the increased participation of women in the work force. The debate over women's status revolved primarily around this "scapegoating" for most of the period preceding the election. In particular, the opposition parties criticized the government for misdiagnosing the unemployment problem and for systematically discriminating against women when the unemployment insurance program was changed, training allowances available to women were reduced, women were eliminated as a target group in employment policies, and funding for programs to help women find jobs (outreach) and to improve their status (rape crisis centers, family planning programs, shelters for battered wives, and so on) were gradually withdrawn.

With these debates as a backdrop, the National Action Committee on the Status of Women (NAC) said of the 1979 election:

> This was the first federal election in Canada in which women's issues had played any role. The National Action Committee on the Status of Women does not think that any

of the parties gave the issues the kind of attention they deserve, but *all* gave them much more consideration than ever in the past.[21]

The major parties' definitions of women's issues, however, concentrated almost exclusively on women's status—or lack of status—in the federal bureaucracy and the paid work force. Numerous issues about which many organized women's groups expressed equal concern, such as violence against women, child-support security, wages for housework, and abortion, were studiously avoided. In fact, an examination of speakers' notes and candidate manuals of the major parties showed that their candidates were, in general, cautioned to avoid these issues if possible. Even when coalitions of women's groups asked candidates to indicate their positions on issues such as these, candidates were often advised by their parties to avoid taking a definite stand.

Although all the major parties apparently sought to limit debate on women's issues, their actual treatment of these issues varied considerably. The Liberal party, which, as we have indicated, has made greater efforts to ensure the presence of a small but significant contingent of women in the House (and in the cabinet), surprisingly issued no policy statements concerning women during the course of the campa.gn. When the issues were forced upon Liberal candidates in the last month of the campaign, they had to fall back on a document entitled "Towards Equality" published by the Liberal government in February 1979. This document offered no new initiatives in response to the criticisms of government actions in the 1975–1979 period. In fact, the Liberal party's only offering to women was a commitment to act at last on its longstanding promise to permit homemakers to participate on a voluntary basis in the Canada Pension Plan.

It was the NDP, the party with the lowest proportion of women supporters in 1974, that developed the most aggressive and coherent campaign to attract women voters in 1979.[22] This was part of a long-term strategy that began with the hiring after the 1974 election of a full-time researcher exclusively committed to women's issues. The NDP was the first major party to address these issues in the

[21] National Action Committee on the Status of Women, press release, Ottawa, May 16, 1979, p. 3. The National Action Committee on the Status of Women is an umbrella organization of 170 women's groups. It has some 2 million women members.

[22] The 1974 Canadian National Election Study, funded by the Canada Council, indicated that 58.4 percent of NDP voters were male and 41.6 percent were female.

campaign. As early as April 3, Ed Broadbent outlined an eight-point program for women that recognized "men and women as bread-winners of equal importance."[23] Included in the NDP's proposals were affirmative action programs for both the public and the private sectors, a restoration of job-training and counseling services eliminated or scaled down by the Liberal government, federal assistance to new training programs and day-care facilities, and equal treatment for women in the Canada Pension Plan. In addition, a special appeal to women unionists was included as an integral part of the coordinated campaign known as Labour Calling, undertaken by the Canadian Labour Congress in support of the NDP.

The Conservatives were sufficiently impressed by the effectiveness of this strategy to offer a similar program of their own later in the campaign. The party issued a general policy statement on April 11, though Clark himself did not discuss women's issues until a press conference in Vancouver on May 6. The Conservative proposals echoed in many ways the positions taken by the NDP. The Conservatives promised to improve the status of women in the federal bureaucracy, which, they indicated, should set an example for the private sector. They planned no specific actions to improve the status of women in the private sector, because, as Clark said, "Leadership by example is the major thrust of our action plan."[24] In addition, the Conservatives indicated that they would end discrimination against women in existing legislation applying to the tax system, consumer credit, the status of Indian women, and the Canada Pension Plan. They also promised to restore the funds of the Employment Outreach program at an estimated cost of $3 million.[25]

It is difficult to say whether the major parties' positions on women's issues decided many voters, outweighing traditional cues such as religion, ethnic background, and region, but it is clear that these issues drew many women's organizations that had previously tended to avoid partisan politics into the electoral debate. Some small groups endorsed the NDP, and others actively pursued and publicized the positions of local candidates on women's issues. The NAC itself, despite heated debate, refused to endorse any party. This reflects the longstanding practice of women's rights groups in English Canada of moving between the major parties at both the federal and provincial levels for recognition and funding, rather than

---

[23] NDP communiqué, April 3, 1979, p. 2.

[24] *Globe and Mail* (Toronto), May 7, 1979, p. 9.

[25] This promise was confirmed by the Conservative government on October 17, 1979.

working within a single party to provide a clear alternative for voters concerned with the status of Canadian women. This position was articulated by Lynne MacDonald, president of NAC, on the eve of the election: "We have decided that at no time will we support one party. . . . Our members come from all political parties and we have to work with whoever is in government."[26] This is in contrast to the labor movement, which, though it had maintained a similar neutrality in the past, attempted to mobilize its membership behind the NDP in 1979. In fact, the Canadian Labour Congress (CLC) did more to mobilize women to vote for their interests in 1979 than did the mainstream groups of the women's movement. The CLC argued that women's equality, proper child-care services, and decent pensions depended on a vote for the NDP.

Summary and Conclusions

Although for analytic purposes we have treated candidacies and issues separately, any survey of the history of parties shows that the content of electoral discourse and the nature of political recruitment are intimately tied. For example, it was only after the early trade-union movement had forced its concerns into the electoral debate—either through existing parties or with the establishment of new parties— that workers' issues and worker candidates were integrated into electoral politics. Similarly, increased legislation dealing with women's conditions can be observed shortly after women's enfranchisement became part of the dominant political debate.[27] The 1979 election demonstrates in many ways the failure or inability of both party officials and women's groups to forge the kinds of links that would enhance women's recruitment opportunities and encourage the passage of positive legislation. Although there were more women candidates and the women's movement was increasingly vocal in 1979, these factors alone are not likely to lead to a significant increase in the number of women elected or to serious legislative initiatives to improve the status of Canadian women. Most women candidates in 1979 had little chance of being elected, and the established elements of the women's movement did not mobilize their substantial membership to force the major political parties to put up women in winnable constituencies or to make the status of women a central issue in the campaign. Thus, most Canadian women chose among the parties without reference to their status as women.

[26] *Ottawa Citizen*, May 16, 1979, p. 60.
[27] *Report of the Royal Commission*, p. 338.

12

Epilogue: The 1980 Election

William P. Irvine

We may not have the numbers.

Prime ministerial assistant
December 13, 1979

They did *not* have the numbers. The Clark government was unable to prevent Parliament from passing an embarrassing amendment to its first budget. On December 11 the government introduced that budget—a very austere and demanding compilation of tax and price hikes only moderately relieved by some credits and rebates. It was a prescription, in the words of the finance minister, of "short-term pain for long-term gain." The opposition did not see it that way. For them, it was the "budget that stole Christmas," an unwise deflation of the economy and a regressive attack on its disadvantaged citizens. On December 12 the New Democratic party (NDP) moved a sub-amendment to the budget to add the following:

> And this House unreservedly condemns the Government for its outright betrayal of its election promises to lower interest rates, to cut taxes and to stimulate the growth of the Canadian economy, without a mandate from the Canadian people for such a reversal.[1]

The government's House leader, in a move later seen by some as a kind of death wish, scheduled the vote on that subamendment for the very next day. It passed, 139 to 133, supported by the NDP at full strength and the Liberals with but one member missing because of illness. Others were recalled from business trips or from hospital beds for the vote. The government was missing three members: the

---

I should like to record my very deep gratitude to my colleague Edwin Black, who, as usual, shared unstintingly of his knowledge of Canadian politics and his editorial skills. Remaining errors of judgment are my own.

[1] Canada, House of Commons, *Debates*, December 12, 1979, p. 2304.

secretary of state for external affairs on official business in Paris, another ill, and a third on a South Seas vacation. The government's own weakness was enough to defeat it, but its overthrow became unavoidable with the decision of the five-man Social Credit (SC) group to abstain. The vote was quite clearly an expression of lack of confidence in the government. Though the governor general apparently explored other courses of action, in the end he did the conventional thing. The Thirty-first Parliament was dissolved on December 14, 1979, just over two months after its opening. A new election was called for February 18, 1980.

In one sense, the Clark government never did have the numbers. The 1979 election gave Clark's party 136 of 282 seats, 6 short of a majority. This still represented a substantial lead over the Liberal party, which won 114 seats, the NDP, which won 26, and Social Credit, which won 6. Subsequently, the government recruited one Social Credit M.P. and lost one seat in a by-election. The Conservatives also neutralized one Liberal vote by reappointing the former Speaker of the House of Commons. The government was therefore in a strong parliamentary position on December 11.

Though it was not the most short-lived Canadian government, it was the first to fall so quickly from such an apparently secure position. What had gone wrong? How had the Progressive Conservative government managed to turn not only the Parliament but also, as subsequently became clear, the country against it? In answering these questions, one can draw on a range of explanations, from the most systematic to the most idiosyncratic. Reflecting on an earlier period of Liberal party dominance, Donald Smiley wrote:

> Further, under the one-party dominant system the major opposition party is in no sense an alternative government because its leaders are quite unable to speak for the complex of interests that would have to be reconciled should the party succeed to power.[2]

The new Clark government had to learn quickly to manage a whole new social base. An almost equally demanding task for the new government was to adapt psychologically to its new role rather than its customary one of opposition. Smiley's analysis has recently been augmented by that of George Perlin, who argues that the Conservatives' prolonged periods in parliamentary opposition and their reliance on a social base drawn from the periphery of Canadian society are

---

[2] Donald V. Smiley, "One-Partyism and Canadian Democracy," *Canadian Forum*, vol. 38 (July 1958), pp. 79-80.

responsible for many of the conflicts in the party and can explain its apparently compulsive and self-defeating behavior in power.[3]

Dalton Camp has offered a very different explanation. Speaking of the Progressive Conservative government, he claimed:

> By assuming that it could not be defeated, it was prepared to run enormous political risks. The miscalculation was not so much one of arrogance as of innocence. It failed to comprehend the swiftness with which cynicism, opportunism, and an abiding lust for power could combine to revive a defeated Liberal Party and even resurrect its leadership.[4]

Lying behind these explanations are some of the classic questions of political sociology. Canada in the 1980s will be beset by conflicts that will divide the country along three cleavages. The first conflict is by now familiar to observers of Canadian politics: What kind of country is Canada to be? Will it be a country at all? And if it is, what sort of cultural and language policy will it have? The second conflict has been growing in urgency since the 1973–1974 OPEC oil price increases: How are wealth and economic activity to be divided among the West, the center, and the East in Canada? The third source of conflict has not yet been clearly articulated in Canada and is not yet embodied in opposing institutions. Informed observers now agree that, regardless of the territorial shift of wealth, the country must reinvest massively—both in basic technology to produce energy and in areas of manufacturing in which Canada has some natural or technological advantage. Whose consumption shall be curbed to finance this new investment? Shall it be financed regressively or progressively? Will its direction be set by government or by business?

Canada must, in the 1980s, attempt to harmonize these cultural, territorial, and class cleavages, each of which influenced both the

---

[3] George Perlin, *The Tory Syndrome* (Montreal: McGill-Queen's University Press, 1980). Part of the argument was presented in George Perlin, "The Progressive Conservative Party in the Election of 1974," in Howard R. Penniman, ed., *Canada at the Polls: The General Election of 1974* (Washington, D.C.: American Enterprise Institute, 1975), pp. 97-119.

[4] Dalton Camp, preface to Warner Troyer, *200 Days: Joe Clark in Power* (Toronto: Personal Library, 1980), p. 17. Other stories from Ottawa suggested that the Liberal defeat of the government was a form of mass hysteria that many Liberals regretted in the cold light of morning. See, for example, Val Sears, "Top Tories Just Wouldn't Believe Election Threat," *Toronto Star*, December 12, 1979. For a contrary argument, that the defeat of the government was engineered by members of the Trudeau entourage seeking to preserve his and their power in the Liberal party, see Richard Gwyn, "The Resurrection of Pierre Trudeau," *Toronto Star*, January 5, 1980, pp. B1, B5, and Jeffrey Simpson, "Behind the Scenes in a Wild Week in Ottawa," *Globe and Mail* (Toronto), January 7, 1980, p. 9.

1979 and the 1980 election campaigns. This chapter goes beyond the question of why the Clark government fell and attempts an analysis of the consequences of that fall for Canada's future: Will the country be able to hold together, or will it split along one of these three fault lines?

The First Few Days of the Clark Government

Joe Clark heard of his victory and of the Liberals' concession in Spruce Grove, Alberta, part of his home constituency. With aides and advisers, he immediately retired to Jasper Park Lodge to prepare to assume office. In Canada, there are no long transition periods as one government replaces another: the Clark cabinet would be sworn in less than two weeks after election day. The media proved even less patient than the constitution, however, pressing Clark almost immediately on his intentions. He confirmed one campaign promise on May 30, only a week after the election: the government did indeed intend to "privatize" Petrocanada, the state-owned petroleum company. He repeated this at his first press conference following the swearing-in and also affirmed other commitments. During the campaign Joe Clark had promised a $2 billion tax cut, tax deductibility for mortgage interest and local property taxes, small-business tax incentives, and the abolition of some capital gains taxes. While acknowledging that perhaps not all of these could be included in the first budget of his government, the prime minister stated his intention that they should be pursued in years to come. He also confirmed that he would move the Canadian embassy in Israel from Tel Aviv to Jerusalem. Privatization, taxation, and Middle Eastern policy would prove to dominate the Bosch-like triptych that was the backdrop to the decline of the Clark government.

But that was for the future. The cabinet introduced on June 4 was extremely well received. It seemed a most appealing blend of youth, ability, and political breadth. Of the thirty cabinet members, fourteen (including the prime minister) were *not* central Canadians, and they held such key ministries as Finance, Defense, Energy, and Transport. In naming his cabinet, Joe Clark clearly preferred his own cohort, both chronologically and in time of arrival on Parliament Hill. Sworn in the day before the prime minister's fortieth birthday, the government had an average age of forty-nine years. Twenty of the thirty had first been elected in or after 1971.[5]

There was one glaring shortfall: the paucity and weakness of the cabinet positions given to Quebec. This had been easily pre-

[5] Calculated from capsule biographies of members of Parliament in Pierre G. Normandin, ed., *The Canadian Parliamentary Guide, 1979* (Ottawa, 1979).

dictable on election day. Only two Progressive Conservatives were elected from Quebec. Both received cabinet posts, albeit minor ones. Two other Quebecers were appointed from the Senate, and one of these held the traditional post for Quebec lieutenants, the Ministry of Justice. These two had been appointed to the Senate in the dying days of the last Progressive Conservative government, sixteen years before. They were among the few veterans of that earlier period to find their way into government.

The prime minister sought a two-tier cabinet: a larger one to handle the many tasks and to give representation to the country and a smaller, inner cabinet of eleven to facilitate decision making. This innovation quickly proved its potential for divisiveness rather than effectiveness. Apart from Senator Flynn, the minister of justice, all of them had come to Parliament since 1968, and there seemed to be a preponderance among them of "red" Tories, generally to the left of the caucus as a whole. Rural eastern Ontario provided three members of the inner cabinet, Toronto only one. British Columbia was not represented at all, though this was later rectified by appointing a twelfth cabinet member from that province.

Apart from this concession, little was done to assuage the sense that many Progressive Conservatives had of being still out of power. Small decision-making groups are probably a luxury that a faction-ridden party cannot afford. In opposition Clark had bent his efforts to uniting the party and had been strikingly, though not totally, successful. Progressive Conservatives had stopped fighting each other and begun to focus on the Liberals. This détente, however, did not constitute a consensus on policy, and it was almost inevitable that old wounds would be reopened when the enemy was defeated. The inner cabinet innovation provided an unnecessary additional stimulus to internecine warfare.

Building a Policy under Fire

Yet there was no lack of external attack. The reference to Jerusalem in the June 5 press conference brought on the first barrage. During the campaign, this had seemed a rather unnecessary pledge to an area of Ontario where the party would do well in any event. After the campaign, however, it became a question of, Who is in charge here, the government or the professional foreign service? The reaffirmation of the commitment was a general affirmation that the government meant to get its way against the bureaucracy, but it immediately provoked an outcry from Arab countries. On June 6 the statement was denounced by the Arab ambassadors in Ottawa and by the Palestine Liberation Organization (PLO) in Lebanon. Unease was expressed by Bell Canada, which had just negotiated a billion-dollar contract to supply telecommunications equipment to Saudi Arabia. Though Clark reiterated the pledge on June 7 in a telephone conversation with Prime Minister Begin, his secretary of state for external affairs, Flora MacDonald, tried to calm things down. She met with the ambassadors from the Arab countries and assured them both that it was not a high-priority matter and that it would not be done without consultation with Arab and other countries. Though the pledge was again affirmed on June 11 in an interview with the prime minister by Barbara Walters, the MacDonald meeting can be taken as the beginning of the government's disengagement from an ill-considered promise.

Unfortunately for the government, but in large part through its own fault, the issue dragged on until the end of October. With more economic reprisals threatened, the government sought to temporize by appointing former party leader Robert Stanfield as a roving ambassador. He began his mission on June 23, but instead of defusing the issue, he inevitably gave it new media currency every time he met a head of state. Moreover, as long as the issue remained unsettled, Canada was open to business reprisals, followed by condemnation of the policy by the businessmen affected. As Stanfield ended his mid-eastern tour in early October, the minister for international trade acknowledged that $4.5 million worth of contracts had been canceled. On October 29 the prime minister formally abandoned the policy of moving the Canadian embassy to Jerusalem.

Without reaching the same level of intensity, Clark's second trouble spot, the Petrocanada issue, followed a similar path. Many in the Progressive Conservative party were responsive to neoconservative analysis of economic problems. They defined the most pressing problem as the control of inflation and identified government deficits as its major cause. This was simply one aspect of a broader problem: the heavy-handedness of government in the economy and society. The general program of people in this wing of the party was to reduce government transfer payments except for the most glaring cases of need, to cut the number of public servants spending the money and planning new ways to do so, and to provide more scope for private enterprise as a way of making sure that expenditure and investment would be more productive.

Privatization was thus a key policy for furthering a set of interrelated objectives. Its focus was much broader than simply the state oil company. Sinclair Stevens, the president of the Treasury Board and head of the cabinet Committee on Government Operations, was actively seeking to return more than a dozen companies to the private sector. In addition to Petrocanada, study groups were set up to determine how to get rid of two aerospace companies (Canadair and de Havilland Aircraft), Eldorado Nuclear, Northern Transportation, Teleglobe Canada, Nordair, and the Canada Development Corporation (a public-private investment holding company). There may have been cosmetic as well as ideological reasons for this.[6]

The centerpiece of the policy, however—the privatization of Petrocanada—was no statistical wrinkle. The government appeared determined to accomplish it. On July 15 the company was ordered to acquire no new assets and to stay out of new capital ventures; it was also mandated to continue to negotiate oil purchases with Mexico and Venezuela. On September 6 the government named a study group of leading businessmen to give advice on dismantling the company. At this time the government also clarified its intentions somewhat: "a significant portion" of the assets of the company would be turned over to the private sector, but the government would retain the parts dedicated to state-to-state oil contract negotiations, exploration in frontier areas, and the promotion of oil sands and heavy oil development.

Even this was not enough to dissipate the rising current of opposition. The NDP had announced in May that it would oppose the government on this issue. Both the Liberals and the NDP reiterated this position after the September 6 announcement. In early August a Gallup poll showed 48 percent of Canadians opposed to privatization and only 27 percent in favor. Shortly thereafter, the national president of the Progressive Conservative party called for reexamination of the party's policy, and the Progressive Conservative premier of Ontario urged against the sale of the company or offered, as an alternative, to have provinces buy into it. The Canadian Association of Small Business wanted it retained by the government as a supplier of fuel to independent dealers.

The issue outlived the government and became important in the election campaign. On December 20 in Vancouver, Prime Minister Clark announced yet a new version of the policy: no dispersal of the company but its conversion into a publicly traded company in which the government would retain a one-third interest and in which all

---

[6] The Progressive Conservatives had promised to cut 60,000 people from the federal government payroll. Statistics Canada does not count as public sector employees those working for companies less than 50 percent government owned. Stevens announced his intention to reduce the government's ownership of the Canada Development Corporation from 66 percent to just under 50 percent. By a purely statistical act, this would have eliminated 10,000 federal jobs.

Canadians would receive five free shares. They could also purchase more, to a maximum of 3 percent. Though this remained the government's position throughout the election campaign, ministers nevertheless managed to dissipate confidence in their commitment to the decision. In Winnipeg the prime minister said that although the government would retain control of Petrocanada, it might not exercise that control and might sell off more of its holdings at a later time. Late in the campaign the minister of energy reversed field. Capital from the share sale could be used by Petrocanada to buy the Canadian assets of a multinational oil company. Again doubt was sown as to just what policy the party was adopting.

The third serious problem for the government was the question of fiscal and monetary policy. During the 1979 election campaign, the Progressive Conservatives had promised a $2 billion personal tax cut and had objected to rapidly escalating interest rates. Though the prime minister reiterated his support for the tax cut at his first news conference, his ministers were soon saying that the Liberals had left such a fiscal mess that the cut was impossible. The Liberal legacy was also blamed for the government's inability to curb interest rates. Despite opposition from some members of its own parliamentary caucus, the government had to accept four increases in the Bank of Canada's discount rate, which passed from 11¼ percent in mid-July to 14 percent on October 24. Perhaps even more galling to some of its supporters was the government's reappointment of the governor of the Bank of Canada—the architect of the new monetarist policy of high interest rates.

There was even some backpedaling on tax benefits to homeowners. The initial promise had been to allow deductions of up to $5,000 of mortgage interest and up to $1,000 of municipal property taxes—these limits to be reached over a four-year phasing in of the policy. Such an approach clearly benefits homeowners in higher tax brackets. The policy announced by the finance minister in mid-September was cast in terms of tax credits for only a portion of mortgage interest and local taxes. Though again only those able to afford more expensive homes would obtain maximum benefits, this also was perceived as reneging on a campaign promise.

The decisions on all these matters, Jerusalem, Petrocanada, fiscal policy, marked abandonment of commitments made during the election campaign and repeated at least once after the victory. These "flip-flops" seemed to indicate ineptitude, inexperience, or simple political cynicism.

Particular publics had no difficulty discerning other examples. Supporters of foreign aid were disappointed in the tone taken by the new secretary of state for external affairs. Flora MacDonald had for so long demonstrated her concern for the most disadvantaged within Canada or outside it that some of her new positions did not seem in character. Similar disquiet was felt when others whose reputations were more progressive than conservative began to fly social policy trial balloons. In early September it appeared that the government was thinking of cutting unemployment benefits to seasonal workers, to those who quit their jobs or were fired from them, and to those out of work because of illness or pregnancy. Another proposal was that total family income be taken as the test of eligibility for unemployment insurance. Two months later the universality of the family allowance program came into question. None of these should have surprised close followers of Progressive Conservative policy. The proposals were a decade old, though coupled in the past with proposals for a guaranteed annual income. None of them had been prominent in the 1979 campaign, however, and their promotion by the government in power seemed an unexpected attack on what had appeared to be settled policy.

There was one other reversal felt by a relatively small but prestigious and articulate segment of the community. Early in its term, the Clark government announced that Canada would admit 50,000 Vietnamese refugees over two years and that the government would sponsor one family for each one sponsored privately. Almost immediately this decision was assailed in a large-scale advertising campaign by the National Citizens' Coalition. During the Liberal government, this group had espoused many of the same causes as the Progressive Conservative party and probably expressed what many of its supporters felt. The Clark government persisted in its commitment for quite some time, but the heat finally grew too intense, and in early December the government conceded a diminution in its sponsorship of the refugees. This retreat was immediately denounced by church leaders. Though probably pleasing more people than it angered, it was yet another reversal that had to be defended before particular audiences. For them, it probably added to the image of the Clark government as one without a settled policy and excessively swayed by currents of opinion.

Policy Innovation

It is unfair to focus entirely on policy reversal. In many other changes of Liberal policy, some almost equally controversial, the government was very persistent. A prime example is in federal-provincial relations. Joe Clark had long been critical of the Liberals' tendency to turn every intergovernmental disagreement into a bitter confrontation. When he took office, Clark sought both to cool the atmosphere and to give real substance to his view of Canada as a "community of communities." In his more explicitly confederal model, Canada would draw its strength from building strong provinces. Only in this way, he felt, could the alienation and tension obstructing attachment to the country be reduced.

The government's most significant move in this area was to recognize the ownership by coastal provinces of their undersea natural resources. Other steps were to pull out of the lottery business, leaving a clear field for the provinces, and to promise provinces more effective control of their natural resources and a larger role in telecommunications.

Of particular interest to Quebec, the prime minister promised not to reintroduce a bill to allow the federal government to hold referendums on Quebec's constitutional status. He implicitly, therefore, acknowledged the province's right to hold its own referendum and agreed to respect its outcome. Clark also immediately accepted an inquiry commission recommendation that bilingual air-traffic control be allowed in Quebec airspace. He thus ended what had been the most bitter language conflict of recent Canadian history, and did so in such a manner that there was total acceptance of the decision.

The natural resources and referendum decisions were clearly anathema to former Prime Minister Trudeau, whose concept of Canada they directly challenged. As John Meisel observes in chapter 2, the level of trust and respect between parties has been at a very low ebb since Clark took over the leadership of the Progressive Conservatives. It is clear that Trudeau now felt that Clark was simply destroying the country. He said as much in Alberta in late October and told party workers in Ottawa that the party had a duty to defeat the government at the first opportunity. The 1979 change of government was not accepted with the equanimity that is the precondition of democratic government.

Other policy innovations were much more easily accepted. The government was particularly concerned with instituting a more open government. The centerpiece of this thrust was a new Freedom of Information Act, but also included were a strengthening of parliamentary committees, a greater openness in publishing the economic and expenditure forecasts underlying the budget, and explicit estimation of the impact of tax expenditure.

Also important and well received were the strictly managerial reforms the government brought to the public sector. The government promised to introduce a system of "sunset laws" to compel periodic reevaluation of government programs and regulatory activities. For budgetary control, the president of the Treasury Board put into effect a system of spending envelopes for various domains, by means of which total expenditure in each domain would be limited to a certain percentage growth and increased expenditure for one program would have to be financed by cuts in others in the same domain.

If some special publics were disconcerted by the government's activities, others found them almost surprisingly congenial. In mid-November the government announced an increase of one-third in the budget of the natural sciences and engineering research council. This was a step toward the party's goal of channeling 2.5 percent of GNP into research and development. It was a step greeted with enthusiasm by the favored sections of the academic community and with anticipation by the rest, who hoped for equal favor in later announcements.

The party also moved to implement its election commitment to improving the status of women. The Throne Speech (akin to the U.S. State of the Union message) in early October promised amendments to the Indian Act to protect the native rights of Indian women who marry non-Indians. And the budget promised tax-deductibility for a salary paid to a wife working in a small family business.

Energy and Finance: The Government's Downfall

Though relieved here and there by a patch of light, the background to the government's decline was generally somber. In the foreground were the interconnected issues of energy supply, energy pricing, government deficits, and an internationally weak currency. Such issues continue to plague the present government, which, however, has the safety net of a majority that the Clark government lacked. As a minority government it had to be as sensitive to political realities as to economic ones.

Since the major OPEC oil increases, Canada has adopted a policy of holding domestic prices for oil and natural gas at levels significantly below both the world price and the average American price. The wellhead price for domestically produced oil is an administered price, necessitating protracted annual negotiations between the federal government and the governments of the producing and consuming provinces. Although the final price has so far been agreed upon, the producing provinces feel that they have borne the greatest sacrifice for the national economy. They complain of the greediness of consuming provinces, seeing them despoiling the West of a rapidly-diminishing birthright at bargain-basement prices.

The conflicts engendered by oil are among the most serious facing the country. The West literally cannot profitably use all the wealth its oil now generates, even at low prices. The oil-producing provinces would prefer to be able to charge world prices or to leave the oil in the ground rather than exchange it for depreciating dollars. Consuming provinces, on the other hand, need lots of oil, especially when it is cheap. If Alberta and Saskatchewan are to meet the demand, they insist on high prices for oil and the ability to acquire other wealth-producing assets before the wells go dry. In a word, they seek a shift in economic power from central Canada to the West.[7]

Canada does not now produce all the petroleum it consumes, and about one-fifth of the national requirement must be imported at prevailing world prices. Oil companies supplying the five easternmost provinces receive a federal subsidy to bridge the gap between the Canadian and the world price so that all petroleum used in Canada is bought at one artificially low wellhead price. The import subsidy that makes this a reality is one of the fastest growing components of federal spending. It will further aggravate the federal deficit as Canada becomes increasingly dependent on foreign oil, particularly if the gap between world and domestic prices remains at present levels.[8]

Financing the federal deficit requires, of course, high levels of government borrowing, not only in Canada but in New York, London, Zurich, and other capital markets. Another major component of the federal deficit is therefore the interest on the national debt.[9] To the extent that the debt is foreign held, the government must also be concerned with the international value of the Canadian dollar. With a cheap dollar, Canadian exports have increased significantly, but export industries are now operating virtually at capacity. To maintain

---

[7] These issues were explored in some detail at a conference at the University of Alberta in October 1979. For a report, see the special issue of *Canadian Public Policy*, vol. 6 (February 1980).

[8] Incomplete data on the 1979-1980 fiscal year indicated that oil import compensation payments were costing $1.575 billion. Estimates for 1980-1981 put the cost of these payments at $2.6 billion. See Government of Canada, *Estimates for the Fiscal Year Ending March 31, 1981* (Ottawa: Ministry of Supply and Services Canada, 1980), table 8. Federal government borrowing requirements for 1979-1980 were $10.4 billion and were expected to increase to $11.7 billion for 1980-1981. See statement of the minister of finance, Allan J. MacEachen, to the House of Commons, Canada, House of Commons, *Debates*, April 21, 1980, pp. 242-48. Virtually the whole increase in the federal deficit could be attributed to the increase in oil price compensation.

[9] The cost of debt service was about $8.45 billion in 1979-1980 and was estimated to be $10.275 billion in 1980-1981. See Canada, *Estimates*, table 8.

the value of the dollar, Canadian governments have, therefore, maintained high domestic interest rates to attract foreign capital and retain Canadian capital. This, however, increases the cost of developing energy from nontraditional sources, such as nuclear, tar sands, and heavy oil, and increases the cost of expanding capacity in export sectors to take advantage of the current terms of trade.

Any Canadian government faces a nearly impossible task in picking its way around the interregional cleavages and through the economic thickets. Any choice is bound to arouse opposition. It now seems clear that the Progressive Conservatives did not fully appreciate the magnitude of the task ahead when formulating campaign promises for 1979. Once in office, they soon learned, and this explains the retreat on the $2 billion tax cut. Energy pricing was not an issue in the 1979 election but rapidly became one as the Clark government sought to develop a strategy for handling this set of interrelated problems.

The Progressive Conservatives' *Speakers' Manual* for 1979 dealt first with the topic of self-sufficiency under the general heading of "Energy." This was to be achieved through more vigorous conservation measures, encouraging the substitution of natural gas for oil by building new transmission pipelines, and developing sources of oil that are at present quite expensive to exploit. The *Speakers' Manual* noted with much less emphasis that this should be accompanied by domestic price increases phased in in such a way as not to threaten the industrial economy of Canada.

After the government had been elected, it became clear that price increases would move well up on the agenda. They were seen as necessary to encourage conservation, to generate investment capital for the public and private segments of the industry, and, not incidentally, to help curb the budgetary deficit. However congenial the approach was on fiscal and ideological grounds, compromises and trade-offs were clearly necessary. On such a crucial issue, the Progressive Conservative government of Ontario does not start from the same premises as the Progressive Conservative government of Canada or the Progressive Conservative government of Alberta.

By early September there were various policy straws in the wind. A confidential federal report was leaked. It called for immediate and rapid increases in domestic oil prices, subsidies for less well off consumers, and an energy bank to help recycle petrodollars through the national economy. Prime Minister Clark began a series of bilateral meetings with premiers of individual producing and consuming provinces. The press conferences following these showed mainly that agreement was difficult. The prime minister tried to assure Ontarians on September 6 that his energy policy would not threaten the province's industrial power. The premier of Ontario may not have been convinced: within ten days he was publicly speaking of oil price increases as a threat to national unity. Two weeks later he repeated the same caution against too rapid movement to world prices. Prime Minister Clark's meetings with Premier Peter Lougheed of Alberta seemed to go no more smoothly. By the end of October, Alberta discerned a basic threat to its right to control its own resources. It met this with a counterthreat. Alberta would set its own price for in-province consumption and would not sell oil outside the province. A mid-November federal-provincial conference seemed to end in stalemate. The federal government wanted to increase the wellhead price but to tax away most of the private company profits, thus readjusting the sharing of oil revenues (currently 45 percent to Alberta, 45 percent to the producing companies, and 10 percent to the federal government). Premier Lougheed opposed new federal taxes on private companies as an invasion of his province's right to control the industry. Premier William Davis of Ontario opposed any price increases in advance of a broad energy package dealing also with the sharing and recycling of the revenue generated. Back to the bilateral negotiations. In late November there was still no Ottawa-Alberta agreement, and Prime Minister Clark was threatening to act unilaterally. Premier Davis warmly introduced the prime minister at a party fund-raising dinner in Toronto and endorsed an unspecified plan to recycle the revenues.

The long delay in negotiations had forced the federal government to put off introducing its budget. Agreement was still elusive when the new date arrived. Budget night, December 11, 1979, could provide only a partial picture of the government's economic strategy. Unfortunately for the government, it was the darker part.

The Budget That Destroyed a Government

The main surprise in the budget statement read in the House of Commons on December 11, 1979, was an eighteen cents per gallon increase in the federal excise tax on gasoline. Moreover, the excise tax was to apply to aviation and railroad fuel and to gasoline for inter-city trucks and buses, urban transit, farm equipment, and fishing vessels. Farmers, fishermen, and urban transit systems could expect a rebate of ten cents a gallon from a tax that would now total twenty-five cents a gallon. Home fuel oil was not to be taxed and Canadians earning less than $25,000 could get an energy tax credit of $80 for each adult and $30 for each child. This tax had been totally unanticipated. It could be (and was) justified as a conservation measure. Canadians had to pay more of the real cost of their gasoline before they would become more frugal in consuming it. On the other hand, it could be (and was) decried as simply an attempt to force drivers to pay the tax credit to homeowners that the government had introduced some weeks earlier.

Nor was this to be the only increase in energy prices. The pricing agreement for 1980 negotiated by the previous Liberal government had provided for a $2 a barrel increase. The budget now announced a new agreement with producing provinces, by which oil would increase by $4 a barrel in 1980 and by $4.50 a barrel annually thereafter to reach 75 percent of the average American price by January 1, 1983, and 85 percent of the "Chicago price" by January 1, 1984. If the announced price increases were insufficient —and they were in fact overtaken by an OPEC price increase of 33 percent announced two days after the budget was defeated—an escalator clause in the agreed pricing formula would come into operation.

There were other, more minor tax increases as well: taxes on alcohol and tobacco, increased unemployment insurance contributions from employers and employees, a corporate surtax of 5 percent of tax payable, and the closing of some depreciation allowance loopholes. There was also to be a special tax, still to be worked out with Alberta, to allow the federal government to recover from private oil companies half of all annual price increases above $2 a barrel. The government needed more money and, in any case, felt that the companies could not speedily or profitably employ their new income to increase oil resources, and there had been complaints that they were using their profits to diversify into coal or non-energy-related investments. In the absence of agreement with Alberta, there could be no specifics about this tax or its yield and only a general indication of how the money would be used. It would go into a Canadian energy bank for investment in capital projects in energy. How much money, and where it was to be spent, could not be specified.

The budget was not unrelievedly exacting. There would be tax credits for investment in small business, for salaries paid to wives working in family businesses, and for salaries for new employees and some changes in the capital gains tax. Also attractive was the forecast that government spending would increase by only 10 percent (to keep pace with projected inflation) and that the spending deficit would be cut to $4.4 billion by 1983, from $10.2 billion in 1979. Other projections were less inviting: economic growth would slow from 2.8 percent in 1979 to 1 percent in 1980, and unemployment would increase from 7.3 to 8.3 percent. Subsequent developments in the Canadian and American economies suggested that neither the unemployment nor the growth targets would be met.

It was courageous, but was it wise? Wisdom is of two kinds— economic and political. Economically the budget was well received by most in the business community, despite the strong medicine that was being prescribed. The rapid movement to world prices was not welcome news to Ontario business, however. Premier Davis of Ontario focused his criticism on the excise tax, but his provincial treasurer directed a more broad-gauge attack on the amount of money being drained from the province. The Quebec government objected to the excise tax increase as completely negating the tax savings that the provincial government had been able to pass on to Quebecers. Labor leaders also doubted the economic wisdom of such a deflationary budget at a time when all Canadians were waiting for the long-heralded American recession to strike and spill over, as it inevitably does, into Canada. The way of economic wisdom was not entirely unambiguous and depended on how one weighed the long term against the short. Was the patient sufficiently robust to tolerate the medicine being administered?

Discerning the path of political wisdom is as difficult as interpreting the Delphic oracle. The Liberal party had been defeated in part by popular reaction against Prime Minister Trudeau. Even within the party, his popularity was not high, at least with the English-speaking wing. Many Liberals were anxious to schedule the party's national convention, which had been postponed by the imminent election, hoping that it would show a significant, if not a majority, vote for a leadership review. Some Liberals met in Winnipeg in early October, officially only for a study session; however, they invited none of the current Liberal leaders. In mid-November, whether by intent or by bad staff work, Trudeau seemed gratuitously to insult Liberal activists in British Columbia. Shortly after that incident, he surprised everyone by announcing his resignation as party leader. He would stay on as caretaker until the party could elect a new leader, and a leadership convention was scheduled for March. Various hopefuls began making telephone calls to supporters.

It seemed, therefore, that the Liberals were effectively neutralized. The party talked tough but, even before the announced resignation, had not seemed to relish an election. After the Throne Speech debate, the Liberals had failed to support an NDP confidence motion on Petrocanada and had not even got all the parliamentary caucus out to vote for their own confidence motion. After Trudeau's call in late October for an early defeat of the government, the party seemed

FIGURE 12–1

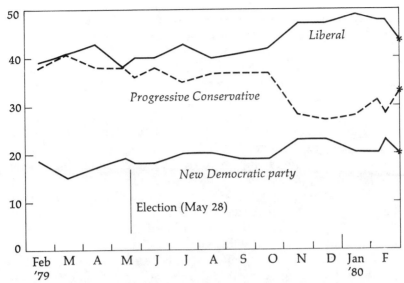

* Indicates actual election results.

Source: Canadian Institute of Public Opinion, monthly news releases.

somewhat more determined, and both Liberals and the NDP were at full strength for a no-confidence motion on November 6. The government survived it only with help from the Créditiste party.

No doubt budget planners felt they could ignore this signal, and even the more ominous one of the Conservative loss of former Prime Minister John Diefenbaker's seat. By November 21 the Liberals were leaderless. Surely the Créditistes would be no more eager for an election in December than they had been the previous month. Such calculations seemed confirmed by the vote on the second reading on the government's mortgage credit plan. Not only were seventeen opposition members absent from the House, but three Liberals broke with their party to support the plan in a vote on December 4, 1979. The Progressive Conservatives undoubtedly knew that their government was attracting little public support. Unlike most new governments, theirs had had no postelection halo. From June through October, as shown in figure 12–1, no party saw its support change by more than sampling error. The Progressive Conservatives had, on a countrywide basis, been the second most popular party in the 1979 election, and their position remained unchanged. Early December brought even more discouraging news: interviews in November

353

indicated that Progressive Conservative support had slipped eight points since election day. They now had the support of only 28 percent of the electorate, their lowest point since the shock of the Parti Québécois election in Quebec, and they were nineteen percentage points behind the Liberal party. The NDP had increased its support to 23 percent of the electorate. Subsequent Gallup polls up to the February election showed no significant variation in these percentages.[10]

Does this support the Camp suggestion? Was a courageous but politically innocent government brought down by a scheming and power-hungry opposition? The Canadian electoral system certainly encourages such behavior by exaggerating the shift in seats corresponding to any given shift in votes. Even discounting the inflation of the Liberal percentage by their solid support in Quebec, the Gallup poll seemed to guarantee a Liberal majority. But the Liberals needed, and obtained, a lot of help to bring the government down. It could not have been accomplished without the votes of the NDP and the abstention of the Créditistes.

Was it a case of an ideologically blinkered government, insensitive to a developing economic recession and to the lack of popular support for an essentially regressive tax (albeit slightly tempered by other tax credits)? The same Gallup survey that charted the sudden Progressive Conservative slump asked two other questions relevant to government strategies for dealing with Canadian difficulties. Questioned whether taxes and government services such as health, education, and welfare should be cut, whether things should be left as they were, or whether services should be increased even if taxes had to be increased, Canadians showed no consensus. Twenty-three percent preferred the cut, 37 percent the status quo, and 29 percent were willing to see higher taxes for more services.[11] Canadians did have a very clear preference, however, for income tax increases rather than increases in "a tax on spending such as a sales tax." Twenty-eight percent thought that a shift in emphasis from an income to a sales tax would be "a good idea." Twice as many (55 percent) thought it "a bad idea."[12]

---

[10] Canadian Institute of Public Opinion, release of December 3, 1979. As also shown in figure 12-1, the Gallup poll seriously underestimated the final vote for the Progressive Conservative party and overestimated that for the Liberals and the NDP. It is incontestable, however, that there was a real change of opinion sometime in October or November.

[11] Canadian Institute of Public Opinion, release of December 12, 1979.

[12] Canadian Institute of Public Opinion, release of December 19, 1979.

Was it a case simply of a government insensitive to the mood of the House of Commons? Repeatedly the NDP introduced tough, uncompromisingly liberal motions of confidence—and the Liberals, afraid of bringing down the government before they had an issue they could campaign on, kept their members away from the chamber and lamely suffered taunts from the NDP. The Social Credit party was swayed by the condemnation of the budget by the Quebec government. Certainly the government seems to have made no effort to meet with the Créditiste leader, Fabien Roy, or even to reschedule the crucial vote until it could have all its members present. No doubt the government was sensitive to the image of indecision raised during the previous election campaign and aggravated by its retreat on election promises. If Canada is entering an era demanding economic sacrifice and possible shifts of economic power, however, governments will have to learn to touch base with all affected parties. The prime minister was quite prepared to negotiate major aspects of his budget (implicitly) with provincial governments; indeed, he took credit for this approach to the provinces, as he took credit for showing new respect for the House of Commons. But building a coalition for its budget within the House apparently was not important to the government.[13]

Asking why the Progressive Conservative government was defeated in the House of Commons is a bit like asking why the United States was caught unawares at Pearl Harbor. Lots of signals were given, but few were received. Politicians had to make guesses as to how adversaries would react. As Dalton Camp has suggested, it is naive to assume that opponents will do what one would like them to do, but this is a common failing. The blame for precipitating the 1980 election is not easy to apportion. It was briefly an election issue but was neither resolved nor judged to be terribly important. The Progressive Conservative government did not make concessions because it felt it did not have to. The Liberals did not yield because it did not seem in their interest to do so.

The Winter Campaign

If the Progressive Conservatives had the problem of selling a tough budget and an apparently weak leader, the Liberals had an equally

[13] In several subsequent campaign speeches, Prime Minister Clark celebrated his refusal to discuss the budget with opposition parties—in particular the Créditistes. Here again, the felt need to build an image of "toughness" led to neglect of the politics of government.

serious problem of deciding whom and what to sell. When the election date was announced on December 14, the Liberals had an undefined policy and a leader who had tendered his resignation. Though some policy discussion had begun, the Liberals were far from having redefined positions on the major issues for the 1980s or from having a new strategy for building a new electoral coalition.

The House of Commons was dissolved on a Friday. Liberals spent the weekend on the leadership issue. Trudeau indicated that if he were to lead the party, it would have to unite behind him. As Liberal M.P.s met first in the full caucus and then in regional caucuses, it was clear that only Quebec fully supported him. Rumbles of discontent from segments of the party association in western Canada, and also in Toronto, were beginning to be heard. In the end, the Liberal M.P.s decided on December 14 to ask Trudeau to resume the leadership. The request was confirmed on December 15 by the party's thirty-six-member national executive, to which the presidents of all provincial organizations, including those in areas of Liberal weakness, belong. The vote of confidence may not have been as unqualified as Trudeau would have liked. He waited until December 18 to announce that he had accepted the challenge, and he made it clear that this was an act of duty rather than of preference and that this would be the last election in which he would lead the Liberals.

The International Context. Rarely since World War II has a Canadian election taken place against such a volatile international background. Rarely, therefore, have campaigners had so little control of the issues to which they had to respond. The first crisis, at the end of December, was the invasion of Afghanistan by the Soviet Union. Trudeau was first off the mark by saying that the whole Western alliance, including Canada under Clark, had failed the United States by giving insufficient backing in response to the taking of hostages by the Iranians. When the United States imposed sanctions, Clark confirmed that Canada would not offer substitute grain to replace that embargoed by the United States. A week later, Canada announced a series of moves against the Soviet Union, largely in the form of limiting exchanges and certain types of trade.[14] The government did not espouse an Olympic boycott at that time, but would explore with other countries the transfer of the Olympic games—possibly back to Montreal.

[14] This initiative unfortunately redounded to the government's discredit as exporters began to complain of their inability to get precise information from the government about the disposition of current contracts.

With the United States seeking a larger defense budget and taking a stronger anti-Soviet stance, broad foreign and defense policy came to occupy an increasing place in the Canadian campaign. The Progressive Conservatives became more hawkish. They accused the Liberals of having allowed Canada's defense forces to shrink in size, in quality of equipment, and in morale. Liberals were portrayed as "soft" on détente, a theme pushed to a quite disgusting extreme in advertising by the National Citizens' Coalition in the last week of the campaign.

The Progressive Conservatives' implicit claim that they were more committed members of the Western alliance than the Liberals got its most significant boost on January 29 with the announcement that six potential hostages from the American embassy in Iran had managed to escape their embassy, find shelter in Canada's, and eventually be smuggled out of the country. The previous day, with international tensions heating up and Canada enigmatically announcing the closing of its Teheran embassy, Trudeau had canceled a trip to Prince Edward Island to make a "major" foreign policy address in Toronto. (It turned out not to live up to its advance billing, being largely a reprise of already made criticism of Conservative ineptitude.)

The speech was, in any case, completely upstaged by the announcement of the "Scarlet Pimpernel" role Canada had played in Teheran. Trudeau did use part of his speech to congratulate the government and the embassy staff on the action. A tremendous sense of pride swept Canadians, a sense to which Americans, from the president and the Congress to many ordinary individuals, contributed. Photographs of Prime Minister Clark taking a telephone call from President Carter or of External Affairs Minister Flora MacDonald welcoming Ambassador Taylor back to Canada were prominently displayed. As we shall see, however, evidence that the government benefited from the publicity over this initiative is somewhat ambiguous.[15]

Not all foreign policy spillovers redounded to the government's benefit. In mid-January, and just as Trudeau was due to speak in Vancouver, President Carter announced that he favored transporting Alaskan oil to the "lower forty-eight" by tanker rather than across Canada through a pipeline. Since the tankers will sail along the

---

[15] There was a "low road" side to this as well. Trudeau had been briefed from the start on the sheltering of the Americans. After their escape, he was accused of irresponsibly needling the government on its Iran policy. His reply was that failure to maintain the usual line of questioning would have more seriously imperiled the "cover" of the operation. This did not spare him from general charges of disloyalty and irresponsibility, however.

British Columbia coast and negotiate tricky tides and passages, serious environmental concerns are raised by such a policy. Economic interests also come into play all across the country. Canadian steel makers had anticipated large orders for pipe. The Liberals used the Carter declaration as further evidence of Conservative ineptitude in foreign policy. They charged that the government had been insufficiently vigorous in pressing on the United States Canada's interest in the overland route.[16]

The Progressive Conservative Campaign. Foreign policy was not the only question on which the Conservative party had little choice of fighting ground. Party strategists knew they would have to defend their budget. They also knew, from party polls going back to August 1979, that they were seen as a party that did not keep its promises. The party chose to meet both challenges head on.

Prime Minister Clark conceded that mistakes had been made and that promises had had to be shelved when the government learned the true state of the Canadian economy. He claimed, however, that it was unfair to judge his government on so short a record. His government had quickly appreciated the situation in which Canada found itself and had changed the general direction of the country. The Progressive Conservative course was responsible and prudent, he assured the voters, and the party would be proud to be judged on it in four years' time. The one encouraging feature in internal party polls was that voters agreed that the party had not had a chance to govern. Party advertising was therefore focused on this theme. Each broadcast and ad ended with the slogan: "Real Change Deserves a Fair Chance."

The budget was defended as a part of the record that the future would applaud. It was not only fiscally responsible but absolutely necessary if Canada was ever to enjoy self-sufficiency in petroleum. The theme of self-sufficiency was repeated throughout the campaign. Sometimes it was tied to local issues. Near Quebec City, Prime Minister Clark promised that the new energy bank would invest up to $200 million in Quebec on energy-related projects. Speaking to Prince Edward Island farmers, upset by the way the excise tax increased the cost of trucking potatoes to market, the prime minister tried to redirect attention to producing gasohol from substandard potatoes. Sometimes self-sufficiency was tied to the international

---

[16] After the hostage drama, the NDP suggested that it might be time to open negotiations on Alaskan oil policy with the United States and to seek prompt ratification of the fisheries treaty.

climate. Progressive Conservative policy was promoted as freeing Canada from Khaddafis and Khomeinis.

However the future might judge the budget, Prime Minister Clark had considerable difficulty in getting important elements of his party to buy it. Before the defeat of the government in the House, the premier of Ontario and his provincial treasurer both condemned the extra burden being placed on Ontario consumers. The Ontario Progressive Conservative party had become expert at attacking the provincial Liberals with the faults of their federal party. Now the provincial Liberal leader was not slow to return the compliment. Local Conservatives wished to distance themselves as best they could from Clark's Conservatives, but Ontario was where the federal election would be won or lost, and Prime Minister Clark badly needed help from its provincial organization.

Here he was badly served by the timing of his government's defeat. Ontario could accept increased oil prices at the wellhead, could even accept excise taxes if the money was recirculated back to low-income consumers or to capital goods industries. Ontario has more than its share of the latter and a large number, if not a large share, of the former. The budget did include some relief for those with low incomes, but it was not able to report how much of the new value of a barrel of oil would go to the federal government, nor could it report in detail on the government's strategy for using that share.[17] There were leaks by aides to the prime minister, but the premier of Alberta never confirmed their version, and Clark never spelled it out either. The revenue-sharing agreement just around the corner began to take on the dimensions of the fish that got away, and Ontario audiences gave it about as much credence. Prime Minister Clark held a meeting with the Progressive Conservative members of the Ontario legislature in which he successfully rallied their support. It was reported that he asked them to accept higher oil revenues for Alberta now in return for broad-gauge revision of the sharing of provincial revenues, including resource royalties, in the future. The meeting was behind closed doors and had little public impact. Probably it could not have had much even in the most open of circumstances. Ontario voters are not ornithologists; birds in the bush, and in particular studies to establish their dimensions, are no more appealing than fugitive fish.

---

[17] The party was embarrassed when an Ontario strategist announced a commitment to spend $900 million from the energy bank on mass transit vehicles. He later had to admit that he had made this up and there was no such party commitment.

To be fair to Clark, he spoke both in Alberta and in Ottawa of the need for a fiscally strong central government with the capacity to redistribute revenues whose incidence is now highly skewed. It is not an easy matter to persuade the energy-producing provinces that a strong Ottawa is a policeman, not an attacker. Nor was it easy for Clark to persuade the voters in the consuming provinces that he was on their side: the Progressive Conservative government seemed to favor the producer, and it would take more than a few statements to change its image.

The political difficulties arose in part because even the current agreement was not fully in place, and also because the general policy had not been completely thought through. Though Clark wanted a strong federal government, he also wanted to give coastal provinces full ownership of their offshore energy.[18] One can make a case that all provinces should be put in the same position with respect to resource revenues before beginning to redistribute the wealth. This is attractive as a moral proposition but may not be effective bargaining or redistributive strategy.

Energy pricing (as distinct from revenue sharing) also redounded upon the party. The minister of finance suggested that the OPEC price increases announced after the introduction of his budget might necessitate price increases beyond those contemplated in December, a suggestion that had to be repudiated by the prime minister. The reversals on the Petrocanada side of the energy issue have already been described.

The other major strategy of the Progressive Conservative campaign was to revive the attack on Pierre Trudeau and the Liberal party that had served them well in the 1979 campaign. It fitted nicely with the general advertising slogan, since the Liberals could be depicted as a party whose arrogance and lust for power had denied a fair chance to a government seeking to reorient the country. The Progressive Conservatives were assisted in this strategy by the Liberals themselves: Trudeau refused to debate Clark and the NDP leader on television, and the Liberals were unable (or unwilling) to produce a comprehensive policy document for the campaign. Some Progressive Conservative speakers claimed that Liberal policies were too unspecific to judge and that the Liberals were thus seeking a blank check from the electorate. Other speakers, however, found them specific enough to put an inflationary price tag on them. Some

[18] The Progressive Conservative premier of Newfoundland was apparently not very sanguine about Clark's chances in the 1980 election. During a Clark campaign stop in that province, Premier Brian Peckford sought to have the undersea resource agreement signed and sealed before election day.

party television advertising quite blatantly sought to fan the old anti-Trudeau flame. Foreign policy issues also gave occasion both to reexamine the record of the past Liberal government and to question the patriotism of Liberal leaders. It also helped heal links with Ontario Progressive Conservatives, to whom Clark's hawkish views were quite congenial.[19]

There were other, minor themes to the Progressive Conservative campaign. In Quebec Prime Minister Clark announced that a highly respected Quebec senator, whom he had appointed, was at work on the government's constitutional policy, beginning from the well-received report of the Task Force on Canadian Unity. Clark was able to point to his concessions to provinces generally, and on bilingual air-traffic control in particular, as evidence that he had the capacity to avoid federal-provincial confrontation. His ability to speak (and be interviewed) in French is truly impressive for one with no better school opportunities than are typical in English Canada. That and his evident sympathy for Quebec provided strong support for his claim that his was the only party able to interpret Quebec's aspirations to all the rest of Canada. His model of Canada as a "community of communities," while not further specified, was consistent with his guaranteeing to those communities control over their own natural resources. But there were a couple of lower notes. Prime Minister Clark tried to break Quebecers' Liberal habit by stressing Trudeau's planned retirement and saying that they did not know who might become Liberal leader. He also cautioned that the Progressive Conservatives could not go again to the Senate to find Quebec representation. If Quebec wanted to be part of a Clark government, they would have to elect Progressive Conservative candidates.

There were other more specialized points for particular audiences. Pork-barrel politics were not neglected. One of the test cities for metrification of supermarkets was promised that metrification would be abandoned. A group of policemen's wives was promised a free vote (no party lines drawn) on the reestablishment of capital punishment. The hard defense line was the centerpiece for a speech at Ukrainian Independence Day festivities in Toronto. The prime minister was well received when he outlined his government's accomplishments and plans to a meeting of the National Action Committee on the Status of Women.

---

[19] Hawkishness extended, after President Carter announced the reestablishment of the draft, to statements by Conservatives that new American draft dodgers could not expect to find refuge in Canada. The prime minister later qualified this by saying that no decision had been taken.

Despite a few communications gaffes and crossed signals, the Progressive Conservatives ran a very strong campaign. The prime minister was indefatigable. Even political opponents had to admire the grace with which he bore the discouragement of the polls and the meanness of repeated jokes. In the end, of course, it was a successful operation, but the patient died. The fatal incisions had been made well before the campaign began.

The Liberal Campaign. Many Liberals felt that the 1979 campaign had been poorly fought. The party had had no program, no vision of the future. Non-Quebecers, more concerned with economic than constitutional problems, had felt the Liberal party had nothing to say. With this diagnosis, the prescription was clear: though Christmas would allow a hiatus in campaigning, Liberal activists could take no such break; they had to define a new program.

Other Liberals reacted differently. They believed that the 1980 election was already won—if the party made no mistakes. What might those mistakes be? One clearly would be to return to a focus on the constitution, language rights, and the need for a strong central government. These were important issues, but when they were raised, these Liberals feared that the voters would hear other things, such as a celebration of French power and Trudeau's arrogance. Liberal planners felt that anti-Trudeau feeling had been largely exorcised by the May defeat, but they did not want to summon the ghost again.

This basic cleavage could not be entirely ignored, though Trudeau argued that his position was known and did not need futher elaboration. Here again, the matter was not entirely in the federal politicians' hands. Just after the fall of the Clark government, the Parti Québécois premier of Quebec made public the question he intended to put to Quebecers in a referendum. The party's objective is to achieve a radically different constitutional status, including some elements of sovereignty, for Quebec, an objective it is approaching one step at a time. The referendum question proposed sought only a mandate to negotiate a new agreement with Canada, and the party promised to hold another referendum before attempting any change in constitutional status.

From Ottawa, this was not an issue: Prime Minister Clark called it "absolutely unacceptable," and Trudeau and Broadbent took the same position. The next injection of this cleavage into the campaign was the mid-January release of the Quebec Liberal party position on the constitution, which might have become an issue.[20] This document contained a number of points that Trudeau could endorse. In particular, it was the first document from a Quebec politician to articulate a defense of federalism in language other than that of pure expediency. It took a strong position on civil liberties and the rights of the English-speaking minority in Quebec. On the powers of the federal and provincial governments, however, and on some of the new institutions proposed, there might have been sharp disagreement between Trudeau and the Quebec Liberal leader, Claude Ryan. As we have seen, it is part of Canadian political sport to embarrass a politician at one level by citing the stated positions of his copartisan at the other. Liberals played this game on energy, but neither the Progressive Conservatives nor the NDP returned the blow. All joined Trudeau in greeting the Ryan document in as noncommittal a fashion as possible. They then joined a "cartel of silence" on the matter for the rest of the campaign. For fear of provoking quarrels among the profederalist forces in Quebec just before a referendum, Clark and Broadbent had to acquiesce in the Liberal low-profile strategy during the federal campaign. Such self-denial is clearly to their credit and confirms their statesmanship.

For Liberals, avoiding issues that focused on Trudeau would avoid one mistake. The second could be skirted by not allowing the voters' focus to shift from the record of the Progressive Conservative government. This meant that the party had to be very cautious in announcing new policies. The government had to be kept on the defensive. "The speech" for Trudeau was to be an attack on the budget and on the record of the government. It was given at every opportunity.

By and large, the Liberals ran a brilliant campaign. The party managed to keep to "the speech" and on the attack despite criticism from opponents and from bored reporters, whose ingenuity was taxed to find a new angle for their stories on a virtually unchanging performance. The policy-oriented party activists got their moment in the spotlight also, but only toward the end of the campaign. The Liberals were able to end with positive promises for the future, without having had to spend too much time defending them.

Arising out of the mainstream strategy was a decision to avoid participating in a televised debate among the party leaders. In 1979 the Liberals had been desperate to get Clark in the same television

[20] Liberal Party of Quebec, Constitutional Committee, *A New Canadian Federation* (Montreal, 1980).

studio with Trudeau. In 1980 the Conservatives were the ones eager for the debate. They felt that a debate would bring the negative side of Trudeau's personality into the spotlight and give Clark an opportunity to demand policy details from the Liberals.

So eager were the Conservatives for a debate that the Liberals were able to protract the negotiations in a teasing way. At first the Liberals countered with a proposal for several debates on specific topics among members of party teams. When the networks demurred, the Liberals made several suggestions for changes in format before finally, on January 11, announcing that they would not participate in a debate unless they could get a format that had already been rejected by the others.[21]

Though the strategy was to keep the government on the defensive, the Liberal campaign was not as devoid of issues as this summary might suggest. Even early in the campaign, the Liberals promised not to reintroduce the excise tax on gasoline (in 1980, as Liberals are now stressing after the election) and promised to give Petrocanada its full budget request (which had been cut by the Conservatives).

On January 12, to a meeting of party workers in Toronto, Trudeau laid out the five themes of the Liberal campaign:

1. better management of public finances
2. energy security at fair prices
3. a new industrial strategy
4. greater economic strength for Canada's regions
5. better social security for individuals

Opposition spokesmen could easily burlesque this as asking for a mandate to deal with all the things that past Liberal governments had neglected to do. Certainly no one could dissent from such objectives. The party was sufficiently imprecise about means of achieving them to leave little for the Progressive Conservatives and the NDP to criticize, except the vagueness itself.

More specific promises were forthcoming, however. At a later speech in Toronto, Trudeau promised to increase the income supplement for poorer pensioners. The audience for the speech, a club of middle-class women, was not the most appropriate, but the strategy was exquisite: announcing the increase obviated the need to talk about women's issues.[22]

---

[21] Val Sears, "The Cardboard Campaign: How the Liberals Backed Out of the National TV Debate," *Toronto Star*, February 16, 1980, p. B1.

[22] Trudeau was the only one of the three party leaders to decline to speak to a meeting of the National Action Committee on the Status of Women.

A more disastrous promise was made a couple of days later in Saskatchewan. Trudeau promised to double-track the rail line of the government-owned Canadian National Railways from Winnipeg to Vancouver. This became pretty much of a joke for the rest of the campaign. For much of the line, the terrain simply does not permit double-tracking. Moreover, the real problems in moving western wheat to market are more closely related to shortages of hopper cars and inadequate port facilities than to clogged rail lines. Later, Prairie Liberals tried to reduce the promise to the status of a metaphor and to interpret it simply as an indicator of concern for the West.

Promises for the Pacific coast were somewhat better directed. Liberals promised support for a commercial seaplane that had been designed and would be built on Vancouver Island. They also promised to expand port facilities in the north of the province, to allow more autonomy for the port of Vancouver, and to post an assistant deputy minister of fisheries to be resident on the west coast.

By the end of January, Liberal energy strategy was taking more positive form. It was clearly to be an interventionist and nationalist approach. In Winnipeg Trudeau suggested that explicit rationing would be a fairer way of dealing with shortages or promoting conservation than rationing through price. On April 25, in Halifax, Trudeau stated the Liberal commitment to a "blended price" concept, according to which the Canadian price was to reflect the prices of all oil being used in Canada. There is no problem in establishing the price of imported oil, but the blended price was also to make allowance for different kinds of domestic oil. That produced from northern tar sands or recovered by applying new technology to long-exploited wells is much more costly than oil from newly discovered land basins. Offshore oil and Arctic oil have yet other cost structures. Since there is no domestic market to establish the price for these various domestic sources, the Liberals' "blended price" would continue to be largely an administered price. Presumably, however, it would adjust more automatically to shifts in the mix of oil used in Canada. A Petroleum Pricing and Auditing Agency would study the books of private producers. Liberals would also aim to achieve at least 50 percent Canadian ownership of the domestic oil industry and to encourage the switch from oil to gas and eventually to other energy sources (through an Alternate Energy Corporation by which the government would coordinate research and development of such sources).

This plan would require much greater government involvement in the energy sphere. It also included elements of greater federal as opposed to provincial government action. Certainly the Liberals were concerned with the wealth implications of any energy strategy.

In one of his best speeches of the campaign, Trudeau told Newfoundlanders that they could not have complete ownership and control of energy resources off their coast. He made a powerful plea for the erection of a Canadian community based on sharing—sharing the different forms of wealth that natural endowment produces in each province. The theme was repeated in Alberta a week later, showing at least some willingness to enter various lions' dens waving raw meat.

Politically, the plan gave the Progressive Conservatives and the NDP something to attack. The NDP doubted the Liberals' ability to follow through on all aspects of the plan, while the Conservatives kept trying to force the Liberals to specify the price that would emerge from the complex calculations they seemed to envisage. By and large, the Liberals avoided entering into debate over their proposal. In a television interview, Trudeau suggested that Liberals would keep oil price increases under $3 a barrel, but this was repudiated by other Liberals and admitted by Trudeau to be a mistake.

Having seen the shadow of controversy, the Liberal policy groundhog rapidly took cover until the last week of the campaign, when Trudeau broadened the party's nationalist and interventionist commitment to spheres beyond the oil industry. Indeed, he suggested that the mixed publicly and privately owned Canada Development Corporation should play a role in manufacturing analogous to the role of Petrocanada in energy. He also promised to strengthen the Foreign Investment Review Agency by requiring it to assess the performance of foreign-owned firms, to publicize proposed foreign takeovers of Canadian firms, and to assist Canadian companies in repatriating foreign ownership of Canadian assets. Government would also take a more active role in defining an industrial strategy. These principles were related more directly to the auto industry in a speech a few days later in Windsor.

These themes certainly satisfied those Liberals who thought the party had strayed too far from its liberalism in the latter years of the previous government. Though no report of the hastily convened policy committee was ever released, no doubt these themes were prominent in the deliberations. That this was not merely a sop to make sure activists worked wholeheartedly on election day is perhaps indicated by inclusion of the same points in the new government's Throne Speech. The party seemed, at least, to have a sense of direction in areas other than the constitutional. Thanks to the timing of the announcement, Trudeau was able to grab some headlines without having to defend the policy against substantive questioning or comparison to the record of his previous government.

The New Democratic Party Campaign. All NDP campaigns are motivated by a "maybe this time" hopefulness. In 1980 it seemed to have some basis. However short the voters' memories, they should extend over at least twelve months. The NDP felt that both major party leaders and policies had been discredited within that time span. But 1980 also brought the classic pitfall for the NDP: to be the third party when the Canadian electorate wanted to reject somebody.

There was considerable overlap in the policy themes between the two elections. On the resource side, there was the call for the expansion of Petrocanada. The NDP had been prepared to fight strongly against the privatization of the company, but this issue was taken away from them early in the campaign by Clark's change of position. On industrial strategy, the NDP became much more specific than it had been nine months before, urging much greater state involvement in industrial planning and investment on the Swedish model. The NDP has always been strongly supported by the United Auto Workers, and the NDP industrial strategy took concrete form in its proposals for government assistance to the Chrysler corporation. Help would be given only in return for equity in the company or for performance guarantees by it in matters of employment, investment, and research development. Another concrete industrial policy was also a carry-over from 1979: support for Canadian shipbuilding and for a Canadian merchant marine. Medicare, help for low-income homeowners, small business assistance, and interest-rate policy all looked familiar.

What was perhaps different was the backdrop for these policies. Though always nationalistic, the New Democratic party gave much more emphasis to an explicitly nationalist imagery for the 1980 election. It was not enough to lower interest rates: there had to be a "made-in-Canada" interest-rate policy that was other than a simple tracking of Federal Reserve Board policies. The NDP applied the "made in Canada" label to energy and employment policy as well. Much of this was directed against multinational corporations. While the NDP looked favorably on nationalization of the Canadian assets of some of these, the main approach was to be through greater state control of company investment, employment, and environmental performance. To a minor extent, the NDP's nationalism was directed against the United States: opposition to American tanker traffic off the British Columbia coast, renegotiation of the Canada–United States Auto Pact to obtain more benefits for Canada, limitation of energy exports to the United States.

When foreign affairs became prominent in the campaign, the NDP's mildly anti-American stance became a liability. Broadbent had quickly to affirm his support for sanctions against the Soviet Union and, more broadly, for NATO and the North American Air Defense Command (NORAD). This, in turn, angered some NDP candidates, who called Broadbent back to respect for the foreign policy planks passed at party annual meetings. These planks call for Canada's withdrawal from both NATO and NORAD. While Broadbent had to concede this traditional position of the party, he also devoted time to arguing against the proposition that the NDP was a pacifist party. This perception was clearly not salable among the voters the NDP hoped to attract in 1980. While nationalism in economic policy could be attractive, lack of foreign policy support for the United States was not.

Also different from traditional NDP appeals, though similar to the strategy of the 1979 election, was the much reduced emphasis on social policy. Only after the Liberals promised to increase the guaranteed income supplement did the NDP promise a general pension increase. Though doctors were to be brought back into the Medicare scheme, the theme was not particularly prominent, and there was no mention of a guaranteed income or a negative income tax. The focus, instead, was on economic policy both in the form of an industrial and energy strategy and in the form of macroeconomic stimulus.

Strategically, too, the NDP campaign in 1980 echoed that of 1979. Similar was the emphasis on the leader, who carried the full burden of the national campaign and was the centerpiece of all the party advertising. He was becoming an increasingly polished performer, both at meetings and before the television cameras. The NDP could claim, with considerable justification, that it was the only party to be proud of its leader. Less pleasing to the party, perhaps, were the voters who told Ed Broadbent they liked him "if only you were head of another party."[23]

As in 1979, the Canadian Labour Congress (CLC) again tried to mobilize union members for the New Democratic party. This time the CLC campaign was much lower profile. Its president did not make cross-country tours speaking to union members, but leaders of union locals were active in distributing kits to members to show that

---

[23] Analysis of a postelection study of the 1979 election suggests that Broadbent may not have been able to translate his personal popularity into many additional votes for the NDP. Jon H. Pammett, Harold Clarke, Jane Jenson, and Lawrence LeDuc, "Change in the Garden: The 1979 Federal Election" (Paper presented at the Annual Meeting of the Canadian Political Science Association, Montreal, June 2, 1980), p. 38.

their real standard of living declined under both Liberal and Progressive Conservative governments. More affiliated unions, and more locals and officials in each, were claimed to be active in 1980 than had been active in 1979.[24]

The Advertising Campaigns. All three parties returned to their traditional advertising teams: the Conservatives to Media Buying Services; the Liberals to an ad hoc consortium, Red Leaf Communications, for English-language advertising and to BCP for French advertising; and the NDP to Lawrence Wolf.[25] Thanks to the Election Expenses Act, all parties, including the NDP, had sufficient funds to run extensive media campaigns. The agencies, for the major parties at least, had a lot at stake. One change quickly made by the new Progressive Conservative government had been a reallocation of federal government advertising contracts.

The Election Expenses Act limits election advertising in mass media to the last twenty-eight days (ending twenty-four hours before polling day) of the campaign. In 1980 the advertising campaign could legally begin the day of the Super Bowl, and both major parties tried to reach that audience.[26] Tackling was the order of the day. The Progressive Conservative party returned to its 1979 focus on the popular antagonism to Trudeau. One ad showed him surrounded by former Liberal ministers whose pictures disappeared one by one. An announcer said, "Let's face it. If you vote Liberal, you're getting Trudeau and nothing else." Other English-language advertising also attempted in both picture and voice to keep anti-Trudeau voters in the Progressive Conservative fold. This could not be done with an entirely negative campaign, and it was here that the Con-

[24] Wilfred List, "Unionists Are Switching to Lunchroom Lobby in Bid for NDP Support," *Globe and Mail*, January 21, 1980, p. 9; and John Deverell, "Less Talk, More Troops As Labour Hits Campaign Trail," *Toronto Star*, February 5, 1980, p. A10.

[25] I pass directly from an account of the three main parties to a description of the advertising. The Social Credit party was unable to mount an effective campaign in 1980, even in Quebec. Its five remaining members of Parliament campaigned largely as individuals. In some cases they did not want the nominal party leader to come into their constituencies. To give his campaign some national flavor, Fabien Roy did make one trip to the traditional heartlands of Social Credit, Alberta and British Columbia. Members of that party in the provincial legislatures did not even bother to meet him. His trip was largely ignored by the media in those provinces.

[26] Advertising on the Super Bowl was apparently at bargain rates on Canadian channels: $6,800 for a thirty-second spot as compared with $238,000 in the United States. In general, however, advertising rates were higher for the 1980 than for the 1979 election because winter audiences are significantly larger than spring audiences.

servatives attempted to implant their theme that the party had not been given a fair opportunity to show what it could do. The French-language campaign in Quebec could not be so blatantly anti-Trudeau and was focused on constitutional change rather than economic or energy-related issues. The Progressive Conservative slogan there was "Un Canada meilleur, ça se fait. Votons Conservateur, on va l'faire."[27]

Liberal advertising was equally negative, though not directed personally against Clark. It was directed against his policy "flip-flops," however, and against his budget. Stars on the Liberal antibudget ads (those shown in Ontario at any rate) were all Conservatives. Voices were heard predicting dire consequences for Ontario from the Clark budget. The camera then turned to the speakers—in different ads these were the Progressive Conservative premier of Ontario and his provincial treasurer. Again the Quebec advertising was different—in concept and theme, if not totally in substance. The English advertising had used more image-creating tricks, a magician flipping over cards whose message changed every time, for example, and it did not show any Liberal personalities at all. The French advertising eschewed such tricks and focused completely on Trudeau speaking in a very relaxed manner in very familiar French. The Liberal slogan there was "Une équipe pour ramener le bon sens au pouvoir."[28]

The NDP campaign was not negative. To be sure, it was critical of both the major parties, but the focus was on the party leader speaking in very common-sense terms about particular issues of concern. The belief was that major party advertising would anger voters. The NDP sought to be upbeat and direct—no special camera work or image making. Its advertising focused on economic and energy issues but also tried to deal with two points that might lead voters to avoid the NDP. For those afraid of another minority government, the ads claimed that the NDP deserved credit for pushing the other parties to more constructive policies. For those who feared that the NDP was too far to the left, Broadbent was shown saying, "Many aspects of our economy should be left entirely in the private sector. We don't want the state controlling all kinds of things and directing people's lives."

Candidates. Most of those who had been elected in 1979 chose to run again. There were ten dropouts, three for the Liberals and seven for the Progressive Conservative party. In each case, these were divided about evenly between those who would normally be retiring

27 A better Canada is possible. Vote Conservative; we'll do it.
28 A team to bring common sense back to power.

and those who were clearly disaffected from the party leader.[29] Some Liberals were uncomfortable with Trudeau's continued leadership and felt that the defeat of the government had been a mistake. Some Progressive Conservatives felt that they personally, or their views in the party, had been slighted by Joe Clark in his cabinet building and other action. No one withdrew from candidacy proclaiming any of these feelings. Newspaper reports claimed that they were at work in some withdrawals, but it is probable that more Clark and Trudeau opponents chose to run again than chose to drop out.

Disaffection from the leader probably limited Liberal attempts to recruit for certain candidacies. In the press, in the advertising by opponents, and in other commentary, there was a claim of weakness in Liberal leadership. The outgoing cabinet in 1979 had seemed much weaker than earlier Trudeau cabinets. Able men appeared disinclined to work with him. Liberal advertising in 1980 tried to dispel this image, but to do so successfully would have required the recruitment of new and strong candidates. This need may have militated against renewed candidacies of former cabinet ministers defeated in 1979. Of thirteen of these, only five contested the 1980 election, two successfully. There was no rapid transfusion of new blood into the Liberal team. A former Liberal premier of Nova Scotia ran, as did some important municipal politicians from Toronto. Neither of the leading Liberals mentioned in the brief interim of the Trudeau retirement as possible new Liberal leaders chose to run in 1980. While there is no easy way to assess the strength of a set of candidates, those seeking election as Liberals did not immediately grab the voters' attention.

The Progressive Conservatives enjoyed much more success in recruiting prominent people to their colors in Quebec. Given the regionalism of the Canadian electorate and its exaggeration by the electoral system, Canadian parties have a tradition of relying on local stars rather than local organization in their most barren regions. The search for Conservative candidates in Quebec is the epitome of this pattern. It must be said, however, that Prime Minister Clark had no difficulty finding a dozen very impressive candidates for Quebec, including several former members of the Quebec assembly.

The Liberals ran twenty-three women candidates in 1980, two more than they had in 1979; the Progressive Conservatives the same number, fourteen, and the NDP fourteen fewer, thirty-three. Overall there were slightly more women candidates in 1980 than in 1979, and more—fourteen—were elected. In the Liberal party, the success rates

[29] There was also one ouster of a Progressive Conservative who had been successful in 1979. See chapter 4, note 63.

were most nearly equal: 43 percent of women and 53 percent of men were victorious. In the NDP, 6 percent of the women and 12 percent of the men seeking office were elected, but the greatest imbalance was between Progressive Conservative male and female candidates: 38 percent of the men but only 14 percent of the women were successful. As Vickers and Brodie point out in chapter 11, these differences are largely due to the traditional partisanship of the constituencies contested. The Liberals make more effort to recruit women to safe constituencies than the other parties. Certainly the variation in the success rate for any party is much greater across provinces than it is between the sexes.

Parties, Issues, and Leaders

Canadian voters are not burning partisans. When asked, only two-thirds of them claim strong party ties; when their behavior is examined, it belies even that claim. Still, the Canadian voter is not entirely rudderless, and party identification is quite stable in the aggregate. Measuring the precise level of attachment is a bit more difficult, however, because of the people who claim indecision in surveys between elections yet profess to support the leading party, if there is one, in election-time surveys.

As conceived by the Survey Research Center at the University of Michigan, party identification is the long-run attachment voters feel to one of the parties bidding for support. By definition, then, it should not change much during short periods. This seems to hold for the Canadian electorate, when allowance has been made for possible contamination by bandwagon-climbing respondents. There are very few statistically significant differences in party identification between 1979 and 1980 (see table 12–1). Where they occur, in the Liberal increases in Quebec and Ontario for instance, they are offset by declines in the number of undecideds or noncommittals. The increases for both the Progressive Conservatives and the NDP in British Columbia came from an unusually high level of professed independence in 1979. Despite the overall increase in the number of declared partisans, it is still true that one voter in five supports no party or cannot say which party he supports. As suggested, this probably underestimates the true number of "apoliticals" or "non-partisans" in Canada, but the stated figure has remained at that level for about fifteen years.

The catalog of issues shifted slightly from one election to the other. The classic symptoms of stagflation—high inflation and high unemployment—had dominated public consciousness in 1979. The

TABLE 12–1

PARTY IDENTIFICATION, CANADA AND REGIONS, 1979–1980
(percent)

	Lib.	PC	NDP	SC	Other	None[a]
All Canada						
February 1980	40	23	14	2	1	20
May 1979	36	21	11	3	1	27
Atlantic						
February 1980	41	29	12	0	0	18
May 1979	47	22	5	0	2	23
Quebec						
February 1980	59	9	5	4	2	21
May 1979	52	6	5	7	2	28
Ontario						
February 1980	36	25	16	b	1	22
May 1979	31	27	13	b	1	27
Prairies						
February 1980	27	37	15	1	1	19
May 1979	24	34	15	3	0	25
British Columbia						
February 1980	22	25	27	4	2	20
May 1979	22	17	19	4	1	37

NOTE: Respondents were asked: "Thinking of federal politics, do you usually think of yourself as Liberal, Progressive Conservative, NDP, or Social Credit?"
[a] Includes "no party" and "not sure/not stated."
[b] Less than 0.5 percent.
SOURCE: Gallup poll, reported in *Toronto Star*, February 11, 1980, p. A12.

Progressive Conservative government, probably aided by the crisis in Iran, shifted the debate slightly to concern over energy. By February 1980 a quarter of Canadians felt that was the most important task for the new government. The unemployment rate declined, but only very slightly, over most of the period of Conservative government. Popular attention to it fell much more quickly, though the unconcern was only temporary; between January and February, the number of people attaching importance to it almost doubled. The troubles of the auto industry in general and of Chrysler in particular were doubtless edging forward in public consciousness. Against the competition of these two issues, fewer mentioned inflation, even if we count mentions of the defeated budget as concern for inflation. National unity never held much of the electorate's attention. It was an elite concern, perhaps even an elite pastime. The Clark government was successful in raising the issue of government size somewhat higher on the overall agenda.

Issues are evaluated differently in different regions. Inflation is not a major problem for Atlantic Canadians—just getting a job is the most immediate problem there. As an index of economic activity engendered by the Prairie resource boom, unemployment is of even less concern than national unity in that region. The size of the government concerned the Prairies particularly, suggesting that

TABLE 12–2

PUBLIC CONCERN ABOUT ISSUES, CANADA AND REGIONS, 1979–1980

(percent)

Issue	All Canada			
	April 1979	August 1979	January 1980	February 1980
Inflation	49	50	49	36
Unemployment	27	22	10	18
Energy	3	8	15	27
Size of government	3	5	11	—
National unity	8	6	4	—
Budget	—	—	—	5
Foreign policy	—	—	—	8
Other	11	12	12	19

	Region, January 1980				
	Atlantic	Quebec	Ontario	Prairies	British Columbia
Inflation	39	55	44	52	51
Unemployment	26	12	9	2	7
Energy	13	11	19	12	15
Size of government	8	5	14	19	9
National unity	3	7	2	6	2
Other	7	10	14	17	14

Dash (—): Category not reported.

NOTE: Respondents were asked: "What do you think is the most important problem facing this country today?" except in February 1980, when the question was: "What do you think will be the most important job the new government —to be elected on February 18—will have to deal with?" Multiple responses were permitted, and nonresponses have been omitted from the table.

SOURCES: April 1979 to January 1980 reported in *Toronto Star*, February 6, 1980, p. A7. February 1980 reported in *Toronto Star*, March 1, 1980, p. B3.

Conservative partisans were the main people attending to issues promoted by the government. Government size was the second most important issue in that region, a position held by energy in Ontario and British Columbia.

Though similar data are not available for 1979, it is probable that concern over unemployment was even more regionally unbalanced than appears in the second part of table 12–2. This reinforces the analysis in chapter 3 of the impact of unemployment on that election. West of Quebec, the 1980 survey suggests a larger audience for what had been the Conservative issues of 1979, but by 1980 they were no longer Conservative issues. As can be seen in table 12–3, which repeats figures from table 3–5, the Progressive Conservative party had been rated overall as equal to the Liberals in dealing with inflation and unemployment in 1979. Linguistic breakdowns (unavailable for 1980) show that English speakers had rated Conservatives far ahead of Liberals on these issues. By 1980 the preference for the Liberals over the Conservatives on these issues was so large that it probably extended to English speakers as well. Even the NDP was rated even with, or slightly ahead of, Conservatives on unemployment. Energy and national unity had been Liberal issues in 1979. They remained so in 1980.

TABLE 12–3

PARTY PERCEIVED AS BEST ON ISSUES, 1979–1980

(percent)

Issue	Lib.	PC	NDP	Other, None, Don't Know
Inflation				
January 1980	29	22	14	34
May 1979	24	26	14	37
Unemployment				
January 1980	29	18	20	33
May 1979	24	24	17	36
National unity				
January 1980	48	18	7	26
May 1979	45	21	7	27
Energy				
January 1980	33	20	16	31
May 1979	29	20	11	40

SOURCE: Canadian Institute of Public Opinion, release of January 23, 1980.

TABLE 12–4

ATTITUDES TOWARD PARTY LEADERS, CANADA AND REGIONS,
1979–1980
(percent)

| | All Canada | | |
Leader	November 1979	December 1979	January 1980
Trudeau			
Yes	65	73	64
No	28	21	27
Clark			
Yes	32	28	24
No	52	57	62
Broadbent			
Yes	64	60	57
No	10	13	12

| | Region, December 1979 | | | | |
	Atlantic	Quebec	Ontario	Prairies	British Columbia
Trudeau					
Yes	76	87	73	62	57
No	16	10	24	31	33
Clark					
Yes	29	20	25	46	31
No	57	59	62	45	53
Broadbent					
Yes	71	45	65	63	64
No	7	10	16	15	17

NOTE: The question for Clark was: "Are you satisfied or dissatisfied with the job Joe Clark has been doing as prime minister?" For the other two leaders, the question was: "Do you think _____ is or is not a good leader of the _____ party?" "Don't know" was omitted from the table but not from the percentage base.

SOURCE: Canadian Institute of Public Opinion, releases of December 3, 1979, January 9, 1980, and January 26, 1980, for the three months respectively.

Liberals also had, in Pierre Trudeau, a highly respected party leader, though he was not the leader with the most independent impact. Ed Broadbent was his equal in November 1979 in popular satisfaction, and he provoked much less dissatisfaction (see table 12–4). His party was quite right to center its advertising on him. On balance, his image was the most positive of the three leaders' though it fell somewhat over the three months November 1979 through January 1980. Broadbent's support, moreover, was virtually the same in all the regions of English Canada. Trudeau's performance was judged positively across the country, but he was clearly more highly thought of in the East than in the West.

Like Pierre Trudeau, Joe Clark did best in his home region; but unlike the other leaders, Clark's best was none too good. As many in the country were dissatisfied as were satisfied with his performance as prime minister. Support fell, moreover, and opposition increased during the three-month period (of which only the last month was based on postbudget interviewing). In central Canada, three times as many were dissatisfied as satisfied.

It would seem from table 12–5 that Trudeau received more respect for his prime ministerial qualities than Broadbent, but these figures must be compared with those in table 12–1. Trudeau's supporters for "best prime minister" may have been slightly more numerous in each region than identifiers with his party, but the sets of figures between the two tables are statistically indistinguishable. This is in some contrast to 1979, when Trudeau ran ahead of the Liberal party in the Prairies and in British Columbia. In contrast, Broadbent was clearly ahead of his party from Ontario eastward. Identification with the NDP in 1980 was at 5 percent in Quebec, 12 percent in the Atlantic region, and 16 percent in Ontario. Support for Broadbent as likely to make the best prime minister of Canada was at 11, 20, and 24 percent respectively. This was quite different from the situation the previous year, when Broadbent's popularity exceeded his party's only in the Atlantic provinces. Except for Trudeau in Quebec, Broadbent was the only leader whose popularity increased between the two elections.

Support for Joe Clark as prime minister had never been strong, and estimates of his ability were probably shaped by partisanship. Only in British Columbia can one say that there were, in 1979, more people who liked Clark than supported the Conservative party. In contrast to the response to the question about satisfaction with Clark's performance as prime minister, estimates of his ability to be prime minister remained essentially unchanged—with one very significant exception. In Ontario one-quarter of the voters in 1979 thought he would be best; seven months later this had fallen to one-fifth. He ran behind his party, again comparing tables 12–1 and 12–5, in the Atlantic provinces, Ontario, and the Prairie provinces. This is very dangerous for a minority party. The difference between Trudeau's support and Clark's support was largely what we might expect

TABLE 12–5

LEADER PERCEIVED AS BEST PRIME MINISTER,
CANADA AND REGIONS, 1979–1980

(percent)

	Trudeau	Clark	Broadbent
All Canada			
January 1980	45	18	20
May 1979	43	21	11
Atlantic			
January 1980	41	22	20
May 1979	48	17	13
Quebec			
January 1980	66	5	11
May 1979	59	8	6
Ontario			
January 1980	41	19	24
May 1979	36	27	11
Prairies			
January 1980	29	30	18
May 1979	31	30	11
British Columbia			
January 1980	28	26	30
May 1979	36	26	19

NOTE: Respondents were asked: "Forgetting for a moment which political party you happen to prefer or like right now, which of the following do you feel would make the best prime minister for Canada today?" "Don't know" and "no answer" were omitted from the table.

SOURCES: For 1979, questions commissioned by the *Toronto Star* for the May Gallup poll; results published in the *Toronto Star*, May 13, 1979, p. A26. For 1980, Canadian Institute of Public Opinion, release of January 23, 1980.

between any Liberal and Conservative leader. But, where Trudeau added marginally to his party's support, Clark subtracted slightly from his. The 1979 and 1980 elections should confirm that Canadian elections are not decided on personality. The truism remains: in close contests even small advantages are important. In Quebec and Ontario, the Progressive Conservatives were at a disadvantage in having the third most popular leader. As he himself complained, with much justification, these levels of esteem stemmed from image problems that were in part induced by the media. It will take more detailed surveys to decide where to apportion the blame for the Conservatives' loss. Certainly their government had taken or proposed a number of actions to which central Canadians might strongly object. Surveys may find, however, that their objection was not so much to actions as to personal style. For these, it is less fair to attach the blame to Clark.

The Traditional Majority Returns to Power

During the eighty years of this century, the Liberal party has formed the government for fifty-seven. In the thirty-five years since World War II, Liberals have been out of office for less than seven. Thanks especially to its hold on Quebec voters, the Liberal party is by far the strongest party in the country. The Liberals did not really have to win the 1980 election—it had been won many generations ago—all they needed was not to lose it. We have seen that Liberal campaign strategy was largely based on this premise. The strategy worked.

The Liberals now have 147 of the 282 seats in the House of Commons. Surely it is meanness, then, to say that they did not really win. Yet the evidence shows the limits of the victory. In the first place, it was hardly a joyous acclamation. At somewhat less than 70 percent, turnout was at its lowest since 1953. The party increased its share of the vote from 40 to 44 percent, about on a par with its share in other recent majority victories, and this can be accounted for largely by Quebec. As we see in figure 12–2, Trudeau should be immensely gratified by the support of his home province. The Liberal vote increased from 54 percent in 1974 to 62 percent in 1979 to 68 percent in 1980. Not since 1917 and 1921, when Quebec first moved massively to the Liberal party over the issue of conscription, has its popularity been so high in the province. In Ontario, support for Trudeau, as though determined by some downward ratchet, never seems to come back from a loss to quite the level of his earlier popularity. In 1968 Liberal support in Ontario was almost 47 percent. It fell to 38 percent in 1972, returned to 45 percent in 1974, fell to 36 percent in 1979, and reached only 42 percent in 1980.

More provinces were like Ontario than like Quebec, and this qualifies the endorsement given the Liberals by their victory. From Manitoba eastward, the Liberal party made gains of five or six percentage points. Only New Brunswick joined Quebec in giving the Liberals more than a 1 percent gain over 1974. The strength of the Liberals is significantly less than it was in 1974 in four provinces, Ontario, Saskatchewan, Alberta, and British Columbia. No Liberals were elected in the last three provinces.

The Progressive Conservative party lost in all provinces but Newfoundland, where the NDP was unable to consolidate its spec-

FIGURE 12-2
MAJOR PARTY VOTE, CANADA AND PROVINCES, 1974–1980

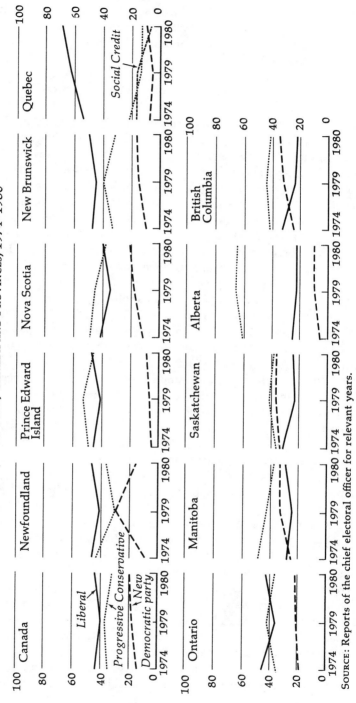

SOURCE: Reports of the chief electoral officer for relevant years.

380

tacular 1979 gain and fell back by twelve points, seven of them going to the Conservatives. If the 1979 election really seemed to be two, one in Quebec and one elsewhere, so did the 1980 election. In 1980 the boundary was between Manitoba and Saskatchewan: west of that, no party's fortunes changed very much; east of that, the Progressive Conservative loss was at least five points. By far the largest segment of this loss went to the Liberal party.

Overall, the Progressive Conservative party fell slightly short of its 1974 percentage, but provincial differences are noteworthy. In three provinces, Newfoundland, Nova Scotia, and Manitoba, the party suffered losses of eight, nine, and ten points respectively. In Prince Edward Island, too, it lost ground, though not quite so seriously. These are four of the six poorest provinces of Canada. In the other two, Quebec and New Brunswick, the party was already at historic lows. For a long time, the only really rich province had been Ontario. It was later joined by British Columbia, then by Alberta and Saskatchewan. In those four provinces, the Progressive Conservative party was in a much healthier position, though even here one must make distinctions. In the two westernmost provinces, British Columbia and Alberta, the party was at historic highs, only slightly below the levels of the previous year. In the other two, the party was slightly above its 1974 vote but, as we shall see, not at any notable level of strength. At present the Progressive Conservative party is unchallenged only in Alberta. It is still typically second to the Liberals in Ontario and only slightly ahead of the NDP in Saskatchewan and British Columbia.

In the last two federal elections, the Canadian Labour Congress actively sought to direct the votes of trade unionists to the New Democratic party. From the aggregate data, its attempts seem to have had only minor impact. In the most heavily unionized province, Ontario, the party gained but a single point over 1979 and only three points over 1974. Though its gain over 1974 in British Columbia has been impressive, that year was an unusually bad one for the NDP, and present levels of support are not much above normal levels. Where the support has grown has been in the poor (and less unionized) provinces: since 1974 the NDP has gained more than six points in Newfoundland, Nova Scotia, New Brunswick, and Manitoba. In none has it made as spectacular a gain as its twenty-point increase in Newfoundland between 1974 and 1979. The last could not be maintained, but NDP support in the three large Atlantic provinces is now likely to stabilize at just under a fifth of the total vote cast. The NDP is traditionally strong in Manitoba, where it now enjoys a third of the vote. The NDP also enjoyed a four-point gain in Quebec between 1979 and 1980, but it is too early to determine if that can be kept. Certainly in provincial politics Quebec can sustain a strong social democratic party. If the major cultural aspirations and fears that underlie support of the Parti Québécois could be met, that strength might be transferable to the NDP in the federal arena.

Better perspective on these results can be gained from the data in table 12–6, which make it possible to compare 1980 with the postwar high and average vote for each of the three parties. Two trends are immediately discernible: an east-west bifurcation in support of the major parties and a steady growth in support for the New Democratic party. Though its support is spreading, it is hardly more national than the other parties. The Liberals are clearly the party of French Canada; they are at, or just below, their postwar peak in both Quebec and New Brunswick, where a third of the population is French speaking. But they are also the party of the poorer eastern provinces more generally. To be sure, the Progressive Conservative party remains competitive with the Liberals in Prince Edward Island and Nova Scotia, but in both the Conservatives are almost at their postwar low points, as they are also in New Brunswick.

Ontario support for the Liberal party in 1980 is about average, somewhat closer to its postwar high than to its postwar low. The Liberals benefited from the vote swing between 1979 and 1980 and made a net gain of twenty seats—almost two-thirds of their total gain. West of Ontario the picture is rather bleak for the Liberals. Though the party is somewhat above its postwar low, support in 1980 was everywhere below average and well below the highs that had once been possible. In the three Prairie provinces, these highs are almost ancient history, dating from 1949 or 1953; they belong to a previous generation of voters. In British Columbia, however, the high was achieved in 1968 in Trudeau's first election as party leader. It is too early to conclude that the Liberals are extinct in British Columbia, though like the exotic vegetation in that province they will need special care.

The data for the Progressive Conservative party are largely the mirror image of this. Their 1979 and 1980 vote in the East was the lowest since 1945 and far below the postwar average. The party is weakened but by no means moribund in the poorer eastern provinces. It obtained below average support in Ontario in 1980. Its growth from its low point is impressive in each of the four western provinces. In Manitoba, Saskatchewan, and British Columbia, the provinces with a strong social democratic tradition, the Conservatives have been unable to consolidate their postwar highs. The populism of

TABLE 12-6

Party Share of the Vote, by Province, through Thirteen Elections, 1945–1980
(percent)

Province	Liberal				Progressive Conservative				New Democratic Party			
	Average	High	Low	1980	Average	High	Low	1980	Average	High	Low	1980
Newfoundland[a]	51	72	41	47	34	53	28	36	7[b]	29	1	17
Prince Edward Island	45	51	38	47	51	62	46	46	4[c]	7	2	7
Nova Scotia	43	53	34	40	46	57	37	39	11	21	5	21
New Brunswick	47	54	43	50	42	54	32	32	5[d]	16	4	16
Quebec	50	68	40	68	23	50	8	13	7[d]	12	4	9
Ontario	42	47	33	42	40	56	32	36	17	22	11	22
Manitoba	32	48	23	28	38	57	22	38	25	33	17	33
Saskatchewan	28	44	20	24	35	54	12	39	33	44	18	36
Alberta	25	35	14	22	44	66	15	65	9	18	4	10
British Columbia	29	42	16	22	31	49	14	41	31	35	22	35

[a] Became part of Canada in 1949.
[b] Contested nine elections.
[c] Contested ten elections.
[d] Contested eight elections.

Sources: For 1980, calculated from Chief Electoral Officer, *Preliminary Statistics of the 1980 General Election* (Ottawa, 1980), table 9. Other figures calculated from Hugh G. Thorburn, ed., *Party Politics in Canada*, 4th ed. (Scarborough, Ont.: Prentice-Hall, 1978), appendix.

John Diefenbaker had attracted bearers of that tradition, but subsequent leaders have not had the same breadth of appeal.

In 1980 the New Democratic party pushed its support to postwar highs in six provinces. Only Quebec, Alberta, Newfoundland, and Saskatchewan, the first two becoming one-party provinces, failed to join this movement. Even there, NDP support in 1980 was at average levels. The NDP does not, however, "own" any province in the way that the other parties do. Many of its greatest improvements over average performance came in provinces where the party started from a very low base. It is not in a position to threaten the other parties seriously for seats in the six eastern provinces.

The election results did not reflect either the innovation or the drama involved in the abrupt fall of a new government and the new fiscal and social policy orientations that had provoked that fall. The results were consistent with general trends and with the basic divisions within each province. Though the Gallup poll underestimated overall support for the Progressive Conservative party, we have no strong evidence that the high drama during the campaign—the smuggling out of the Teheran hostages—had any great impact on the electorate. At best, it firmed up hard-core support and may have dispelled some of the doubts Conservatives had about their own party leaders.

To confirm these impressions of a reorganization of the party system along an "economically prosperous/economically depressed" cleavage, it is useful to examine a finer unit of aggregation than the province. Tables 12–7 to 12–9 give the same shifts as tables 3–7 to 3–9, but for the full period 1974–1980. In effect, they suggest how the base of support for this Liberal government differs from the base for the previous one. At the same time, they allow us to test the proposition that the 1979 election was an idiosyncratic interlude in an otherwise unchanging party system. If that were true and if the 1980 election simply restored the status quo ante, all the 1974–1980 shifts should be close to zero, and there should be no consistent trends by language or by unemployment and homeownership.

We look at language in table 12–7. In 1979 linguistic effects differed. In Quebec, the Liberals gained most (and Conservatives and NDP lost most) in the less French constituencies. Outside that province the effect was reversed, and a strong French-speaking presence inhibited the flow of support to the Progressive Conservative party. When the full period 1974–1980 is considered, this divergence of pattern disappears. The more Francophone a constituency, the larger the Liberal gain from 1974 to 1980. Outside Quebec, there is evidence of strong linguistic polarization. Liberals in 1980 were

TABLE 12-7

CHANGE IN PARTY SUPPORT, BY LINGUISTIC COMPOSITION
OF CONSTITUENCY, 1974–1980
(percentage points)

French Speakers in Constituency	Lib.	PC	NDP	SC	Number of Constituencies
Quebec					
Less than 67 percent	+11	−11	+1	−4	(14)
More than 67 percent	+15	−8	+3	−13	(61)
Rest of Canada					
Less than 10 percent	−4	−1	+5	−1	(180)
10–25 percent	0	−4	+4	−1	(13)
More than 25 percent	+4	−2	+4	−3	(14)

NOTE: Changes may not add to zero because other candidates are omitted.
SOURCES: Calculated from unpublished data on the 1974 and 1980 elections supplied by the chief electoral officer of Canada. Constituency language data taken from the 1976 census, Statistics Canada, *1976 Census of Canada* (Ottawa: Ministry of Supply and Services, 1978), Bulletin 1.9.

still short of their 1974 support in the most English-speaking areas but were ahead of 1974 in areas with relatively high concentrations of French speakers. Comparison of table 12–7 with table 3–7 suggests that the 1979–1980 gains, though general, were largest among French speakers and were drawn from the Conservatives.

As in 1974–1979, there are no strong trends for the other parties for the period 1974–1980. Liberal gains and losses were quite catholic in source and direction. No party was particularly involved, with the unsurprising exception of heavy Social Credit losses to the Liberals in the Francophone Quebec constituencies, the areas where the party had the most to lose.

In comparing areas of Canada with very high male unemployment with more prosperous constituencies in 1979, we found a trend to polarization. The Liberals lost least between 1974 and 1979 and the NDP gained most in the worst-hit areas, while trends in Progressive Conservative support were the reverse of this. Table 12–8 shows that the trend is confirmed, even strengthened, for Liberal and Conservative support in 1980. The 1980 election did not simply restore the status quo. Over the six-year period, the Liberals remain net losers in areas of low unemployment and large net gainers in areas of high unemployment. The Progressive Conservative party loses in all classes of constituency but loses most in disfavored areas. The disappearance of the Créditistes produces a profile for them like

TABLE 12–8

Change in Party Support, in Constituencies with Low, Medium, and High Unemployment, Canada and Regions, 1974–1980

(percentage points)

Unemployment Level	Lib.	PC	NDP	SC	Number of Constituencies
All Canada					
Low	−1	−1	+4	−2	(102)
Medium	+2	−4	+5	−4	(150)
High	+6	−6	+6	−8	(30)
Atlantic					
Low	—	—	—	—	(0)
Medium	−1	−4	+8	[a]	(18)
High	+3	−7	+6	−2	(14)
Quebec					
Low	+16	−12	+3	−10	(13)
Medium	+14	−9	+2	−11	(50)
High	+15	−5	+2	−15	(12)
Ontario					
Low	−4	+1	+3	[a]	(43)
Medium	−2	−1	+3	[a]	(52)
High	—	—	—	—	(0)
Prairies					
Low	−3	[a]	+4	−2	(43)
Medium	+1	−9	+9	−1	(6)
High	—	—	—	—	(0)
British Columbia					
Low	−5	−4	+9	0	(1)
Medium	−12	[a]	+12	−1	(23)
High	−9	−2	+13	−2	(4)

Note: "Low," up to 4.9 percent male unemployment according to the 1976 census; "medium," 5.0 to 9.9 percent; "high," 10 percent or more. Neither Ontario nor the Prairies had constituencies of high male unemployment as defined here, and the Atlantic region had no low unemployment.

[a] Less than 0.5.

Sources: As for table 12-7.

that of the Conservatives, though this is somewhat misleading. The collapse of the Créditistes arose less from abandonment of the party for economic reasons than from its problems of leadership and organization.

An examination of the data disaggregated into regions qualifies the conclusion. Outside Quebec the trend is as it has been seen: toward abandonment of the Liberal party in areas of below average unemployment, a generally stronger attachment to the party in less favored areas, and reorganization of Conservative support in complementary fashion. In both instances the disaggregated shifts of votes are far from dramatic. The overall figures are produced more by movements in regions as a whole than by local characteristics. This is not true for western Canada, however. There it is the NDP rather than the Liberal party that is favored in areas of high unemployment and does less well in more fortunate parts of the regions.

Assessing the Quebec data is made more difficult by the disappearance of the Créditistes. If Progressive Conservative losses are added to theirs, a defection of about 20 percent of voters in each set of constituencies is found. About the same proportion of these drifting voters is netted by the Liberals, whatever the employment status of the area. The 1974–1980 movement confirms that of 1974–1979 for the Conservatives, however: during both periods, the party was more successful in holding its vote in disadvantaged areas than in prosperous areas.

Table 12–9 shows that movement associated with the issues of property-tax deductibility was a "one-election" wonder. In chapter 3, dealing with the 1979 election, a suggestive correlation was found: areas of high homeownership, especially in the wealthier parts of Canada from Ontario westward, showed particularly strong movement to the Progressive Conservative party. This was all lost during the next year. In aggregate, Progressive Conservative support in Ontario was slightly stronger in 1980 than in 1974, but this is completely unrelated to the homeownership variable. West of Ontario, Conservatives in 1980 were ahead of their support in 1974 in all provinces but Manitoba. Looking generally at the regions, some residual trace of a possible "homeownership" effect supporting the Conservatives is found, but it is very much weaker than in 1979.

Overall, then, the apparent class reorganization of Canadian politics that seemed to surface briefly in the 1979 election has proved, as was suggested in chapter 3, to be a regional reorganization. There are, of course, class issues, and there are certainly differences among Canadians in wealth and other advantages. The sense of regional community is strong, however, since regional economies are highly interrelated. Any class cleavage, therefore, will for a long time be first an interregional cleavage. There has been a quite dramatic reorganization of regional attachments to Canadian parties, as was shown in figure 12–2. The data in tables 12–8 and 12–9, along with data on Liberal and NDP shifts by home-owning status, show some trace of intraregional cleavage as well. This is, however, very much at the "first swallow" stage of political development.

TABLE 12–9

CHANGE IN PROGRESSIVE CONSERVATIVE VOTE, BY HOMEOWNERSHIP
AND REGION, 1974–1980
(percentage points)

Proportion of Homeowners in Constituency in 1976	Change in PC Vote	Number of Constituencies
Atlantic		
Less than 60 percent	−7	(4)
60–75 percent	+3	(6)
75 percent and over	−8	(22)
Ontario		
Less than 60 percent	−1	(28)
60–75 percent	a	(44)
75 percent and over	a	(23)
Prairies		
Less than 60 percent	−3	(8)
60–75 percent	−2	(20)
75 percent and over	+1	(21)
British Columbia		
Less than 60 percent	−4	(5)
60–75 percent	+1	(16)
75 percent and over	−1	(7)
Quebec[b]		
Less than 33.3 percent	−13	(18)
33.3–66.7 percent	−7	(29)
More than 66.7 percent	−7	(28)

[a] Less than 0.5.
[b] Different cutting points are used for Quebec because barely 50 percent of dwellings in the province were owned by occupants in 1976.
SOURCES: As for table 12-7.

Canadian Problems and the Trudeau Government

Elections not only register movement along the fault lines of a society. They also produce the teams that will have to govern (and to criticize the government of) the society. In the first chapter of this volume, Alan Cairns pointed out that the Canadian electoral system is a particularly faulty instrument for linking a society to its government. The sensitivity of the electoral system was no more acute in 1980 than in 1979. Table 12–10 describes the regional distribution of party caucuses in the Thirty-first and Thirty-second parliaments.

TABLE 12–10
DISTRIBUTION OF PARLIAMENTARY SEATS, BY PARTY, 1979 AND 1980

Province	1979				1980				Total
	Lib.	PC	NDP	SC	Lib.	PC	NDP	SC	
Newfoundland	4	2	1	0	5	2	0	0	7
Prince Edward Island	0	4	0	0	2	2	0	0	4
Nova Scotia	2	8	1	0	5	6	0	0	11
New Brunswick	6	4	0	0	7	3	0	0	10
Quebec	67	2	0	6	74	1	0	0	75
Ontario	32	57	6	0	52	38	5	0	95
Manitoba	2	7	5	0	2	5	7	0	14
Saskatchewan	0	10	4	0	0	7	7	0	14
Alberta	0	21	0	0	0	21	0	0	21
British Columbia	1	19	8	0	0	16	12	0	28
Yukon, Northwest Territories	0	2	1	0	0	2	1	0	3
Total	114	136	26	6	147	103	32	0	282

SOURCE: Chief Electoral Officer, *Reports on the 1979 and 1980 General Elections* (Ottawa, 1980), table 6 in each report.

It is immediately apparent that the regionalization of major party support just examined is badly exaggerated at the level of parliamentary seats. It is at least a plausible hypothesis that the effect at the one level strengthens that at the other. In addition, the New Democratic party got very little representation in 1979 for its increased support in Atlantic Canada and lost even those seats in 1980.[30]

The first constant, then, is that Canadian governments cannot find, in their own ranks, spokesmen for the various conflicts affecting Canada. Alan Cairns commented that the 1979 election produced a government that had to "confront the nationalist demands of the Parti Québécois with the fewest Quebec members of any government party since 1867." Quebec is now well represented. As can be seen from table 12–10, it makes up more than half the government caucus. Quebec also supplies twelve of the thirty-three cabinet ministers, as many as Ontario. But Cairns's characterization of the Clark government needs only small modification to be applied to the

---

[30] One of the quirks of our electoral system is that the NDP managed to lose a seat in both Nova Scotia and Ontario despite increasing its vote. The NDP also lost its seat in Newfoundland and so has no member of Parliament from east of Ontario despite its improved showing.

current one. The Trudeau government must negotiate the economic and other grievances of the West with the fewest western members of any government since that area gained parliamentary representation. The Liberals elected only two members west of Ontario—both of them from greater Winnipeg and one representing a constituency with a large French Canadian minority. The West has only four members in the Trudeau cabinet, one for each province.[31] In three of the cases, Trudeau had to follow the Clark strategy of naming nonelected senators to his cabinet to represent provinces where the Liberals had failed to elect anyone.

There is, of course, no difficulty in finding out what the grievances are. Provincial premiers are only too eager to make them known. Opposition members in the federal Parliament do the same in only slightly more muted terms. The difficulty lies in fashioning a response to these complaints in ways consistent with the partisan history and, even more crucial, with the partisan interest of the government. This can only come from the party itself—in caucus and cabinet—and obviously cannot come easily in the situations of the present and past governments. Grievances are only partly attributable to policy failures, moreover; quite often they arise from the centralist bias of the federal public service, headed by a minister who is himself insensitive to local complaints about the administration of government programs. A minister with roots in the West and sensitive to its views of federal practices might do much to reduce western alienation, even in the absence of substantial policy change. None of the present western ministers, because of their inexperience or because they are senators, has been given major administrative responsibilities. The situation was not much different in the Clark cabinet. The present electoral system robs governments of talent and sensitivity, as well as policy advice.

Moreover, even if the federal government is able to devise a national policy that does take the needs of particular regions into account, it is hard for it to defend that policy in the regions where it is weak. It has no one with a local political base to make the arguments against the more province-centered views of the premiers. The federal opposition is hardly likely to do so. The result is that the federal cabinet stresses the need for a strong federal government but has to defend its claim with a personnel that lacks acceptance, possibly even lacks trust, in some regions. Given Canada's constitutional evolution, it is impossible to prevent provincial premiers from making policy that has countrywide implications. Their constitutional

---

[31] The Atlantic provinces have five ministers in the cabinet.

powers guarantee them such a role. The situation is aggravated, however, when these premiers are the only power holders accepted as legitimate, as they are now in the West and were in Quebec during the Clark government. No recent Canadian government has had within its own ranks the capacity to deal legitimately with all three of the cleavages discussed at the outset of this chapter.

The new Liberal government has no problem in arguing its case on the issues separating English-speaking and French-speaking Canadians. This cleavage is now front and center. Shortly after Trudeau resumed the prime ministership on March 3, 1980, Lévesque inaugurated a prescribed period of debate in the Quebec legislature on the question he planned to submit to Quebecers by referendum. In the judgment of reporters, the Parti Québécois got the better of the provincial Liberal party in that debate.

The referendum campaign itself, begun on April 15, 1980, and limited by law to thirty-five days ending on May 20, 1980, was fought by two committees. It seemed that the "yes" committee had every advantage: its members were unified (at least for the first stage); the question asked little enough so that the cautious could still be comfortable;[32] and the committee initially seemed to monopolize the claim to French Québécois pride and solidarity. Indeed, as the referendum campaign progressed, the "yes" campaign was focused more and more on themes of solidarity, the need for the bargaining power that a mandate would confer, and the need to break the constitutional logjam. What concrete results it would seek with this solidarity and bargaining power faded more and more into the background of the "oui" campaign.

The committee for the "no" tried desperately to keep the substance in the forefront and to paint it in the most strident colors. They claimed that the "yes" forces wanted sovereignty primarily to destroy Canada, and in doing so were recklessly denying Quebecers their

---

[32] The official English translation of the referendum question was as follows:
The Government of Québec has made public its proposal to negotiate a new agreement with the rest of Canada, based on the equality of nations; this agreement would enable Québec to acquire the exclusive power to make its laws, levy its taxes and establish relations abroad—in other words, sovereignty—and at the same time, to maintain with Canada an economic association including a common currency; no change in political status resulting from these negotiations will be effected without approval by the people through another referendum; on these terms, do you give the government of Québec the mandate to negotiate the proposed agreement between Québec and Canada?
The promise of the second referendum to ratify the agreement was the only unexpected feature. It was clearly designed to persuade the cautious that they had little to lose by voting "yes" this time.

heritage as Canadians. Prime Minister Trudeau spoke four times in Quebec during the referendum campaign: once as prime minister of Canada and three times as a Quebecer participating under the umbrella of the "no" committee. He was clearly at the height of his form and was able to appeal emotionally to Quebecers, as well as to explain their interest in remaining part of Canada. More important, he dedicated himself to the process of constitutional change and pledged that the Liberals from Quebec would resign their seats if it were not brought to a rapid and successful conclusion.

These pages are being written after the May 20, 1980, referendum. The "non" won a more striking victory than most of the polls had predicted. More than 59 percent of Quebecers voted not to give the Parti Québécois government a mandate to negotiate a loose confederal association with the rest of Canada. A margin so large means that a majority, slim to be sure, of French-speaking Quebecers must have voted "non." Non-French Quebecers did so with virtual unanimity. The Parti Québécois still claimed the support of the most vital members of the Francophone community but conceded defeat and expressed willingness to participate loyally in discussions for constitutional reorganization. As Premier Lévesque said in his concession, the ball was now in the federalist court.

It will not be an easy one to play. In the sixteen months since his election, Prime Minister Trudeau has been the only committed French Canadian federalist at the bargaining table. His legislative action on the constitution has provoked dissent in and outside Quebec. His views on Canadian federalism, and on the place of the French within Canada, differ greatly from those of other Québécois political leaders, even the other federalists. His views are strongly liberal and pluralist. Government must seek to develop not one but two flourishing cultures in Canada, while protecting the civil rights of all Canadians and the freedom of Canadians to choose in which culture they will live. In more concerte terms, he seeks to guarantee to Canadians from coast to coast an effective right to choose the language of instruction, English or French, for their children.

This is difficult to sell to almost all the other participants. English Canadian premiers, whose provincial French minorities have been eroded by assimilation and whose electorates may include more Italians or Ukrainians or Orientals than French, appear unwilling to spend either the money or the political capital needed to give reality to the Trudeau vision of Canada. But perhaps the most resistant are French Quebecers themselves. Public opinion polls in Quebec consistently show that the leading demand made of a "renewed federalism" is more cultural rights for the province. Quebecers accept the demographers' projections that the province will become a smaller and smaller segment of the Canadian population. There is probably also a quite widespread fear that, without an active cultural policy on the part of the provincial government, French speakers could be seriously weakened within Quebec itself.[33] These views, reflecting and feeding their basic anxiety about survival as a people, lead to fundamental resistance to erecting a constitutional shield to protect cultural rights from provincial majorities. Prime Minister Trudeau has already announced that constitutional protection of language rights is not negotiable. Premier Lévesque's position is that he is duty bound to protect the fundamental rights that French Quebecers now possess. Of these a large measure of cultural autonomy is probably the most crucial. The referendum has changed nothing in this basic conflict, and both sides try to claim mandates from the referendum campaign. Furthering the constitutional protection of access by Canadians to English-language institutions in Quebec will provoke a monumental battle, even if the package includes corresponding rights for the French outside Quebec. These are no longer highly valued by the Québécois.

During the referendum campaign, politicians from outside Quebec stressed their commitment to change. They greeted the victory of the "non" with a promise to Quebecers that they would not now simply go back to sleep. These leaders realize that they must use the current breathing spell to persuade Quebecers that their vote was not a mistake. In federal and provincial meetings following the referendum, however, the demands of other parts of Canada were also brought to the negotiating table. This meant that the cleavage between provinces enriched by oil prices and those becoming poorer became intertwined with the cultural one.

There are a number of dangers in this. Progress on one front almost inevitably becomes hostage to progress on the other. Western premiers, whose populations are least likely to see the necessity of expanding French language rights outside Quebec, demanded a strengthening of economic powers for the provinces. Ontario, which strongly backs Trudeau's constitutional change, is also a major backer of his second nonnegotiable position: a federal government with important economic powers. Though Quebec is a major consumer of energy, its provincial premier preferred to back western economic demands in return for western support on his cultural positions. At a policy level, the two cleavages are thus brought together with a

---

[33] This is a subject of considerable debate among demographers, but popular fears do not always wait for academic consensus.

confrontation of Quebec and the West against Ottawa, Ontario, and New Brunswick. To break the impasse, Trudeau is fighting a constitutional package through the federal Parliament, the Supreme Court, and the British Parliament. As already noted, the Liberal government can carry its point of view effectively into the Quebec segment of its opponents' camp. It cannot do so with anywhere near the same authority in the West. It will take imagination and rapid movement to assuage western grievances at a policy level and to overcome the feelings engendered by the constitutional debate. These have already stimulated western separatist movements whose growth has so far been hampered by a lack of effective leadership.

The third cleavage—in shorthand the class cleavage—is not effectively represented at the constitutional bargaining table. Indeed, the interests of workers as workers and unionists have never been strongly represented in Canada. As we have seen, the Liberal party has reaped benefit from its representation of poorer Canadians: the aged, residents of the Atlantic provinces, and small primary or secondary producers in eastern Canada. None of these beneficiaries are highly organized.

They are partly represented by the forces for a strong federal government. Strength is defined in part by redistributive capacity. Should questions of the powers of federal and provincial governments be negotiated, the Liberal cabinet will insist on retaining federal power to redistribute from richer to poorer provinces and from active, employed Canadians to older, unemployed Canadians. Having the capacity is one thing, using it quite another. At the outset of this chapter, I speculated that Canada is entering an era of strong pressure for cutting current consumption and diverting it to investment in productive capacity for industry and for energy generation. Governments are unlikely to be able to resist the trend, but it may be assumed that they will follow paths of least resistance.

This would mean that the least well organized groups will have their consumption cut most sharply. They would then be motivated to organize more extensively. If real consumption by current workers is threatened, it is possible that Canada will be pushed to follow the European route and develop councils representative of workers and owners of corporations. Redistribution from rich to poor provinces will be incorporated in a new constitution, but welfare, pensions, and unemployment insurance will continue to be subject to a political process wherein the recipients are poorly organized. It is possible that the Liberal government will return to the Progressive Conservative strategy of more precise allocation of welfare payments, a strategy the Liberals themselves began with child tax credits. This, however, would do considerable violence to the tradition of the Liberal party. The whole issue is emerging on the current intergovernmental agenda, and the Liberal government will resist the attack on interpersonal redistribution, at least in the short run. It will, however, seek more political credit for its health, welfare, and educational expenditures.

This was clearly foreshadowed in the Throne Speech of the Trudeau government. Read in mid-April, the speech emphasized sharing wealth, increasing the guaranteed income of the elderly, and calling a pension conference "to design better methods of providing flexible, portable and secure pensions both in the private and public sectors." This was much more prominent than the investment concern. The federal government did promise to reduce its deficit, but not to the exclusion of fighting unemployment.

Still, no government can ignore investment considerations. The Throne Speech spoke of producing new domestic energy, switching from oil to gas, improving the transportation infrastructure, and increasing research and development. Any government that promotes investment, either by subsidy or by permitting very large profits on easily extracted energy, is bound to ask who will own and control the assets. The investment-consumption cleavage inevitably brings into question the issue of foreign (primarily American) ownership in Canada. The Throne Speech raised this question in calling for at least 50 percent Canadian ownership of the petroleum industry by 1990, the use of government procurement to encourage Canadian-owned enterprises, a strengthening of the Foreign Investment Review Act, and assistance to Canadian corporations bidding against foreign ones for control of Canadian assets.

Simply raising issues does not indicate how they will be resolved. Perhaps one clue to the government's stance on the nationalist aspect of this third cleavage can be gained from its action on the Chrysler issue. This company is a major employer in the constituencies of no fewer than three cabinet ministers, all from the Windsor, Ontario, area. The requested assistance was given, but clearly with reluctance and after some lobbying of Ottawa by American Treasury officials. As in the United States, Chrysler's request to the Canadian and Ontario governments had to be scaled down. It was acceded to only with the proviso that the traditional ratio between employment in Canadian operations and employment in the United States be maintained. In Ontario's case, the provincial government could take over new assets built with the government funds in the event of any default.

Unlike the cultural and East-West cleavages, neither the producer-consumer aspect nor the Canadian-foreign aspect of this third division is highly institutionalized. Indeed, this is the only major cleavage adequately and primarily contained within the political parties. All sides of the division are represented within the Liberal and Progressive Conservative parties, while the nationalist, proconsumer side predominates in the NDP. Canadian parties have been celebrated as the brokers of conflict within society; for this one, they are probably up to the task, though it is much too early to forecast the shape of the bargains to be made. Throne Speeches and initial decisions provide straws in the wind, but the gusts swirling around the constitutional issues may jumble the initial disposition of these straws. Certainly, it is unlikely that there will be much active—as opposed to reactive—policy making in this area as long as the focus is on the other two.

It is too early to make confident forecasts about the future of Canadian politics. Can a final appraisal of the short-lived Progressive Conservative government be made? It can—within limits. Precisely because it was so short-lived, its capacity for adding to its voting base or the ultimate effectiveness of its strategy for resolving Canadian problems cannot be definitively appraised. Trudeau's opposition to Clark was fundamental; probably he really believed that Conservative policy and intentions would weaken the federal government. He may have been right, though Clark was quickly learning the limits of his policy of decentralization. It is still an open question, moreover, whether weakening the federal government weakens Canada. The Liberal government has substantially different goals from those of the Clark government on both the cultural and the East-West cleavages, and the differences in style are even sharper: there is likely to be much more resort to showdown tactics now than under the previous government. The probable ultimate policy differences are still unknown, and the stylistic differences, though easier to predict, are even more difficult to appraise. Judgments must therefore remain conjectural and personal.

The line that the Progressive Conservative government seemed committed to pursue will be reversed in another field also. It would probably have favored investment over consumption and the middle class over those who are slightly above poverty levels. Though probably as nationalistic as the Liberals on questions of economic ownership, it would have pursued deficit cutting, setting targets for social programs, and rapid price increases in energy.

Less controversially, the Progressive Conservative government contributed to public management and gave impetus to fuller disclosure of public business. These actions had sufficient support for the new government to be unlikely to depart fundamentally from them, and they should therefore be lasting contributions. The appointments of the Clark government will also outlive it.[34]

While political scientists may be reluctant to judge the Clark government, party activists share no such inhibition. With Clark himself continuing to fare badly in public opinion polls,[35] delegates meeting in convention at the end of February 1981 showed their impatience. The Progressive Conservative party constitution requires that a motion be put asking delegates if they wish a convention to determine who should be leader. This motion was defeated, but not by a sufficiently large margin. The two-to-one vote in Clark's favor was held by most commentators to be too small to permit him to stay in office. By May 1981, he had not resigned, but he might be forced to do so—continuing his party's sacrifices to the god of electoral victory.[36]

Inability to predict the future of Canadian politics need not preclude the raising of questions about it. This has been done at several points in the preceding pages. Two final questions might encapsulate many. Can Canadian politics be conducted in the normal manner over the next decade? It has been seen that each federal party alone can mediate only one of the three major conflicts that divide the country. There would thus seem to be a strong case for a grand coalition strategy at the federal level to devise nationally acceptable policy and subsequently promote it. Former Prime Minister Clark, for instance, campaigned effectively against the Parti Québécois referendum in Quebec. The alliances that that battle compelled could possibly be prolonged, despite differences of personal style. Alternatively, the Liberal party might seek long-term cooperation with the New Democratic party to acquire deeper roots in, and more personnel from, western Canada. This is the strategy adopted in the 1981 constitutional debate. In addition to explicit alliances for constitutional change, Canada may, in the long run, have to develop

[34] Among these, we should note that a contributor to this volume, John Meisel, was appointed chairman of the Canadian Radio-television and Telecommunications Commission.

[35] Interviewing in mid-March, the Gallup poll found 37 percent approving and 43 percent disapproving of "the way Joe Clark is handling his job as leader of the Opposition." These figures had not notably changed since September 1980 and included majority disapproval in the electorally crucial province of Ontario. See *Toronto Star*, May 6, 1981, p. A7. Note, however, that this is much more favorable than his ratings as prime minister reported in table 12-4.

[36] The Liberals may also soon have to choose a new leader. Trudeau's departure will not tear the party. It is he who wishes to go, and he will be allowed to pick the time. He has groomed no obvious successor, however, and the Liberals too will be divided, primarily on issues of economic policy and economic nationalism, but also on past loyalty to the team and its leader.

similar institutions for economic and social policy. Since the parties are still able to encompass these cleavages, however, and since the level of organization of the affected groups is low, this departure from business as usual is unlikely in the near term.

It is also open to question whether Canada has a sufficient level of community feeling to eliminate the acrimony from the bargaining that will take place. Constitutional change would be a far different process if the question were, How do we rearrange *our* affairs? Unfortunately, the question animating each participant seems to be, How much do I have to give them, and what can I get in return? A more nationalistic economic policy, *had it been pursued in the past*, might have made the first question as likely as the second. Such a policy might still capture some imaginations, but considerable time will be required before it affects the context of constitutional bargaining. Time is the scarcest resource, though trust among federal and provincial leaders is also in short supply. Though the election of February 1980 may be decisive for Canada's future, it has not made it clear what that future will be.

Appendix A

Canadian Ballots, 1979 and 1980

General election ballots in Canada's single-member districts carry the candidates' names, in alphabetical order, followed by their party affiliation. Except for parties registered in only one language (such as the separatist Union Populaire in Quebec and the Parti Rhinocéros) the party affiliation is given in both English and French, with the English first in every province but Quebec. A candidate not affiliated with a registered political party is automatically listed as an independent unless he requests that no affiliation be stated.

The front and back of the ballot used in Prince Albert, Saskatchewan, in the 1979 general election are reproduced on the next two pages. This is the last ballot to have carried the name of John Diefenbaker, prime minister of Canada from 1957 to 1963, who died in August 1979. The other three ballots reproduced here all show the proliferation of small parties and independent candidates that was under way in 1979 and became even more marked in 1980.

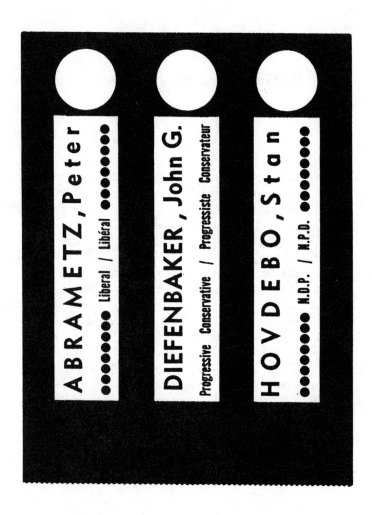

Prince Albert, Saskatchewan, 1979 (front, actual size)

400

№ 10825

№ 10825

GENERAL ELECTION
ELECTORAL DISTRICT OF
PRINCE ALBERT,
SASK.

1979

ÉLECTION GÉNÉRALE
CIRCONSCRIPTION DE
PRINCE-ALBERT
(SASK.)

POLLING DAY / JOUR DU SCRUTIN

May 22 mai 1979

Printed by: Imprimé par:

Write Way Printing Co Ltd.
24-15th Street West
Prince Albert, Saskatchewan

CANADA

Prince Albert, Saskatchewan, 1979 (back, actual size)

Rosedale, Ontario, 1979 (actual size 6″ x 11″)

Surrey–White Rock–North Delta, British Columbia, 1980 (actual size 6" x 6½")

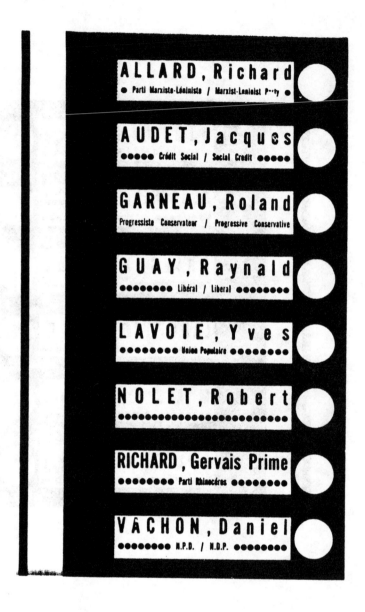

Lévis, Quebec, 1980 (actual size 6″ x 9″)

Appendix B

Canadian Election Returns, May 1979 and February 1980

Compiled by Richard M. Scammon

Election Returns, Canadian House of Commons, May 1979

Province	Total Valid Vote	Liberal	PC	NDP	Social Credit	Other[a]
Alberta	853,177	188,295	559,588	84,236	8,164	12,894
Percentage of vote		22.1	65.6	9.9	1.0	1.5
Number of seats	21	—	21	—	—	—
British Columbia	1,195,912	274,946	530,380	381,678	1,885	7,023
Percentage of vote		23.0	44.3	31.9	0.2	0.6
Number of seats	28	1	19	8	—	—
Manitoba	513,773	120,493	222,787	167,850	1,044	1,599
Percentage of vote		23.5	43.4	32.7	0.2	0.3
Number of seats	14	2	7	5	—	—
New Brunswick	337,532	150,634	134,998	51,642	—	258
Percentage of vote		44.6	40.0	15.3	—	0.1
Number of seats	10	6	4	—	—	—
Newfoundland	201,732	81,861	59,893	59,978	—	—
Percentage of vote		40.6	29.7	29.7	—	—
Number of seats	7	4	2	1	—	—
Nova Scotia	425,609	151,078	193,099	79,603	—	1,829
Percentage of vote		35.5	45.4	18.7	—	0.4
Number of seats	11	2	8	1	—	—
Ontario	4,142,995	1,509,926	1,732,717	873,182	1,002	26,168
Percentage of vote		36.4	41.8	21.1	[b]	0.6
Number of seats	95	32	57	6	—	—

Prince Edward Island	64,613	26,231	34,147	4,181	—	54
Percentage of vote		40.6	52.8	6.5	—	0.1
Number of seats	4	—	4	—	—	—
Quebec	3,204,029	1,975,526	432,199	163,492	512,995	119,817
Percentage of vote		61.7	13.5	5.1	16.0	3.7
Number of seats	75	67	2	—	6	—
Saskatchewan	489,404	106,550	201,803	175,011	2,514	3,526
Percentage of vote		21.8	41.2	35.8	0.5	0.7
Number of seats	14	—	10	4	—	—
Yukon-Northwest Territories	26,926	8,779	9,948	7,926	—	273
Percentage of vote		32.6	36.9	29.4	—	1.0
Number of seats	3	—	2	1	—	—
All Canada	11,455,702	4,594,319	4,111,559	2,048,779	527,604	173,441
Percentage of vote		40.1	35.9	17.9	4.6	1.5
Number of seats	282	114	136	26	6	—
Metropolitan Montreal	1,069,849	752,271	116,176	65,526	86,478	49,398
Percentage of vote		70.3	10.9	6.1	8.1	4.6
Number of seats	24	24	—	—	—	—
Metropolitan Toronto	1,005,244	390,196	394,505	208,174	125	12,244
Percentage of vote		38.8	39.2	20.7	b	1.2
Number of seats	23	10	12	1	—	—

[a] Includes Rhinoceros party, 62,600; Independent, 52,152; Union Populaire, 19,444; Libertarian, 15,852; Marxist-Leninist, 14,231; and Communist, 9,162.

[b] Less than 0.5 percent.

SOURCE: Canada, Ministry of Supply and Services, Thirty-first General Election 1979: Report of the Chief Electoral Officer, Ottawa, 1980.

ELECTION RETURNS, CANADIAN HOUSE OF COMMONS, FEBRUARY 1980

Province	Total Valid Vote	Liberal	PC	NDP	Social Credit	Other[a]
Alberta	795,445	176,601	516,079	81,755	8,158	12,852
Percentage of vote		22.2	64.9	10.3	1.0	1.6
Number of seats	21	—	21	—	—	—
British Columbia	1,209,812	268,262	502,088	426,858	1,763	10,841
Percentage of vote		22.2	41.5	35.3	0.1	0.9
Number of seats	28	—	16	12	—	—
Manitoba	475,904	133,253	179,607	159,434	—	3,610
Percentage of vote		28.0	37.7	33.5	—	0.8
Number of seats	14	2	5	7	—	—
New Brunswick	335,730	168,316	109,056	54,517	—	3,841
Percentage of vote		50.1	32.5	16.2	—	1.1
Number of seats	10	7	3	—	—	—
Newfoundland	203,045	95,354	72,999	33,943	—	749
Percentage of vote		47.0	36.0	16.7	—	0.4
Number of seats	7	5	2	—	—	—
Nova Scotia	422,242	168,304	163,459	88,052	—	2,427
Percentage of vote		39.9	38.7	20.9	—	0.6
Number of seats	11	5	6	—	—	—
Ontario	4,000,841	1,675,519	1,420,436	874,229	804[b]	29,853
Percentage of vote		41.9	35.5	21.9	—	0.7
Number of seats	95	52	38	5	—	—

	Total						Other[a]
Prince Edward Island							
Number of votes	66,205	31,005	30,653	4,339	—	—	208
Percentage of vote		46.8	46.3	6.6	—	—	0.3
Number of seats	4	2	2	—	—	—	—
Quebec							
Number of votes	2,957,042	2,017,156	373,317	268,409	174,583	—	123,577
Percentage of vote		68.2	12.6	9.1	5.9	—	4.2
Number of seats	75	74	1	—	—	—	—
Saskatchewan							
Number of votes	455,774	110,517	177,376	165,308	178	—	2,395
Percentage of vote		24.2	38.9	36.3	[b]	—	0.5
Number of seats	14	—	7	7	—	—	—
Yukon-Northwest Territories							
Number of votes	25,874	9,627	7,924	8,143	—	—	180
Percentage of vote		37.2	30.6	31.5	—	—	0.7
Number of seats	3	—	2	1	—	—	—
All Canada							
Number of votes	10,947,914	4,853,914	3,552,994	2,164,987	185,486	—	190,533
Percentage of vote		44.3	32.5	19.8	1.7	—	1.7
Number of seats	282	147	103	32	—	—	—
Metropolitan Montreal							
Number of votes	931,841	687,054	91,501	95,872	13,441	—	43,973
Percentage of vote		73.7	9.8	10.3	1.4	—	4.7
Number of seats	24	24	—	—	—	—	—
Metropolitan Toronto							
Number of votes	958,221	429,482	325,833	191,044	—	—	11,862
Percentage of vote		44.8	34.0	19.9	—	—	1.2
Number of seats	23	17	4	2	—	—	—

[a] Includes Rhinoceros party, 110,597; Independent, 30,067; Marxist-Leninist, 14,717; Libertarian, 14,656; Union Populaire, 14,474; and Communist, 6,022.

[b] Less than 0.5 percent.

SOURCE: Canada, Ministry of Supply and Services, *Thirty-second General Election 1980: Report of the Chief Electoral Officer*, Ottawa, 1980.

Contributors

M. Janine Brodie is assistant professor of political studies at Queen's University, Kingston, Ontario. She is the author of several articles on women in Canadian politics, the Canadian party system, and political party organization and is coauthor of *Crisis, Challenge, and Change: Party and Class in Canada*.

Alan C. Cairns is professor of political science at the University of British Columbia. He has written numerous articles on federalism and Canadian politics.

Steven Clarkson is professor in the Department of Political Economy at the University of Toronto. His most recent book is *The Soviet Theory of Development* (University of Toronto Press, 1978). Active in the Liberal party in the late 1960s and early 1970s, he is now completing a book on the Liberals under Pierre Trudeau.

John C. Courtney is professor of political science at the University of Saskatchewan. His works include *The Selection of National Party Leaders in Canada* and articles on Canadian political parties and political leadership.

Jean Crete is associate professor of political science at the Université Laval and has published articles in Canadian and French journals on urban affairs, electoral behavior, and public policy. He is coauthor and editor of *Le comportement électoral au Québec* (forthcoming).

Frederick J. Fletcher is associate professor of political science and research development officer of the Faculty of Arts at York University, Ontario. His studies of the mass media have included numerous articles and papers on public opinion, voting, and the media.

William P. Irvine is associate professor of political studies at Queen's University, Ontario. He is the author of *Does Canada Need a New Electoral System?* and has served as a consultant to the Task Force on Canadian Unity.

VINCENT LEMIEUX is professor of political science at the Université Laval. He is the author or editor of several books on Quebec political parties, elections, and patronage. His current fields of research are social networks and public policy.

JOHN MEISEL is chairman of the Canadian Radio-television and Telecommunications Commission. Long a professor of political science, he is the author of *The Canadian General Election of 1957* and *Cleavages, Parties and Values in Canada.*

KHAYYAM ZEV PALTIEL is professor of political science at Carleton University in Ottawa. His writings include *Political Party Financing in Canada* and chapters in *Democracy at the Polls: A Comparative Study of Competitive National Elections* and the first At the Polls study on Canada, which dealt with the general election of 1974.

RICHARD M. SCAMMON, coauthor of *This U.S.A.* and *The Real Majority,* is director of the Elections Research Center in Washington, D.C. He has edited the biennial series *America Votes* since 1956.

F. LESLIE SEIDLE is a legislative assistant in the Office of the President of the Privy Council in Ottawa. He has recently completed his doctoral thesis in Canadian and British party finance and electoral law at Oxford University.

JILL VICKERS is associate professor of political science at Carleton University in Ottawa. She is a coauthor of *But Can You Type?* and has written articles on women in politics, political theory, and feminist epistemology.

ROBERT J. WILLIAMS is assistant professor of political science at the University of Waterloo. He has studied parliamentary candidates in two federal and several provincial elections in Canada. His most recent publication is "The Role of Legislatures in Policy Formulation," in Rejean Landry, ed., *Introduction à l'analyse des politiques.*

WALTER D. YOUNG is professor of political science at the University of Victoria and has written about the New Democratic party and politics in western Canada. He is presently coordinator of a research project examining the impact of government turnover on politics and administration in British Columbia.

Index

Page numbers in italics indicate tables.

413

Contents of

Canada at the Polls:

The General Election of 1974

Edited by Howard R. Penniman

ISBN 0-8447-3178-1
Published in 1975. Paperback. 310 pages. Index.

Available from

American Enterprise Institute for Public Policy Research
1150 Seventeenth Street, N.W., Washington, D.C. 20036

AEI's *At the Polls* Studies

Australia at the Polls: The National Elections of 1975, Howard R. Penniman, ed. (1977, 373 pp.)

The Australian National Elections of 1977, Howard R. Penniman, ed. (1980, 367 pp.)

Britain at the Polls: The Parliamentary Elections of 1974, Howard R. Penniman, ed. (1975, 256 pp.)

Britain Says Yes: The 1975 Referendum on the Common Market, Anthony King (1977, 153 pp.)

Britain at the Polls, 1979: A Study of the General Elections, Howard R. Penniman, ed. (1981, 345 pp.)

British Political Finance, 1830–1980, Michael Pinto-Duschinsky (1981, 339 pp.)

Canada at the Polls: The General Elections of 1974, Howard R. Penniman, ed. (1975, 310 pp.)

France at the Polls: The Presidential Elections of 1974, Howard R. Penniman, ed. (1975, 324 pp.)

The French National Assembly Elections of 1978, Howard R. Penniman, ed. (1980, 255 pp.)

Germany at the Polls: The Bundestag Election of 1976, Karl Cerny, ed. (1978, 251 pp.)

Greece at the Polls: The National Elections of 1974 and 1977, Howard R. Penniman, ed. (1980, 220 pp.)

India at the Polls: The Parliamentary Elections of 1977, Myron Weiner (1978, 150 pp.)

India at the Polls, 1980: A Study of the Parliamentary Elections, Myron Weiner (1982, 195 pp.)

Ireland at the Polls: The Dáil Elections of 1977, Howard R. Penniman, ed. (1978, 199 pp.)

Israel at the Polls: The Knesset Elections of 1977, Howard R. Penniman, ed. (1979, 333 pp.)

Italy at the Polls: The Parliamentary Elections of 1976, Howard R. Penniman, ed. (1977, 386 pp.)

Italy at the Polls, 1979: A Study of the Parliamentary Elections, Howard R. Penniman, ed. (1980, 335 pp.)

Japan at the Polls: The House of Councillors Election of 1974, Michael K. Blaker, ed. (1976, 157 pp.)

A Season of Voting: The Japanese Elections of 1976 and 1977, Herbert Passin, ed. (1979, 199 pp.)

New Zealand at the Polls: The General Elections of 1978, Howard R. Penniman, ed. (1980, 295 pp.)

Scandinavia at the Polls: Recent Political Trends in Denmark, Norway, and Sweden, Karl H. Cerny, ed. (1977, 304 pp.)
Venezuela at the Polls: The National Elections of 1978, Howard R. Penniman, ed. (1980, 287 pp.)
Democracy at the Polls: A Comparative Study of Competitive National Elections, David Butler, Howard R. Penniman, and Austin Ranney, eds. (1981, 367 pp.)
Referendums: A Comparative Study of Practice and Theory, David Butler and Austin Ranney, eds. (1978, 250 pp.)

Studies are forthcoming on the latest national elections in Australia, Belgium, Denmark, France, Germany, Greece, Ireland, Israel, Jamaica, Japan, the Netherlands, New Zealand, Norway, Portugal, Spain, Sweden, and Switzerland and on the first elections to the European Parliament, women in electoral politics, candidate selection, and parties of the left.

SEE ALSO the first in a new series of studies of American elections: *The American Elections of 1980,* edited by Austin Ranney.

A NOTE ON THE BOOK

The typeface used for the text of this book is
Palatino, designed by Hermann Zapf.
The type was set by
Hendricks-Miller Typographic Company, of Washington.
Bookcrafters, Inc., of Chelsea, Michigan, printed
and bound the book, using Glatfelter paper.
The cover and format were designed by Pat Taylor,
and the figures were drawn by Hördur Karlsson.
The manuscript was edited by Kate Tait and
by Gertrude Kaplan, of the AEI Publications staff.

Selected AEI Publications

AEI Associates Program